Management Information Systems

PRENTICE-HALL, INC., *Englewood Cliffs, N. J.*

MANAGEMENT

WILLIAM A. BOCCHINO

Associate Professor of Management and Computer Science
College of Business Administration
Fairleigh Dickinson University

President
Advanced Management Institute, Inc.

INFORMATION SYSTEMS

Tools and Techniques

Management Information Systems
Tools and Techniques

WILLIAM A. BOCCHINO

ISBN: 0-13-548693-9

Library of Congress Catalog Card Number: 73-38416

Printed in the United States of America

10 9 8 7 6 5

PRENTICE-HALL INTERNATIONAL, INC., *London*
PRENTICE-HALL OF AUSTRALIA, PTY. LTD., *Sydney*
PRENTICE-HALL OF CANADA, LTD., *Toronto*
PRENTICE-HALL OF INDIA PRIVATE LIMITED, *New Delhi*
PRENTICE-HALL OF JAPAN, INC., *Tokyo*

To

Lucia

CONTENTS

7 CHARTING TOOLS
FOR SYSTEMS ANALYSIS 114

The Organization Chart. The Systems Flow Chart.
The Work Distribution Chart. The Work Count. The Gantt Chart.
Line of Balance (LOB). Review Questions. Bibliography.

8 FORMS ANALYSIS,
DESIGN, AND CONTROL 141

Principles of Forms Analysis. Forms Analysis Procedure.
Principles of Forms Design. Forms Control.
Records Retention—How Long to Keep? Review Questions.
Bibliography.

9 STATISTICAL TECHNIQUES FOR MANAGEMENT
INFORMATION SYSTEMS 160

Measurement—The Basis for Statistical Analysis.
General Applications of the Statistical Method.
Other Application Areas. The Critical Management Question—
What Are the Chances? The Normal Curve—A Design for
Decision. Specific Statistical Tools and Techniques.
Review Questions. Bibliography.

10 SYSTEMS CONTROL TECHNIQUES 184

The ABC Concept of Control. The Learning Curve.
Inventory Control Systems.
Program Evaluation and Review Technique (PERT).
Review Questions. Bibliography.

11 OPERATIONS RESEARCH
FOR THE SYSTEMS ANALYST 224

A Commonsense Look at Operations Research.
General Steps in Applying OR. Tools and Techniques of OR.

PREFACE

Management Information Systems have existed from that moment in history when people first joined together to reach a common objective. As the years went by, the MIS came to take the form of after-the-fact status reporting. But instead of helping managers run their organizations, it resulted in the almost universal phenomenon of managers chasing their organizations from crisis to crisis.

This state of affairs continued more or less unchanged until the advent of the electronic computer and the concurrent development of a burgeoning array of quantitative decision tools. This combination of management tools and techniques seemed to indicate that an MIS revolution was finally in the making. But nothing really happened!

An impassable chasm seemed to exist between concept and implementation—between the tools and the techniques and a pragmatic understanding of how they should be used to create a viable Management Information System, an MIS that actually encompasses the planning, analysis, and control network that has always been envisioned but never attained. This book is a contribution toward bridging that chasm.

As is always the case, a great many people contributed to this effort—too many to name them all individually. I take this opportunity to thank them all for their help. In particular, Mr. Irving Sklansky gave unstintingly of his time and talent in coordinating the final typing, proofreading, and general administrative effort to help me finish the manuscript on schedule. Mrs. Betty Clark provided her critical typing talent and her usual charm and good humor.

I especially want to thank Mr. Victor Lazzaro, of Merrill Lynch, Pierce, Fenner & Smith Inc, and Professor H. Weiman, of the Bronx Community College, for their constructive comments on this book when it was in manuscript.

A number of sources cooperated with regard to illustrations for this book. Unless otherwise specified, pictures of equipment were provided through the courtesy of International Business Machines.

WILLIAM A. BOCCHINO

1

THE MANAGEMENT
INFORMATION SYSTEM

THE EVOLUTION
OF A MANAGEMENT INFORMATION SYSTEM

An *organization* is a grouping of elements to accomplish a purpose. For example, a *business organization* is a grouping of men, materials, machines, and money. These elements are interrelated by operating management to convert human effort and raw materials into goods and services to satisfy human needs at a profit.

This definition includes the key ingredients of every business organization:

1. It is made up of men, materials, machines, and money.
2. The organizers invest money, time, and creative energy.
3. The organization converts human effort and raw materials into goods or services.
4. Its objective is to satisfy human needs at a profit.
5. There is risk of loss as well as hope for profit.

TABLE 1-1

Examples of Organizations and Their Elements

Organization	Men	Materials	Machines	Money
Grocery store	Clerk	Shelf stock	Calculator	Inventory, salaries, supplies
Doctor's practice	Doctor	Medicines	X ray	Education, salaries, rent, insurance
Hardware wholesaler	Warehousemen	Warehouse stock	Lift trucks	Inventory, rent, light, heat, salaries
Manufacturer	Workers	Raw materials	Metal working	Plant and equipment, operating costs
Computer programming school	Teachers	Books, reference materials	Computer	Supplies, computer rental, salaries
Airline	Flight crew	Fuel and lubricants	Planes	Equipment, fuel and lubricants, repairs
Rest home	Nurses	Food and bedding	Beds and furniture	Building and equipment, operating costs
New car dealer	Salesmen	Sales literature	Car Lifts, wheel balancer	Automotive inventory, salaries, repairs and maintenance
Hospital	Nurses, doctors	Medicines, linens, instruments	Diagnostic equipment	Salaries, wages, food, linens, operating costs
Infantry division	Officers, soldiers	Guns, ammunition, clothing, food	Tanks, trucks	Pay, supplies, repairs and maintenance, fuel and lubricants
U.S. Post Office	Postmen, clerks	Stamps, envelopes, forms, paper	Cancelling machines, trucks	Equipment, salaries, operating costs
Public library	Librarians, typists	Books	Carts, typewriters	Fixtures, books, salaries

It is important to note that with the deletion of any reference to *profit* in the foregoing definition, everything that has been stated applies equally well to any organization, be it governmental, institutional, charitable. This general applicability of concepts will hold true throughout this book. The tools and techniques that will be discussed are universally applicable wherever men, materials, machines, and money come together (in whatever proportions) to accomplish a purpose.

A Man with an Idea   + brainstorm

Another characteristic of every organization is that it usually begins as an idea in the mind of one man (or woman) who then brings together others of a like point of view (or goes it alone) and invests the financial and human resources. The genesis of a typical business organization can be a useful example of the evolution of all organizations.

The *beginning* is usually characterized by crisis and confusion. It is the rare organization that follows the textbook requirement of having, at its start, a detailed written set of objectives, plans, budgets, organization charts, procedures manuals, or any of the other formal paraphernalia that make grist for the theoretician's mill. The beginning of most organizations is characterized by crude and primitive operating plans and controls.

The principal operating guideline in the early stages of most businesses is "to play it by ear." But if that really is the case, how do they survive? The answer is a simple one. The major reason for the survival of many embryonic business organizations is the entrepreneur. He is the secret ingredient who combines incredibly long hours, very hard work, and his best thinking—modified by experience—into the survival and eventual growth of his original idea into a viable organization. This is true for all organizations. They very often are "the elongated shadow of one man."

The Emergence of an Information System

As the business survives and grows, supervision of the activities associated with it develops beyond the scope of one man. He finds that he must be in more than one place at the same time to plan, direct, coordinate, analyze, and control (i.e., to *manage*) all the different activities of his enterprise. The face-to-face encounters for solving problems, transferring information, and checking on performance that were adequate when the business was very small become too numerous and time-consuming. In other words, the one-man owner-manager finds himself over his head in a complex network of interrelated duties that must be discharged.

His response is predictable and practical. He recognizes his need for help if his business is to continue to grow, and he hires another man to assist him in his management functions. It should be recognized that because he was the sole owner-manager, all his actions up to this point were, by definition, *management*. But, with a second manager on the scene, managing begins to require more definition.

Suddenly, problems of authority and responsibility, and communication and organization, begin to assume serious proportions. Where does one man's area of authority and responsibility begin and where does the other man's end? Who tells whom to do what? Who reports to whom? The whole spectrum of organizational problems appears on the horizon, and the need for a Management Information System (MIS) begins to take shape.

Ideally, the evolution of an MIS would be guided by knowledgeable people, careful to structure the information system to meet the objectives of the organization and the realities of its internal and external environment. But experience indicates that an MIS evolves in fits and starts to meet sudden needs and to respond to unforeseen crises.

The result, as may be expected, is a system that grows with little attention to the overall needs of the total organization. It usually takes shape as a patchwork of information subsystems, some connecting with others, some overlapping, some duplicating, and many working at cross-purposes.

As the organization develops, the managers establish better communications channels to meet their needs for accurate, timely information. Formal, semiformal, and even informal reporting habits are standardized, proceduralized, and scheduled. Information flows are structured for early warning of problems, quick response to crises, and clear pathways for management directives to the critical action points of the organization. A viable Management Information System is born!

The criterion for an effective Management Information System is that it provide accurate, timely, and meaningful data for management planning, analysis, and control to optimize the growth of the organization. Neither the glamour of the equipment nor the sophistication of the decision techniques can offset the failure of a Management Information System to meet that test. It must enhance the *management* of the organization.

The Essential Elements of Management

The realities of operating a business not only provide the impetus for the development of a Management Information System but also cause the thoughtful manager to begin to think seriously about the management of his business. But what is it? How does one define it? This word *management* is one of the most popular of the age. It is a highly acceptable "buzz-word." But its definition is rarely made explicit, although the word is used, overused, and abused.

A useful operational definition is that *management is the rational selection of courses of action to optimize the interrelationships of men, materials, machines, and money for the survival and growth of the organization.* This definition is usful because it encompasses the three essential elements of all management activity—planning, analysis, and control.

1. Planning
   a. Sets specific goals for the organization.
   b. Selects the courses of action to reach the goals.
2. Analysis
   a. Evaluates alternative courses of action.
   b. Compares operating results with plans.
3. Control
   a. Interrelates men, materials, machines, and money for optimum results.
   b. Modifies the plan or the operating conditions that produced the results that are at variance with the plan.

Of course, the essential elements of management existed when the owner-manager was alone. They still exist as more managers join the organization, but each additional manager adds new complexities to the task of managing. The more people operating as managers, the higher the demands on the information system. Management problem solving, information exchange, and checking on performance require the setting up of more formal channels of information flow designed not only for status reporting of conditions in the system but for the key critical data for managing—planning, analysis, and control.

Whereas previously the lone owner-manager carried the affairs of the business around "in his hat," now that other decision makers have arrived on the scene, the planning, analyzing, and controlling activities require very careful coordination. There is a need for specifying the areas of authority and responsibility. Channels of information must be provided between the decision makers, so that "one hand knows what the other is doing." The relatively simple personal involvement of one human being has been replaced by the infinitely more complex interaction of two or more human beings attempting to administer parts of the same organization. In other words, when an organization grows beyond the scope of the single manager it also reaches the point where its survival requires the development of an effective Management Information System.

It probably doesn't require emphasis, but it should be noted that the same logic that requires the institution of an effective information network in a business is also valid for any organization, whether profit oriented or not. The network of information that constitutes a Management Information System not only provides data for the conduct of day-to-day operations but, even more significantly, provides the action data for management planning, analysis, and control.

The Management Information System

The lifeblood of any organization is the flow of intelligence, information, and data. This "plasma" moves along channels from point to point through the interrelated network of the operating elements of the organization. This flow of information includes data on supplies, operations, costs, customers, competitors, and, in fact, the total internal and external environment. The flow units may be in the form of telephone calls, memos, reports, forms, face-to-face encounters, electric or electronic signals, or any other medium that moves intelligible symbols from one place to another in the system.

This flow of information, or data, is a continuous record of the status of all the pertinent elements that affect the survival and growth of the organization. It is important to recognize that a tremendous number of these pieces of information, these bits of data, are generated almost every minute of every day in the interaction of an organization with its environment. Every activity in every organization contributes to the generation of this information. Receipts, disbursements, communications, sales orders, purchase orders, production schedules, design changes, standard times and costs, changes in salaries and wages, tax reports, government regulations are all examples of the different activities that contribute to the flood of data that is generated and processed daily. Part of management's responsibility is the setting up of a method for the selection of the key/critical data from this flood of information and the means to have it captured, processed, and fed back to assist management to make more effective decisions. This feedback-decision network is an integral part of the anatomy of an effective Management Information System.

In summary then, a Management Information System develops in response to the needs of management for accurate, timely, and meaningful data in order to plan, analyze, and control the organization's activities and thereby optimize its survival and growth. The MIS accomplishes this mission for management by providing means for input, processing, and output of data plus a feedback-decision network that helps management respond to current and future changes in the internal and external environment of the organization.

ANATOMY OF A MANAGEMENT INFORMATION SYSTEM

An effective Management Information System captures data as close to its point of origin as possible and then channels it to the information-processing stations where it is arranged, calculated, summarized, and otherwise prepared for communication to the decision makers. In many of the more sophisticated information systems much of this is done electronically, utilizing electronic computers and associated equipment. In most information systems, however, it is still done manually or electro-mechanically, that is, by human beings alone or assisted by mechanical devices (adding machines, typewriters, etc.) that utilize electricity for motive power.

The particular equipment used, though important to the timeliness and the level of sophistication of the data processing, does not change the essential nature of the Management Information System. The MIS is still the network of communications channels in an organization from the points of data origination through the processing procedures to the decision makers (feedback); then from the points of decision back through the information channels to the points of implementation of the decisions (control).

The key components of the Management Information System are the sensing devices that capture the data at the point of origin, the channels for processing and feedback of the data, the analysis of the data by comparison with plans and standards, and the action decisions that, when implemented, result in management control of the organization. Data capture, processing, feedback, analysis, decision, and control— these are the major structural elements in the anatomy of a Management Information System.

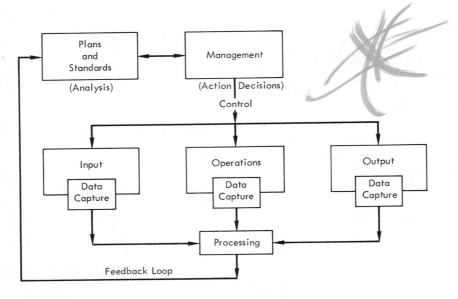

FIGURE 1-1
Anatomy of a Management Information System

Data Capture and Processing

(Refer to Fig. 1-1.)

Input data (quantities of raw materials, deliveries, prices, labor costs, etc.), *operations data* (production rates, machining costs, work-in-process, inventory, etc.), and *output data* (finished goods, inventory levels, sales, shipping dates, etc.) are captured either by manual methods or by mechanical, electromechanical, and electronic sensors (data recording devices) and are transmitted along the communications channels to a *processing* unit or units (perhaps a computer).

Feedback Analysis

Processed input, output, and operations data are compared with the *plans* and operating *standards* set by management in the form of manning tables, output levels, sales forecasts, expense budgets, production schedules, and other specific quantitative standards.

The *feedback loop* consists of the information channels that transmit the processed input, operations, and output data to the *analysis* and *decision* steps and the transmittal of *control* directives back down to the operating levels of the organization. Based on the analysis of the variations of the feedback data when compared with the plans and standards, management may decide on one of three courses of action.

1. To change the plans and standards to reflect changes in the basic assumptions that were made when they were set up.
2. To change the input, operating, or output conditions (when possible) so as to bring actual performance back into line with plans and standards.
3. To do nothing.
4. A combination of the above.

Action Decision and Control

The alternative selected is the management decision. It is important to emphasize that the third alternative is very much a decision, although it is often considered a compromise between the first and the second. In reality, it may be a sensible alternative, but more often than not it is an abdication of responsibility, with the result that uncoordinated action is taken at the operating level where it contributes to confusion and working at cross-purposes. For effective management, the "do-nothing" decision should be communicated to those closest to the operations to guide them in controlling their reaction to conditions.

It has been said that the mark of experience is not wasting effort on things that cannot be significantly changed. But since perspectives differ as one moves from one level to another in an organization, it is important that any management decision, even to do nothing, be communicated back down the feedback control network to avoid wasted effort.

Communication and implementation of the alternative chosen are the essence of control in the management decision process and the basic reason for the existence of the MIS. Unless the decision is communicated and implemented it is not an *action decision* and management control has not been exercised. Selecting an alternative and then seeing to it that it is implemented is the essence of control and the justification for having a Management Information System. *Control* is the "moment of truth" for managers. Only to the extent that the organization responds to their action decisions are they the managers of that organization. It is understood, of course, that this exercise of control

may be in the context of authoritarian, democratic, participative, motiva-
tional, or any of the other concepts of management theory. Whatever
form *managing* has in a particular organization is unimportant to the
concept. The exercise of control is the exercise of management.

The function of the MIS is to provide the mechanism for the
exercise of management.

THE OBJECTIVE
OF A MANAGEMENT INFORMATION SYSTEM

In designing an effective network of channels of communication (the
Management Information System) management must determine:

1. What data is needed.
2. When it is needed.
3. Who needs it.
4. Where it is needed.
5. In what form it is needed.
6. How much it costs.
7. The relative significance of data elements for priority treatment
   in the processing cycle.
8. The mechanics of sorting the information, collating it, manipulating it into meaningful form, and presenting the synthesized
   information in minimum time to the operations decision makers
   for action. (This is the prime area for evaluation of automatic
   data processing.)
9. The requirements of a feedback control loop to provide for
   dynamic management.
10. The mechanism for constantly evaluating and improving the
    Management Information System.

Once designed, the function of a Management Information
System is to provide decision makers with timely and accurate data to
allow them to make and implement the necessary decisions to optimize
the interrelationships of men, materials, machines, and money to most
effectively reach the organization's predetermined goals. In other words,
the primary objective of a Management Information System is to provide
the organization with a mechanism for the exercise of management.
The balance of this book will concern itself with a number of the tools
and techniques that will help to design and implement Management
Information Systems to reach this objective.

REVIEW QUESTIONS

1.   If you were going to start a particular business or organization, what would you need in terms of men, materials, machines, and money? Be specific.

2.   Visit a small business or local organization in your area and talk to the owner or principal administrator. See if the pattern of growth of the organization followed the general outline described in this chapter. Discuss the probable reasons for any variations that you found.

3.   Describe a Management Information System with which you are familiar. Identify the major elements.

4.   Draw the "anatomy" of the Management Information System you described above.

5.   What is a useful definition of *management?*

6.   Why is *control* defined as *action decision?*

7.   What is the basic function of a Management Information System? What is the basic objective of an MIS?

8.   Give five specific examples of the *channels* that may be used in a Management Information System.

9.   Prepare a five-minute explanation of what a Management Information System is and how it might be used in an organization.

10.   "A Management Information System allows management to utilize the principle of feedback control." Explain.

BIBLIOGRAPHY

BLUMENTHAL, SHERMAN, C., *Management Information Systems.* Englewood Cliffs, N.J.: Prentice-Hall, Inc. 1969. A philosophical treatment for the planning of the MIS.

DRUCKER, PETER F., *The Age of Discontinuity.* New York: Harper and Row, Publishers, 1968. A very perceptive and provocative treatment of the environment with which the MIS must cope in the last third of this century.

————, *The Practice of Management.* New York: Harper & Brothers, 1954. A classic in the sense of provoking useful ways of thinking about the functions of management and indirectly of the MIS.

HOPEMAN, RICHARD J., *Systems Analysis and Operations Management.* Columbus, Ohio: Charles E. Merrill Publishing Co., 1969. Emphasizes the systems concept and explores the nature and dynamics of Management Information Systems. Applications concentrate on materials management.

KOONTZ, H., and O'DONNELL, *Principles of Management* (4th ed.). New York: McGraw-Hill Book Company, 1968. One of the classics in the field of management.

SCHODERBEK, PETER P., *Management Systems.* New York: John Wiley & Sons, Inc., 1967. A book of readings by authorities in the field that provides an excellent overview of the various facets of the subject.

SCHUCHMAN, ABE, *Scientific Decision Making in Business.* New York: Holt, Rinehart & Winston, Inc., 1963. Thorough treatment of decision making. Applicable to all organizations.

2

MANAGEMENT INFORMATION
SYSTEMS GLOSSARY

There are a number of authoritative glossaries that can be depended upon to keep up to date with the evolution of the terminology in the field.[1] Terminology in the field of Management Information Systems is particularly crucial because the essence of an MIS is communication.

The glossary that follows in this chapter is not meant to be exhaustive. It is meant to highlight the more important terms and will help the reader to understand the balance of the book. A few minutes spent in reading this glossary now will repay significant dividends.

Access time: (1) The time it takes a computer to locate data or an instruction word in its storage section and transfer it to the destination

[1] Glossaries can be obtained from the following sources, among a number of others:
American National Standards Institute, Inc., 1430 Broadway, New York, N.Y. 10018.
International Business Machines, 112 East Park Road, White Plains, N.Y. 10601.
Superintendent of Documents, Government Printing Office, Washington, D.C. 20402.

specified. (2) The time it takes to transfer information that has been operated on, or directed to be stored, to the location in storage where it is to be stored.

Acronym: A word formed from the initial letter or letters of the words in a name or phrase, e.g., ALGOL from ALGOrithmic Language, COBOL from COmmon Business Oriented Language.

Address: An identification, represented by a name, label, or number for a location in storage.

ADP: Automatic Data Processing.

ALGOL: An arithmetic language by which numerical procedures may be precisely presented to a computer in a standard form. Popular in Europe but not widely used in the United States.

Algorithm: A series of steps in a procedure to solve a problem.

Algorithmic: Pertaining to a calculating process usually assumed to lead to the solution of a problem in a finite number of steps.

Alphabetic-numeric: The characters that include letters of the alphabet, numerals, and other symbols such as punctuation or mathematical symbols.

Alphameric: A contraction of alphanumeric and alphabetic-numeric.

Analog computer: A computer that represents variables by physical analogies. Thus, it is any computer that solves problems by translating physical conditions such as flow, temperature, pressure, angular position, or voltage into related mechanical or electrical quantities and uses mechanical or electrical equivalent circuits as an analog for the physical phenomenon being investigated. In general, it is a computer that uses an analog for each variable and produces analogs as output. Thus, an analog computer measures continuously, whereas a digital computer counts discretely.

Analyst: A person skilled in the definition and development of techniques for the solving of a problem—especially those techniques for solutions on a computer.

Argument: An independent variable. For example, in table look-up operations, the arguments are the numbers that are used to identify the locations of the desired items in the table.

Arithmetic unit: The portion of the hardware of a computer in which arithmetic and logical operations are performed.

Array: A series of items arranged in a meaningful pattern.

Artificial intelligence: The capability of computers or other devices to perform functions that are normally associated with human intelligence, such as reasoning, learning, adapting to environmental changes, and self-improvement.

ASCII (American Standard Code for Information Interchange): A 7-bit code adopted as a U.S.A. standard to facilitate the interchange of data among various types of data-processing and data communications equipment. Note: Because of the very large investment in equipment and programs that use earlier codes, ASCII has not been widely used to date, but a steady trend toward its usage may be expected.

Assemble: To integrate subroutines into the main routine by adapting or changing relative and symbolic addresses to absolute form.

Assembler: A computer program that operates on symbolic input data to produce machine instructions by carrying out such functions as translation of symbolic operation codes into computer operating instructions, assignment of locations in storage for successive instructions, computation of absolute addresses from symbolic addresses.

Assembly routine: Same as *assembler.*

Asynchronous computer: A computer in which each operation starts as a result of a signal generated by the completion of the previous operation or by the availability of the equipment required for the next operation. Contrast with *synchronous computer.*

Audit trail: A system of providing a means for tracing items of data from processing step to step, particularly from a machine-produced report or other machine output back to the original source data.

Automatic data processing: Data processing performed by a system of electronic or electrical machines so interconnected and interacting as to reduce to a minimum the need for human assistance or intervention.

Automatic data-processing system: The term is descriptive of an interacting assembly of procedures, processes, methods, personnel, and automatic data-processing equipment to perform a complex series of data processing operations.

Automation: The investigation, design, development, and application of methods of rendering processes self-controlling. Smooth, continuous production through feedback analysis and control.

Auxiliary equipment: The peripheral equipment or devices not in direct communication with the central processing unit of a computer.

Auxiliary storage: A storage device in addition to the main storage of a computer, e.g., magnetic tape, disk, data cell, or drum. Auxiliary storage usually holds much larger amounts of information than the main storage, but the information is accessible less rapidly.

Background program: A program, usually of the batch-processing type, that is not subject to any real-time constraints and can be executed whenever the facilities of a multiprogramming computer system are not required by real-time programs or other programs of higher priority. Contrast with *foreground program.*

Batch processing: A technique by which items to be processed must be coded and collected into groups prior to processing.

Batch total: The sum of certain quantities, pertaining to batches of unit records, used to verify accuracy of operations on a particular batch of records, e.g., in a payroll calculation the batches might be departments, and batch totals would be number of employees in the department, total hours worked in the department, total pay for the department. Batches, however, may be arbitrary, such as orders received from 9 A.M. to 11 A.M. on a certain day.

Baud: A unit of signaling speed equal to the number of discrete conditions or signal events per second. Note: In the case of a train of binary signals, and therefore in most data communications applications, one baud equals one bit per second.

Binary: A characteristic in which there are but two possible alternatives, e.g., the binary number system using two (2) as its base and using only the digits zero (0) and one (1).

Binary code: (1) A coding system in which the encoding of any data is done through the use of bits, i.e., 0 or 1. (2) A code for the ten-decimal digits, 0, 1, . . . 9, in which each is represented by its binary equivalent.

Binary coded decimal: Describing a decimal notation in which the individual decimal digits are represented by a pattern of ones and zeros, e.g., in the 8–4–2–1 coded decimal notation, the number twelve is represented as 0001 0010 for 1 and 2, respectively, whereas in pure or straight binary notation it is represented as 1100. Related to *binary.*

Binary digit: A numeral in the binary scale of notation. This digit may be zero (0) or one (1). It may be equivalent to an on or off condition, a yes or a no. Often abbreviated to BIT.

Binary notation: A number system written to the base two notation.

BIT: (1) An abbreviation of binary digit. (2) A single character in a binary number. (3) A single pulse in a group of pulses. (4) A unit of information capacity of a storage device.

Block diagram: A graphical representation of the hardware in a computer system. The primary purpose of a block diagram is to indicate the paths along which information and/or control flows between the various parts of a computer system. It should not be confused with the term *flow chart.*

Block sort: A sort of one or more of the most significant characters of a key to serve as a means of making workable-sized groups from a large volume of records to be stored.

Boolean algebra: A process of reasoning using a symbolic logic and dealing with on-off circuit elements. It employs symbols to represent AND, OR, NOT, IF . . . THEN, etc., to permit mathematical calculation. Named after George Boole, an English mathematician (1815–64).

Bootstrap: A technique for loading the first few instructions of a routine into storage, then using these instructions to bring in the rest of the routine. This usually involves either the entering of a few instructions manually or the using of a special key on the console.

Branch: The selection of one of two or more possible paths based on some criterion.

Branch instruction: An instruction that enables the computer to choose between alternative subprograms, depending upon the conditions determined by the computer, during the execution of the program.

Breakpoint: A point in a computer program at which interruptions to permit visual checking, printing out, or other analyzing may occur. Breakpoints are usually used in debugging operations.

Buffer: An internal portion of a data-processing system serving as intermediary storage between two storage or data-handling systems.

Bug: A mistake in the design of a routine or a computer, or a malfunction.

Byte: (1) A generic term to indicate a measurable portion of consecutive binary digits, e.g., an 8-bit or 6-bit byte. (2) A group of binary digits usually operated upon as a unit. (3) Eight adjacent bits that represent one alphanumeric character or two decimal digits.

Card field: A set of card columns, either fixed as to number and position or, if variable, then identifiable by position relative to other fields. Corresponding fields on successive cards are normally used to store similar information.

Card-to-tape converter: A device that converts information directly from punched cards to punched or magnetic tape.

Cathode-ray tube: An electronic vacuum tube containing a screen on which information can be stored or displayed. The abbreviation CRT is frequently used. Note: Cathode-ray tubes served as the principal storage medium in some of the early digital computers; they now serve as the basic component of most display units.

Central processing unit: The central processor of the computer system. It contains the main storage, arithmetic unit, and special register groups.

Centralized data processing: Data processing performed at a single central location on data obtained from several geographical locations or managerial levels or geographical points throughout the organization.

Character: One symbol of a set of elementary symbols, such as those corresponding to the keys on a typewriter. The symbols usually include the decimal digits 0 through 9, the letters A through Z, and punctuation marks, operation symbols, and any other single symbols that a computer may read, store, or write.

Character recognition: The technology of using a machine to sense and encode, into a machine language, characters that are written or printed to be read by human beings.

Check: A process of partial or complete testing of the correctness of machine operations, the existence of certain prescribed conditions within the computer, or the correctness of the results produced by a program. A check of any of these conditions may be made automatically by the equipment or may be programmed.

Check bit: A binary check digit; often a parity bit.

Check digit: One or more redundant digits carried along with a machine word and used in relation to the other digits in the word as a self-checking or an error-detecting code to detect malfunctions of equipment in data-transfer operations.

Checkpoint: A point in time in a machine run at which processing is momentarily halted to make a magnetic tape record of the condition of all the variables of the machine run, such as the position of input and output tapes and a copy of working storage. Checkpoints are used in conjunction with a restart routine to minimize reprocessing time occasioned by functional failures.

Chi-square test: Statistical test used to determine how well theoretical distributions fit empirical ones, i.e., those obtained from sample data.

Circuit: (1) A system of conductors and related electrical elements through which electrical current flows. (2) A communications link between two or more points.

Clear: To erase the contents of a storage device by replacing the contents with blanks or zeros.

Closed loop: Pertaining to a system with feedback type of control, such that the output is used to modify the input.

Closed shop: A computer installation that may be operated (and, in some cases, programmed) only by personnel on the staff of the associated computer department. Contrast with *open shop.*

COBOL: See Common Business Oriented Language.

Code: (1) A system of symbols for meaningful communication. (2) A system of symbols for representing data or instructions in a computer or a tabulating machine. (3) To translate the program for the solution of a problem on a given computer into a sequence of machine-language instructions and addresses acceptable to that computer. (4) A machine-language program.

Code line: A single instruction written usually on one line, in a code for a specific computer to solve a problem. This instruction is usually stored as a whole in the program register of the computer while it is executed, and it may contain one or more addresses of registers or storage locations in the computer where numbers or machine words are to be obtained or sent and one or more operations are to be executed.

Coded program: A program that has been expressed in the code or language of a specific machine or programming system.

Coding: The ordered list in computer code or pseudocode of the successive computer instructions representing successive computer operations for solving a specific problem.

Collate: To merge two or more ordered sets of data or cards in order to produce one or more ordered sets that still reflect the original ordering relations.

Collator: A device used to collate or merge sets or decks of cards or other units into a sequence.

Command: (1) An electronic pulse, signal, or set of signals to start, stop, or continue some operation. It is incorrect to use *command* as a synonym for instruction. (2) The portion of an instruction word that specifies the operation to be performed.

Comment: An expression that explains or identifies a particular step in a routine but has no effect on the operation of the computer in performing the instructions for the routine.

Common Business Oriented Language (COBOL): A specific language by which business data-processing procedures may be precisely described in a standard form. The language is intended not only as a means for directly presenting any business program to any suitable computer for which a compiler exists but also as a means for communicating such procedures among individuals.

Compare: To examine the representation of a quantity to discover its relationship to zero, or to examine two quantities, usually for the purpose of discovering identity or relative magnitude.

Compatibility: The characteristic of computers by which one computer may accept and process data prepared by another computer without conversion or code modification.

Compile: To produce a machine-language routine from a routine written in source language by selecting appropriate subroutines from a subroutine library as directed by the instructions or other symbols of the original routine. Translating the subroutines and linkage into machine language. The compiled routine is then ready to be loaded into storage and run, i.e., the compiler does not usually run the routine it produces.

Compiler: A computer program more powerful than an assembler. In addition to its translating function, which is generally the same process as that used in an assembler, it is able to replace certain items of input with series of instructions, usually called *subroutines.* Thus, where an assembler translates item for item, and produces as output the same number of instructions or constants that were put into it, a compiler will do more than this. The program that results from compiling is a translated and expanded version of the original.

Computer: (1) A device capable of accepting information, applying prescribed processes to the information, and supplying the results of these processes. It usually consists of input and output devices, storage, arithmetic, and logical units, and a control unit. (2) A high-speed adding machine that can recognize 0 and 1, whether one number is greater than, less than, or equal to another number, and can store data, all under its own control.

Confidence interval: Used in interval estimates to indicate estimate dependability or accuracy.

Configuration: A group of machines that are interconnected and are programmed to operate as a system.

Console: A portion of the computer that may be used to control the machine manually; correct errors; determine the status of machine circuits, registers, and counters; determine the contents of storage; and manually revise the contents of storage.

Control: The part of a digital computer or processor that determines the execution and interpretation of instructions in proper sequence, including the decoding of each instruction and the application of the proper signals to the arithmetic unit in accordance with the decoded information.

Control chart: Graphic method of presenting a sequence of observations. Used to decide if changes are due to chance or to actual process changes.

Control field: A constant location where information for control purposes is placed; e.g., in a set of punch cards, if columns 79 and 80 contain various codes that control whether or not certain operations will be performed on any particular card, then columns 79 and 80 constitute a control field.

Control unit: The portion of a computer that directs the sequence of operations, interprets the coded instructions, and initiates the proper commands to the computer circuits preparatory to execution.

Control word: A word, usually the first or last word, of a record, or first or last word of a block, which carries indicative information for the following words, records, or blocks.

Conversational mode: A mode of operation that implies a "dialogue" between a computer and its user, in which the computer program examines the input supplied by the user and formulates questions or comments which are directed back to the user. Often the mode with a remote computer terminal.

Core storage: Same as *magnetic core storage.*

Correlation: Relating one factor to another to find out how much of the relationship is due to chance. Correlation is expressed as a decimal between zero and one. A correlation of one would mean that none of the relationship was due to chance—a direct relationship. A correlation of zero would mean that all the relationship was due to chance—no relationship at all.

Counter: A device, register, or location in storage for storing numbers or number representations in a manner that permits these numbers to be increased or decreased by the value of another number, or to be changed or reset by zero or to an arbitrary value.

CPU: Central Processing Unit, same as *main frame.*

Cryogenics: The field of technology in which devices utilizing properties assumed by metals near absolute zero are used. At these temperatures, large current changes can be obtained by relatively small magnetic field changes.

Cybernetics: The field of technology involved in the comparative study of the control and intracommunication of information-handling machines and nervous systems of animals and man in order to understand and improve communication.

Cycle: (1) To repeat a set of operations indefinitely or until a stated condition is met. The set of operations may be subject to variation on each repetition, as by address changes obtained by programmed computation. (2) An occurrence, phenomenon, or interval of space or time that recurs regularly and in the same sequence; or time that recurs regularly and in the same sequence, e.g., the interval required for completion of one operation in a repetitive sequence of operations.

Data: A general term used to denote any or all facts, numbers, letters, and symbols that refer to or describe an object, idea, condition, situation, or other factors. It connotes basic elements of information that can be processed or produced by a computer.

Databank: The system of data files containing records that provide information to access other files in the same system. Each record in any file has at least one field that relates it to a record in another file.

Database: The common pool of all data elements. It consolidates all data files so that data elements required by different functions do not need to be stored in more than one place. All organization applications have access to the same central databank.

Data processing: (1) The preparation of source media that contain data or basic elements of information and the handling of such data according to precise rules of procedure to accomplish such operations as classifying, sorting, calculating, summarizing, and recording. (2) The production of records and reports. (3) Converting input to output.

Data reduction: The process of transforming masses of raw, test, or experimentally obtained data, usually gathered by automatic recording equipment, into useful condensed or simplified intelligence.

Debug: (1) To locate and correct any errors in a computer program. (2) To detect and correct malfunctions in the computer itself.

Decision: (1) Selection between alternative courses of action. (2) The computer operation of making comparisons by use of arithmetic to determine the relationship of two terms (numeric, alphabetic, or a combination of both), e.g., equal, greater than, or less than, and taking an alternative course of action based on this comparison.

Decision table: A table that lists all the contingencies to be considered in the description of a problem, together with the corresponding actions to be taken. Note: Decision tables permit complex decision-making criteria to be expressed in a concise and logical format. They are sometimes used in place of flow charts for problem definition and documentation. Moreover, compilers have been written to convert decision tables into programs that can be executed by computers.

Deck: A collection of cards, commonly a complete set of cards that have been punched for a definite service or purpose.

Decrement: The quantity by which a variable is decreased.

Density, packing: (*See* Packing density).

Detail file: A file containing information that is relatively transient, such as records of individual transactions that occurred during a particular period of time. Synonymous with *transaction file.* Contrast with *master file.*

Diagnostic routine: A routine used to locate a malfunction in a computer or to aid in locating mistakes in a computer program. Thus, in general, any routine specifically designed to aid in debugging or trouble-shooting.

Digit: A sign or symbol used to convey a specific quantity of information either by itself or with other numbers of its set, e.g., 2, 3, 4, and 5 are digits.

Digital: Pertaining to the utilization of discrete integral numbers in a given base to represent all the quantities that occur in a problem or a calculation. It is possible to express in digital form all information stored, transferred, or processed by a dual state condition, e.g., on-off, open-closed, and true-false.

Digital computer: A computer that processes information represented by combinations of discrete or discontinuous data, as compared with an analog computer for continuous data. More specifically, it is a device for performing sequences of arithmetic and logical operations, not only on data but on its own program.

Diode: A device used to permit current flow in one direction in a circuit and to inhibit current flow in the other. In computers, these are primarily germanium or silicon crystals.

Disk storage: The storage of data on the surface of magnetic disks.

Display: A visual presentation.

Display tube: A cathode-ray tube used to display information.

Document: A form, voucher, or written evidence of a transaction.

Documentation: Supporting instructions and explanations of a program, such as flow charts, block diagrams, operator directions, etc.

Downtime: The period during which a computer is malfunctioning or not operating correctly due to mechanical or electronic failure, as opposed to available time, idle time, or standby time, during which the computer is functional.

Duality theory: Every linear programming problem has associated with it another related LP problem called the *dual.*

Dump: Transferring all or part of internal storage to external storage or print-out.

Dynamic programming: A quantitative technique that has proved useful for making a sequence of interrelated decisions. It provides a systematic procedure for determining the combination of decisions which maximizes overall effectiveness.

EAM: Electrical Accounting Machine.

EBCDIC (Extended Binary Coded Decimal Interchange Code): An 8-bit code that represents an extension of a 6-bit BCD code that was widely used in computers of the first and second generations. Note: EBCDIC can represent up to 256 distinct characters and is the principal code used in many of the current computers.

Echo check: Received data are returned to point of transmission for comparison with original data.

Econometrics: Mathematics and statistics applied to economic problems. Mathematical models of economic situations are manipulated to see what the economic effects of changing variables will be.

Edit: To rearrange data or information. Editing may involve the deletion of unwanted data, the selection of pertinent data, the application of format techniques, the insertion of symbols such as page numbers and typewriter characters, the application of standard processes such as zero suppression, and the testing of data for reasonableness and proper range.

EDP: Electronic Data Processing.

Electronic data processing (EDP): Data processing performed largely by electronic equipment.

End of file (EOF): Termination or point of completion of a quantity of data. End-of-file marks are used to indicate this point.

Erase: To replace all the binary digits in a storage device by binary zeros.

Error: Any variance between a processed quantity and the true condition.

Execute: To interpret a machine instruction and perform the indicated operation(s) on the operand(s) specified.

Executive routine: A routine that supervises other routines.

Exit: A way of momentarily interrupting or leaving a repeated cycle of operations in a program.

External storage: (1) The storage of data on a device that is not an integral part of a computer but in a form prescribed for use by the computer. (2) A facility or device, not an integral part of a computer, on which data usable by a computer is stored, such as off-line magnetic tape units or punch-card devices.

Feed: To supply the material to be operated upon to a machine.

Feedback: The part of a closed loop system that automatically brings back information about the condition under control.

Feedback control: A type of system control obtained when a portion of the output signal is operated upon and fed back to the input in order to obtain a desired effect.

Field: An assigned area in a record to be marked with information.

File: An organized collection of information directed toward some purpose. The records in a file may or may not be sequenced according to a key contained in each record.

File protection: A device or method that prevents accidental erasure of operative data on magnetic tape reels.

Fixed point: The position of the decimal point is set with respect to one end of the numerals in the numbering system.

Flag: (1) A bit of information attached to a character or word to indicate the boundary of a field. (2) An indicator used frequently to tell some later part of a program that some condition occurred earlier.

Floating point: The position of the decimal point is not set with respect to one end of the numerals in the numbering system.

Flow chart: A graphic representation of the steps of a procedure.

Font: A family or assortment of graphic character representations (i.e., a character set) of a particular size and style, e.g., Font E–13B, the MICR font adopted as a standard by the American Bankers Association, and the U.S.A. Standard Optical Font for OCR.

Foreground program: A program that requires real-time responses or has a high priority and therefore takes precedence over other concurrently operating programs in a computer system using multiprogramming techniques. Contrast with *background program.*

Format: The predetermined arrangement of characters, fields, lines, page numbers, and punctuation marks, usually on a single sheet or in a file. This refers to input, output, and files.

FORTRAN (FORmula TRANslator): A machine-independent programming language designed for problems that can be expressed in quantitative notation. The FORTRAN compiler is a routine for a given machine which accepts a program written in FORTRAN (source) language and produces a machine-language (object) program.

Frame of reference: Talking about the same thing or speaking in the same terms. Refers to the mathematical base from which values are taken. For example, labor costs will vary throughout your plant. To use labor costs as a frame of reference, you would have to convert all labor costs to a standard labor cost for the plan—departmental labor costs would then be percentages of this.

Function: (1) A characteristic action or purpose of an entity. (2) A rule that assigns values to a variable.

F-test: Statistical test of significance of differences between two variances of proportions.

Game theory: (1) A mathematical process of selecting an optimum strategy in the face of an opponent who has a strategy of his own. (2) A mathematical approach for dealing with competitive situations with the emphasis on the decision-making process of the competitors.

Gang punch: To punch identical or constant information into all of a group of punch cards.

General-purpose computer: A computer designed to solve a large variety of problems, e.g., a stored-program computer that may be adapted to any of a very large class of applications.

Hang-up: A nonprogrammed stop in a routine. It is usually an unforeseen or unwanted halt in a machine pass. It is most often caused by the improper coding of a machine instruction or by the attemped use of a nonexistent or an improper operation code.

Hard copy: A printed copy of machine output, e.g., printed reports, listings, documents, and summaries.

Hardware: The physical equipment, or devices, forming a computer and peripheral equipment.

Hash total: A sum of numbers in a specified field of a record or of a batch of records used for checking purposes. No attention is paid to the significance of the total. Examples of such numbers are customer numbers or part numbers. If alphabetic characters have a numerical interpretation to a computer, they can also be added.

Head: A device that reads, records, or erases information in a storage medium —usually a small electromagnet used to read, write, or erase information on a magnetic drum or tape, or the set of perforating or reading fingers and block assembly for punching or reading holes in paper tape or cards.

Heuristic: Pertaining to trial-and-error methods of obtaining solutions to problems.

Hexadecimal: Pertaining to the number system with a radix of 16, or to a characteristic or property involving a choice or condition in which there are sixteen possibilities. Synonymous with *sexadecimal.* Note: Hexadecimal numerals are frequently used as a "shorthand" representation for binary numerals, with each hexadecimal digit representing a group of four bits (binary digits), e.g., the binary numeral 1001 0111 0100 can be represented as hexadecimal 974.

Hierarchy: A specified rank or order of items; thus, a series of items classified by rank or order.

Histogram: Graphic representation of frequency distributions.

High-order: Pertaining to the digit or digits of a number that have the greatest weight or significance, e.g., in the number 53276, the high-order digit is 5. Contrast with *low-order.*

Hollerith: A widely used system of encoding alphanumeric information onto cards; hence, *Hollerith cards* is synonymous with *punch cards.* Such cards were first used in 1890 for the U.S. Census and were named after Herman Hollerith, their originator.

Housekeeping: For a computer program, housekeeping involves the setting up of constants and variables to be used in the program.

Hunting: A continuous attempt on the part of an automatically controlled system to seek a desired equilibrium condition. The system usually contains a standard, a method of determining deviation from this standard, and a method of influencing the system such that the difference between the standard and the state of the system is brought to zero.

Hypothesis testing: Procedures to validate certain assumptions about populations.

Idle time: (1) The period between the end of one computer run and the start of a subsequent programmed computer run. (2) The time normally used to assemble cards, paper, tape reels, and control panels required for the next computer operation. (3) The time between operations when no work is scheduled.

Illegal character: A character or combination of bits that is not accepted as a valid representation by the machine design or by a specific routine. Illegal characters are commonly detected and used as an indication of machine malfunction.

Immediate access: Obtaining data from or placing data into a storage device directly and without delay.

Independent events: Events whose occurrence or nonoccurrence does not depend on one another.

Indicators: The devices that register conditions, such as high or equal conditions resulting from a comparison of plus or minus conditions resulting from a computation. A sequence of operations within a procedure may be varied according to the position of an indicator.

Industrial engineering: The design, improvement, and installation of integrated systems of men, materials, and equipment. It draws upon specialized knowledge and skill in the mathematical, physical, and social sciences together with the principles and methods of engineering analysis and design, to specify, predict, and evaluate the results to be obtained from such systems.

Information retrieval: The recovering of desired information or data from a collection of documents or other graphic records.

Information theory: The mathematical theory concerned with information rate, channels, channel width, noise, and other factors affecting information transmission. Initially developed for electrical communications, it is now applied to management systems and to phenomena that deal with information units and flow of information in networks.

Initialize: (1) To set various counters, switches, and addresses to zero or other starting values at the beginning of, or at the prescribed points in, a computer routine. (2) Used as an aid to recovery and restart during a long computer run.

Input: Information or data transferred or to be transferred from an external storage medium into the internal storage of the computer. It is often used to refer to the data to be processed.

Input-output: A general term for the equipment used to communicate with a computer and the data involved in the communication. Synonymous with I/O.

Inquiry: A technique whereby the interrogation of the contents of a computer's storage may be initiated at a keyboard.

Inquiry station: The remote terminal device from which an inquiry into computing or data-processing equipment is made.

Instruction: (1) A set of characters that defines an operation together with one or more addresses, or no addresses, and, as a unit, causes the computer to perform the operation on the indicated quantities. The term instruction is preferable to the terms *command* and *order*: command is reserved for a specific portion of the instruction word, i.e., the part that specifies the operation to be performed; order is reserved for the characters (implying sequence), or the order of the interpolation, or the order of the differential equation. (2) The operation or command to be executed by a computer, together with associated addresses, tags, and indices.

Instruction code: The list of symbols, names, and definitions of the instructions that are intelligible to a given computer or computing system.

Integrated circuit: A complete, complex electronic circuit, capable of performing all the functions of a conventional circuit containing numerous discrete transistors, diodes, capacitors, and/or resistors, all of whose component parts are fabricated and assembled in a single integrated process. The resultant assembly cannot be disassembled without destroying it.

Integrated data processing (IDP): (1) A system that treats as a whole all data-processing requirements to accomplish a sequence of data-processing steps, or a number of related data-processing sequences, and strives to reduce or eliminate duplicating data entry or processing steps. (2) The processing of data by such a system.

Interface: A common boundary between automatic data-processing systems or parts of a single system.

Internal storage: (1) The storage of data on a device that is an integral part of a computer. (2) The storage facilities forming an integral physical part of the computer and directly controlled by the computer. In such facilities all data is automatically accessible to the computer, e.g., magnetic core and magnetic tape on-line.

Interpret: (1) To print on a punch card the information punched in that card. (2) To translate nonmachine language into machine-language instructions.

Interrupt: To disrupt temporarily the normal operation of a routine by a special signal from the computer. Usually the normal operation can be resumed from that point at a later time.

Inventory: The stock held for future use in operations, production, or sales. It serves the vital function of decoupling each of the steps in the conversion process from each other and from the suppliers at one end and the customers at the other.

I/O: The abbreviation for input/output. Synonymous with *input-output*.

IOCS (Input/Output Control System): A standard routine or set of routines designed to initiate and control the input and output processes of a computer system, thereby making it unnecessary for users to prepare detailed coding for these processes.

Iterative: Describing a procedure or process that repeatedly executes a series of operations until some condition is satisfied. An iterative procedure can be implemented by a loop in a routine.

Keypunch: (1) a special device to record information in cards or tape to represent letters, digits, and special characters. (2) To operate a device for punching holes in cards or tape.

Label: A set of symbols used to identify or describe an item, record, message, or file. Occasionally it may be the same as the address in storage.

Lacing: Extra multiple punching in a card column to signify the end of a specific card run. The term is derived from the lacework appearance of the card.

Language: A set of rules for conveying information.

Leader: The blank tape at the beginning of a reel of tape.

Least squares: Method of finding a line that best fits a set of data by minimizing the sum of the squares of the deviations between known data and the line being considered.

Level of confidence: Probability, normally in percentages, of the central tendency of the data.

Library: (1) A collection of information available to a computer, usually on magnetic tapes. (2) A file of magnetic tapes.

Library routine: An often-used routine kept in the program library.

Linear programming: A technique of operations research for the optimum allocation of limited resources among competing activities. All the mathematical expressions used are to the first degree, that is, they are linear. Programming refers to the step-by-step procedure for developing the optimum solution.

Load: (1) To put data into a register or storage. (2) To put a magnetic tape onto a tape drive, or to put cards into a card reader.

Load-and-go: Refers to an automatic coding procedure which not only compiles the program, creating machine language, but also proceeds to execute the created program. Load-and-go procedures are usually part of a monitor.

Location: A storage position in the main internal storage which can store one computer word and is usually identified by an address.

Logical flow chart: A detailed solution of the work order in terms of the logic, or built-in operations and characteristics, of a specific machine. Concise symbolic notation is used to represent the information and to describe the input, output, arithmetic, and logical operations involved. The chart indicates types of operations by use of a standard set of symbols. A coding process normally follows the logical flow chart. Synonymous with *program flow chart.*

Loop: A self-contained series of instructions in which the last instruction can modify and repeat itself until a terminal condition is reached.

Low-order: Pertaining to the digit or digits of a number that have the least weight or significance. In the number 53276, the low-order digit is 6.

LPM: Lines per minute.

Machine language: (1) A language designed for interpretation and use by a machine without translation. (2) A system for expressing information which is intelligible to a specific machine, e.g., a computer or class of computers. Such a language may include instructions that define and direct machine operations, and information to be recorded by or acted upon by these machine operations. (3) The set of instructions expressed in the number system basic to a computer.

Machine operator: The person who manipulates the computer controls, places information media into the input devices, removes the output, and performs other related functions.

Macroinstruction: (1) An instruction consisting of a sequence of microinstructions which are inserted into the object routine for performing a specific operation. (2) The more powerful instructions that combine several operations in one instruction.

Magnetic core storage: A storage device in which binary data is represented by the direction of magnetization in each unit of an array of magnetic material, usually in the shape of toroidal rings but also in other forms, such as wraps on bobbins. Synonymous with *core storage.*

Magnetic disk storage: A storage device or system consisting of magnetically coated disks, on the surface of which information is stored in the form of magnetic spots arranged in a manner to represent binary data. These data are arranged in circular tracks around the disks and are accessible to reading and writing heads on an arm which can be moved mechanically to the desired disk and then to the desired track on that disk. Data from a given track are read or written sequentially as the disk rotates. Related to *storage, disk.*

Magnetic drum: A cylinder having a surface coating of magnetic material which stores binary information by the orientation of magnetic dipoles near or on its surface. Since the drum is rotated at a uniform rate, the information stored is available periodically as a given portion of the surface moves past one or more flux-detecting devices which are called *heads* and are located near the surface of the drum.

Magnetic drum storage: The storage of data on the surface of magnetic drums. Related to *magnetic drum.*

Magnetic storage: A device or devices that utilize the magnetic properties of materials to store information.

Magnetic tape: A tape or ribbon of any material impregnated or coated with magnetic or other material on which information may be placed in the form of magnetically polarized spots.

Magnetic tape storage: A storage device in which data is stored in the form of magnetic spots on metal or coated plastic tape. Binary data is stored as small magnetized spots arranged in column form across the width of the tape. A read-write head is usually associated with each row of magnetized spots, so that one column can be read or written at a time as the tape traverses the head.

Magnetic tape unit: The mechanism, normally used with a computer, that handles magnetic tape and usually consists of a tape transport, reading or sensing, and writing or recording, heads, and associated electrical and electronic equipments. Most units may provide for tape to be wound and stored on reels; however, some units provide for the tape to be stored loosely in closed bins.

Main frame: The central processor of the computer system. It contains the main storage, arithmetic unit, and special register groups.

Main storage: Usually the fastest storage device of a computer and the one from which instructions are executed.

Malfunction: A failure in the operation of the hardware of a computer.

Management Information System (MIS): (1) The channels of information flow that feed back operations data for analysis, managment decision, and implementation to exercise control in order that the organization reach its objectives. (2) A system designed to supply the managers of an organization with the information they need to keep informed of the current status of the organization to understand the implications, and to make and implement the appropriate operating decisions.

Map: To transform information from one form to another; to establish a relation between one set of elements and another set.

Markov chains: Mathematical models of physical processes that have a particular kind of stochastic process (events with associated probabilities) associated with them. The stochastic process must have the conditional probability that any future *event* given any past event and the present state is independent of the past event and depends only on the present state of the process.

Mark sensing: A technique for detecting special pencil marks entered in special places on a punch card and automatically translating the marks into punch holes.

Master data: A set of data that is infrequently altered and supplies basic data for processing operations. The data content of a master file. Examples include names, badge numbers, or pay rates in personnel data; or stock numbers, stock descriptions, or units of measure in stock-control data.

Match: A data-processing operation similar to a merge, except that instead of producing a sequence of items made up from the input, sequences are matched against each other on the basis of some key.

Mathematical model: The abstract representation of the essence of a problem in terms of mathematical expressions. This enables the manipulation of variables utilizing mathematical theory in order to evaluate alternative solutions and determine the optimum.

Matrix: An array of quantities in a prescribed form—in mathematics, usually capable of being subject to a mathematical operation by means of an operator or another matrix according to prescribed rules.

Mean value: A characteristic of data which gives a measure of the central tendency of the data.

Measure of effectiveness: Evaluating how close to the right answer you are. Determining probable errors and impact of results. The means by which you can tell how effective results will be—for instance, hours lost through plant accidents is a measure of the effectiveness of your safety program. Operations research may develop an elaborate formula to measure the effectiveness of results in a complex situation.

Median: The middle value, or arithmetic mean of the two middle values, of a set of data arranged in order of magnitude.

Medium: The physical substance upon which data is recorded, e.g., magnetic tape, punch cards, and paper.

Megabit: One million binary digits.

Memory: Same as *storage.*

Merge: To combine items into one sequenced file from two or more similarly sequenced files without changing the order of the items.

MICR (Magnetic Ink Character Recognition): The automatic reading by machine of graphic characters printed with magnetic ink.

Microinstruction: A small, single, short, add, shift, or delete type of command.

Microsecond: One millionth of a second, 10^{-6} seconds; abbreviated *microsec.*

Millisecond: One thousandth of a second, 10^{-3} seconds; abbreviated *msec.* or *ms.*

Minimax: Solving problems so as to minimize the maximum possible loss. Following a course of action that would minimize ill effects caused by wrong predictions or by circumstances over which you have no control.

Mnemonic: Pertaining to the assisting, or intending to assist, human memory. Thus a mnemonic term is usually an abbreviation that is easy to remember, e.g., mpy for multiply.

Mode: (1) A computer system of data representation, e.g., the binary mode. (2) A selected mode of computer operation. (3) The value that occurs with the greatest frequency, i.e., the most common value.

Module: (1) An interchangeable plug-in item containing components. (2) An incremental block of storage, or other building block, for expanding the computer capacity.

Monitor: To supervise and verify the correct operation of a program during its execution, usually by means of a diagnostic routine used from time to time to answer questions about the program.

Monte Carlo method: A trial-and-error method of repeated calculations to discover the best solution of a problem. Often used when a great number of variables are present, with interrelationships so extremely complex as to forestall straightforward analytical handling. Utilizes random number procedures.

Multiplex: The process of transferring data to a storage device operating at a high transfer rate from several storage devices operating at relatively low transfer rates in such a manner that the high-speed device is not obliged to wait for the low-speed devices.

Mutually exclusive events: Events that cannot occur simultaneously.

Nanosecond: One thousandth of a millionth (one billionth) of a second, 10^{-9} seconds.

Noise: The meaningless extra bits or words that must be ignored or removed from the data at the time the data is used.

Normal distribution: Symmetrical distribution of data about its central value, forming the familiar bellshaped curve.

Null: (1) An absence of information, as contrasted with zero or blank for the presence of no information. (2) Zero.

Numerical analysis: The study of methods of obtaining useful quantitative solutions to problems that have been expressed mathematically, including the study of the errors and bounds on errors in obtaining such solutions.

Numerical control: Descriptive of systems in which digital computers are used for the control of operations, particularly of automatic machines, e.g., drilling or boring machines.

Object language: A language that is the output of an automatic coding routine. Usually object language and machine language are the same; however, a series of steps in an automatic coding system may involve the object language of one step serving as a source language for the next step, and so forth.

Object program: The program that is the output of an automatic coding system. Often the object program is a machine-language program ready for execution, but it may well be in an intermediate language.

OCR: (Optical Character Recognition): The automatic reading by machine of graphic characters through use of light-sensitive devices.

Off-line: Descriptive of a system and of the peripheral equipment or devices in a system in which the operation of peripheral equipment is not under the control of the central processing unit.

On-line: Descriptive of a system and of the peripheral equipment or devices in a system in which the operation of such equipment is under control of the central processing unit, and in which information reflecting current activity is introduced into the data-processing system as soon as it occurs. Thus, directly in-line with the main flow of transaction processing.

Open shop: A computer installation that may be programmed and operated by any qualified employee of the organization. Contrast with *closed shop.*

Operand: A quantity entering or arising in an instruction. An operand may be an argument, a result, a parameter, or an indication of the location of the next instruction, as opposed to the operation code or symbol itself. It may even be the address portion of an instruction.

Operation: A defined action. The action specified by a single computer instruction or pseudoinstruction.

Operation code: The part of a computer instruction word that specifies, in coded form, the operation to be performed.

Operations research: The use of analytic methods adopted from mathematics for solving operational problems. The objective is to provide management with a more logical basis for making sound predictions and decisions. Among the common scientific techniques used in operations research are the following: linear programming, probability theory, information theory, game theory, Monte Carlo method, and queuing theory. Synonymous with OR.

Optical scanner: A device that scans printed or written data, using optical techniques, and converts the data into digital representation.

Optimal solution: A feasible solution that maximizes the objective function.

Optimalization: Determining what to do with variables in order to achieve a desired goal—which may be the greatest dollar saving, minimum hours, or maximum return on investment. The answer may not be to maximize or minimize the variables themselves.

Output: (1) The information transferred from the internal storage of a computer to secondary or external storage, or to any device outside of the computer. (2) The routines that direct item 1. (3) The device or collective set of devices necessary for item 1. (4) To transfer from internal storage on to external media.

Overflow: The condition that arises when the result of an arithmetic operation exceeds the capacity of the storage space allotted in a digital computer.

Packing density: The number of units of useful information contained within a given linear dimension, usually expressed in units per inch, e.g., the number of binary-digit magnetic pulses, or the number of characters stored on tape or drum per linear inch on a single track by a single head.

Paper tape: A strip of paper capable of storing or recording information. Storage may be in the form of punched holes, partially punched holes, carbonization or chemical change of impregnated material, or by imprinting. Some paper tapes, such as punched paper tapes, are capable of being read by the input device of a computer or a transmitting device by sensing the pattern of holes that represents coded information.

Parallel operation: The performance of several actions, usually of a similar nature, simultaneously through provision of individual, similar, or identical devices for each such action, particularly flow or processing of information. Parallel operation is performed to save time over serial operation. Parallel operation usually requires more equipment.

Parity bit: A check bit that indicates whether the total number of binary "1" digits in a character or word (excluding the parity bit) is odd or even.

Parity check: A summation check in which the binary digits in a character or word are added and the sum is checked against a single digit, i.e., a check that tests whether the number of ones in a word is odd or even.

Pass: A complete cycle of reading, processing, and writing, i.e., a machine run.

Patch: A section of coding inserted into a routine to correct a mistake or to alter the routine.

Pattern recognition: The identification of shapes, forms, configurations, or sounds by automatic means, e.g., Optical Character Recognition (OCR), machine recognition of human speech.

Payoff table: In game theory, an array showing the value of payoffs to each competitor versus the particular strategy employed.

Peripheral equipment: The auxiliary machines that may be placed under the control of the central computer. Examples of this are card readers, card punches, magnetic tape feeds, and high-speed printers. Peripheral equipment may be used on-line or off-line, depending upon computer design, job requirements, and economics.

Picosecond: One thousandth of a nanosecond (i.e., 10^{-12} second), abbreviated psec.

PL/1 (Programming Language 1): A process-oriented language designed to facilitate the preparation of computer programs to perform both business and scientific functions. Note: Developed jointly by IBM and the SHARE users' organization between 1964 and 1966, PL/1 represents an attempt to combine the best features of existing programming languages (such as ALGOL, COBOL, and FORTRAN) with a number of facilities not available in previous languages.

Plotter: A visual display board in which a dependent variable is graphed by an automatically controlled pen or pencil as a function of one or more variables.

Population: Universe from which we take samples.

Preedit: To edit the input data previous to the computation.

Preset: (1) To set the contents of a storage location to an initial value. (2) To establish the initial control value for a loop.

Probability: Relative frequency of occurrence of an event when the total number of observations is extremely large.

Probability density function: Mathematical function giving probabilities of a random variable.

Problem definition: The art of compiling logic in the form of general flow charts and logic diagrams which clearly explain and present the problem in such a way that all requirements involved are presented.

Procedure: A precise step-by-step method for effecting a solution to a problem.

Process: A general term that covers assemble, compile, generate, interpret, compute, etc.

Process control: Descriptive of systems in which computers, most frequently analog computers, are used for the automatic regulation of operations or processes.

Processor: (1) A generic term that includes assembly, compiling, and generation. (2) A shorter term for automatic data processor or arithmetic unit.

Program: (1) The complete plan for the solution of a problem; more specifically, the complete sequence of instructions and routines necessary to solve a problem. (2) To plan the procedures for solving a problem. This may involve, among other things, analyzing the problem, preparing a flow diagram, preparing details, testing, and developing subroutines, allocating storage locations, specifying input and output formats, and incorporating a computer run into a complete data-processing system. Related to *routine.*

Program check: A system of determining the correct program and machine functioning, either by running a sample problem with similar programming and a known answer or by using mathematical or logic checks, as comparing A times B with B times A.

Program step: A phase of one instruction or command in a sequence of instructions. Thus, a single operation.

Program test: Before running any problem, a system of checking in which a sample problem of the same type with a known answer is run.

Programmer: A person who devises programs. Note: The term *programmer* is most suitably applied to a person who is mainly involved in formulating programs, particularly at the level of flow chart preparation. A person mainly involved in the definition of problems is a *systems analyst*, while a person mainly involved in converting programs into coding suitable for entry into a computer system is a *coder*. In many organizations, all three of these functions are performed by *programmers*.

Pseudoinstruction: (1) A symbolic representation in a compiler or an interpreter. (2) A group of characters having the same general form as a computer instruction, but never executed by the computer as an actual instruction.

Pulse: A significant and sudden change of short duration in the level of some electric variable, usually voltage.

Punch: (1) To shear a hole by forcing a solid or a hollow sharp-edged tool through a material into a die. (2) The hole resulting from item 1.

Punch card: A heavy stiff paper of constant size and shape, suitable for punching in a pattern that has meaning and for being handled mechanically. The punched holes are sensed either electrically by metal fingers or photoelectrically by photocells.

Punch tape: A tape, usually paper, upon which data may be stored in the form of punched holes. Hole locations are arranged in columns across the width of the tape. There are usually five to eight positions (channels) per column, with data represented by a binary-coded decimal system. All holes in a column are sensed simultaneously in a manner similar to that for punch cards.

Punch-tape code: A code to represent data on punch tape.

Queuing theory: A mathematical study of waiting lines which occur whenever current demand exceeds current capacity to provide service. Assists management decisions regarding amount of capacity. Requires predicting arrival of units for service and amount of service time so as not to have too much or too little capacity or too much waiting. The objective is to balance the cost of service with the cost of waiting for service.

Random access: (1) The process of obtaining information from or placing information into storage where the time required is independent of the location of the information most recently obtained or placed in storage. (2) Each location can be reached in the same amount of time as can any other location.

Random-access storage: A storage technique in which the time required to obtain information is independent of the location of the information most recently obtained. This strict definition must be qualified by the observation that we usually mean *relatively* random. Thus, magnetic drums are relatively nonrandom access when compared with magnetic cores for main storage but are relatively random access when compared with magnetic tapes for file storage.

Random number: Number in a series of possible numbers generated so that each number has an equal chance of occurring in any position.

Random variable: Variable that takes on specific values, with corresponding probabilities for each.

Raw data: Data that has not been processed. Such data may or may not be in machine-sensible form.

Read: (1) To sense information contained in some source. (2) The sensing of information contained in some source.

Read-out: To sense information contained in some internal storage and transmit this information to a storage external to the computer.

Real-time data processing: (1) The processing of information or data in a sufficiently rapid manner so that the results of the processing are available in time to influence the process being monitored or controlled. (2) Transactions are captured and the whole system updated the instant the transaction occurs.

Reel: A spool of tape, generally magnetic tape.

Regression: Similar to correlation, but goes further. A measure of how much relationship exists between variables, and also the nature of the relationship. Shows the effect of one variable on another.

Relative frequency: Frequency of a class divided by total frequency of all classes (usually percentage).

Relative frequency distribution: Tabular list of class intervals and their relative frequencies.

Reliability: (1) A measure of the ability to function without failure. (2) The amount of credence placed in a result.

Reperforator: (1) The contraction of the words *receiving perforator.* (2) Any tape punch that automatically converts coded electrical signals into perforations in tape.

Report generator: A technique for producing complete data-processing reports, based only on a description of the desired content and format of the output reports and certain information concerning the input file. The computer language used is called Report Program Generator (RPG).

Reproducer: A device that reproduces a punch card by punching another similar card.

Rerun: To repeat all or part of a program on a computer.

Restart: To go back to a specific planned point in a routine, usually because of machine malfunction, the portion of the routine in which the error occurred.

Rewind: To return a film or magnetic tape to its beginning or passed location.

Rewrite: The process of restoring the information in a storage device to its state prior to reading.

Round: Deletion of the last significant digit(s), with or without modifications to reduce bias.

Rounding error: The error resulting from rounding off a quantity by deleting the less significant digits and applying some rule of correction to the part retained, e.g., 0.2751 can be rounded to 0.275, with a rounding error of 0.0001.

Routine: A set of coded instructions arranged in proper sequence to direct the computer to perform a desired operation or sequence of operations. A subdivision of a program consisting of two or more instructions that are functionally related; therefore, a program. Clarified by *subroutine* and related to *program*.

Run: The performance of one program on a computer; thus, the performance of one routine or of several routines linked so that they form an automatic operating unit, during which manual manipulations by the computer operator are zero, or at least minimal.

Saddle point: In game theory, when one entry in the payoff table is the minimum in its row and the maximum in its column.

Sample: Group of members of a population taken for purposes of analysis based on a random selection procedure.

Scan: To examine every reference or every entry in a file routinely as a part of a retrieval scheme.

Scanner: An instrument that automatically samples or interrogates the state of various processes, files, conditions, or physical states and initiates action in accordance with the information obtained.

Search: To examine a series of items for any that have a desired property or properties.

Seek: To look for data according to information given regarding that data; occasionally used interchangeably and erroneously for *search, scan,* and *screen.*

Self-checking number: A number with a suffix figure related to the figure(s) of the number, used to check the number after it has been transferred from one medium to another.

Sensitivity analysis: A method of determining the effect on a solution by changing the values of the parameters over a range.

Service routines: A broad class of routines that are standardized at a particular installation to assist in the maintenance and operation of the computer, as well as in the preparation of programs, as opposed to routines for the actual solution of production problems.

Setup time: The portion of the elapsed time between machine operations that is devoted to such tasks as changing reels of tape and moving cards, tapes, and supplies to and from the equipment.

Simplex method: An algebraic procedure in linear programming which progressively approaches the optimal solution through a well-defined iterative process.

Simulation: (1) The abstract representation of physical systems and phenomena by computers, mathematical models, or other equipment, such as an imitative type of data processing in which a computer program is executed as a model of some entity, e.g., a chemical process. Information enters the computer to represent the factors entering the real process; the computer program produces information that represents the process itself. (2) In computer programming, the technique of setting up a routine for one computer to make it operate as nearly as possible like some other computer.

Software: The totality of programs and routines used to extend the capabilities of computers, such as compilers, assemblers, narrators, routines, and subroutines. Contrast with *hardware.*

Solid state: The electronic components that convey or control electrons within solid materials, e.g., transistors, germanium diodes, and magnetic cores. Thus, vacuum and gas tubes are not included.

Solid-state computer: A computer built primarily from solid-state electronic circuit elements, i.e., transistors. Often referred to as "second-generation" computer.

Sort: To arrange items of information according to rules dependent upon a a key or field contained in the items or records, e.g., to digital sort is to sort first the keys on the least significant digit and then to re-sort on each higher order digit until the items are sorted on the most significant digit.

Sorter: A machine that puts items of information into a particular order, e.g., it will determine whether A is greater than, equal to, or less than B and will sort or order accordingly.

Source document: A document from which basic data is extracted.

Source language: The original form in which a program is prepared prior to processing by the machine.

Source program: A computer program written in a language designed for ease of expression of a class of problems or procedures by human beings, e.g., symbolic or algebraic. A generator, assembler, translator, or compiler routine is used to perform the mechanics of translating the source program into an object program in machine language.

Special-purpose computer: A computer capable of performing sequences of permanently wired instructions.

Standard deviation: Square root of the variance of data. Gives a measure of the dispersion about the mean, or central value, of a collection of data.

Statistic: A characteristic of a sample.

Statistical inference: Deals with the conditions under which inferences about the population can be made from analysis of a sample.

Stochastic: Processes with random variables where the results are affected by conditions such as time. For example, the diameter of parts machined on a lathe might first vary in a random way according to a standard distribution about some average value. As cutting tools wear, the average value will shift. This makes it a stochastic process and difficult to analyze mathematically.

Storage capacity: The number of elementary pieces of data that can be contained in a storage device. Frequently defined in terms of characters in a particular code, or words of a fixed size that can be so contained.

Storage dump: A listing of the contents of a storage device, or selected parts of it. Synonymous with *memory dump, core dump,* and *memory print-out.*

Store: (1) To transfer an element of information to a device from which the unaltered information can be obtained at a later time. (2) To retain data in a device from which it can be obtained at a later time.

Stored-program computer: A computer capable of performing sequences of internally stored instructions.

Subroutine: (1) The set of instructions necessary to direct the computer to carry out a well-defined mathematical or logical operation. (2) A subunit of a routine. A subroutine is often written in relative or symbolic coding, even when the routine to which it belongs is not. (3) A portion of a routine that causes a computer to carry out a well-defined mathematical or logical operation.

Symbolic instruction: An instruction in an assembly language directly translatable into a machine code.

Symbolic logic: Intuitive, generalized reasoning and analysis. Unmathematical in nature but often serves as a basis for mathematical analysis by placing logical restrictions on variables. Defines problems or factors that affect a situation.

Symbolic programming: The use of arbitrary symbols to represent addresses in order to facilitate programming.

Synchronous computer: A computer in which all operations are controlled by equally spaced pulses from a clock.

Synergism: The effect of the whole is greater than the sum of the independent effects of its parts.

System: (1) Elements interrelated for a purpose. (2) An assembly of procedures, processes, methods, routines, techniques, or hardware united by some form of regulated interaction to form an organized whole.

Systems analysis: The examination of an activity, procedure, method, technique, or organization to determine what must be accomplished and how the necessary operations may best be accomplished to optimize the attaining of predetermined objectives.

Systems flow chart: A graphical representation of the major steps in a procedure.

Systems test: (1) The running of the whole system against test data. (2) A complete simulation of the actual running system for testing the adequacy of the system. (3) A test of an entire, interconnected set of components for determining proper functioning and interconnection.

Table: A collection of data in a form suitable for ready reference, frequently as stored in sequenced machine locations, or written in the form of an array of rows and columns for easy entry, in which an intersection of labeled rows and columns serves to locate a specific piece of data or information.

Table look-up: To obtain a function value corresponding to an argument, stated or implied, from a table of function values stored in the computer.

Tabulating equipment: The machines and equipment using punching cards. The group of equipment is called tabulating equipment because the main function of installations of punch-card machines for some twenty years before the first automatic digital computer was to produce tabulations of information resulting from sorting, listing, selecting, and totaling data on punch cards. This class of equipment is commonly called PCM, PCDP, or tab equipment.

Tabulator: A machine that reads information from one medium—e.g., cards, paper tape, and magnetic tape—and produces lists, tables, and totals on separate forms or continuous paper.

Tape: A strip of material which may be punched, coated, or impregnated with magnetic or optically sensitive substances and used for data input, storage, or output. The data is stored serially in several channels across the tape, transversely to the reading or writing motion.

Tape drive: Same as *tape transport* and *tape unit.*

Tape-to-card converter: A device that converts information directly from punched or magnetic tape to cards.

Tape transport: The mechanism that moves magnetic or paper tape past sensing and recording heads, usually associated with data-processing equipment. Synonymous with *tape drive,* and *feed;* related to *tape unit, magnetic tape unit,* and *paper tape unit.*

Tape unit: A device consisting of a tape transport, controls, a set of reels, and a length of tape, which is capable of recording and reading information on and from the tape at the request of the computer under the influence of a program. Clarified by *tape transport, magnetic tape unit,* and *paper tape unit.*

Test data: A set of data developed specifically to test the adequacy of a computer run or system. The data may be actual data taken from previous operations or artificial data created for this purpose.

Throughput: The total amount of useful work performed by a data-processing system during a given period of time.

Time-sharing: (1) The use of one central processing unit by two or more terminals during the same overall time interval, accomplished by interspersing component actions in time. (2) The use of a given device by a number of other devices, programs, or human users, one at a time and in rapid succession. (3) A technique or system for furnishing computing services to multiple users simultaneously while providing rapid responses to each of the users. Note: Time-sharing computer systems usually employ multiprogramming and/or multi-processing techniques, and they are often capable of serving users at remote locations via a data communications network.

TLU: See Table Look-Up

Total systems concept: The performance of every element affects the performance of the whole.

Tracing routine: A diagnostic routine used to provide a time history of one or more machine registers and controls during the execution of the object routine. A complete tracing routine would reveal the status of all registers, and locations affected by each instruction, each time the instruction is executed. Since such a trace is prohibitive in machine time, traces that provide information only following the execution of certain types of instructions are most frequently used.

Track: The path along which information is recorded on a storage device, e.g., the track on a drum or a tape.

Transcribe: To copy, with or without translating, from one storage medium to another.

Transcriber: The equipment associated with a computing machine for the purpose of transferring input or output data for a record of information in a given language to the medium and the language used by a digital computing machine, or from a computing machine to a record of information.

Transistor: An electronic device utilizing semiconductor properties to control the flow of currents.

Translate: To change information from one form of representation to another without significantly affecting the meaning. Related to *transform.*

Troubleshoot: To search for the cause of a malfunction or an erroneous program behavior in order to remove the malfunction.

Truncate: To drop digits of a number of terms of a series, thus lessening precision, e.g., the number 3.14159265 is truncated to five figures in 3.1415, whereas one may *round off* to 3.1416.

Truncation error: The error resulting from the use of only a finite number of terms of an infinite series, i.e., 1.333 instead of 1.33333, etc.

T-test: Statistical test used to test the significance of the difference between two means.

Ultrasonics: The field of science devoted to frequencies of sound above the human audio range, i.e., above 20 kilocycles per second.

Unit record: (1) A record that is similar in form and content to other records on a punched card. (2) Pertaining to equipment or techniques for dealing with unit records as described in item 1, especially to punched-card equipment.

Update: (1) To put into a master file changes required by current information or transactions. (2) To modify an instruction so that the address numbers it contains are increased by a stated amount each time the instruction is performed.

Utility routine: A standard routine used to assist in the operation of a computer by performing some frequently required process such as sorting, merging, report program generation, data transcription, file maintenance, etc. Synonymous with *service routine.* Note: Utility routines are important components of the software supplied by the manufacturers of most computers.

Validity: Correctness, especially the degree of the closeness by which iterated results approach the correct result.

Variable: (1) A quantity that can assume any of the numbers of some set of numbers. (2) A condition, transaction, or event that changes or may be changed as a result of processing additional data through the system.

Variance: The sum of the squares of the differences between the mean and the individual values in a collection of data, divided by the total number of observations (values) in the collection.

Verify: To check a transcribing operation by a compare operation. It usually applies to transcriptions that can be read mechanically or electrically.

Vocabulary: A list of operating codes or instructions available to the programmer for writing the program for a given problem for a specific computer.

Word: An ordered set of characters that occupies one storage location and is treated by the computer circuits as a unit and is transferred as such. Ordinarily, a word is treated by the control unit as an instruction, and by the arithmetic unit as a quantity. Word lengths may be fixed or variable, depending on the particular computer.

Word-mark: An indicator to signal the beginning or the end of a word.

Write: (1) To transfer information, usually from main storage, to an output device. (2) To record data in a register, location, or other storage device or medium.

X-punch: (1) A punch in the X, or 11, row of an eighty-column card. (2) A punch in position 11 of a column. The X-punch is often used to control or select, or to indicate a negative number as if it were a minus sign. Also called an 11-punch.

Xerography: A dry copying process involving the photoelectric discharge of an electrostatically charged plate. The copy is made by tumbling a resinous powder over the plate. The remaining electrostatic charge is discharged and the resin is transferred to paper or an offset printing master.

Y-punch: (1) A punch in the Y, or 12, row of an eighty-column card, i.e., the top row of the card. (2) A punch in position 12 of a column. It is often used for additional control or selection, or to indicate a positive number as if it were a plus sign.

Zero suppression: The elimination of nonsignificant zeros to the left of significant digits, usually before printing.

Zone: (1) A portion of internal storage allocated for a particular function or purpose. (2) The three top positions, 12, 11, and 0 on certain punch cards. In these positions, a second punch can be inserted so that with punches in the remaining positions 1 to 9, alphabetic characters may be represented.

3

THE SYSTEMS ANALYST
AND CREATIVITY

THE SYSTEMS ANALYST

The person who plans the Management Information System, analyzes its performance, and designs improvements in the system is usually referred to as a *systems analyst*. In most organizations where this position exists, more often than not it is in a staff capacity. Although the systems analyst plans, analyzes, and designs information systems for operating management, he rarely has any responsibility for these operations. Furthermore, his formal training and experience are such that he usually has little, if any, practical knowledge of how to operate a business or manage an organizational unit. This is one of the great anomalies in the information-processing field. Management Information Systems, which are the lifeblood of an organization, are often designed and implemented by people who are operational novices in the running of the organizations for which they design these information systems. This obvious contradiction has a rather dramatic resolution. The key to it is contained in the definitions of the terms *Systems Analyst* and *Manager*.

A *systems analyst* is a person who designs information systems to optimize the interrelationships of men, materials, machines, and money. This is actually very similar to the definition of manager. If you recall, a *manager* is a person who selects courses of action to optimize the interrelationships of men, materials, machines, and money for the survival and growth of the business. Since the manager is the systems operator, and since he is the only one who can specify the critical specifications of the needed information system, he is also, in reality, the systems analyst.

THE MANAGER AS A SYSTEMS ANALYST

The manager, by virtue of his job, is therefore a practicing systems analyst. His awareness of all the technical aspects of information processing may be missing, but this can be taken care of by appropriate technical support.

This possible role of the manager underscores an existential reality in the design of Management Information Systems. Operating managers, the doers, must be intimately involved in the structuring of the network of information channels and in the design of the form, the content, and the timing of the information flow in these channels. They, the operating managers, are the major reason for the existence of the Management Information System. They best know the subtle interactions in their areas of responsibility and authority. Therefore, the managers concerned must set up the operating specifications for the design of the information system that will directly affect their operating effectiveness. It is the manager who must be the key systems analyst. This is fundamental to the successful planning, analysis, and design of an effective Management Information System.

The professional systems analyst should be viewed as a technical specialist who understands the technical ramifications of information theory and the strengths and weaknesses of the various types of information-processing equipment. He also should be well versed in the tools and techniques of systems analysis. In these areas he should be superior to the operating manager. But his role is clear—it is that of technical adviser. The strategic planning, operational analysis, and fundamental design of the Management Information System must reside in the hands of those whose survival depend upon it—the operating managers.

CREATIVITY—THE BASIC TOOL OF THE SYSTEMS ANALYST

The manager who accepts his role as a systems analyst will find that his experience has already provided him with training in the most basic tool of systems planning, analysis, and design—creativity.

The importance of creativity to management is underscored by recognizing a universal characteristic of the management function in all organizations. It is simply that the solutions to yesterday's problems will not work on today's! The manager often finds that he must come up with new solutions daily because it seems that every day there are new problems. Coming up with new solutions to old problems, or adapting old solutions to new problems, is a definition of *innovation*. Therefore, managers must be innovators. But innovation is just another name for *creativity.* So it is safe to say that the occupational common denominator of managers is creativity.

If creativity is really as important for the manager-systems analyst as all the evidence indicates, developing an understanding of creativity makes sense. Understanding it better will help the manager-systems analyst use it better in the effective application of the techniques of systems planning, analysis, and design.

Definition of Creativity

Some currently useful definitions of creativity are as follows:

1. To cause something to exist
2. To produce that which would not otherwise be
3. The formulation of the whole that is greater than the sum of its parts
4. The rearrangement of past experience

The fourth definition is probably the most provocative, the most surprising, and the most specific.

But if creativity is thought of in the concrete terms of "the rearrangement of past experience," how does one develop a rich and varied background of experience to provide the raw material for creativity? Research indicates that it is most often done by:

1. Exposure to the provocative ideas of others by reading, travel, TV, conversation
2. Personal experiences in professional activities
3. Formal education to provide an organized and systemized expansion of experiences
4. Research in the field through trade sources, conferences, literature, and experimentation

Yet, thinking about it, it may be disturbing to consider that people with the same experiences and background often exhibit different degrees of creativity! How does that square with the concept of creativity that has been described? People who have studied the matter indicate that creative results depend upon:

1. *How you think*—Not how you think you think, but how you really think. Whether your thought processes are based on hunches or logical analysis or emotions. Whether your conclusions depend on who spoke to you last or what fits in best with your preconceptions, or the most popular current generality. Or combinations of all of these.
2. *How you apply your energy*—Do you immobilize yourself with the bromides "play it safe," or "the innovator is the mistake maker," or, possibly, "conforming is more comfortable"?

All of these tend to channel creative energy into the well-worn grooves that dissipate that energy without generating new solutions. Therefore, the answer to the question, How is it that people with similar past experiences exhibit significantly different degrees of creativity? really depends on the answers to the questions, *How do you think?* and *How do you apply your energy?*

A good test of whether or not you have been answering these questions in a creative way is to look back on the record of your past activity for a period of, say, two, three, or even five years. Examine the major decisions you have made during this time span. Are you satisfied with the results? Where could you have done better—dramatically better? Were those decisions based on self-deception? Self-hypnosis by the bromides mentioned? A drawing back from the new and untried?

If your answers are disturbing, if you feel things could have gone better, the following section will give you some specific steps to help harness your creative energy—the universal systems tool that is within us all.

Steps in Developing Creativity

1. Test "how you think."
2. Develop an understanding of creativity.
3. Develop your creativity—by practice.
4. Apply your creative energy.

Step 1: Test How You Think.   Here is a simple test using nine dots, which may give you some idea about how you think.

Without lifting your pencil from the paper, connect all nine dots with four straight lines. Take a minute or two to try it. Then look at the solution on page 56.

Step 2: Develop an Understanding of Creativity.   Eight generally accepted qualities of creativity have been identified. A person who has developed them will probably exhibit creative effectiveness.

1. *Sensitivity*—to problems, needs, attitudes, and feelings of others. The creative person uses his eyes for observing as well as seeing, his ears for listening as well as hearing, his hands for feeling as well as touching.
   Test yourself: Which shoe do you put on first in the morning? How many steps in the stairway in your home? Which statesman's picture is on a ten-dollar bill?
2. *Fluency*—the ability to take advantage of a developing situation, to use each completed step as a vantage point for the next.
   Test yourself: List quickly as many words as possible that express enthusiasm.
   Examples: zealous, fervent, fanaticism, inspiration.

3. *Flexibility*—the ability to adjust quickly to a new development and changed situations—bad breaks, market changes, luck.
   Test yourself: Write down all the things you can think of that might happen if people could suddenly read each other's minds.

4. *Originality:*—the capacity to come up with new ideas that work.
   Test yourself: List six unusual uses to which newspaper can be put—starting a fire or wrapping garbage is unacceptable.
   Examples: to write a kidnap note, to use as a language-training aid, to use as insulation—acoustical and thermal.

5. *Skill at redefinition*—the ability to rearrange ideas, concepts, people, and things—using old things for new purposes.
   Example: The way 3M Company developed uses for scotch tape. The way some businessmen turn waste into profit.

6. *Skill of analysis*—proficiency in breaking down a problem into its parts, and relating the parts to each other and to the whole.
   Example: Noncreative people look at a problem as one big, stubborn mass. The creative person will break it into bite-size chunks.

7. *Ability to synthesize*—the other side of the coin, that is, the combining of several elements to form a new whole.
   Example: The bringing together of different manufacturing operations for the smoothly integrated production of a new product.
   Test yourself: Put scrambled words into a meaningful sentence.
   Example: Fundamental creativity planning is in management.

8. *Ability to organize*—to plan a project, to create a design, to organize a department.
   Test yourself: Compose a story using as many as possible of a list of random words. Use the last words of each sentence on this page.

Step 3: Develop your Creativity—By Practice. Now that the key attributes of creativity have been defined, you may want to know how they can be developed. We know that there are techniques for improving memory, such as association, writing things down, repetition. We know that there are techniques for improving vocabulary, such as learn ten words a day, use them daily. We know that by practicing courtesy we become courteous. There is a basic similarity in all of these techniques. The secret ingredient seems to be practice. And that is exactly how creativity can be improved. You must practice using your creative energy to develop it and to learn to apply it better. Here are some specific suggestions.

GAMES: There are about 250 sedentary games, and of these about 50 involve creative exercises.

1. *Chess and checkers.* If not played "by the book," they are excellent creative exercises.

2. *Twenty Questions.* Not much good for those who answer yes or no, but fair for the questioner. He has to think of perceptive questions.

3. *Charades.* This game provides creative exercise for all participants. It challenges the ingenuity of those who have to act out their ideas, and viewers have to try hard to interpret gestures and expressions.

4. *Puzzles.* All of the following are useful.
   a. Crossword puzzles require working the mind.
   b. Double-crostics, Scrabble, cryptograms.
   c. Anagrams—developing words from scrambled letters.

5. *More active games*—The catcher in baseball and the quarterback in football are the really creative positions on the team.

HOBBIES: Most are acquisitive and of little creative value, but they build knowledge and, to some extent, judgment rather than creativity directly. But embossing, wood carving, and metalworking, for example, stimulate the imagination and help creativity.

FINE ARTS: Painting and drawing—excellent for developing creativity.

READING:

1. Read one-half of a story, then think up and write an outline for the second half.

2. Make notes as you read and you will find that you get ideas from passages wholly unrelated to the particular subject that provoked them. It will seem that ideas and solutions to problems were "cooking" on your brain's "back burner."

WRITING: Writing does much to exercise the imagination. Try writing your own gag lines for cartoons. Try short stories, articles. Prepare advertising copy for a company. For different media.

OBSERVATION: Look at a picture. Cover it. Try to recall as many things about it as you can.

Step 4: Apply Your Creative Energy.   Now that we have defined creativity and have presented some ideas on how to develop it, let us look at some specific techniques of systems analysis that are closely identified with the creative process. Managers intuitively used these techniques long before they became glamorized with names like *scientific method* and *brainstorming.* Whatever their names, they are real down-to-earth systems tools and they work!

SOME CREATIVE TOOLS FOR THE SYSTEMS ANALYST

The Scientific Method of Problem Solving

A systematic approach can help you to think creatively and to apply your energy effectively.

1. *Identify the problem*—not the symptoms, but the problem. Write a tentative statement of the problem. Yes, write it down!
2. *Gather data*—the more the better. Use a checklist to help you gather data. What is being done? Where is it being done? When is it being done? Who is doing it? How is it being done? Organize data as you collect it. Estimate its reliability. Is it fact? Opinion? Hunch?
3. *List possible solutions*—let your imagination roam freely. Jot down all possibilities, even the absurd ones. Provoke your thinking by considering the following:
   a. Put to new uses.
   b. Adopt—what else is similar, what could be copies?
   c. Modify—new twist? Change color, shape, odor, motion, sound, other changes.
   d. Magnify—add, more time, frequency, stronger, higher, longer, duplicate, exaggerate, multiply.
   e. Minify—make smaller, subtract, omit, lower, thinner, lighter, split up, understate, streamline.
   f. Substitute—who else instead, what else, other ingredient, material, process? Other place, approach, tone or voice.
   g. Rearrange—interchange components, other patterns.
   h. Reverse—positive and negative, opposite, turn backward, upside down, turn the tables, turn other cheek.
   i. Combine—blending, assortment? Combine units, appeals, ideas.

The greater the quantity of ideas you generate, the more workable and sound the ideas that are likely to result. Develop in greater detail any ideas that look good and then evaluate.

4. *Test the solutions objectively*—
   a. Suitability—Will it do the job fully, partially, permanently, temporarily?
   b. Feasibility—Is it practical? What will it cost?
   c. Acceptability—Will the interested parties go along? You could set up a rating chart to help test solutions on some quantitative scale.

5. *Select the best solution*—Decide, perhaps by using the strong points of one solution with the particular virtues of another.
6. *Put your solution into action*—Put theory into practice. If the problem disappears, it is solved. If not, recycle, that is, start back at step 1. If this seems strange, remember, you know a lot more about the problem now than you did the first time.

Brainstorm Sessions

Brainstorm sessions are another specific systems analysis technique that depends on creativity. There are times when management knows that it would be productive to tap the uninhibited creative thinking of the members of a group. Different, better, or unique solutions are desired for a problem under consideration. However, in most discussions or conferences the participants are inclined to be conservative in their contributions. One reason for this is that most people have trained themselves to censor their ideas before they speak. This is because of the opposition, criticism, or kidding they are usually sure to get from their associates if they generate a wild idea. The purpose of the brainstorm method is to provide for complete freedom of contributions and to eliminate opposition. It can be used as the creative portion of a meeting, with more conventional methods being used for the remaining time. The method has been variously labeled *brainstorming, bright idea session, creative discussion*. As *brainstorm sessions*, its origin and use is described in *Your Creative Power*, by Alex Osborn.[1]

Here is how it works:

1. Number of People:
   The method seems to work best with from five to ten people, but often it is productive with as many as twenty. It is helpful if there are two or more members who can "let themselves go."
2. Type of Subject:
   The more specific the subject, the better—so that the idea can be aimed at a small target.
3. Rules of the Game:
   a. Any contribution is welcome, however wild.
   b. Criticism or argument regarding another member's idea is out of order.
   c. Questions for the purpose of understanding are in order but are not to imply doubt or ridicule.

[1] Alex F. Osborn, *Your Creative Power* (New York: Charles Scribner's Sons, 1948).

      d. Assistance to another member in building up his idea is to be encouraged.

      e. A large number of suggestions is desired with very little time spent on each.

   4. Leader Action:

      a. He establishes a free, informal atmosphere.

      b. He encourages contributors in any way possible.

      c. He holds the group to the above rules, first gently warning offenders, then firmly stopping them.

      d. He avoids like poison any "masterminding" and any belittling.

   5. Tests of a Good Session:

      a. The number of ideas produced.

      b. The feeling of the members "after the picnic."

If you have never tried the foregoing on a problem, you have a very satisfying and surprising experience in store.

Creative Use of Time

Time is of the essence in all aspects of management and systems analysis. But the ancient adage Time Is Money should not mean the maintaining of a hurried and frenetic atmosphere. Systems analysts must learn how to provide themselves with the time they need to try new tools and techniques, as well as time to think. But where can they find the time? Here are some suggestions that have worked for others:

   1. Increase your reading and writing skills.

   2. Make good notes and keep them.

   3. Use a surefire reminder system.

   4. Make up your mind first time around.

   5. Answer your correspondence at once.

   6. Specify who is to do what and when.

   7. Make weekly and daily plans—in writing.

   8. Control that telephone.

   9. Make dates and times specific.

  10. Give advance notice of meetings.

  11. Keep chitchat under control.

  12. Review this list periodically.

The Activity Profile Analysis

An excellent source for finding time is to analyze where you are now spending it. Although the method was designed for managers, it can be used by students, housewives, anyone. The way to do it is misleadingly simple. You keep a detailed and systematic log of everything you do, every minute of every day—for two weeks. Every telephone call, conference, interruption. What correspondence you received, read, answered, initiated. Wherever you spent your time. In other words, everything that requires time during every day is recorded.

It may seem like a lot of work, but the results are dramatic! After the first few hours you will find that you have developed a quick shorthand method for noting time, subject, conclusions, participants, and so forth. It really is not as impossible as it sounds. Do not be too disturbed if you miss a few items, the two weeks of recording will take care of that.

After you have compiled the raw data, the next step is to categorize. The particular categories you use will depend on the unique characteristics of your activity. Here are some ideas: Segregate what you have done by importance. Those you must do, should do, nice to do, should not do. Then categorize by timeliness, that is, items that must be done immediately, should be done reasonably quickly, need not be done for some time, have no time limit. Other categorizations might involve activities that could only be done by you, or could be done by others. It is important that whatever categories you select, you segregate what you did within these categories and then indicate the percentage of your total time you spent on each of these categories. Unless you are the rare exception, you will be amazed at where you are spending your time. Especially when you compare it with where you think you are spending your time and with those responsibilities where you know you should be spending your time.

You will be amazed, not only at the things you are doing that you should not be doing but at the time you will find you are spending on very low-priority items. The criterion to use in developing a new activity schedule for yourself is to apply the most basic yardstick—Am I putting my efforts where they will maximize results?

Writing in the Dark

Writing in the dark is a tool that has been used by a number of the most successful executives in the world. It is based on the fact that many of our best ideas occur just before we drop off to sleep. This phenomenon seems to occur often to many people. They have a problem that has been bothering them, or a decision that must be made, and as they drift off to sleep the solution occurs to them. Most people, when this happens, just go to sleep. When they get up in the morning, they cannot remember what it was that they had conjured up before dropping off to sleep. If they had learned to write in the dark, using a pad tied to the side rail of the bed, they could have jotted down a quick note, and it would have been enough to remind them of the solution the next morning. You can shed quite a bit of light on your problems by developing the rather eccentric skill of learning to write in the dark.

Solution to test in Step 1, p. 49:

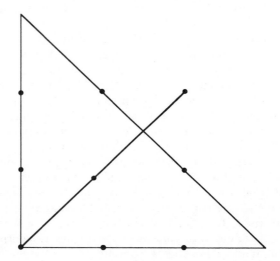

Most people limit their possible solutions within the confines of the dots, as if there were a wall around them. This shows that we often confine our thinking and, therefore, our energy to preconceived channels. Yet the solution is easy and obvious once we leap these self-imposed barriers. How did you think?

REVIEW QUESTIONS

1.   What is a systems analyst?
2.   How would you defend the position, "a manager is a systems analyst"?
3.   Define *creativity*.
4.   Why understand creativity?

5.   What two basic factors determine creative effectiveness?

6.   Comment on the procedure for the development of creativity.

7.   Apply the scientific method of problem solving to a specific Management Information Systems application.

8.   Describe the mechanics of a *brainstorm session*. Try it out. Report on the experience.

9.   What is an activity profile analysis? Try it in shortened form. Criticize it.

10.   What possible reason can a systems analyst have for learning to write in the dark?

BIBLIOGRAPHY

BELLOWS, ROGER M., *Creative Leadership*. Englewood Cliffs, N. J.: Prentice-Hall, Inc. 1959. Provides a number of interesting and helpful insights into the role of creativity in management.

HAEFELE, JOHN W., *Creativity and Innovation*. New York: Reinhold Publishing Corp., 1962. Provocative and helpful.

KRICK, EDWARD V., *Methods Engineering*. New York: John Wiley & Sons, Inc., 1962. Provides considerable details on the industrial engineering approach to problem solving, i.e., problem formulation, analysis, and then development of alternatives before selection and implementation.

OSBORN, ALEX F., *Applied Imagination*. New York: Charles Scribner's Sons, 1953. One of the first and still one of the greatest treatments of the subject by a successful practitioner and world-recognized authority.

PARNES, SIDNEY J., and HAROLD F. HARDING, *A Source Book for Creative Thinking*. New York: Charles Scribner's Sons, 1962. Comprehensive and useful.

TAYLOR, CALVIN W., *Creativity: Progress and Potential*. New York: McGraw-Hill Book Company, 1964. Additional material for innovation.

WEIL, RICHARD, JR., *The Art of Practical Thinking*. New York: Simon and Schuster, Inc., 1940. Just as the title implies. It is wide ranging and still worthwhile and contains a number of down-to-earth illustrations from the author's experience.

WHITING, CHARLES S., *Creative Thinking*. New York: Reinhold Publishing Corp., 1958. A source book that stresses fundamentals.

4

THE PLANNING FUNCTION AND THE MANAGEMENT INFORMATION SYSTEM

THE PLANNING FUNCTION

Planning is the rational selection of courses of action to reach pre-determined goals. A more detailed, more systems-oriented way of thinking about planning is that it is the systematic evaluation of the different degrees of risk associated with alternative combinations of men, machinery, materials, and money and the selection of courses of action to maximize the organization's effectiveness in reaching its predetermined goals.

An effective Management Information System must be integral to the planning function. The planners must make provision for a network of communication channels for feedback, analysis, and control information. In addition, if the volume and type of data to be handled plus the frequency and timing of feedback reports and action decision directives require it, planning may also have to encompass a feasibility study for an automated data-processing system. Chapter 14 will discuss this aspect in detail.

The objective of the planning function is to develop a blueprint for action and standards for performance measurement. The plan that results usually takes the form of quantitative operations plans, forecasts, schedules, budgets, and proposals. These represent, in numbers, the actual resources of men, materials, machines, and money that make up the organization. These plans are quantitative representations of the organization. By definition, a *model* is an abstract representation of reality. The representations of reality developed by the planning function are therefore quantitative models of the total system. The manipulation of these quantitative models by management can be a powerful aid in pretesting alternative courses of action. Although managements have been trying to do this for generations, it is only with the advent of the electronic computer that the actual manipulation of masses of quantitative data has become practical. This aspect of the role of the computer in the planning function and its relation to the Management Information System will be discussed in Chapter 13. What is important to recognize at this time is that the planning function sets the stage, as it were, for the operation of the Management Information System.

Not only does the planning function in an organization structure the operations of that organization, provide standards for performance measurement, and even create models for pretesting management decisions, but it also provides a unique method for the coordination of effort in the organization's management system. This comes about when the planners are the key decision makers. Then the mechanics of developing the overall organization plan helps them get in tune with the objectives and operational realities of the system of which they are a part. In a very real sense the planning process acts as a master compass which each of the participants uses to orient his own perspective and his decision criteria for his own area of responsibility. This is one of the more subtle but one of the most important side effects of the planning process that is explained in this chapter.

THE PLANNING CYCLE

As was outlined in Chapter 1, the Management Information System provides the means for the implementation of the key management functions.

Planning—the conscious determination of courses of action.

Analysis—the detailed examination of the performance of each of the elements in the plan by comparing actual performance against the plan.

Control—the action decisions required, as indicated by the *analysis*, to accomplish the *plan*. The planning cycle provides the step-by step procedure for structuring the organizational environment that will be given life by the Management Information System.

An understanding of the fundamentals of the planning cycle will give the systems analyst useful insights regarding the planned environment with which he must interact. His area of operations and the effectiveness of the information systems he helps design will be determined, to a large extent, by the planning or lack of it in the organization of which he is a part. Understanding the planning procedure will help him understand the management system of an organization.

Although planning procedures are as varied as the organizations themselves, the planning cycle can usefully begin by considering the method of setting the organization's objectives and then determining a time span for the plan, followed by organizing the planning group itself, forecasting key/critical statistics, detailing the quantitative elements of the plan, and finally designing the Management Information System to process data, analyze results, and control the operations.

In many organizations, the planning is carried out by people other than those directly involved. However, the concept of planning that is gaining wider and wider acceptance is that of having each of the decision makers concerned participate in the planning that affects his area of responsibility. In other words, the doers have a hand in setting the goals and the constraints that determine the climate within which they will work. Each decision maker can then base his specific decisions on a deeper understanding of what went into the elements of the plan that he is expected to follow. In a sense, the advance planning on an organization-wide level sets the "rules of the game," while each functional area manager interprets the rules and converts them into the specific guidelines and objectives that pertain to the observed reality of his situation. Involvement in the planning process generates interest for more involvement which can develop into enthusiastic cooperation. This is the planning philosophy that will be assumed in the steps that follow.

Determining Systems Objectives

The first step in setting up a plan is to establish objectives, that is, to set the long-term goals of the company or organization. One method used in developing goals is to have the top executive put out a general statement of what he believes the goals are of the organization. This statement is usually phrased in very general terms and emphasizes the satisfying of a human need by the product or service rendered. Much like a commencement day speech, it is given respectful attention as a traditional element of the occasion and then discreetly ignored.

One way of using such a statement of goals and objectives to generate more meaningful specifics is to distribute it down the line to all management and staff personnel for their detailed written recommendations of what they believe the goals and objectives should be. The results of their thinking are then integrated by top management into a statement that embodies the best points of all the ideas expressed. It should be pointed out that although this approach attempts to obtain the participation of those most concerned in setting objectives, the statement of the chief executive who initiated the process usually exerts a significant "blanketing" effect.

Another approach is to have key decision makers meet with the chief executive with the stated purpose of developing the organization's goals. Once again, however, unless the chief executive is aware of the inordinate effect his opinions have on his subordinates and restrains himself accordingly, he will find, more often than not, that the goals and objectives that result will be reworded reflections of his own point of view.

As difficult and as frustrating as it may be during the process, the potentially most useful method of setting objectives and goals is to have it done in concert by the operating executives, without the presence of the chief executive. His absence will provide them with the opportunity to examine their own and each other's points of view with a minimum of concern about reflecting the official position. The concern is by no means eliminated, but it is reduced.

This group approach has important side effects. It provides the key executives with the opportunity to compare their thinking with the thinking of their colleagues on a very important subject, the future of the organization. But even more significant, the very process of developing goals and objectives in this manner can produce the important by-product of having the key people get "in tune" with each other on the organization's objectives—a major contribution toward cooperation when the plan must finally be implemented by the same people. Goals and objectives can be articulated in a variety of ways. In terms of the specific service that the organization hopes to perform; growth with security; maximization of profit with medium, low, or high risk; promotion from within; doubling volume every ten years; product diversification; responsibility to the public and, to stockholders, return on investment; markets to be developed; sources of supply to be discovered; company organization; research and development; financial policies; personnel policies; and a host of others. Any or all could be made a part of the statement of the goals and objectives of the company.

It is interesting to note that as subtle as they are, these general attitudes influence the day-to-day decisions of the various executives at all levels in the organization. The cumulative effect of the daily decisions, influenced by the organization's objectives, can determine the success or the failure of the enterprise. Yet in most companies and organizations, these general decision guidelines are rarely written down for the guidance for all concerned. Furthermore, even a smaller percentage of organizations include key managers and department heads in the development of goals and objectives. Yet these same key people are the ones who, by their day-to-day decision making, can de-emphasize or give priority to the intent of the organization's goals and objectives. When they are not part of the goal-setting process, their day-to-day decisions may effectively modify and rearrange the goals and objectives envisioned by the highest levels of management. In effect, the operating decision makers set the real goals of the organization, so that including them in the formal process is simply combining form and substance. The results can be very gratifying.

The planning function rests squarely on the determination of the objectives and goals of the organization. Participative development of these goals is insurance that they will be understood by the decision makers who have the responsibility for making them happen. The greater their understanding, the greater their role in setting the targets against which they will be measured, and the greater the possibility for enthusiastic cooperation.

Organizing for Planning

The previous comments about utilizing key decision makers for setting objectives also provide a clue as to the best approach for setting up an effective planning organization. It is axiomatic that the planning concept requires an overall, integrated approach. That is, planning must be "total systems" oriented, since every aspect of the organization is affected and must be considered. Whatever mechanism is to be set up to do the planning must, therefore, reflect all functions, levels, and interests within the total organization system. These criteria can best be satisfied by that much-maligned entity known as a committee. The keystone of the planning organization is therefore a carefully selected *planning committee.*

In one company, a very effective planning committee was set up with a staff vice-president in charge. The balance of the committee consisted of a manager from each of the following departments: product development, engineering, finance, purchasing, sales, production, and personnel. The existing staff personnel in each of the departments handled any studies, reports, and research that were required. In addition, an outside consultant was retained to meet with the committee and act as technical adviser. In another organization, each operating manager who was to be on the planning committee was given a leave of absence from his regular job while he served on the committee. A bold and drastic step, but the plan developed by that committee worked out well for that organization's survival and growth.

A third approach that has been used is the setting up of a planning department reporting to the president. Members of this department acted as chairmen of subcommittees that handled different aspects of the planning effort. Operating personnel were members of these subcommittees. The subcommittee reports were finalized and integrated into the total plan by the planning department. The track record of this type of approach has been spotty at best. Where it has been tried it has usually evolved into an informal management development program under the guise of a planning function.

Variations in each of these approaches have been tried with varying degrees of success. The important thing to recognize is that the development of the plan is an exercise in futility unless it is implemented with the necessary systems for analysis and control. Implementation begins with understanding and develops quickest where there is involvement and active participation. These principles reinforce the observation made with regard to the setting of objectives, which also applies here —the doers should be the planners. This same basic principle provides the clue as to the best organization for effective planning. The touchstone must be to maximize participation and involvement in the planning cycle by those who will have key roles in the implementation of the plan.

Although the name, ground rules, and *modus operandi* may vary, the coming together of key decision makers to prepare the plan for their organization must be the result. The professional systems analyst in the guise of a staff employee or as an outside consultant has the important role of providing technical input to insure that the planning decisions make provision for the necessary information channels and processing and feedback to ensure management analysis and control.

Setting the Time Span

The next step in planning is the setting of a time period for the plan. Usually, any planning under six months is considered short-term or short-range planning, while anything over two years is considered long-range planning.

In the dress business or in the bathing suit industry, six months might be considered long-range planning. In the telephone and utility industries or in hospital construction, long-range cycles are ten and twenty years. Every organization has a planning time period that is natural to its own unique situation. A good approach for determining the time span for any organization is to dimension the time cycle in which the key influences in that organization's environment go through major changes. These are then interpreted in terms of the organization's unique situation.

For instance, the increase in leisure time is a key influence in the travel and recreation industry, and the increased proportion of the young and of the aged in the United States population is having a great impact on school and hospital construction. It is also affecting the composition of the labor force and the number of women that are working. On a more restricted regional basis, the space complex at Cape Kennedy and the Space Center at Houston, Texas, were key influences in their respective areas. Realization of the impact of such key influences provides the planning group with the necessary information to select a planning time span that has a direct relationship to the realities of the organization's environment.

In many situations, the time span selected is based on the time period that governs the return on investment of resources. Since these are key influences in those situations, this approach can be considered an extension of the preceding comments.

The setting of the time span is particularly significant because planning can be viewed as the process of making things happen that would not otherwise occur. Planning sets the stage and provides the script, actors, and props for the show to go on. Timing and scheduling are therefore fundamental to the whole concept of planning. The time span is the ingredient in planning that answers the key question—*When will it happen?*

It is, of course, basic to the concept of planning that no matter what the time cycle of the plan, it will have to be reviewed periodically —monthly, quarterly, or yearly. A useful guideline is to review the plan whenever a basic assumption changes. This review concept needs emphasis because there is a mystique that builds up around "the plan" and gives the impression that the plan is inflexible and untouchable and once set up must be followed to (what often is) the bitter end. This is a sure formula for self-liquidation. There is nothing as certain as uncertainty; there is nothing as unchangeable as change. Right at the start, the philosophy of planning must encompass the attitude that plans are but "best guesses" and should be modified as reality unfolds to replace imagination. As conditions change, the effective organization adjusts itself and its plan to meet changing conditions. It takes advantage of those developments that seem to be to its benefit and avoids those that seem to be obstacles.

In summary then, the planning time period varies with the type of organization. The most common periods for "long-range" planning are from two to five years. There is a tendency in many organizations toward lengthening this term because of governmental regulations and tax policies. However, the greatest number of formal plans use a planning time span of five years.

Short-range plans are generally governed by the need to conform to accounting periods such as fiscal years or quarters. Short-range plans are integrated with long-range plans. In essence, short-range (tactical) plans implement long-range (strategic) plans. The decisions of the short-range plans have the cumulative effect of contributing to the achievement of the long-range plan or of slowing it down or of even changing it.

A particular dividend of having management think in terms of a time cycle that is longer than the normal cycle for day-to-day operations is that it encourages the consideration of the impact of decisions on the long-range goals of the organization. It helps management balance its concentration on close-in objectives with an awareness of the effects on long-range planning.

The actual setting of the time span for an organization is best developed in the same way as the goals and objectives were developed, by having the participation of all key management personnel. The resulting time span then has the advantage of reflecting the critical realities that determine the survival and growth of the organization.

Evaluating Strengths and Weaknesses

The basic rationale on which planning rests is that it is possible to anticipate circumstances, devise methods for dealing with them, and control their impact on the survival and growth of the organization.

In order that the setting of objectives and the evaluating of alternatives to attain them are not simply an exercise in imagination, it is mandatory that the strengths and weaknesses of the company be identified and dimensioned. It is only by knowing the resources and potentials of the company that feasible ways of utilizing them most effectively can be developed. Planning must proceed in terms of reality: not considering things as they should be—but as they really are.

The following checklist is a start for identifying and measuring strengths and weaknesses. It should be added to as necessary to fit the specific situation.

Strengths and Weaknesses Checklist

1. Technical capability and know-how
2. Financial position—cash, accounts receivable, accounts payable, liabilities, assets, etc.
3. Equipment and plant capacity—physical factors limiting company growth
4. Assurance of sources of supply
5. Product mix matched to marketing and production capability
6. Wage levels and labor pool
7. Technological developments, patents—special problem areas
8. Competitive position related to capabilities of competitors
9. Customer acceptance, demand profile
10. Management accomplishments, backup depth
11. Supplementary and complementary goods and services
12. Market conditions, growth potential

A Practical Forecasting Procedure

The fundamental problem of planning is the accurate forecasting of significant events and activities over the planning cycle. It has been said that a good forecast is a lot like a good salad: one part experience, two parts science, with a good bit of judgment thrown in.

If we could forecast perfectly, companies would be able to produce within perfect schedules, achieve perfect inventories, and always be in a healthy cash position. Management's batting average would be phenomenal. As forecasts vary from perfection, the problems of management increase and seemingly erratic fluctuations occur in all those carefully laid out programs.

Planning demands the application of the most improved forecasting techniques commensurate with the situation to minimize the introduction of error at the foundation of the whole planning process. Though accurate forecasts are obviously of great value, few companies have made any significant efforts to improve their techniques of forecasting. Many of them still make a half-hearted "sales forecast" based on hopes and then discount that by 50 percent (salesmen are born optimists!) for actual production planning.

The following procedure provides a practical approach to forecasting. It is a basic approach that can be augmented by advanced techniques to make it as sophisticated as the situation demands.

1. Determine the Key Influences

Population growth, changing consumer habits, per capita consumption, technological developments, aging population, increasing leisure time, rising expectations of minorities, and so forth—What effects will they have on the organization?

The influences identified will be modified by experience in later forecasts. But it is most important to discover those external factors that will cause profound changes in the organization's environment, over which it has little control. The significance of identifying them and then assessing their impact on the organization is simply to provide early warning to maximize results while minimizing the risk of disaster.

Examples of key external influences:

a. Car registrations this year influence tire purchases in two years.
b. Baby boom in the fifties meant "pop" record sales in the sixties and "young marrieds" needs in the seventies.
c. Aging population means emphasis on geriatrics.
d. Farm income and savings affect farm machinery sales.
e. Acceleration of automation means more relays, switches, motors, computers, etc.
f. Increased leisure time means increased demand for garden and sporting goods, vacation homes, travel, etc.

2. Identify the Indexes That Chart the Key External Influences (External Indicators).

The quantification of the key external influences over time is usually provided by a variety of sources, for instance, the government, trade associations, banking houses, universities, newspapers, and industrial publications. To be useful, these statistics should meet certain requirements:

a. Be available and up to date.
b. Be presented in usable form.
c. Have a history of publication.
d. Be reliable—from an authoriative source.

Some examples of indexes that quantify key influences follow:

a. Employment—available from *Survey of Current Business*, United States Government Printing Office.

b. Bank Debits—keeps tabs on the number of checks that are active (a good indication of the level of business activity). *Survey of Current Business.*

c. Disposable Income—the personal income available to the consumer after taxes. *Survey of Current Business.*

d. Savings Bonds and Personal Savings—*Treasury Bulletin,* United States Government Printing Office.

e. Building Construction—F. R. Dodge Corporation Reports.

f. Department Store Sales—*Survey of Current Business.*

g. Industry Sales Figures—trade associations, the Department of Commerce, certain business magazines.

Sources of Statistical Forecasting Information

Statistic	*Source*
Economic Indicators	Joint Council of Economic Advisors
Economic Indexes	Industrial Conference Board
U.S. Statistical Abstract	U.S. Government Printing Office
U.S. Income and *Output*	U.S. Department of Commerce
Survey of *Current Business*	U.S. Department of Commerce
American Trucking Trends	American Trucking Association
Statistics of Railways	Association of American Railroads
Transport Statistics of U.S.	U.S. Superintendent of Documents
Fortune's "500" Directory	*Fortune* Magazine
Business in Brief	Chase Manhattan Bank
Growth Trends in Manufacturing Industry	U.S. Department of Commerce
Current Population Reports	U.S. Department of Commerce
Federal Reserve Bulletin	U.S. Superintendent of Documents
Business Statistics	U.S. Department of Commerce
Monthly Labor Review	U.S. Department of Labor
Moody's Industrial Manual	Moody's, Inc.
Thomas Register	Thomas Publishing Co.
Vital Statistics of the U.S.	U.S. Department of Health, Education, and Welfare
Sunday *New York Times*	New York Times Company
Facts for Industry	U.S. Bureau of the Census

3. Develop an Internal Indicator of the Organization's Activity.

An internal indicator might be dollar sales per week or units shipped per month, or hospital admissions per week or dollar sales per man-hours of direct labor, or kilowatt hours of electricity used, or whatever internal indicator best measures the fluctuations in quantity and timing of the conversion effort of the men and materials of the organization; that is, a standard unit of measure that best reflects the human energy and material resources that are combined to produce the goods or services that are the reason for the existence of the organization. This is a very important measure and should be developed very carefully because it will be the key to converting any external indicator's forecast into the specifics that are germane to the organization's operations.

Using historical records, plot on regular graph paper the internal indicator that has been identified. It will graph the variations of the organization's fundamental activity over time. This graph in turn can be used to relate to external indicators.

4. *Correlate your internal indicator to external indicators.*

    a. *Leading indicators*—those that lead the internal indicator trend of your organization by weeks, months, or years.

    b. *Coincident indicators*—those that seem to be in phase with the trend of the internal indicator. They fluctuate at the same time, with about the same relative amplitude.

    c. *Trailing indicators*—those that seem to fluctuate weeks or months behind the internal indicator. They are useful in gauging what has happened in retrospect.

5. *Combine Indicators and Experience.*

This is the step that utilizes the comparison of the internal indicator with those external indicators that have been isolated. The historical record of the company and its expected future activity are tempered by the implications of the external indicators.

Based on the analysis of past history, future activity can be forecast by straight line extrapolation, regression analysis, correlations, simulation, or some of the other quantitative techniques that are widely available today. This is then coupled with feedback from industry sources, competition, customers, and suppliers. The raw estimate is tempered by the factual, systematic application of what the indexes relating to the external indicators tell us. The internal and external indicators provide the mass of statistical input, while actual experience and reasoned judgment provide the pragmatic leavening.

Certainly, situations unique to each organization must be given every consideration, but the cry "we're different" is often the hallmark of a management hiding from the risks inherent in trying new approaches to old problems.

The steps outlined in this practical approach of forecasting have the avowed purpose of reducing the area of uncertainty in decision making. But judgment is still the essential ingredient for the key/critical decisions. The steps discussed can be modified to fit each company's or organization's unique situation while still providing a systematic approach for forecasting the environment within which the organization must survive and grow.

STRUCTURING THE PLAN

The preceding section outlined a useful approach to determining, dimensioning, and forecasting the organization's key influences. Then the forecast of the external indicators was related to the internal indicators and interpreted using management judgment in regard to the specifics of the organization's operating parameters. When all of the foregoing has been done, the detailed structure of the plan can take shape. The traditional method of detailing the plan in a company is to set up sales forecasts, production schedules, inventory guidelines, *pro forma* profit and loss statements and balance sheets, and a variety of other charts, schedules, and reports. These project the quantitative directions and targets for operating management. Actual performance is then recorded and reported periodically in the same format as the plan for ease of analysis.

Some specific examples of operating plan outlines for a typical company follow. Although they will not be representative of all the kinds of plans that would apply to all kinds of organizations, they will provide an idea of the scope and detail that should go into actual plans.

I.   Market position plan
   A. Define the market—Put dimensions on potential business. Needs that may be satisfied by the company's product or service whether or not currently utilized to do so. Additional needs that may be created by product development and market development.
   B. Market penetration—The portion of the total need being met and to be met by the company's product or service. New uses (market development) and new users considered for each year of the plan. Product development and diversification must also be considered and reflected in quantitative terms.
   C. Competition—What other products are available to satisfy the customer's needs? Not necessarily limited to direct competition. Potential competitive developments that will give other companies significant advantages must also be considered.

II. Sales forecast
   A. Unit sales by product by year.
   B. Dollar sales by product by year.
   C. Company sales by product versus industry sales by product.
   D. New orders by customer (or type of customer), units and dollars by product by year.

   Note: Assuming a five-year plan: The first year is shown monthly; the second and third, quarterly; the fourth, semiannually; and the fifth, as one figure for the year.

III. Profit and Loss Statement (Monthly, Quarterly, Yearly)

	Present Products		New Products		Total	
	$	% to Sales	$	% to Sales	$	% to Sales
A. New orders	—	——	—	——	—	——
Sales	—	——	—	——	—	——
Material	—	——	—	——	—	——
Labor	—	——	—	——	—	——
Overhead	—	——	—	——	—	——
Manufacturing cost	—	——	—	——	—	——
General and Administrative expense	—	——	—	——	—	——
Engineering	—	——	—	——	—	——
Total cost	—	——	—	——	—	——
Pretax profit	—	——	—	——	—	——
B. Refinements	—	——	—	——	—	——
1. Overhead labor	—	——	—	——	—	——
Overhead other	—	——	—	——	—	——
2. Sales labor expense	—	——	—	——	—	——
Sales other expense	—	——	—	——	—	——
Advertising	—	——	—	——	—	——
Service labor	—	——	—	——	—	——
Service other	—	——	—	——	—	——
Administrative labor	—	——	—	——	—	——
Administrative other	—	——	—	——	—	——
3. Engineering labor	—	——	—	——	—	——
Engineering other	—	——	—	——	—	——
4. Total payroll/sales $	—	——	—	——	—	——

IV. Profit measurement and financial ratios
   A. Profit as a percentage of sales by product.
   B. Dollars output per man-hour, direct, indirect, total.
   C. Return on investment by product (Return on investment = Profit/investment).
      Isolating investment in plant and equipment by product may require arbitrary decisions. The advantage of having a basis of comparison of what might otherwise be incomparable is

worth the effort. The companies that use it find it very valuable.

Note: Investment to include:
1. Prior years' engineering on the product.
2. Percentage of depreciated plant and equipment used in producing the product.
3. Inventory (raw material, work in process, and finished goods).

V. Cash flow: A running forecast of working capital in detail, showing the generation of money to meet obligations, month by month in the first year, quarter by quarter in the second, half-yearly in the third, and yearly from then on.

Cash balance at beginning	_____
Receipts from receivables	_____
Total available cash	_____
Cash out: trade payables	_____
Direct labor	_____
Sales expense	_____
General and administrative expenses	_____
Other manufacturing expenses	_____
Note payments	_____
Other	_____
Total cash out	_____
Total available cash less total cash out is cash balance	_____

VI. Departmental expense budgets. Detailed forecast of expense by department by major expense category. It is an excellent tool for spotlighting areas where overhead is getting out of line. It also helps to bring all departments into the planning program.

VII. Engineering
    A. Costs by program by year.
    B. Manpower by program—direct and indirect.
    C. Cost by product sales by year.

VIII. Purchasing
    A. Raw material purchases by product by year.
    B. Finished parts purchases by product by year.
    C. Total material purchases.

IX. Manpower
    A. By type of product by year.
    B. Sales volume per employee by product by year.
    C. Ratio of indirect to direct employees by year.
    D. Payroll percentage of sales by year.

E. Personnel development—Evolution of the organization chart as the plan is implemented during the planning cycle.

X. Editorial Content: An excellent selling tool for the plan.
   A. A summary of the plan to precede the charts, graphs, and schedules.
   B. An introduction to explain the basic assumptions and the approach used may precede each section.
   C. Conclusions and recommendations may very well be the last section of the summary presentation.

PLANNING THE FEEDBACK CONTROL SYSTEM

The implementation of the plan is the only real proof of its effectiveness. The key to this implementation is the Management Information System that provides all levels of management with timely, accurate feedback data on actual operations—for comparison with the plan and also provides channels for implementing management control decisions. This feedback control network must be designed to provide an accurate reflection of reality and then provide action decision data as close to the point of control as possible. That is, the feedback data must be captured in a form and at a point of activity that most reflects the significant operations generating the data at that juncture of the organization. Furthermore, after processing, analysis, and action decision, the control signals must be routed back to the point where they will maximize their impact on the operations that produced them.

The detailed plans that have been prepared in the form of schedules, budgets, forecasts, targets, and so forth, are the quantitative specifics that provide the foundation upon which the Management Information System is constructed. Each of these quantitative planning guides also contains within it the identity of these elements of operations data that must be captured and fed back to the decision points of the Management Information System for review and possible control action.

In production schedules, for example, the quantity produced per time period is a rather obvious but important data element that will be very revealing to the knowledgeable observer (i.e., management) if brought to his attention. A daily report of units of production routed to the production supervisor would be an elementary example of an element in the feedback information system. A series of such reports on all production units, summarized and organized for ease of understanding and sent up the line for higher management review, would be a natural extension of the system. Variance from the plan might initiate a decision to authorize overtime or to utilize idle equipment, and this decision transmitted down to the point of implementation completes the feedback control loop.

Expense budgets detail the various dollar requirements for office supplies, telephone expenses, travel expenses, dues and subscription, salaries, insurance costs, and so forth. Once again, the plan, in the guise of an expense budget, identifies the elements of management information that will be of use to decision makers. The Management Information System would provide the feedback control system that would be appropriate to each particular level of the decision hierarchy. For instance, at first level supervision, the MIS might set up an elementary system of keeping tabs on each category of expense charged to the supervisor's area of responsibility. It might be done very simply, by requiring his initials on any expenditure. At the next higher level, say the department manager, the Management Information System involving expense budgets might be a weekly report of total expenditures by department, by category. The factory manager might require monthly reports for all his departments summarized and processed so that he could quickly spot those departments that varied from the plan by a particular amount. He could then investigate those further for possible corrective action by means of the feedback control system.

Each of the specific plans (budgets, schedules, forecasts, etc.) that were developed as part of the overall planning effort become the basis for identifying the data that will be captured, processed, and fed back to the decision points throughout the Management Information System.

At these decision points, the Management Information System has set up the mechanism to compare the results of actual performance with what had been guessed (planned!) would be the actual performance. The analysis mechanism might be human, automated, or a combination of the two. Variation from the plan may result in the requesting of additional information, or applying judgment and experience and reaching a decision, or perhaps attempting a revision of the plan. The decision may be to change operating conditions to get performance back on plan, or to change the plan, or to do nothing. When the decision is made, the control information is transmitted through the Management Information System channels to the control points involved.

Through the operation of the feedback control network of the Management Information System, which is designed to implement the organization's long-range plan, management is able to monitor performance, coordinate operations, and take appropriate control action, as necessary, to insure the survival and growth of the organization.

REVIEW QUESTIONS

1.   What is planning? How does planning relate to the organization's predetermined goals?

2.   If given the planning responsibility of an organization, how would you implement the planning cycle?

3.   What is the difference between *short-term* and *long-term* planning? Does the nature of the organization determine the time span for planning? Explain.

4.   What are the advantages and disadvantages of having all echelons participate in planning?

5.   How can advanced quantitative techniques assist in planning?

6.   Why is feedback important to control?

7.   Define *leading, lagging,* and *coincident indicators.* How can they be used in planning?

8.   What specific plans, budgets, and forecasts would be useful when preparing a plan for a hospital? A city? An aircraft company?

9.   What are the criteria for determining the usefulness of sources of statistical data?

10.   What is the relationship between an organization's long-range plan, its management information system, and the feedback control system?

BIBLIOGRAPHY

FORRESTER, J., *Industrial Dynamics.* New York: John Wiley & Sons, Inc., 1961. This book caused quite a stir when first published, and its ability to provoke constructive thinking has not diminished.

LIEN, ARTHUR P., *Technological Forecasting: Tools, Techniques, Applications.* New York: American Management Association, 1968. A brief overview with an interesting bibliography.

NEMMERS, ERWIN E., and JOHN H. MYERS, *Business Research.* New York: McGraw-Hill Book Company, 1966. Very useful treatment of procedures of forecasting and research including many sources of information.

PRINCE, THOMAS R., *Information Sytems for Management Planning and Control* (rev. ed.). Homewood, Ill.: Richard D. Irwin, Inc., 1970. The case studies included in this book are valuable for placing the content in an operational environment. The emphasis on economics and costing does not detract from the major thrust of the book which is the planning and implementation of a decision-information system.

RICHARD, MAX D., and PAUL S. GREENLOW, *Management Decision Making*. Homewood, Ill.: Richard D. Irwin, Inc., 1966. Integrates the behavioral science, quantitative, and traditional management approaches to decision making. Presents a total systems view of the organization.

WOLFE, HARRY D., *Business Forecasting Methods*. New York: Holt, Rinehart & Winston, Inc., 1966. Discusses a number of specific techniques of forecasting in an understandable way. Provides many explanatory examples.

5

MANAGEMENT INFORMATION
SYSTEMS ANALYSIS

CONCEPT AND OBJECTIVES OF SYSTEMS ANALYSIS

As has already been discussed in detail, the Management Information System exists to implement the plans that were designed to meet the organization's objectives. The MIS in turn is made up of subsystems, each of which supports a major activity of the organization. These major subsystems are in turn made up of sub-subsystems, and so on. In actuality, the MIS is made up of an infrastructure of interlocking subsystems.

Each of the systems that make up the overall MIS is made up of a set of methods and procedures which are part of the decision network that performs one of the major activities of the organization.

A *procedure* is a sequence of data-processing operations designed to handle recurring transactions in a standard manner. The procedure for generating payroll checks is a case in point.

A *method* is a manual, mechanical, or electrical means by which specific individual operations are performed. An example is the encoding of information into cards by means of the card punch machine.

Each of the systems that support the MIS has the same set of objectives:

1. It constrains its part of the organization to ensure coordination of the overall effort.
2. It provides sensing devices to capture operations data and then feeds this information through the MIS to decision centers and then routes directives from management to points of control.
3. It integrates efforts to get the organization's work done.

Furthermore, the universal characteristic of all systems throughout the organization is that they all need constant improvement.

Improving the systems that make up the MIS improves the total MIS. This is the objective of systems analysis. It is implemented by the constant evaluation of all systems, procedures, and methods in the MIS to insure that each is making a maximum contribution to the objectives of the organization. The key concept in the systems analysis approach is to gauge each system's operation from the perspective of the organization's reason for existence. The question that the systems analyst seeks to answer is, Can this system be improved to help meet changing conditions in order to optimize its contribution to the organization's survival and growth?

In more succinct terms, and repeating an observation made in an earlier chapter, the systems analyst constantly strives to have the system put the effort where the results are maximized. The criterion used to determine whether a systems change is warranted is to measure the potential benefits against the cost of the change.

In summary, then, the systems analyst must be aware of the need for constant evaluation of each system in terms of the organization's overall objectives. He must also measure system's efforts in terms of system's results, and finally he must balance potential improvements against costs of implementation.

However, although these concepts of systems analysis seem obvious enough once stated, they are difficult to implement. The reason is easy to understand. There is a great deal of complexity in attempting to analyze the multilevel interrelationships of authority, responsibility, talents, knowledge, skills, experience, and results in the systems, procedures, operations, and methods. But the systems analyst must begin somewhere and, although the challenge seems overwhelming, there is a rationale that can help discover an analysis approach that can be used. It consists of recalling that the Management Information System's function is to provide channels of communication for all the elements of the organization and to provide management with the means for implementing plans, analyzing operations, and exercising control. This is the systems perspective the analyst must acquire.

The key to an approach for analyzing systems for improvement is therefore understanding that systems exist to attain objectives through the enhancement of management planning, analysis, and control. They are a means to an end. They are designed to facilitate the adjustment of the organization to the reality of its environment. In a very real sense, systems can be thought of as problem-solving devices. Therefore the most effective approach for systems analysis must relate to a basic procedure for solving problems. Just such a procedure is embodied in the classical approach to systems analysis.

THE CLASSICAL APPROACH TO SYSTEMS ANALYSIS

The classical approach to systems analysis is based on what has been known for decades as the *scientific method of problem solving*. The major steps in this method have been adapted to the terminology and the realities of systems analysis. These steps are as follows:

1. *Define the problem*—the objectives of the system.
2. *Collect the facts*—the key/critical data.
3. *Analyze the facts*—apply the relevant techniques.
4. *Develop Alternatives*—synthesize facts and forecast.
5. *Apply the solution*—modify the system, test, and follow up.

This basic approach gives the systems analyst a framework which will guide him no matter what the systems problem or the tools and techniques he applies. All will fit the basic approach of the classical procedure.

The variety of tools and techniques of systems analysis that are discussed in the other chapters of this book can prove bewildering to assimilate even without the procedural framework provided by the classical approach. An additional simplification happily exists. That is, most of the tools and techniques of systems analysis fit into one of three major categories.

THE THREE MAJOR CATEGORIES
OF SYSTEMS ANALYSIS TOOLS AND TECHNIQUES

Different tools and techniques may be required by the systems analyst, depending on the particular facet of the system that is under analysis. Since a broad spectrum of systems, procedures, and methods within the

Management Information System involve production operations and clerical and administrative activities, the tried and proven techniques of industrial engineering constitute one of the three major categories of systems analysis tools and techniques. These industrial engineering tools include statistical quality control, methods analysis, work simplification, work sampling, and plant layout. All will be discussed in subsequent chapters.

A second vital function within the MIS involves data capture, categorization, processing, storage, retrieval, and rapid transmitting of the digested data to decision centers. This emphasis on the manipulation of numbers, letters, and symbols within very short time frames requires the use of automatic data-processing equipment, including electronic computers, with their own powerful contribution to the systems analyst's repertory. They can be categorized under the general heading of computer-oriented tools and techniques. Chapters 12, 13, 14 and 15 relate to this area of interest.

The combination of larger, more complex organizations, the information explosion, and the need for much more demanding optimization requirements for organization growth and survival dramatically underscores the limitations of the traditional techniques of management decision making. Based on a proven record of success during and since World War II, a body of quantitative decision techniques (linear programming, queuing theory, simulation, PERT, etc.) has been developed and is being applied to management problems. These tools and techniques of the third category are generally referred to by the term *Operations Research* (OR). Many of these OR techniques have now been combined with the power of the electronic computer to provide the systems analyst with an imposing array of very powerful management decision tools. Chapter 11 provides an overview of OR and a detailed explanation of a number of OR tools.

In summary, then, the three major categories of tools and techniques in the repertory of the systems analyst are:

1. Industrial engineering
2. Computer oriented
3. Operations research

Each has its own particular contribution to make to help the systems analyst meet the challenge of analyzing and improving a particular part of the MIS.

Notwithstanding this segregation of the analytical tools into three categories, they all operate on parts of the same structure. The unifying systems concept still applies. A change in any element will affect the whole. Whether the systems analysis effort emphasizes the computer and information processing or whether it relates to procedures improvement, design of man-machine systems, or other industrial engineering techniques, or whether the analysis emphasizes the mathematical approach of Operations Research, the underlying objective is still the same. It is to optimize the interrelationships of the elements of the MIS to maximize their contribution to attaining the organization's objectives. That is, in essence, the systems analysis approach. Each aspect of the MIS is evaluated in terms of its relationships to optimizing the effect of the whole.

RELATING THE THREE CATEGORIES TO THE CLASSICAL APPROACH

The foregoing discussion may imply that complexity and sophistication are the hallmarks of Management Information Systems analysis. This need not be the case. Relating the elements of each of the three major categories of tools and techniques to the classical approach to systems analysis (Table 5-1) will emphasize the refreshing simplicity of this unifying concept.

Table 5-1 includes some terms that have been defined in the Glossary in Chapter 2 and will be discussed in detail in subsequent chapters. Each of these tools and techniques has a large body of literature devoted to it that includes specific applications in various kinds and sizes of organizations. The material in this book will provide enough information to understand the general structure of the tools and techniques and the particular types of MIS problems that are vulnerable to them. With this as a start, the serious student of systems analysis will want to utilize the Bibliography at the end of each chapter for an in-depth investigation of those tools and techniques that are of most interest to him.

Now that the classical approach to systems analysis has been briefly described, and the spectrum of tools and techniques available to the systems analyst has been categorized and each category related to the classical approach, the balance of this chapter will add detail to the classical approach and the balance of the book will detail the applicable tools and techniques of the three major categories.

STEPS IN SYSTEMS ANALYSIS

Step 1: Define the problem. This step is often considered the most important in systems analysis. If the problem is properly identified, stated, and dimensioned, all the subsequent steps are focused on target

TABLE 5-1

Relating the Three Major Categories of Tools and Techniques to the Classical Approach

The Classical Approach	Industrial Engineering	Computer Oriented	Operations Research
1. Define the problem.	Identify application	Determine output/input	Specify objectives (Measures of effectiveness)
2. Collect the facts.	Observe and record	Systems flow chart	Relate the variables
3. Analyze the facts.	Work simplification	Program, test, debug	Construct the model
4. Develop alternatives	Proposed procedure	Run program	Simulate/solve
5. Apply the solution.	Apply improvement	Utilize output	Implement results

and the probability is high that a feasible solution will be developed. To insure this, the systems analyst makes a preliminary investigation to define the scope of the problem and the specifics of the situation and to identify carefully and completely the objectives of that part of the MIS he is to analyze and improve. This preliminary investigation results in a concise but comprehensive statement of the problem and an evaluation of the resources available to resolve it. It assesses the skills, talents, and time available: the organizational, environmental, and legal constraints, if any, that may impinge on the analysis and resulting systems design. The analyst attempts to clarify the results desired, whether a management report, an operating condition, or a level of costs or profits. He reviews the available sources of input that he will examine in much greater detail later. He mentally outlines the probable route of his problem-solving path and concludes this phase of his analysis with a careful integration of his understanding of the objectives of the system he is studying with the objectives of the overall system.

Step 2: Collect the Facts. The systems analyst uses whatever leads were generated during the preliminary investigation phase to identify sources of information having reference to the problem under analysis. Usually, his major sources are his own observations and his own direct interviews with the key people involved. Very often, this step is the most time-consuming, but it is well worth the effort. All that comes after depends on the accuracy and comprehensiveness of this step.

The systems analyst must be particularly careful not to be misled. He must continually ask himself if what he has been told as fact is really fact. A useful definition of *fact* from a systems analysis point of view is that it is an agreement on something that exists and is real, is based on a series of observations, and can be verified at any time. If the analyst has prepared himself for his assignment and has developed an understanding of the operating realities of the system he is analyzing, he can protect his work from spurious "facts" by rigorously challenging and cross-checking and by being sure that the checking results in close agreement.

For example, a report may indicate a problem with regard to inventory quantities. The experienced analyst will search for additional sets of figures that verify and corroborate the report. He will check the figures with those who use them as well as those who generated them.

Another example involves a verbal opinion regarding excessive machine downtime. The analyst is told that it is inoperative 50 per cent of the time. However, maintenance records do not substantiate this opinion. The only fact that can be verified is that the machine is now inoperative, but there are no records as to how often or how long it has been broken down in the past.

Direct observation includes studying available reports within the organization as well as reviewing similar situations in the literature of the field. Direct interviews are often the most valuable sources of facts, but there is always the chance of getting half facts, opinions, and even downright lies.

The systems analyst's attitude is the key to his success. If he attempts to gain understanding from the point of view of the person he is interviewing, he will have a much better chance of establishing two-way communication. If his attitude is that of someone cross-examining a hostile witness, he will engender just that type of response.

Some currently useful generalities that may help a systems analyst to maintain a respectable interviewing batting average follow:

a. Think positively and not negatively.
b. Train yourself to recognize your own prejudices and offset them to maintain an open mind.
c. Give credit wherever it is due.
d. Find good points in the present way of doing things.
e. Publicly acknowledge help.
f. Emphasize courtesy and respect by your attitude.
g. Respect the worker's skill. He knows more about his job than you will ever discover.
h. Work through supervisors, not around them.
i. Listen more than you talk.
j. Gain confidence a little bit at a time.
k. Collect forms as you interview. Forms are facts.
l. Take notes as you go along—rewrite them later.

In summary, interviewing is a very important tool for the systems analyst, especially when he is collecting the facts on a system under study. He will be much more effective when interviewing if he remembers to be uncritical, helpful, well-balanced, and friendly.

Step 3: Analyze the Facts   This is the phase of the systems analysis procedure that will call on all the resources of the analyst. Whereas the preceding steps and the succeeding steps can be supplemented, bolstered and redone if necessary, the analysis phase is lonely, challenging, difficult to structure, and totally professional. It is that part of systems analysis that is closest to being an art. Effective analysis leads to viable solutions. Superficial, misdirected, mediocre analysis results in the kind of solutions that quickly fall of their own weight.

The mechanics of analysis begins with breaking the problem into its smallest component parts and then thoroughly questioning each of these parts in terms of its own requirements and with regard to its relationship to the whole.

You generally gather more facts than you need. Some will have no bearing on the improved system. Others will have been superseded or will require updating. Those that apply to the system under study should be grouped under major points in the analysis. Relate each group of facts to the whole and keep restructuring the system in your mind in terms of its objectives.

Evaluate the information you are organizing from several points of view. Challenge the assumptions you make as you continue your analysis. For example, if purchasing in palletized lots is part of the system under study, do not just consider cost, but include handling, damage, warehouse aisle sizes, and other aspects of the problem that may be involved.

The systems analyst must train himself to seize on ideas as they are born as he goes through the analysis. Since these ideas can come to the analyst at any moment, it behooves him to have a pencil and paper handy at all times. As was explained in Chapter 3, learning to write in the dark is an occupational must for the systems analyst.

As you gather ideas, test them as soon as possible on the people who are actually doing the work. Let them help by criticizing the ideas, adding to them, and suggesting others. Remember to be realistic in considering the feasibility of the ideas in terms of the present and future talents and abilities of those concerned. The key criterion of all ideas must be that they are ideas that work within the context of the system under study.

Step 4: Develop Alternative Solutions   Defining the problem, collecting the facts, and analyzing them have all produced a variety of inputs to the systems analyst. His mental processes have been consciously and unconsciously relating, evaluating, integrating, discarding, absolving, confirming, eliminating, and synthesizing—always in terms of the objectives of the system under study and the objectives of the MIS.

Each alternative that survives should be listed along with the advantages and disadvantages that apply. A quantitative value should be assigned to each. The impact of the implementation of each alternative should be evaluated in terms of short-range and long-term goals. The analyst should always consider the possibility of a stopgap to fill an immediate need while the more elaborate new system is being finalized. A further warning to the systems analyst is to be careful to fit the treatment to the malady. That is, do not drive a tack with a sledge-hammer.

Finally, the systems analyst must remember that the new system requires management approval. Therefore, his proposal should be in general terms, emphasizing the results in terms of the organization's objectives. Be factual, be businesslike, be brief.

Step 5: Apply the Solution, Test It, Modify if Necessary   When one of the alternatives developed in Step 4 is selected for implementation, a step-by-step program for installation of the new system should be planned in detail. The plan should include:

a. The time schedule for each step of the conversion from the present system to the new system.

b. The training requirements necessary, who will prepare the training program, and how it will be administered.

c. The procedure for testing the change, who will test it, what are the criteria for testing.

d. The lead times necessary for ordering new forms, getting equipment, staffing.

e. The finalization of all procedures and methods that apply.

f. The parallel operation of the old and of the new system during the conversion phase.

Modifications are made as the operating results of the new system are evaluated under actual conditions. Sometimes the development of the modfications requires a recycling through the same steps that were used to develop the original solution. But if that is necessary, the systems analyst will know a great deal more about the situation the second time around.

A thorough follow-up phase is obviously an absolute necessity. The improvement that may have appeared as the answer to everyone's prayer may actually be nothing more than a combination of the halo effect that attends any innovation, the personality of the systems analyst, and the general euphoria surrounding an effort that was conducted professionally. The real professional will not consider his assignment complete till it has been tested under the unrelenting pressure of day-to-day operating demands. Once the new system is operating smoothly, the systems analyst, like the old soldier, simply fades away.

REVIEW QUESTIONS

1.   What is systems analysis?
2.   What is the role of the systems analyst? What is his objective?
3.   What are the objectives of each of the systems that are part of the MIS?
4.   Differentiate each of the three major categories of systems analysis.
5.   What is the classical approach to systems analysis?
6.   Apply the steps in the classical approach to a situation you are familiar with. Discuss.
7.   Conduct a fact-gathering interview. Criticize.
8.   What is meant by "understanding from the other person's point of view"?
9.   Why is follow-up necessary—no matter what technique is used?
10. How does systems analysis relate to the MIS?

BIBLIOGRAPHY

BARNES, R. M., *Motion and Time Study*. New York: John Wiley and Sons, Inc., 1963. An understandable treatment of one of the great tools of industrial engineering.

BOWMAN, EDWARD H., and ROBERT B. FETTER, *Analysis for Production and Operations Management* (3rd ed.). Homewood, Ill.: Richard D. Irwin, Inc., 1967. The emphasis is on tools for the analysis of industrial operations. A workmanlike, no-nonsense approach that does not over-simplify. The methods are quantitatively oriented and involve some mathematics but are not too complex. Good examples scattered throughout.

DEARDON, JOHN, and F. WARREN McFARLEN, *Management Information Systems: Texts and Cases*. Homewood, Ill.: Richard D. Irwin, Inc., 1966. The text combined with case studies provides a very useful comparison of theory and practice.

JOHNSON, RICHARD A., FREMONT E. KAST, and JAMES ROSENZWEIG, *The Theory and Management of Systems*. New York: McGraw-Hill Book Company, 1967. Includes a very interesting philosophical treatment of the subject.

LAZZARO, VICTOR, *Systems and Procedures* (2nd ed.). Englewood Cliffs, N. J.: Prentice-Hall, Inc., 1968. An excellent compendium of tools and techniques in the area of industrial engineering. Each chapter prepared by an authority in the field.

SCHELLENBERGER, ROBERT E., *Managerial Analysis*. Homewood, Ill.: Richard D. Irwin, Inc., 1969. Explains the procedures and tools of managerial analysis. Somewhat mathematical, but much of the book is easily understandable.

STARR, MARTIN K., *Production Management Systems and Synthesis*. Englewood Cliffs, N. J.: Prentice-Hall, Inc., 1964. A very useful and comprehensive treatment of systems analysis. Although set in the production environment, the treatment and content have universal application.

6

A BASIC SYSTEMS TOOL—
WORK SIMPLIFICATION

THE WHY OF WORK SIMPLIFICATION

The philosophy underlying the application of the systems tool known as *work simplification* is perhaps best summed up in the old saying Work Smarter, Not Harder. It is a philosophy that has proved very effective over the years. The procedure for implementing the work simplification philosophy is often described as the organized application of common sense. Its objective is to find better and easier ways of doing a job.

All the steps in using this technique are rather elementary, yet it is one of the most powerful of the basic tools in the arsenal of the systems analyst. Although elementary, work simplification is systematic, rigorous, and comprehensive in seeking out improvements. The more it is used, the more all concerned become conditioned to viewing all aspects of their areas of responsibility in terms of working smarter— not harder. This attitude, once developed, is the most effective systems improvement tool of them all. Work simplification can be a key change agent in bringing about this attitude.

In essence, work simplification is a systematic way of eliminating all unnecessary work and then streamlining what is left to make it move faster and more effectively. It really is the organized application of common sense to help everyone work smarter—not harder. In the past, work simplification was generally identified with factory work, and it accomplished a great deal in improving work activities on production lines. However, the same principles can be a great help to the systems analyst in the improvement of the methods and procedures that make up the systems in all types of organizations and enterprises.

Interestingly enough, the same steps that simplify work also tend to raise its quality. Complex, time-consuming, hard-to-execute procedures are inherently costly, and they also become the breeding grounds for mistakes, misunderstandings, bottlenecks, and delays. When such procedures are simplified, many benefits may result. For instance:

> *Greater accuracy*—the simpler the procedure, the less chance for error.
>
> *Increased speed*—needless operations are eliminated and necessary operations are simplified.
>
> *Improved morale*—hectic peaks and valleys in work load and work distribution are smoothed out.
>
> *Easier training*—simplified procedures are easier to learn.
>
> *Lower costs*—help the organization survive and grow.
>
> *Job security*—a successful organization is a good place to work.

THE PRINCIPLES OF WORK SIMPLIFICATION

1. All activities should be productive, that is, they should directly accomplish results.
2. Activities should be interrelated to provide for smooth work flow.
3. Activities should be as simple as possible.
4. Participation of those concerned develops understanding. This, in turn, encourages their enthusiastic cooperation.
5. The man doing the job is closest to the job and is in a very good position to help improve it.
6. People do things because it is in their enlightened self-interest. That is, if they can satisfy their basic need for security, recognition, and self-expression by doing something, they will do it enthusiastically.

THE TOOLS OF WORK SIMPLIFICATION

A great number of specific tools and techniques have been developed and used under the general heading of work simplification. A number of those that are most applicable to the analysis and design of Management Information Systems will be covered in this book. These include:

1. The flow process chart
2. The flow diagram
3. The work distribution chart
4. The work count
5. Forms design

The flow process chart and the flow diagram will be discussed in detail in this chapter.

THE WORK SIMPLIFICATION METHOD

The work simplification method follows the same basic procedure that has been referred to in the preceding chapter as the scientific method of problem solving and also as the classic approach to systems analysis.

1. Select the specific application.
2. Collect the facts.
3. Analyze the facts.
4. Develop the improved method.
5. Apply the improvement.
6. Follow up, evaluate, and recycle, if necessary.

Selecting the Specific Application

Selecting the specific application is the first step in the work simplification procedure. A job or an activity or a procedure is selected for possible improvement. High-cost operations, bottlenecks, troublesome activities, procedures involving much walking, movement, or material handling, areas of confusion or misunderstanding, all provide clues to possible work simplification projects. Other high-potential applications are those operations where quality is not up to standard, productivity is low, schedules are rarely met, or other unsatisfactory conditions exist.

It is a good idea to select the first project with the objective of making it an example of the benefits of work simplification. Therefore, to build confidence in the method, the first application should be made in an area where cooperation seems most probable, goals are modest, and results will be highly visible. Nothing succeeds like success, and the most effective programs of work simplification are those that build on small successes.

Collecting the Facts

Common sense indicates that we should use all the facts that are readily available and add other facts that can be gathered within the time and effort constraints that exist. A word of caution about facts: One of the most sobering definitions of the word *fact* is that it is a phenomenon that has not yet been proved false. Another definition is that it is a quantum of observed information on which investigation as to its validity has stopped by general consent. Perhaps the most cynical definition is that a *fact* is simply something that has been written so that someone else can read it!

All of the foregoing emphasizes one thing to the conscientious systems analyst—beware of accepting "facts" too readily. Check and double-check. It is not the lies that people tell you that will cause the most trouble, it is the information they give you that they sincerely believe is correct when it is not.

Most organizations usually, have more information available than is being used for analysis and improvement. Specifications, procedure write-ups, historical cost data, blueprints, drawings, time studies, production records, schedules, sales data, payroll data, job descriptions, forecasts, and budgets are just a few of the data elements available. Although these general resources must be tapped, the systems analyst must also be prepared to get specific information on the application in question. One of the major tools of work simplification, the flow process chart, will be of great help in obtaining this information in an organized way.

THE FLOW PROCESS CHART   The flow process chart is both a record of the present situation as observed by the systems analyst and a blueprint for the improvement to come. It is also an effective outline of the steps in work simplification:

1. Select the specific application.
2. Collect the facts.
3. Analyze the facts.
4. Develop the improved method.
5. Apply the improvement.
6. Follow up.

When completed, the flow process chart represents the area of application for work simplification. It is an abstract representation of the real situation—which is a succinct definition of the word *model*. The Flow Process Chart can therefore be thought of as a model of what is actually happening in a method of operation or a procedure. The systems analyst operates on the chart by using analysis, creativity, and experience and produces a model of the improved method or procedure which he then implements and evaluates in the real world. Viewed in this perspective, the flow process chart is as new and sophisticated a tool as any that may be available to the systems analyst.

Flow process chart—explanation of Figure 6-1

Job.   After the job, procedure, or activity has been selected, identify it at the top of the flow process chart on the *job* line. "No. ——" and "Page —— of ——" are further aids in identifying the application and indicating the number of chart pages used.

Man or Material.   Check whether man or material, depending on which is to be studied. A more complicated flow process chart is available to follow several people or several material parts at the same time. Once enough experience has been gained, the more complex chart can be used. For the regular chart, however, a person, a single piece of material, or a document will be followed through the entire process that is to be improved. Remember, once a particular subject has been selected, do not be diverted, no matter how enticing—and there will be many temptations.

Chart Begins . . . Chart Ends.   Select and identify a specific starting point and ending point. Do not try to do too much. There will be a surprisingly large amount of detail in what at first looks like a very short process. Later, as work simplification skills improve, more complex procedures may be charted so that several simple charts can be combined into one comprehensive chart. Be sure to identify the beginning and the end of the application that is to be analyzed and improved and then *stick to it.*

FIGURE 6-1

FLOW PROCESS CHART

FIGURE 6-1 (cont'd)

DETAILS OF (PRESENT / PROPOSED) METHOD	OPERATION	TRANSPORT	INSPECTION	DELAY	STORAGE	DISTANCE IN FEET	QUANTITY	TIME	ANALYSIS WHY?						NOTES	ACTION CHNGE				
									WHAT	WHERE	WHEN	WHO	HOW			ELIMINATE	COMBINE	SEQUENCE	PLACE	PERSON
	○ ⇨ □ D ▽																			
	○ ⇨ □ D ▽																			
	○ ⇨ □ D ▽																			
	○ ⇨ □ D ▽																			
	○ ⇨ □ D ▽																			
	○ ⇨ □ D ▽																			
	○ ⇨ □ D ▽																			
	○ ⇨ □ D ▽																			
	○ ⇨ □ D ▽																			
	○ ⇨ □ D ▽																			
	○ ⇨ □ D ▽																			
	○ ⇨ □ D ▽																			
	○ ⇨ □ D ▽																			
	○ ⇨ □ D ▽																			
	○ ⇨ □ D ▽																			
	○ ⇨ □ D ▽																			
	○ ⇨ □ D ▽																			
	○ ⇨ □ D ▽																			
	○ ⇨ □ D ▽																			
	○ ⇨ □ D ▽																			
	○ ⇨ □ D ▽																			
	○ ⇨ □ D ▽																			
	○ ⇨ □ D ▽																			
	○ ⇨ □ D ▽																			
	○ ⇨ □ D ▽																			
	○ ⇨ □ D ▽																			
	○ ⇨ □ D ▽																			
	○ ⇨ □ D ▽																			
	○ ⇨ □ D ▽																			
	○ ⇨ □ D ▽																			
	○ ⇨ □ D ▽																			

Charted by and Date.   Self-explanatory.

"Details of (Present-Proposed) Method

Initially, the systems analyst will observe the way the job is actually being done and will record it in exact detail. Therefore, the word *proposed* at the head of the column is crossed out. Then the systems analyst lists every step that occurs in the process, no matter how small or insignificant. Every time something happens to the material or is done by the person who is being charted, it should be recorded.

Every operation performed or movement or inspection or delay or storage should be recorded exactly as it occurs and in the sequence in which it occurs. These five elements are the five universal categories into which all work activities can be placed. This is one of the great contributions of the flow process chart. It enables the systems analyst to dissect any job into its basic elements for analysis and improvement. These basic, universal job elements are identified by five special symbols.

The Flow Process Chart Symbols

The flow process chart symbols are a very helpful shorthand method of describing the job. They also aid in providing a bird's-eye view of the entire process, and they graphically portray the present process for quick visual comparison with the results of the analysis and improvement.

The written description of the particular step in the process determines the symbol that will be associated with it. A connecting line is drawn between each of the symbols associated with each step. If one detail step seems to require more than one symbol, it is a sign that the step has not been broken down into fine enough detail.

Make Ready, Do, and Put Away Steps

An operation step that actually gets something done to the material being charted is called a *do* step. Either the condition, shape, or appearance of the part is changed or value is added. If we are charting a person, it is a *do* step whenever that person does something of the same nature. *Make ready* steps are those that are preparatory to or lead up to the performance of a *do* step. *Put away* steps are those that occur after and because of a *do*.

Since experience has shown that most *make ready* and *put away* steps depend on the *do* steps, the questioning and development of the preferred solution will be simplified by concentrating on the *do* steps first. Therefore, before going on to the analysis phase, each detailed step should be evaluated to see whether or not it is a *do*. If it is, the operation symbol associated with it is shaded in. If there is any doubt as to whether

Symbol	Explanation

OPERATION

(circle)

When something is done by or to the subject being followed. When something is changed, created, added to, picked up or laid down, or otherwise manipulated within a specific work area. Examples include typing a letter, filling out a form, driving a nail, or picking up a tool.

TRANSPORTATION

(arrow)

When something is moved from one work area to another. A letter being carried from one desk to another, a box of material moved from a truck to a warehouse bin, a part conveyed from one work station to another -- all would be transportation. (Usually pick-ups and lay-downs within a work area are not considered transportations, but are considered operations.)

INSPECTION

(square)

When something is checked or verified against a predetermined standard of quality or examined for information, or compared for agreement to the original. Inspections are simply specialized types of operations which govern the quality of the product. Because of the importance of quality these steps are segregated specifically. Checking a requisition for completeness, checking a part against a blueprint, gauging or observing the appearance of a part -- all are inspections and are designated by the square symbol.

DELAY

(D)

When the object or person is interrupted or delayed in its flow or movement -- an interference. An unplanned inactivity. A letter in an "out" box, a carton awaiting transportation, a supply of parts on a production bench -- all are considered delays.

STORAGE

(triangle)

When an object is kept and protected against unauthorized removal. A planned inactivity. Goods in a warehouse, supplies in a stockroom, or a letter in a filing cabinet are examples of storage.

or not the step should be considered a *do,* it should be shaded in any-way. The major purpose of the shading is to identify those steps that should be considered first in the analysis phase of the work simplification procedure.

Distance in Feet

This column is provided to record the distance of each transportation. It is rarely necessary to measure these distances exactly. Pacing it off or sight estimating is usually close enough. The method of transportation is usually indicated in the description by using the proper verb, such as carried, trucked, conveyed, or hoisted.

Quantity

The quantity of material or product being handled should be recorded where appropriate. The number of pieces in a tote box or the number of documents in a pile. and so forth, may be useful information later on when the chart is analyzed. It might be important, for example, to know that in one instance each piece was handled by itself and in another it was handled as part of a box of fifty units.

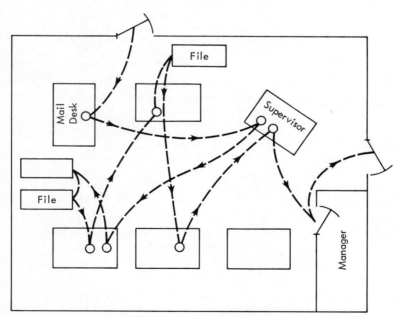

BEFORE: Note backtracking.

FIGURE 6-2

Flow Diagram

Time or Production Rate

If the time or production per hour or time period for each detail step is available, the information should be recorded in the column provided. This kind of information is particularly helpful when considering the unit cost of an operation or comparing one method with another.

Summary

Summarize the activities portrayed by the flow process chart by totaling each category of activity in the space provided in the upper left-hand corner. The total number of operations, transportations, inspections, delays, and storages in the body of the chart should check exactly with the total number in the appropriate column. Total distance, as well as the total time for each category of activity, should also be recorded.

THE FLOW DIAGRAM   At this point in the work simplification procedure it is often helpful, if there is any amount of transportation involved, to sketch a flow diagram of the process. This consists of a simple outline drawing of the department or the area in which the process being studied occurs. Indicate roughly the location of equipment, benches,

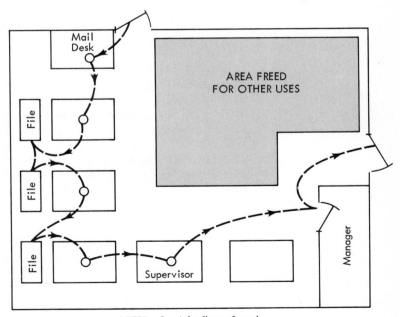

AFTER: Straight flow of work.

Flow Diagram (continued)

tables, or desks involved. Draw a line along the route from each work station to the next corresponding to the transportation steps on the flow process chart. An example of a flow diagram is shown in Figure 6-2.

Flow diagrams help tremendously to visualize the present process and the proposed process. Bear in mind that the diagram should indicate the transportations exactly as recorded on the flow process chart. To be even more elaborate, models of the machinery, benches, or desks may be made and placed on the flow diagram. Models of this sort are more readily understood than conventional engineering drawings and are particularly useful when employees are involved in the discussion of the present method and of the proposed changes.

It is almost axiomatic that there is too much walking and waiting time in almost all industrial activities. The flow diagram combined with the flow process chart is a very effective way of spotlighting this fact in the specific job being studied. The flow diagrams in Figure 6-2 show how useful they are in illustrating work flow and thereby helping the analyst to improve the situation.

Summarizing the Fact Collection Phase

1. The flow process chart breaks down a process into its simple, individual details in an organized, systematic way.
2. The *make ready, do,* and *put away* phases are clearly indicated for quick comparison.
3. As a "still picture" it separates the job from its background and surroundings for subsequent intensive analysis.
4. Its condensed form enables the process to be visualized easily in its entirety and in context.
5. Through the mechanics of making the on-the-scene observations required to prepare the chart, ways and means of introducing improvements often become apparent.
6. A fundamental premise that underscores the use of a flow process chart is that any process when charted in full detail and then analyzed can be improved.

Analyzing the Facts

After the flow process chart (and flow diagram—if used) of the present method is completed, it is then studied for possible improvement. This is done by challenging every single detail of the job. Each step is "put on the witness stand" and cross-examined.

The Six Useful Servants   A good guideline is the list of questions used by news reporters—*What? Where? When? Who? How?* Each answer is then subjected to the real clincher—*Why*? As these questions are asked, notes are made of the answers in the *notes* column of the flow process chart for later synthesis into the proposed improvements.

The following expansion of the key questions is an indication of the possible variations that can be developed to trigger innovation.

1. *What* is done? *Why* should it be done? This determines the purpose of doing the particular step being analyzed. Does this step do what it is supposed to do and for the reason it is done?
2. *Where* is this step done? *Why*? Where is the best place to do this step in the process? *Why* should it be done there? Where else could it be done?
3. *When* is this step done   What comes before? After? When is the best time to do it? *Why* should it be done then? Perhaps it should be done at the same time as some other step? Should it be done before some other step? After some other step? Should it be juxtapositioned?
4. *Who* does this particular step? Who should do it? *Why* should this person do it? Can less-skilled people do the job? More-skilled?
5. *How* is this step done? *Why* is it done this way? Can we make it easier, pleasanter, faster, slower, etc.?

In summary:

Flow Process Chart Facts	*Analysis of the Facts*
What is done?	*Why* is it done?
Where is it done?	*Why* is it done there?
When is it done?	*Why* is it done then?
Who does it?	*Why* does that person do it?
How is it done?	*Why* is it done that way?

CHALLENGE EACH STEP   A good way to begin the analysis is to challenge the existence of the whole job that is being studied. Why is it done? Perhaps it has outlived the reason for its existence. If satisfied on that point, you can begin by questioning each *do* operation. This approach can save analysis time because each *do* step eliminated also automatically eliminates all the *make ready* and *put away* details that go with it. Therefore, take each "shaded-in" step in the process in the order that it occurs and ask each of the five questions and the underlying *Why*? Carefully explore all the possibilities that arise as a result. Remember— thoughts, ideas, and questions are entered in the *notes* column of the flow process chart for future reference when developing the improved method.

With the information resulting from analysis of the *do* steps, each *make ready* and *put away* detail is questioned in turn. Ask the five questions and *Why?* Explore the possibilities that suggest themselves and make pertinent notes.

After the *do* and the *make ready* and the *put away* details have been challenged, the transportations and delays are next. Whenever we see a part carried an appreciable distance, the question *Why?* should immediately suggest grouping of the equipment or the work stations so as to eliminate this travel. Delays should alert the analyst to fertile areas for improvement.

One very useful approach to improvement is to have several people challenge each step of the chart in a group session. A very rich source of improvement ideas comes from those working directly on the operation. If their enthusiastic cooperation can be engendered, many of the most valuable workable ideas will come from the people doing the job. The real criterion for improvement must utimately be *ideas that work*.

THE ACTION COLUMN   As a result of the intensive questioning of the analysis phase of this work simplification procedure, ideas for the improved method are developed. The flow process chart itself provides some useful and provocative guides in the *action* column. *Eliminate, combine, change sequence—place—person, improve.* Each of these key words can provoke a positive contribution to improvement.

Can We Eliminate?

In far too many instances a good deal of time is invested in studying operations for possibilities of improvement without ever asking the overall question, Why do we perform this operation at all?

It is for precisely this reason that the viewpoint of someone outside the area concerned is so valuable. The flow process chart provides an opportunity to take an objective, analytical view of the whole situation.

In all this questioning, if it seems at all possible that the step can be eliminated, or if a good answer cannot be found to the question, Why can't it be eliminated?, put a check mark in the appropriate column to the right of that step.

Can We Combine?

When two operations can be combined they are often performed for considerably lower cost. Also, all transportatons and storage between the two operations are automatically eliminated. Combination of operations frequently results in the improvement of quality, since the responsibility for both operations is concentrated at one work station and in one person. Unnecessary inspections between the two operations may automatically be eliminated. If the operations cannot be combined, perhaps it is possible to combine a transportation and an operation. Modern conveyor systems have made this quite practical in many instances. Until recently, it was thought that if an object was being moved, say, from one conveyor to another, and a mechanical handling means was provided, this was about as far as it could go. However, even this practice has been questioned, and in many instances certain operations may now be performed while the product is being moved from one location to another.

Inspections may often be combined with an operation. When inspecting, it is sometimes necessary to remove the piece from its container and then return it to another container. This usually either follows or precedes an operation. If the inspection can be combined with one of the operations, the additional handling is eliminated.

A check mark should be placed in the appropriate column to the right of the step being questioned if it seems likely that it may be combined with another.

Can We Change the Sequence?

Here is where the flow diagram of the department, plant, or office is particularly helpful. If the sequence of an operation is changed, it may be possible to eliminate backtracking or to improve the flow of material. Most of the time the sequence in which the operations are performed is a necessary part of the process. On the other hand, this cannot be assumed in all cases because it may result in missing some spectacular savings.

Can We Change the Place?

The question *Where?* is directed toward the place where the step is performed. Why is it done there? Could it be done better some other place? Why not? All too often, work is done in one place or within a certain department mainly because it has always been done there, or perhaps the building of "little kingdoms" has prevented it from being moved elsewhere. The question Where should the job be done? often leads to interesting possibilities for improvement.

Can We Change the Person?

Again, the challenging of each step with the question *Who?* often results in the discovery that it could be done to better advantage by some other person. Who does the step? Could someone else do it inasmuch as he already has it in his hands? Who inspects it? Why? Perhaps an inspection could be done by the operator who performed the step. It pays to stay with this question until it has been shown that no other person could possibly do the step to advantage. If possibilities do come to light during this challenging, place a check mark in the appropriate box opposite the detail. Each time a possibiilty is checked it may suggest another, in which case go back and also check this off.

Can We Improve the Steps?

The *notes* column will list suggestions as well as further questions. There may also be many different possibilities for improving each step. It should be emphasized that these are *only possibilities* for improvement. But they must be evaluated individually to decide which are preferable for use under existing conditions.

Past experience with similar situations, reference material, comments from others, as well as the raw material supplied by the *notes* section of the flow process chart, all combine with the innate creativity of the systems analyst to develop the improved method.

Developing the Improved Method

After each detail on the chart has been challenged as outlined above, the next step of the work simplification procedure applies—develop the improved method.

1. *Work with facts—not opinions.* Opinions are very difficult to work with. They are the cause of many arguments. Facts, on the other hand, are easy to work with and tend to produce definite conclusions. A fact does not vanish when we ask *Why?* Be careful—people may mask opinion as fact, and as was pointed out previously, facts are few.

2. *Work on causes—not effects.* A bucket under the leak is not the cure for a leaky roof. Get at the causes of the difficulty in order to make the best improvements. Try to get at the disease—do not be fooled by the symptoms.

3. *Work with reasons—not excuses.* Excuses dodge the question and often cover up the facts. Find out why every detail is handled the way it is. Teamwork in an atmosphere of approval usually minimizes excuses.

The questioning that has been gone through in developing the flow process chart will be effective only if the best and most searching judgment is properly used to evaluate the information obtained.

THE PROPOSED METHOD CHART   A *proposed method* flow process chart can usually be made directly from the information that is on the *present method* flow process chart if it contains the notes made during the analysis and if it contains comments on the evaluations of the different possibilities for improvement. A new chart would then be filled out except that the word *present* would be crossed out at the head of the *details* description column. The chart would thus be identified as a *proposed* method.

Each detail step in the proposed method is then entered on this new flow process chart. The steps are listed on the chart in their proper order indicating any combinations or changes of sequence, place, or person that may have been introduced. The symbols are identified by connecting lines as before with appropriate changes in distances and times.

A quantitative summary of the proposed method is made in the space provided in the upper left hand corner of the flow process chart. In addition, a summary of the net savings is made in the *difference* column. The number of activities eliminated, the total distance shortened, and the time saved are valuable assets for helping to gain acceptance of the proposed method both by management and by those who will be doing the work.

Implementing the Improved Method

The *proposed* flow process chart serves as an instruction sheet for trying out the new method in a pilot run and for training operators in the new method. It may also be used for comparison with an even more radical change which may yet be developed. It also serves as a reference source for use at some future date when conditions may have changed again. Finally, it becomes a "follow-through" check sheet by which the new method may be reviewed after a reasonable amount of time has passed to see if it is being implemented properly.

The proposed flow process chart should be checked over carefully with all who may be affected, especially those who may not have been involved in the problem-solving activity. This will frequently reveal new considerations. If special care has been taken to get those concerned involved each step of the way, all well and good; if not, inviting participation at this point may be too late for their wholehearted support.

TECHNICAL AND HUMAN FACTORS   Two major areas must be considered in the implementation phase of work simplfication: the technical and the human factors.

The technical problems are concerned with the practicability of the proposal in terms of the realities of the situation. Will it reduce costs? Will it increase production? Will it improve quality? Does it require special tooling? training? testing? Is it a "good buy," all things considered? What is the probable payback period? That is, how long will it take for estimated savings to equal total investment costs? Is the proposed method technically sound? Engineers and specialists inside as well as outside the company may be required to evaluate changes from this technical point of view.

The human problems to be considered in putting the improved method to work are equally as important as the technical problems. Every time a method is changed people are affected. Change generates two big difficulties—people resist what they do not understand and people resent criticism. A change can imply criticism to those who are identified with the old method. The best way to build acceptance of change rather than resistance is to obtain the participation of those involved during the early steps of applying work simplification. This holds true whether using the flow process chart or other work simplification tools. If the security of the workers concerned is protected, if their ideas are recognized, and if they are given the opportunity to express themselves all during the procedure, their enthusiastic cooperation is almost guaranteed.

Following Up, Evaluating, and Recycling If Necessary

After an improvement has been installed, it is essential that it be monitored to see if the anticipated benefits actually result. This means continual contact with everyone involved. A regular report of the results of the proposed method will be very helpful in building credibility for the systems analyst. Be generous in giving credit to those who participated. It means so much, it requires so little effort, and it generates a reservoir of goodwill that every systems analyst will need as he pursues his career as an agent of change.

Where the proposed method does not result in the expected improvements, the systems analyst may be chagrined but need not be discouraged. The flow process chart, the flow diagram, and other systems analysis tools that will be covered in later chapters are at his disposal to find out why. Furthermore, as he recycles the steps of the work simplification procedure and as he retraces his collecting of facts, analyzing of facts, and developing of the improved method, he will have the added ingredient of experience—he has been over this ground before. He knows a lot more about it than he did the first time around. So even the "misses" provide dividends when the organized application of common sense—work simplification—is applied.

As redundant as this follow-up step may seem to the inexperienced, it is probably the step that separates the professional from the amateur. The follow-up phase of work simplification can do a great deal for the systems analyst in building up respect for his professionalism. "He cared enough to come back to see that it really worked." The analyst who scoffs at this seeming incidental does so at his own peril.

WORK SIMPLIFICATION CASE STUDY

The flow process charts that follow represent the actual application of the work simplification method to a particular procedure in a relatively large hospital.

The first flow process chart, Figure 6-3, represents the analyst's record of the *present* method. A careful study of this chart will provide much food for thought about the procedure being charted. But perhaps even more provocative are the second thoughts one has regarding the choice of steps the analyst recorded, how he recorded it, what he included or left out, and what other notes he should have included if only he had thought of them. The notations on the flow process chart, Figure 6-3, reflect the result of the analysis-of-the-facts step in work simplification. The use of the printed aids on the flow process chart are obviously very useful. The analyst's ideas, possible modifications, and candidates for elimination are identified by his comments to himself.

The second flow process chart, Figure 6-4, represents the *proposed* method. The savings are significant and they are summarized in the upper left hand corner. Even a cursory comparison of the *present* method with the *proposed* method will demonstrate that the work is really being done smarter, not harder.

A final word on the case study. It should be evident that the *present* method could have been charted in many different ways. Other improvements might have resulted from analysis by other investigators. The *proposed* method that resulted is a direct outgrowth of the background, experience, and training of the particular analyst. Another analyst would probably come up with a different result—perhaps slightly different, perhaps significantly different.

The point that must be emphasized (and the reader can easily prove it by analyzing the case himself) is that the systems analyst is the key ingredient in the work simplification technique. A well-trained, aware, creative analyst can provide any organization with a powerful weapon to help all facets of the operation to find better ways of doing what must be done.

FIGURE 6-3

		NO _____
SUMMARY	FLOW PROCESS CHART	PAGE 1 OF 2

	PRESENT		PROPOSED		DIFFERENCE	
	NO.	TIME	NO.	TIME	NO.	TIME
○ OPERATIONS	34	38.1				
⇨ TRANSPORTATIONS	15	8.1				
☐ INSPECTIONS	1	1.0				
D DELAYS	1	1.0				
▽ STORAGES	2	.2				
DISTANCE TRAVELLED	420 FT.		FT.		FT.	

JOB **ADMISSION OF HOSPITAL PATIENT (WOMAN IN LABOR)**
☒ MAN OR ☐ MATERIAL **PATIENT AND NURSE**
CHART BEGINS **PATIENT ARRIVES AT HOSPITAL**
CHART ENDS **PATIENT READY FOR DELIVERY RM.**
CHARTED BY **ART YORK** DATE **5 MAY 1972**

DETAILS OF (PRESENT) METHOD	Operation/Transport/Inspection/Delay/Storage	DISTANCE IN FEET	QUANTITY	TIME MIN	WHY?	NOTES	ACTION
1 Patient Wheeled to Office	○⇨☐D▽	55	1			To Labor Room?	X
2 Helped Into Chair	●⇨☐D▽			.2	X X	Straight to Room Ask Questions Later	X X
3 Hospital Forms Taken from Desk	●⇨☐D▽			.1	X	Set of Forms	
4 Fill In Forms by Interview	●⇨☐D▽			3	X	Get Advance Info from Dr.	X X
5 Transfer Data to Labor Record	●⇨☐D▽			2	X	Get Advance Info	X X
6 Fill In Clothing Form	●⇨☐D▽			2	X	Later	X
7 Nurse and Patient Review Forms Info	○⇨☐D▽			1	X	Later	X
8 Fill In Bottle/Breast Card	●⇨☐D▽			1	X	Get from Dr.	X
9 Patient Helped Into Wheelchair	●⇨☐D▽			.2			
10 Patient Taken to Labor Room	○⇨☐D▽	45	2			By Nurse	
11 Nurse Helps Patient Change Clthg	●⇨☐D▽			3			
12 Nurse Gets Thermometer	○⇨☐D▽	25	2	X		Storage Room...Closer?	X
13 Get Preparation Set (Razor, etc.)	○⇨☐D▽	15	.1			Medicine Cabinet Closer?	X
14 Go to Files Get Pre Natal Rcd	○⇨☐D▽	20	1	X		Do On Arrival?	X
15 Return to Labor Room	○⇨☐D▽	20	.2				
16 Patient's Temperature Taken	●⇨☐D▽			2			
17 Record Pulse, Respiration, Bld Pressure	●⇨☐D▽			3			
18 Measure Fetal Heart Rate	●⇨☐D▽			2			
19 Ask Patient About Allergies	●⇨☐D▽			.1			
20 Shave Patient	●⇨☐D▽			2			
21 Rectal Examination	●⇨☐D▽			.5			
22 Bed Card Filled Out	●⇨☐D▽			.5			
23 Fill Out Personal Property Tags	●⇨☐D▽			.5			
24 Nurse Disposes of Preparation Kit	●⇨☐D▽	10	.2				
25 Nurse Stores Thermometer	●⇨☐D▽	15	.1			Medicine Cabinet	X

DETAILS OF (PRESENT/PROPOSED) METHOD	Symbol	Distance in Feet	Time	Analysis Why?	Notes	Action Change
26. Nurse Goes to Telephone	Transport	20	.2	X	1 Phone ... Addt'l Lines?	X
27. Looks Up Doctor's Number	Inspection		1	X ... X	Pre-Pchd Phone Cards?	X
28. Inform Dr. of Patient's Status	Operation		2			
29. Return to Labor Room	Transport	20	.2			
30. Obtain Urine Sample	Operation		1			
31. Pour Urine Into Test Tube	Operation		.1			
32. Prepare Label for Sample	Operation		.1	X ... X	Part of Form Set?	X
33. Put On Test Tube	Operation		.1			
34. Carry Test Tube to Utility Room	Transport	15	.1			
35. Place Test Tube In Rack	Transport		.1			
36. Go to Storage Room	Transport	20	.2		Store Closer?	X X
37. Get Enema Equipt.	Operation		.1			
38. Bring to Labor Room	Transport	20	.2			
39. Start Enema	Operation		.3			
40. Go to Desk	Transport	45	.5	X X ... X	Do In Labor Room?	X
41. Locate Addressograph Plate	Operation		.5			
42. Apply Plate to Records	Operation		2		9 or 10 Stampings	X
43. Fill In Balance of Records	Operation		3			X
44. Fill Out Urinalysis Form	Operation		.5			X
45. Fill Out Blood Test Form	Operation		.5			X
46. Go to Utility Room	Transport	30	.2			
47. Put Urinalysis Form With Sample	Transport		.1			
48. Go to Labor Room	Transport	15	.1			
49. Assist Patient Use Bed Pan	Operation	20	1	X	Nurse's Aid?	X
50. Clean Bed Pan	Operation		.5		By Nurse?	X
51. Put Bed Pan In Cabinet	Transport	10	.1			
52. Record Fetal Heart Rate	Operation		1			X
53. Begin Timing Labor Pains	Operation		3			

FIGURE 6-4

FLOW PROCESS CHART

PAGE 1 OF 2   NO _____

JOB: ADMISSION OF HOSPITAL PATIENT (WOMAN IN LABOR)

[X] MAN OR [ ] MATERIAL: PATIENT AND NURSE

CHART BEGINS: PATIENT ARRIVES AT HOSPITAL

CHART ENDS: PATIENT READY FOR DELIVERY ROOM

CHARTED BY: ART YORK   DATE 6 MAY 1972

SUMMARY

	PRESENT		PROPOSED		DIFFERENCE	
	NO.	TIME	NO.	TIME	NO.	TIME
OPERATIONS	34	38.1	24	22.9	10	15.2
TRANSPORTATIONS	15	8.1	5	1.7	10	6.4
INSPECTIONS	1	1.0	–	–	1	1.0
DELAYS	1	1.0	–	–	1	1.0
STORAGES	2	.2	2	.2	–	–
DISTANCE TRAVELLED	420 FT.		280 FT.		140 FT.	

DETAILS OF (PRESENT / PROPOSED) METHOD

#	Details	Distance in feet	Quantity	Min. Time	Notes
1	Patient Wheeled To Delivery Room	65		.4	By Nurses Aide
2	Nurse Gets Prepared File			.5	Contains Info From Patient's Dr.
3	Nurse Reviews Patients File			2	
4	Nurse Goes to Labor Room	45		.3	
5	Clothing Form Filled Out			2	
6	Clothing Form Signed			.1	
7	Nurse Gets Preparation Kit & Thermometer	10		.1	In Labor Room
8	Takes Patient's Temperature			–	
9	Record Pulse, Respiration, Bld Pressure			2	
10	Measure Fetal Heart Rate			3	
11	Shave Patient			2	
12	Rectal Examination			.5	
13	Dispose of Prep. Kit	10		.1	In Labor Room
14	Nurse Stores Thermometer	10		.1	
15	Nurse Picks Up Telephone	15		.1	
16	Uses Pre Pchd Call Card			.2	
17	Inform Dr. of Patient's Status			2	
18	Obtain Urine Sample			.5	Part of Prep Kit
19	Pour Urine Into Test Tube	10		.2	
20	Put Prepared Label On Tube			.1	
21	Put Test Tube In Rack In Room			.1	
22	Get Enema and Start It	15		2	In Labor Room
23	Go To Desk	45		.5	
24	Locate Addressograph Plate			.5	
25	Complete Patient's Records			2	

DETAILS OF (PRESENT/PROPOSED) METHOD	OPERATION TRANSPORT INSPECTION DELAY STORAGE	DISTANCE IN FEET	QUANTITY	TIME	ANALYSIS WHY? (WHAT WHERE WHEN WHO HOW)	NOTES	ACTION CHNGE (ELIMINATE COMBINE SEQUENCE PLACE PERSON IMPROVE)
26. Fill Out Urinalysis Request	●▷□D▽		.3				
27. Fill Out Blood Test Request	●▷□D▽		.5				
28. Return to Patient's Room	O▷□D▽	45	.4				
29. Place Urin. Request With Spec.	●▷□D▽		.1			Will Be Picked Up	
30. Call Aide for Bed Pan	●▷□D▽	10	.2				
31. Take Fetal Heart Rate	●▷□D▽		2				
	O▷□D▽						
	O▷□D▽						
	O▷□D▽						
	O▷□D▽						
	O▷□D▽						
	O▷□D▽						
	O▷□D▽						
	O▷□D▽						
	O▷□D▽						
	O▷□D▽						
	O▷□D▽						
	O▷□D▽						
	O▷□D▽						
	O▷□D▽						
	O▷□D▽						
	O▷□D▽						
	O▷□D▽						
	O▷□D▽						
	O▷□D▽						
	O▷□D▽						
	O▷□D▽						
	O▷□D▽						
	O▷□D▽						

REVIEW QUESTIONS

1. Express the philosophy that underlies the work simplification approach.
2. What are the basic principles of work simplification?
3. What are the general steps of work simplification? Apply these steps to a simple situation known to you.
4. Prepare a flow process chart for a procedure or method available for your study. Analyze the present method. Prepare a proposed flow process chart for it.
5. Explain each of the symbols used in the flow process chart.
6. Discuss the relationship of *make ready, do,* and *put away* steps.
7. Prepare a before-and-after flow diagram for a situation with which you are familiar.
8. What is the relationship between creativity and work simplification?
9. How is work simplificatoin compatible with the concept of enlightened self-interest?
10. Discuss the human relations problems that the systems analyst might encounter in work simplification.

BIBLIOGRAPHY

CAPSTONE MANUAL, *Paperwork Flow Charting.* Arvada, Calif.: Capstone Bookpress, 1967. A simplified presentation of a basic system for paperwork flow charting.

LAZZARO, VICTOR, *Systems and Procedures* (2nd ed.). Englewood Cliffs, N. J.: Prentice-Hall, Inc., 1968. One of the best contributions to the development of an understanding of the tools in the field for the novice. Each chapter describes a particular tool or technique and is written by an authority in the field.

LEHRER, ROBERT N., *Work Simplification.* Englewood Cliffs, N. J.: Prentice-Hall, Inc., 1957. Well done, clearly presented, and practical.

NADLER, GERALD, *Work Design.* Homewood, Ill.: Richard D. Irwin, Inc., 1963. A thorough treatment of the design of systems that accomplish work in any organization. It goes far beyond basic work simplification but does not lose sight of the relationship.

————, *Work Simplification*. New York: McGraw-Hill Book Company, 1957. Excellent treatment reflecting the author's wide experience and know-how.

SYSTEMS AND PROCEDURES ASSOCIATION, *Business Systems*. Cleveland, Ohio: Systems and Procedures Association, 1966. The SPA developed the book, utilizing acknowledged experts who were members of their association to develop the materials for each chapter. Strong in work simplification, fair in computers and Operations Research.

7

CHARTING TOOLS
FOR SYSTEMS ANALYSIS

The "glamour treatment" that has been given the computer and advanced quantitative techniques in recent years has tended to relegate the older "pencil-and-paper" systems tools to the background. Work simplification in general and the flow process chart in particular are cases in point. But, like flow process charting, a number of other very useful systems analysis tools utilize the charting approach. One of these systems analysis tools has the unique ability of being able to present an integrated overview of a significant portion of the Management Information System. It is none other than the much maligned but widely used organization chart. Properly prepared and with its limitations clearly understood, the organization chart can be a very valuable systems tool indeed. (See Fig. 7-1.)

THE ORGANIZATION CHART

An *organization* is usefully defined as any group of people working toward a common goal. The work involved in reaching the group's goal is assessed by those instituting and guiding the organization and is then divided among all concerned according to the type and level of the skills required. Then, to coordinate efforts and constrain actions that may be based on lack of information or wrong information or bad judgment and to avoid having the group disintegrate into an aimless do-as-they-please mob, lines of authority, responsibility, and channels of information flow are set up. This network of relationships exists in fact, and its representation is very useful for planning, analysis, and control.

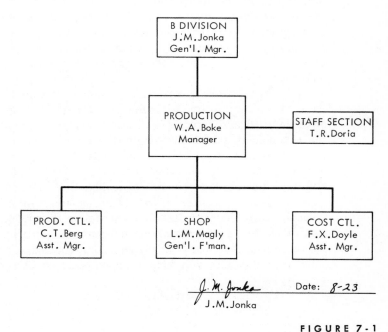

FIGURE 7-1

Organization Chart

The organization chart is a graphical representation of the network of relationships of a group of people working toward a common goal—the division of labor, the level and type of skills required, the lines of authority, the spheres of responsibility, and the channels of information. It is, in reality, a schematic representation of the formal Management Information System. Yet it by no means tells all. It tells who, what, and where, but not how, when, or why. This is a major limitation and emphasizes the point that it should be utilized as an adjunct to other tools of systems analysis.

The general criticism of organization charts is that they are obsolete before they are completed. Since all organizations and their environment are in a constant state of flux, the observation is a valid one. But having a "picture" of the organizational relationships as of a particular point in time can be very helpful. It provides an authorized reference against which to measure the various personal views as to the lines of authority, spheres of responsibility, and channels of information that exist. In any organization, these are as varied as circumstances and situations allow. This state of affairs may be glossed over during the halcyon days, but there comes a time of reckoning for every organization. Then the ignored procedures, the missing information channels, the working at cross-purposes, the duplication, waste motion, and contradictions quickly exacerbate a bad situation into an impossible one. An organization chart, carefully prepared, can act as a continuing guide to provide a record of where the organization was as it grows and changes —to help it get to where it is going.

Organization theory validly points out that an organization is a living, breathing entity, adjusting and changing to meet the challenges of its internal and external realities. A dynamic representation mirroring the ever-changing relationships of the systems elements would be much more valuable to the decision makers than the static organization chart would be. Certainly, decisions based on reality will have a greater probability of meeting the demands of reality. But our technology, both hardware and software, is not up to creating organization charts that instantly reflect changes in organization dynamics, and management must therefore make do with organization charts as they are. The alternative is to do without a tool that has proved itself repeatedly over the years. The following guidelines will help to maximize the usefulness of this tool.

Organization chart guidelines
Refer to Figs. 7 and 7-2:

1. Use standard-size paper (8½ by 11 inches).
2. Different-size rectangles are used to represent the relative significance of the positions.
3. The key position for a particular chart is the largest rectangle and is usually placed at the top center of the chart.
4. Staff positions are shown by smaller rectangles.

5. Connect functional positions by heavy lines representing line of authority and/or communication.

6. Show functional titles for each unit and the current manager's name and title.

7. Include the next level above the key position to the extent of at least one functional rectangle—preferably, two levels are most useful. Use smaller rectangles.

8. Emphasize and chart the work relationships, not the specific people concerned.

9. Usually, charts include from first-line supervisor up to board of directors level, but not necessarily on the same page.

10. Include a signature block to indicate approval of the person to whom the manager of the charted organization reports.

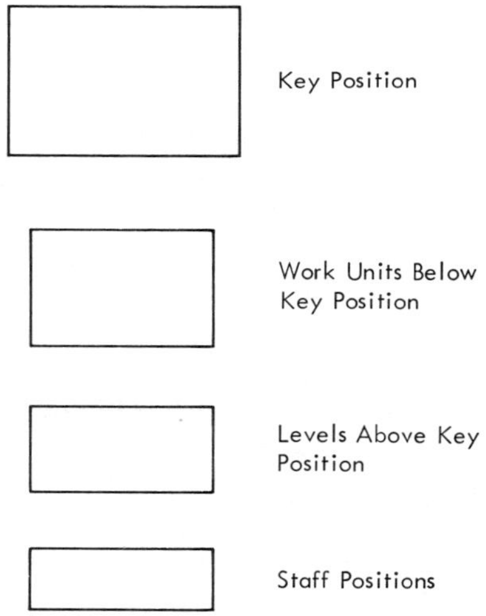

Key Position

Work Units Below
Key Position

Levels Above Key
Position

Staff Positions

FIGURE 7-2

Rectangle Sizes

The criterion for the useful chart is that it not try to include everything. It should strive for simplicity and clarity. If duties are to be listed with functional boxes, another chart should be considered for the purpose. If potential organizational changes are to be charted, it is recommended that *present* and *proposed* charts be constructed.

The overall organization chart will show the major functional divisions of the total system. Supplementary charts are then developed for each of these divisions. In a very real sense, each rectangle on the overall organization chart is "exploded" into its component parts. If there are many such levels in the organization being charted, clarity requires that the process be repeated for each level. The important guideline is not to clutter the chart while aiming for consistency, clarity, and simplicity.

There are a variety of systems applications for this simple but valuable tool. Before-and-after charts can help explain a change. Management succession plans are also easily presented by means of organization charts. There are many others. The systems analyst may find that its construction can be a powerful tool for uncovering Management Information Systems problems that can then be analyzed and improved by other techniques in his repertory.

THE SYSTEMS FLOW CHART

The systems flow chart (see Fig. 7-3) is the symbolic representation of the major steps in the processing and flow of information in the system. Whereas the organization chart identified *who, what,* and *where* in the Management Information System, the systems flow chart shows *how* the information is processed in the channels of the system. Flow charting is a technique in which symbols represent both the sequence of operations and the flow of data and paperwork.

The flow charting symbols are used to record the flow of information from an originating input source through a series of processing steps to some output condition or management report. For example, using the appropriate symbols, an analyst can record the flow of information in the sales department from daily receipt of customer orders to weekly summary report to management of sales by product by type of customer.

The flow chart helps the analyst to understand the information system in terms of the processing operations involved. It will help him to analyze these steps with a view to both improving them and increasing the effectiveness of the Management Information System. Furthermore, and perhaps of signal importance, the symbols used in flow charting are universally recognized and, therefore, are a great help in communicating with the technicians and computer programmers in the information-processing field.

There are two general categories of flow charts—systems flow charts and program flow charts. As was mentioned previously, the systems flow chart presents the overview of the general steps in the information-processing procedure. The program flow chart shows the detailed steps in the procedure.

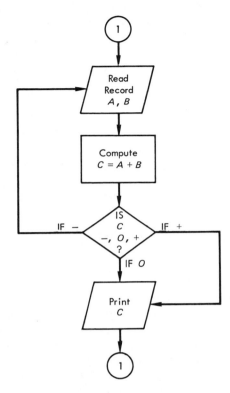

FIGURE 7-3

Systems Flow Chart

The general information processing steps shown in the systems flow chart are "exploded" into the necessary detail for closer analysis in the program flow chart. The program flow chart's details evolve from the general steps of the systems flow chart. How detailed? It depends on the demands of the application and the idiosyncrasies of the computer on which it may run. But it is a moot point; the important thing to understand at this stage is that the systems flow chart is the tool of the systems analyst. It can provide him with an excellent blueprint of the major information flows within the Management Information System. The program flow chart is identified with the computer programmer who prepares it with the help of the systems flow chart just prior to writing the computer program.

In preparing flow charts it is important to emphasize that the same guidelines that were developed for organization charts apply—consistency, clarity, and simplicity.

Flow Charting Symbols

Over the years, systems analysts have developed individualized symbols to represent the steps in processing information. But as flow charts came to be exchanged between analysts and among organizations in government, industry, and education, it was found that misunderstandings occurred because of the lack of uniformity of meaning for the symbols used. After an intensive study by the American Standards Association, a standard for flow chart symbols for information processing was developed. These symbols are designated as the United States of America Standards Institute (USASI) symbols. They are the industry standard.

Although nineteen standard symbols are available for use in flow charting, the following five symbols are all that are necessary for the systems analyst to prepare meaningful systems flow charts. Other standard symbols can be added as the systems analyst becomes proficient in flow charting. Inexpensive plastic templates are available to make drawing the symbols easier.

1. The Input/Output Symbol (Parallelogram):
   Represents the function of making information available for processing (input) or the recording of processed information (output). Specialized input/output symbols are available whose shape suggests the input/output medium being used (punched cards, punched tape, document, magnetic tape, etc.).

Example:

Read
Inventory
Data

2. The Process Symbol (Rectangle):
   Used to represent the processing function, that is, the execution of a defined operation or operations resulting in an arithmetic step or the storage of data, or the transfer of data from one point to another in the information system. Intelligent use of the legend within this symbol makes it a very flexible one indeed.

Example:
Represents the sequence of processing steps to calculate the New Balance (NB) of an item of inventory by adding Receipts (R) to the Balance on Hand (BOH) and subtracting Withdrawals (WD).

$$NB = BOH + R - WD$$

3. The Direction of Flow Symbol (Arrow):
Represents direction of information flow and the sequence of processing operations. It connects one symbol with the next. Normal direction of flow is from left to right and from top to bottom on a systems flow chart.

Example:
Connects the Input information on Inventory to the processing step for calculating New Balance.

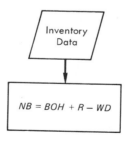

Inventory Data

$$NB = BOH + R - WD$$

4. The Decision Symbol (Diamond):
Whenever the information system provides for a decision step in the processing sequence this symbol is used. It represents a point in the system where a decision, that is, a selection between alternative courses of action, is necessary. It is one of the great insights into decision mechanics to realize that every decision sequence almost invariably involves the necessity of

a. Comparing two numbers (by subtraction)
b. Generating a hierarchy of values (which are the normal result of subtraction —, 0, or +)
c. Selecting an alternative processing sequence depending on whether the result of the subtraction was —, 0, or +

Later it will be shown that this three-step sequence is the essence of computer decision making.

For Example:

In a payroll procedure, previous information-processing steps may have developed a *gross pay* figure. Management may want a list of all piecework employees who earn two hundred dollars or less per week. The *decision* step is illustrated: If the result of the comparison is "greater than," the next processing step is as usual— but if "less than" or "equal to," the next step prints that worker's name on an exception report to management.

Another Example:

Management may have decided that an effective inventory policy requires reordering when the quantity of a particular item falls below two thousand. The *decision* step would show that when the New Balance (NB) is less than two thousand, an order to the supplier must be instituted. If it is equal to or above two thousand, the usual procedure is followed.

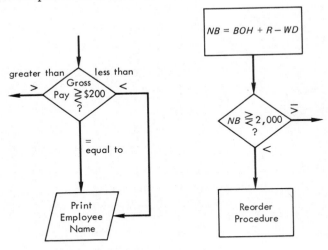

5. The Connector Symbol (Circle):
The small circle with a number (or letter) within it is used when

additional connecting lines will clutter the flow chart or when space is exhausted on one page and the analyst wants to show continuity to another page. Wherever a small circle with the same number (or letter) within it exists on the same page or other pages, those two points are considered to be joined.

That is, they are one and the same point.

Example:

In the inventory example, there may be a number of different items of inventory whose new balance is to be calculated, tested, and the item reordered, if necessary. Therefore, the sequence of

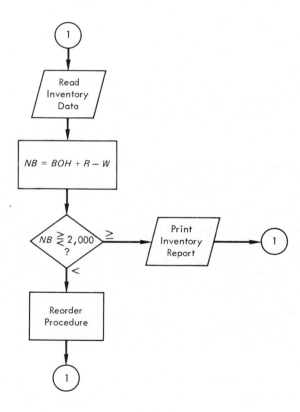

steps must be repeated for each different item of inventory. Rather than redraw the sequence many times, the connector symbol provides an excellent means of representing this necessary recycling. Whether the item being processed is reorderd or not, after one item has been processed the sequence must be repeated for all the inventory items that follow. The portion of the systems flow chart shown details the necessary sequence clearly and succinctly.

As has been pointed out, the systems flow chart is used as the logic guide when the computer programmer prepares the program flow chart. The manager or the systems analyst concerned can insure that his concept of an effective Managment Information System to meet his unique needs is reflected in the computerized "package" if he utilizes the systems flow chart to communicate with the programmers and technicians concerned. It is also an excellent tool to help him prethink his information system specifications.

THE WORK DISTRIBUTION CHART

The work distribution chart details the division of work in the particular part of the Management Information System being analyzed. It is not a total systems tool, but rather it concentrates on one particular unit in the overall system. That unit might be the receiving department of a factory, the outpatient clinic of a hospital, or the circulation department of a library. In essence, the work distribution chart is a list of the major categories of work done in a particular part of the system, how much time each employee spends on each activity, and what specific contribution he makes to that activity.

The systems analyst who uses this tool for the first time may be misled by its simplicity into underestimating its effectiveness. The following experiment will convince both himself and the most skeptical manager of the efficacy of this tool.

1. Have the manager list the major work activities of all persons who report to him. Ask him to include his estimate of the percentage of time each spends on each activity.

2. Then have him ask each person who reports to him to list his work activities and his independent estimate of the time he spends on each activity.

3. Finally, have the manager compare the two lists and the estimates. He will be surprised—perhaps shocked! But what should be even more revealing is the fact that what the workers reported is probably not a very accurate reflection of what they actually do, but rather a composite of what they think they do adjusted by what they think their manager wants them to be doing and the amount of time they guess he wants them to be doing it!

Although the foregoing experiment may appear exaggerated, it is a very likely result in many areas of a typical organization. It dramatizes the lack of precise information on *who* does *what* and *how* long it takes. Not because of malice, laziness, or stupidity, but because the distribution of work tends to "happen" in a haphazard way rather than in an organized, systematic way.

The work distribution chart is a carefully designed tool that helps to spotlight uneven work distribution, improper use of skills, misdirected effort, and activities requiring the most time, as well as whether or not assigned tasks are related, imbalanced, or spread too thinly.

The following procedure provides a step-by-step guide for the application of this tool. Certain associated forms that assist in preparing this tool are also described.

Preparing the Work Distribution Chart

1. The Task List (Fig. 7-4):
   Each employee is requested to prepare a list of tasks and an estimate of the number of hours spent per week on each. The use of a form makes it easier for the employee, encourages accuracy, and emphasizes the importance of the study. The analyst reviews the task list with each employee to further insure reasonable accuracy. The work count should be indicated where possible (number of letters, number of interviews, etc.).

2. The Activity List (Fig. 7-5):
   This is a listing of the major activities of the unit being studied It answers the question, What are the things this unit does? It can be prepared by the supervisor but is reviewed with the analyst and utilizes clues that have been provided by preparation of the task list. Every task on the task list should be classifiable under one of the entries in the activity list. A *miscellaneous* activity is very useful to avoid wasting too much time on categorizing insignificant tasks.

FIGURE 7-4

Task List

TASK LIST OF INDIVIDUAL JOBS					
(For work distribution chart)					
			Page 1 of 1		
Name Smith, M. R.		Working Title Office Supervisor	Dept. Sales	I D No. 5732	
Activity No.	Description of Operation			Work Count	Hours per Week
7	Make travel arrangements				1
8	Plan work (for self and subordinates)				4-30'
8	Coordinate office work				3-30'
2	Answer Telephone			40	2-30'
1	Take dictation and type letters			5	2
1	Prepare all types of correspondence from oral instructions			8	2-30'
8	Plan and conduct office meetings			4	4
8	Review work of subordinates				6-20'
8	Assign work and give instructions				7
3	Take dictation and prepare reports of conferences			3	4-40'
9	Miscellaneous				2
	Total of Work Hours				40
Date 5-14	Function Charted Sales Administration		Approved (signature of supervisor)		

FIGURE 7-5

Activity List

ACTIVITY LIST (For work distribution chart)		Date 5/15
No.	Description of Operation	Weekly Volume
1	Preparation of correspondence	
2	Telephone	
3	Conference Reports	
4	Statistical Tabulations	
5	Maintain Marketing Library	
6	Maintain filing system	
7	Make travel arrangements	
8	Administration and supervision	
9	Miscellaneous activities	
Unit Function Sales Administration	Approved (signature of supervisor)	

3. The Work Distribution Chart (Fig. 7-6):
The data collected in the task lists and the information provided by the activity list are organized for analysis on the work distribution chart.
   a. The heading of the chart is filled in as indicated by the captions.
   b. Employees' names and functional titles are listed across the chart in order of responsibility.
   c. *Activities* are listed in their order of importance in the first column on the left.
   d. Under each employee's name opposite each activity are entered the tasks he does related to that particular activity and the *hours per week* spent on that task. If useful, the *work count* indicating the quantity of items handled can also be recorded.
   e. *Hours per week* and *work count* are totaled and entered in the columns just to the right of the *activity* column.
   f. Man-hours for each employee and for all employees are totaled and entered in the spaces provided.

4. Analyze the Chart:
The analysis is very similar to that described in the work simplification discussion in Chapter 6. If you recall, once the facts had been collected on the flow process chart, they were analyzed by a combination of questioning and applying creativity. Similarly, the analysis of the work distribution chart requires the application of creativity to develop improvements. The following questions and comments will help this process along.
   a. What activities take the most time? Are they commensurate in importance with the effort expended? How do they relate to the overall objectives of the unit? Of the system? Of the organization? When the activities that take significant amounts of total man-hours involve a sequence of steps, the analyst may want to identify them (by circling in red pencil) for future application of the flow process chart which was described in detail in Chapter 6.
   b. Is there misdirected effort? The study of individual tasks and man-hours spotlights relatively small units of effort that are wasted in duplication of effort or in pointless tasks. The *miscellaneous* activity is often the catchall for these wasteful tasks. Identify them, evaluate, then change or eliminate.
   c. Are skills used properly? Review the allocation of activities and tasks to employees to determine whether skills and abilities are matched to the requirements of the *tasks* and the *activities*. This is where the physical organization of the chart comes into its own. The upper left hand portion represents the highest level of employee and the most important activity. The opposite

WORK DISTRIBUTION CHART

Distribution — Present ☐ Proposed ☐

Charted by _____

Function Charted _____

No.	Activity	Work Count	Hrs per Week	Name ____ Position ____ ID No. ____ Task	Work Count	Hrs per Week	Name ____ Position ____ ID No. ____ Task	Work Count	Hrs per Week	Name ____ Position ____ ID No. ____ Task	Work Count	Hrs per Week
Total (Man Hours)												

FIGURE 7-6
Work Distribution Chart

is true for the lower right hand portion of the chart. This lay-out of the chart will help orient the analyst as he studies it for allocation of skills to work.

d. Are employees doing too many unrelated tasks? Crowded *task* columns on the chart are clues to the possibility of waste mo-tion, fatigue, and inefficiency. Few people can do all things equally well. Where possible, a fragmented activity may use-fully be consolidated to reduce the number of different tasks done by one employee. Furthermore, tasks are often intrinsically related, and combining such tasks under the same employee is often conducive to significant improvements in productivity. Additional improvements also result from the efficiencies the employee himself will introduce because of his control over the whole process.

e. Are tasks spread too thinly? This relates to the previous dis-cussion. It merits special emphasis because it is often the case. The same task handled by a number of employees can result in variation of standards, inconsistency, and the ever-present danger of the lack of specific responsibility.

f. Is the work distributed evenly? In analyzing the chart you may get the feeling that the work load of one person is inordinate while that of another person is relatively light. Check into this seeming imbalance, and if it really exists, utilize the work dis-tribution chart to spread the work load more evenly. An ad-ditional aid in determining the actual work load is to use the *work count*. It is described in the following section.

The work distribution chart is a fairly simple tool that gets into the detail of *who* does *what* in the organization. It can be used as a first step in locating areas for the application of the flow process chart, or, as the foregoing discussion has pointed out, it has an important function in its own right.

THE WORK COUNT

The work distribution chart provides a column for recording the *work count* for each task. But the work count can be a useful tool on its own. As simple as its title, the work count is a record of the number of units of work processed in a given time period. These units might be:

Interviews conducted	Documents filed
Inventory items issued	Invoices prepared
Units of product produced	Sales dollars booked
Letters typed	Postings made
Cards punched	Phone calls made

The purpose of the work count is to balance staff and facilities against the unit's work load. Taking the count of work by category provides the necessary data to make work assignments for optimum utilization of available work capacity. It spotlights areas of relative idleness as well as bottlenecks. Furthermore, a work count provides management with quantitative data to support requests for additional personnel.

It is axiomatic that every effort is made to use existing counts. In addition, it is often possible to utilize means other than an individual piece-by-piece count. For instance, a ruler to measure a stack of cards which can then easily be converted to the number of cards by a quick count of number per inch. A scale can be used for bulk weighing of mail or other relatively uniform parts to get a good approximation of piece count, or perhaps the gross weight itself can be used as the work count for a period of time.

Counting may also be facilitated by utilizing data available on existing reports, or by the aid of serially numbered forms, recording counters, or meters, or by actual count, or by other more imaginative methods such as weighing or measuring by ruler as was mentioned previously.

The work distribution chart and the work count, like a number of other charting tools, have a surface simplicity that masks a power that must be experienced to be appreciated. Especially in the early stages of what might become a total Management Information Systems study, it would behoove the systems analysts concerned to invest some time at the operational grass roots level plying the fundamental tools of systems analysis—the work distribution chart, the flow process chart, the work count, the organization chart, and the systems flow chart. The insights gained will often make a big difference in the final design of the organization's Management Information System.

THE GANTT CHART

One of the most widely used charting tools is the Gantt chart developed by a pioneer systems analyst, Henry L. Gantt, who was known in his day as a practitioner of "scientific management." Gantt charts are used to:

1. Relate progress versus a master schedule.
2. Show accomplishment against a plan.
3. Record work load assigned to machines and work stations. Figure 7-7 represents a typical Gantt chart.

Assembly Dept.	Week 7 M T W T F	Week 8 M T W T F	Week 9 M T W T F	Week 10 M T W T F	Week 11 M T W T F
Preparation	13-4 13-7		16-9	19-7	
Degreasing	11-5	13-4	4-31	16-9	2-21
Structural	1-15			13-4	
Mechanical		10-7	1-15		13-4
Welding	3-11	11-5		10-7	
Clean & Polish	1-13	3-11		11-5	
Electric Test	1-3		3-11		11-5
Pressure Test		7-13		3-11	10-7
Final Inspection	4-6	1-3	7-13	9-6 3-11	

FIGURE 7-7

Gantt Chart

The time schedule is usually represented across the top of the chart, with the description of the work to be done identified in the left column.

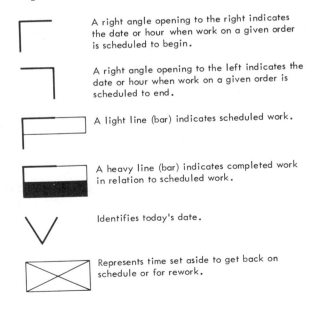

A right angle opening to the right indicates the date or hour when work on a given order is scheduled to begin.

A right angle opening to the left indicates the date or hour when work on a given order is scheduled to end.

A light line (bar) indicates scheduled work.

A heavy line (bar) indicates completed work in relation to scheduled work.

Identifies today's date.

Represents time set aside to get back on schedule or for rework.

Although the Gantt chart is probably the most universal of scheduling and control tools, it has some significant shortcomings.

1. It does not show the sequence of tasks that determines the overall time span of a project that involves a number of interrelated *work orders (tasks)*.
2. Although the Gantt chart identifies each work order, it cannot identify those work orders (tasks) that are related to or depend on each other.
3. There is no provision for alerting management to critical work orders that require special attention by management so that the overall project is not affected.
4. The Gantt chart cannot identify available resources that can be reallocated from one task to another that needs them so that the overall project can be completed on schedule.

A number of techniques have been developed to overcome these shortcomings, and Line of Balance and PERT are two of the most successful and the most widely used. Line of Balance will be discussed in the following section and PERT will be discussed in Chapter 10.

LINE OF BALANCE (LOB)

What It Is

Line of Balance (LOB) is a technique for assembling, selecting, interpreting, and presenting in chart form the essential factors involved in a production process. The charts cover the process from raw materials to completion of the end product, presented against the dimension of time. It is essentially a project control-type tool, utilizing the principle of management by exception to show only the most critical facts to its users.

What It Does

1. It relates the actual status of the elements of a production program to planned progress to meet delivery requirements. It identifies those elements that are lagging and may delay delivery of the end item.
2. It specifies time relationships between the various tasks in the manufacturing process and identifies deficiencies in the availability of materials, parts, and assemblies at selected control points along the production line.
3. It provides an indication to project management as to how well the various phases of manufacturing are synchronized.

What It Is Used For

1. Its basic use is to measure the current relationship of production progress to scheduled performance and to predict the feasibility of meeting the scheduled deliveries.
2. It is a positive means for identifying those areas of the process that need corrective action. Furthermore, successively updated LOB studies provide checks on the effectiveness of remedial action.

Elements of a Line of Balance Study

The Line of Balance (LOB) technique is comprised of the following four phases listed in the sequence in which each is normally developed when conducting a Line of Balance study of a production process.

1. The Objective: the cumulative delivery schedule
2. The Program: the production plan
3. Program Progress: the current status of production performance
4. Comparison of Program Progress with Objective: the Line of Balance study

THE OBJECTIVE   The objective of a production process, where the end item is being produced under contract, is the required delivery schedule. The delivery information used and needed in a Line of Balance analysis is of two kinds, *planned*, the contractual delivery requirement, and *actual*, the deliveries actually made by the producer up to the time of the LOB analysis. Planned delivery and actual delivery of end item sets are always collected and plotted in cumulative terms.

Objective Chart Construction (Fig. 7-8). Chart representation of the objective is accomplished by a simple graph using cumulative completed units plotted against time. The actual deliveries are plotted on the same graph.

THE PROGRAM (PRODUCTION PLAN)   Following the preparation of the objective chart, the second important step in a LOB study is to chart the programmed production plan (Fig. 7-8). The production plan, or "assembly tree," is developed in terms of key plant operations or critical assembly points and their lead-time relationship to final completion dates. This is the most vital stage in a Line of Balance study. These operational control points are steps in the manufacturing cycle, the completion of which can be used to monitor the intermediate progress of production toward the ultimate delivery goal.

Accumulation of Data.   The production plan should cover the span of operations peculiar to the particular manufacturing process, from work on raw materials through assembly operations to point of shipment. The systems analyst utilizing the LOB should make a tour of the plant to observe the physical layout and the actual processes involved, as well as to observe the physical attributes of the operations. This trip should be made "in reverse," beginning at the shipping room door and ending at the stockroom where incoming materials are received. This unusual approach will enable the analyst to obtain a more accurate concept of the entire production plan. It is also essential in order to establish an accurate concept of lead time for operations and materials.

As a further basis for developing the information necessary for the production plan, the guides that the manufacturer has developed to produce his product should be utilized to the utmost. These frequently consist of:

Shop drawings
Bills of material
Process charts
Machine loading charts
Assembly line layouts
Shop orders

The production plan is developed from three aspects:

1. The Determination of Operations to Be Monitored

A determination is made of various operations to be performed on major components, purchased parts, company-furnished parts, government-furnished parts, subcontracted parts, and raw materials. Using the principle of monitoring by exception, only the key operations plus other potentially limiting steps need be included in the production plan. Care should be exercised to eliminate as many as possible of the similar, less-troublesome operations.

The parts of the production plan selected for inclusion in the LOB study are not stereotyped, nor are they standardized in number, but they may vary considerably as determined by local knowledge of the manufacturing process.

2. The Determination of the Sequence of Operations

A determination is made of the sequence, or order, in which the parts and hence the subassemblies are directed into the final assembly stage.

The first step is to examine the list of parts shown on the bill of material. They are usually arranged according to the major assemblies

which, in turn, are further divided into subassemblies. A general chrono-
logical determination of flow can be made at this stage concerning the
approximate sequence, or order, in which these materials and subassembly
groups flow into final assembly operations. This should then be consolidated onto a flow chart which will delineate the steps of the process
in sequence.

3. The Determination of Processing and Assembly Lead Time

A determination is made of the total time interval, in each case,
between the required availability of raw material, purchased parts, manu-
factured parts, and subassemblies and the date of shipment of the completed end item. This time is inclusive, and in addition to required processing time it includes other aspects, such as in-plant storage or handling
time. In this manner, the time is established by which each operation,
subassembly, or other event must take place in advance of ultimate delivery of the end item. This is expressed in definite time units (weeks,
days, etc.). The longest lead time for any one part within a subassembly
group becomes the governing lead time for that entire subassembly group
when constructing the production plan.

Production Plan Construction (Fig. 7-8).   Having determined
the raw materials, parts, fabrication stages, subassemblies and assemblies
with which the Line of Balance study is concerned, and having obtained
the applicable sequence of operations and lead time information, the
data is presented graphically in the following manner. The production
plan is constructed by using a time scale in units commensurate with the
overall lead time. The time scale is normally set down in working days
rather than in calendar days. A week, therefore, consists of five days
and a month consists of twenty-two days if the plant is operating on
a forty-hour week. For ease of interpretation, the production chart is
often coded by symbol, color, and number to indicate the type of operations being performed at each control point.

The production plan is developed by setting down the selected
events and operations in their proper sequence, commencing at the point
of delivery and moving backward through the entire production process.
The control points are numbered from left to right and from top to
bottom. This will usually result in four or more general sequential phases
as follows: The final assembly process, preceded by major subassembly
work, preceded by manufacture of parts, preceded by acquisition and
preparation of raw materials and purchased parts.

PROGRAM PROGRESS CHART   The preceding sections have thus
far developed:

1. A graphic presentation of planned manufacturing goals (objective chart).

2. A graphic presentation of the planned manufacturing process by which attainment of the delivery goal is contemplated (production plan).

The following section explains the development of the program progress portion of the Line of Balance study (see Fig. 7-8).

The program progress phase of the LOB study pertains to the determination of the status of actual production performance and consists of a bar chart which shows the quantities of materials, parts, and subassemblies available at the control points at the specific time of "striking the LOB."

Accumulation of Program Progress Data   Production progress is depicted in terms of the quantities of materials, parts, and subassemblies that have passed through the individual control points specified in the production plan, including those contained in end items already completed. This information is accumulated by a physical inventory for each control point. The count is normally available from appropriate stock records, but if such is not the case a physical tally must be made.

The count must be in end item sets and, therefore, must be factored whenever two or more units of an item are required in the completed assembly. Where a single symbol or a single control point represents the beginning of an assembly process (either subassembly or final assembly), the quantity tallied and used for that control point shall be the quantity of the least available component or part of that assembly or subassembly.

Program Progress Chart Construction   On the program progress chart the same quantity scale is used as the ordinate (vertical axis) as was used for the objective delivery chart. The abscissa scale (horizontal axis) corresponds by duplication of numbers to the numbered control points depicted in the production plan. Numbering and coloring of the status or quantity bars is keyed to correspond with and to duplicate the numbered control points of the production plan. Scale numbering in this instance proceeds from left to right progressively.

If it is desired to show that an appreciable quantity has been nearly completed in addition to that already completed at a given control point, the bar for that control point may be extended upward the appropriate amount but left uncolored. If this is done, an appropriate explanation should be made on the chart. Such bars are normally called *ghost bars*.

COMPARISON OF PROGRAM PROGRESS WITH OBJECTIVE   Development of the objective chart, the production plan, and the program progress chart completes the accumulation of physical information (Fig. 7-8). There remains the task of relating the intelligence already gathered. This is accomplished by striking a *Line of Balance,* which is the basis to be used for comparing the program progress with the objective. The balance line quantity depicts the quantities of end item sets for each control point which must be available as of the date of the study to support the delivery schedule. In other words, it specifies the quantities of end item sets for each control point that must be available in order for progress on the program to remain in phase with the objective.

Striking Line of Balance.   The procedure for striking the Line of Balance is as follows:

1. Plot the balance quantity for each control point.
    a. Starting with the study date on the horizontal axis of the

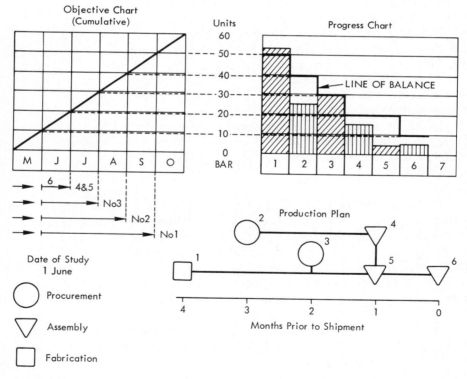

FIGURE 7-8

Striking the Line of Balance

cumulative delivery (objective) chart, mark off to the right the number of working days (or weeks or months, as appropriate) of lead time for that control point. This information is obtained from the production plan.

b. Draw a vertical line from that point on the horizontal axis to the cumulative delivery schedule.

c. From that point draw a horizontal line to the corresponding bar on the progress chart. This is the balance quantity for that bar.

2. Join the balance quantities to form one staircase-type line across the face of the progress chart.

The following paragraph illustrates the procedure for striking the Line of Balance (Fig. 7-8).

A Simplified Line of Balance Analysis

The Line of Balance on the progress chart generated by the combination of lead times and the objective chart determines the necessary status of each critical point in order that the delivery schedule be met. A quick glance at the progress chart indicates that elements 2, 4, 5, and 6 are behind schedule. A study of the production plan will show that element 6 depends on 5, which in turn depends on 4, which is dependent on element 2. Element 2 must be on schedule for the others to get on schedule. The LOB has pinpointed the critical item that must get management's attention.

REVIEW QUESTIONS

1. Draw the organization chart of a group of which you are a part. Take particular care to use the guidelines listed in this chapter.

2. What is a systems flow chart?

3. Interpret the flow chart in Figure 7-3.

4. If A and B had the following values, what would be the result of the process as charted in Figure 7-3?

Value of A	Value of B
20	10
0	1
−5	2
−1	−1
7	−7

5. Ask a manager of your acquaintance to list the major work activities of all persons who report to him and the percentage of the

work week he thinks each spends on each activity. Then have him ask each person who reports to him to list his activities and give his estimate of the percentage of time spent on each. Discuss the results.

6. Which activities in Figure 7-7 are ahead of schedule? Behind schedule? On schedule?

7. What is a Line of Balance study?

8. In Figure 7-8, suppose element 2 was on schedule. Which element would then be a candidate for close review by management?

9. Systems flow chart the procedure for balancing your checkbook and the monthly statement from your bank.

10. Review the literature for alternative methods of representing organizational relationships in chart form.

BIBLIOGRAPHY

BARISH, NORMAN N., *Systems Analysis*. New York: Funk & Wagnalls, 1951. An elementary treatment of certain selected charting tools. Useful for the beginner.

BUFFA, ELWOOD S., *Modern Production Management* (2nd ed.). New York: John Wiley & Sons, Inc., 1965. Excellent treatment of a number of charting tools relating to the production effort in any organization.

IBM, *Flow Charting Techniques* (C20–8152), White Plains, N. Y.: International Business Machines, 1970. A curiously unsatisfactory treatment of the subject by a company that could do better in presenting the material.

JONES, ROBERT L., and GAIL OLIVER, *Basic Logic for Program Flowcharting and Table Search*. Anaheim, Calif.: Anaheim Publishing Company, 1968. Presents an understandable approach to the development of basic logic for computer programs. Useful to both the beginner and the experienced programmer.

LAZZARO, VICTOR, *Systems and Procedures* (2nd ed.). Englewood Cliffs, N. J.: Prentice-Hall, Inc., 1968. Each chapter is written by an authority in the field. Contains a number of descriptions and examples of an array of charting tools.

SCRIBNER, THOMAS J., *Fundamentals of Flow Charting*. New York: John Wiley & Sons, Inc., 1970. Profusely illustrated with examples of the formulation of computer problem-solving procedures by use of flow charts.

SYSTEMS AND PROCEDURES ASSOCIATION, *Business Systems*. Cleveland, Ohio: Systems and Procedures Association, 1966. Written by members of the SPA, it includes authoritative and understandable treatment of a number of charting tools.

8

FORMS ANALYSIS, DESIGN, AND CONTROL

Although largely unrecognized, one of the most essential of the building blocks in every Management Information System is the printed form. It is the medium that transports the data through most of the information-processing steps in organizations.

A *form* is basically a printed document with blank spaces for inserting information. The printed portion does not usually change, but the inserted data varies from form to form. Forms come in all colors, shapes, and sizes; however, many a form is obsolete before it is delivered by the printer because the situation for which it was designed has changed. The reason for this is that most forms tend to be designed by the untrained user, without any partciular attention being paid to a form's relationship to other forms in the system, ease of preparation, or control of its use or retention.

Another characteristic of forms is that their proliferation is endemic in every organization. Unless management recognizes that forms represent one of the most expensive "incidentals" in organizational operations, it may find that all the effort being put into increasing efficiency and lowering costs is being frittered away in the inefficiencies inherent in poor forms design and control.

The printed form is a key ingredient in any serious attempt at developing a viable Management Information System in an organization. It is often the mark of organizational maturity when operations reach the point of proceduralization where a uniform method of recording information is a necessity.

The systems analyst is particularly concerned with forms analysis, design, and control because a rigorous forms program can:

1. Improve information-processing efficiency
2. Simplify employee training
3. Enhance management control
4. Provide an efficient means for recording and carrying data which is the raw material of the Management Information System

An awareness of the principles of forms analysis, design, and control is fundamental to the structuring of an effective Management Information System.

PRINCIPLES OF FORMS ANALYSIS

The design of a form is predicated on a thorough study of *what* goes on the form (analysis) and then determination of *how* it is arranged on the form (design).

In determining what goes on a form it is useful to recall that the basic reason for the existence of a form is to provide a means for carrying accurate, timely, and meaningful information for decision making —information that is essential for directing and coordinating the operations of organizations. The form must also be efficient in terms of the manpower, material, and equipment requirements for its preparation and use.

Reality, however, indicates that most forms currently used in organizations are difficult to read and understand and fill out, inefficient to machine process, and uneconomical to print. The individual cost of producing a blank form is considered trivial, yet it has been estimated by some authorities that the cost of entering data on the form is twenty to thirty times the cost of the form itself. Serious attention paid to *what* should go on the form (analysis) will help determine *how* to arrange the data on the form (design) and will thereby achieve significant dividends in lower costs and more effective information systems.

The systems analyst should play a particularly significant role in the analysis, design, and control of forms because he is interested in improving the overall effectiveness of the Management Information System. He is also trained in the use of methods improvement and work simplification and can therefore utilize his skills of analysis and improvement in the forms area to contribute directly to his major objective.

Effective forms can only result from logical analysis and careful design. The analysis phase concentrates on three specific areas:

1. Evaluation of the need for the information
2. Determination of the most efficient method of getting the needed information on the form
3. Specificaton of the information-processing sequence

It is important to point out that the systems analyst works very closely with operations management in his forms improvement activity. The reason is obvious. Operating management must be the final authority in determining *what* goes on the form. However, the systems analyst can provide an invaluable "total systems" viewpoint in the very important analysis phase of the forms program.

Each systems analyst tends to develop his own style of analysis, one that fits his own unique combination of training, experience, and talent. The following procedure can act as a preliminary guide which can be modified to fit each analyst's training and personality and as his experience indicates.

FORMS ANALYSIS PROCEDURE

The analyst should interview originators, users, and managers and should get answers to the following questions:

1. Is the form really needed?
   a. Is the proposed form needed to the extent that it more than justifies the work required for its preparation?
   b. What if the form did not exist? Is the information on it essential or just nice to have?
   c. Is the same or similar information recorded on another form used elsewhere in the organization?
   d. Determine if the costs for its preparation and use are worth it—the costs to gather information, fill in the form, summarize or extract data from the form, as well as all related administrative and clerical costs.

2. Is each item on the form needed?
   a. What would happen if the item were not included on the form?
   b. Is the item still needed?
   c. Is the item available from another source?
   d. Is the cost of getting the information more than it is worth?
   e. Can this item be combined with another item?

3. Is each copy of the form necessary?
   a. Can each recipient of a copy of the form justify his receiving it?
   b. Can each copy that is filed be justified?
   c. Can the same copy be routed to a number of persons instead of having each receive a copy?

4. Can the form be combined with one or more other forms?
   a. Can one standardized form replace others that are used for essentially the same purpose in different parts of the organization?
   b. Can the addition of a few items to another form allow it to be used in more applications?
   c. Can adding more items to the same form allow it to be used in successive processing steps?
   d. Can the "write it once" approach be used? That is, prepare a multicopy form that is then separated and forwarded to different departments where not all the information is required at each location.

5. Do the procedures related to the forms need improvement?
   a. Do the changes made in the form, or in the number of copies, or in the combining of forms require a revision of the pertinent procedure?
   b. Is the manager concerned agreeable to a procedures review as an extension to the forms analysis?

6. What words should be used on the form?
   Title: Indicates what the form is about.
   Captions: Specify what information is wanted.
   Instructions: Direct the user how to enter the information.
   a. Who will read the words? Beware of technical jargon. Remember that opinion answers require more careful wording than number answers.
   b. Does the title clearly indicate the form's purpose? It should be easily remembered and should reflect the purpose and function of the form.
   c. Are the captions concise and to the point? Try out rough drafts of forms on a sample of users to check clarity of captions.
   d. Where would emphasis be helpful to the user? Type faces, line thickness, and ink color can all help direct the reader's attention.

  e. What instructions would be most helpful to users inside and outside the organization? Extensive detailed instructions should be provided in separate manuals or administrative procedures rather than crowded on the form itself.

7. How can writing the form be made easier?
  a. What is the most logical arrangement of the items on the form from the point of view of the user?
  b. Does the arrangement correspond to the order of items on the document from which the information is taken or to the order of items on the document to which the information is posted?
  c. Is information requested in the sequence normal to people's visual habits? That is, left to right and top to bottom?
  d. For highly repetitive usage, are the items arranged in frequency-of-use sequence?
  e. If a source document for the preparation of punched cards, are the items arranged in the proper sequence for ease of card punching?
  f. Can check boxes be used to save time and space, assist in interpreting data, and reduce errors?
  g. Has enough space been allocated for the maximum number of letters, figures, and punctuation marks that may be entered on the form? Have enough lines been provided on the form?
  h. Are captions printed in the upper-left corners of the answer boxes so that typists can make entries without having to roll the platen up and down to read the captions?
  i. Is the form arranged in columns where possible to allow use of the tabular key on the typewriter?
  j. Can the form be 8½ by 11 inches? If not, why not?

8. How can transmitting of the form be eased?
  a. Can routing information be printed on the form?
  b. Can check boxes be used to make the routing information even more flexible?
  c. Can colored copies on multiple forms help in their distribution?
  d. How is the form addressed and how can that operation be made easier?
  e. Can a window envelope or a self-mailer be used?

9. What can be done to improve filing efficiency?
  a. How will the form be filed? Standard file cabinets, shelves, visible files, or folders?
  b. Will all copies be filed in the same manner? Will other papers be filed with it? How?
  c. How long will the form be retained as a record?
  d. How frequently is the form handled and rehandled after it is filed and what response time is required?
  e. Will the form or copies of it be held in tickler files?

10. Have all existing forms been reviewed?

Part of a comprehensive forms analysis program concerns itself with a review of all the existing forms in an organization to determine the degree of duplication, nonusage, or consolidation that may be possible in the currently used forms. The basic steps involved in this phase of forms analysis are as follows:

a. Collect all forms used by the organization. There are two general sources of information on existing forms—the stationery stockroom and the using departments. First, check with the stockroom and the purchasing department. Many of of the forms will be recorded there—but probably not all. Second, ask all departments to submit copies of every form they use. Since most small organizations store forms in the department where they are used, this should provide the analyst with copies of all the forms.

b. Classify the forms according to the category of information they contain. Then classify the forms according to the person or department using them. Even this rough categorization can lead to consolidation and elimination of forms.

c. Draw up a summary sheet containing, at the left, the list of data elements the forms contain and, across the top, the list of users. The left-hand column should contain the number and title of each form for easy identification. A variation on this summary chart is to list the data elements on the left and the different forms across the top. This quickly identifies duplicate data elements on different forms. This is followed by an investigation into which departments get which forms and why.

d. The summary chart is used in the process of simplifying, combining, and eliminating. It will show who uses what type of form and what data elements are contained on that form. It will often be found that different departments or different people in the same department are using different forms but with nearly identical content. It will also often be found that one form will take the place of two or three after the addition of a few items of information. Finally, with just a little bit of probing, it will be found that there is no justifiable use for some forms at all!

Although these relatively few remarks will not produce an instant forms expert, they will provide the basis for a serious and professional approach to the determination of *what* is required on the form (analysis) to lay the groundwork for a careful specification of *how* it is to be arranged on the form (design).

PRINCIPLES OF FORMS DESIGN

Whereas forms analysis concerned itself with *what* goes on the form, forms design evolves from this effort and determines *how* to arrange and present the information. The forms designer integrates the needs of the persons filling in the form, as well as those who process it, in his determination of *how*. A number of useful principles will help the systems analyst to develop an effective and efficient forms design.

1. The simpler the design of the form, the easier to fill it in.
2. The sequence of information items should be logical.
3. The amount of writing should be minimal.
4. The features of all data-processing devices used should be utilized to their fullest.
5. The resulting layout should achieve a good visual effect.
6. Standardize. Standardize. Standardize.

Although these principles seem simple enough to list, their implementation requires a definite degree of technical skill. To develop that skill, the analyst will need a few tools and a procedure to guide him in the use of the tools to reach his objective of providing the Management Information System with the best forms design possible.

The Basic Tools for Forms Design

1. Graph paper with one-inch squares divided into tenths horizontally and twelfths vertically. The horizontal divisions will be used to measure off the space needed for data entry, with each tenth of an inch representing a number, letter, or symbol of typed copy. The twelfths are used for normal spacing of one-sixth of an inch vertically for each line of typed copy.
2. An ordinary 2H pencil.
3. A plastic triangle and a ruler.

Procedure for Forms Design

1. Count the spaces needed for written and printed entries utilizing the scale provided in Item 1 above (one-tenth of an inch hori-

zontal for characters, one-sixth of an inch vertical for line spacing).

    a. The analysis phase determined the *what*—this rough draft will begin arranging the information on the graph paper.

    b. Add tenths across on each writing line and enter the total in the right margin.

    c. Enter the number of sixths of an inch for each information box in the left-hand margin. Total them in the lower left hand corner.

    d. Using type face sizes (available from your printer), calculate space requirements for printing to be sure there is enough space for written or typed entries.

2. Determine the size of form needed.

    a. Select the longest line across, add its size in tenths to the number of tenths desired for margins. This is the horizontal size requirement.

    b. Total the number of writing lines down the form in sixths, add to it the top and bottom margins in sixths. This is the vertical size requirement.

    c. Juggle a bit to get form size close to the standard size desired—preferably 8½ by 11 inches.

3. Lay out the rough draft.

    a. Using triangle and ruler, draw horizontal lines to represent vertical space requirements.

    b. Do the same horizontally.

    c. Try to remember to allow for the use of tabular stops if a typewriter will be used for data entry.

4. Letter in title, captions, and instructions.

    a. Letter title in approximate position and to approximate size.

    b. Letter instructions and captions as they will appear on the printed form.

5. Select type.

    a. Consult type charts and reference material to select method and style of type.

    b. Indicate rule weights on lines.

Forms Design—The Working Area

The working area is the part of the form that all the rest of forms design is supposed to facilitate. It is the part of the form on which the data is recorded and thereby captured for entry into the Management Information System.

A basic principle for arranging this working area is to design for continuous execution by the person filling in the form. This principle speeds up forms completion and reduces the number of errors. This is done by:

1. Grouping the data by source, by subject matter, or by whatever general category provides for grouping.
2. Establishing the sequence of items in the working area to eliminate unnecessary writing motions, with an awareness of what will make later transcribing easier.
3. Aligning the data on the form to make writing continuous from left to right and from top to bottom. This corresponds to the habit pattern of human beings in Western culture. In addition, items on the form should be aligned vertically to minimize the number of tabular and marginal stops.

Another basic principle of forms design that has already been stated is to use paper stock of a standard size. Your printer will be helpful along these lines. But reduced paper costs are the least of the economies. The greatest economies are in the compatibility of standard paper sizes with processing equipment, supplies, and filing cabinets.

As was discussed earlier in this chapter, horizontal and vertical space requirements are determined by the amount of fill-in material to be entered and by the printed matter such as box captions, column and section heads, and text.

Although the procedure for forms design detailed previously assumed typewritten entries, it is understood that the writing method (hand, typewriter, other machine) determines the amount of space to be allowed for fill-in data, whereas the number of characters per inch of type face used determines the amount of space to be allowed for printed matter. Therefore, horizontal spacing is based on the number of characters written per inch, (one-tenth of an inch used in the *procedure*) which is a direct function of the writing method used to enter the data. Vertical spacing is based on the number of writing lines that can be written per inch. (If typed, six lines per inch is assumed.)

The area set aside for entries is ruled into the familiar *box* configuration with the caption in the upper left hand corner of the box. Experienced forms designers have found that this design format saves space, aligns tab stops, and helps reading, writing, and interpretation of the form.

Forms Design to Facilitate Processing

After a form has exercised its primary function of collecting data, it is usually necessary for the document to be moved from point to point in the Management Information System. It may also be read at a number of the points in the system and eventually stored—probably by filing. These collateral functions of all forms require the attention of the systems analyst interested in forms design. The reading, transmitting, and filing of forms require careful consideration to insure that a design that optimizes the data-collecting function is not offset by poor design from the point of view of the supplementary requirements of every form.

1. Identification of the Form

The title of the form should clearly and concisely indicate to the reader what the form is about. Titles are usually located at the top-left or top-center portion of the form. Form numbers are usually put at the lower left hand margin so that they are not hidden if the form is stapled (usually at the top left) or bound at the top. In addition, the lower left hand location is very useful when forms are stocked flat on shelves.

There are almost as many systems of numbering forms as there are forms. The number system described below will provide useful guidelines for adaptation to a specific situation by the forms designer.

     a. Capitalize the abbreviation of the company: XYCO.
     b. Capitalize the abbreviation of the department: XYCOMFG.
     c. Specify subject classification number and a slash: XYCOMFG271/.
     d. Assign a consecutive number to the form: XYCOMFG271/5.
     e. Put the month and year of issuance in parentheses: XYCOMFG271/5(6–72).
     f. When revised, indicate by date of revision: XYCOMFG271/5(Rev.3–73).

Page numbers should be used for multiple-page forms to assist in collating, in keying instructions to the specific page, and in handling and transmitting if pages are separated.

2. Appearance and Readability

An individual's reaction to a form, to a large extent, depends on the looks and feel of the form, the typography, and the color of paper and ink.

In deciding on the kind of paper, the forms designer selects a surface suitable for the writing method to be used as well as the printing or duplicating processes that may be involved. He also determines if erasures should be facilitated or, possibly, provides a means to prevent attempts at alterations. Futhermore, the weight, thickness, and durability must be determined. These specifications depend on the number of carbon copies required, the handling and processing steps involved, and, finally, the filing method and retention period.

All the foregoing decisions tend toward the know-how of the paper specialist. The typical systems analyst will admit his weakness at this point and call for technical advice from a responsible printer (or two, or three) to help him.

3. Placement of Instructions

Instructions are essential to interpret a form to the reader and also to assist in efficiently processing the form. Brief general instructions are usually placed at the top of the form, near the title, to tell the reader the number of copies required, who should submit the form, and where, when, and to whom copies should be sent. If detailed instructions appear elsewhere on the form they can usefully be referred to in the brief general instructions that appear near the form title.

Lengthy instructions should appear on the front of the form if space permits. If space is not available, they should be put on the back of the form or on a separate sheet or in a booklet. But lengthy instructions should never be placed among entry spaces that must be kept free to expedite fill-in. For maximum readability, a 10- or 12-point Roman type has proved best for instructions. Where space is very limited, it may be necessary to use 8-point type.

Key instructions to the form by the use of item numbers. Use italic or boldface type for reference items. Use sequentially numbered sentences to present the instructions in easy-to-understand outline form rather than put various instructions together in paragraph form.

4. Facilitating Routing and Mailing of Forms

Integrating the routing and mailing provisions in the design of forms will simplify handling and transmitting the forms as well as reduce errors and speed mail delivery. Whenever possible, the form should allow space in which to identify the addressor and the addressee. Distribution of carbon copies can be keyed by color of the copies and by printing at the bottom of the form. When considering the mailing of the form by means of window envelopes or as a self-mailer, it is necessary to become conversant with the pertinent postal regulations.

5. Forms Design and Filing

The preferred position for file or reference data is at the top right of the form. If the form is to be bound filed, the forms designer must dig further to determine the specifics of the filing method used to provide the necessary filing information in the appropriate place. The criterion to be satisfied is that filing or reference information should be placed where it can readily be seen in the type of filing equipment used. Sometimes a bold rule around the box containing filing data is very useful.

Forms Specification and Printing

Detailed forms specifications based on careful design guide the organization's procurement representative as well as help the printer to produce what is wanted. A work sheet containing detailed design specifications accompanied by a mock-up of the form is essential to obtain the precise form desired.

A final caution—*insist on a final review of the printer's proof.* This rather simple proviso can save a great deal of time and money. As in most things in life, all the analysis and design effort expended can come a cropper if the results do not fit the need. Close follow-up with the printer will insure that all the work that has gone before will be converted into the correct form for the job.

FORMS CONTROL

A vigorous forms analysis and design effort is an excellent beginning for an effective forms control program. It demonstrates the support of top management that is an essential prerequisite for effective forms control. A realistic program must encompass the following:

1. A forms analysis effort that includes a review of all existing forms as well as proposed new forms.
2. A forms design capability that will be applied to all new forms and will also provide for redesign of old forms on a regular basis— perhaps when they are due for replenishment.
3. A forms procurement procedure that can act as a review and control point for all forms whether purchased outside the organization or prepared inside.
4. An inventory control procedure for forms that can monitor order quantities, usage, and stocks on hand.
5. A carefully structured records retention schedule, periodically updated, to keep the organization from drowning in a flood of old records.

The first two parts of the forms control program have already been outlined in this chapter. The balance of the program will be described now. The emphasis will be on simplicity and practicality because such a program has the best chance of working.

1. Forms Procurement

Effective procurement does not depend on getting the lowest price. Professional purchasing people have learned through bitter experience that the three characteristics that must be weighed in doing business with a supplier are quality, service, and price.

In the forms area especially, a first-class supplier may not be the lowest priced, but his is often the lowest cost. He will provide consistency and reliability in the paper stock, printing, packaging, and identification of the forms. He will allow for warehousing your forms and envelopes to allow you to order large quantity runs but will only ship and bill as you require them. He will also provide usage records that will allow you to reduce the amount of record keeping in your own forms control program.

Since the supplier is an integral part of the forms control program it is worth the time and money to search out a reliable vendor and plan your program with him in mind. In selecting the supplier, do not hesitate to ask for names of satisfied customers and call them for information on his quality, service, and price. Use his competitors to help evaluate him and, although this may be unusual, ask the forms supplier about his own in-house forms control program.

Once a forms supplier has been selected, have him agree to do the following:

a. Stock all forms and deliver them as needed.
b. Set up a reorder system to automatically replenish his supply using economical printing setups and runs.
c. Invoice your organization quarterly.
d. Alert you to forms usage below an agreed-upon rate for investigation to determine if the form is becoming obsolete.

The foregoing arrangements will dovetail with your organization's internal forms inventory control program so that all aspects of forms generation are covered. A few other suggestions about forms procurement will also help keep costs down and service and quality up.

a. Check specified paper stock carefully. For instance, translucent bond paper is much less expensive than vellum. Furthermore, 16-pound No. 4 sulfite paper is significantly lower priced than No. 1 and can usually do the job. On heavier-weight material, 100-pound tag stock can provide a real cost saving over card index stock. These are examples of what can be done with just a minimum amount of investigation.

b. Standardize the organization's envelopes with regard to type, size, color, paper weights, and stock and end or side opening. This can lead to larger quantity orders and perhaps save on postage.

c. Standardize the type style for all forms.

d. Group forms by category (such as tags, snapouts, multilith masters, and continuous forms), to take advantage of lower-cost, gang-run printing.

e. Avoid specials of all kinds, whether "no carbon required," special sizes, special type styles, or special paper. They often raise the cost with little or no improvement in performance.

f. Keep in mind the possibility of using standard forms for computerized reports, with the computer printing the necessary headings.

Unless your organization has a regular reproduction department, purchasing is a useful department in which to centralize the monitoring of new forms. All departments will be notified, as part of the forms control program, that all forms will require a forms control number issued by purchasing. This number can embody the originating department's number and the month and the year. Depending on the ground rules in a particular organization, it may be necessary to obtain the systems analyst's approval of the proposed form. This would be a must for certain categories of forms, (i.e., intedepartmental, customer service, large quantity, etc.), but for temporary and "one-shot" forms for use within a department, it may be enough to send a copy to the analyst concerned with the explanation as to its status. He can then decide if his attention is warranted.

Purchasing is in an excellent position to review the forms from a "make or buy" point of view as well as being able to advise the departments concerned on costs, quantity, and delivery if such data is helpful in arriving at a better forms decision.

2. Forms Inventory Control

If the purchasing department has been successful in setting up a supplier relationship as outlined in the preceding section, internal inventory control has a reduced work load. The objective of forms inventory control is to maintain an adequate stock of forms for the usage requirements of the organization, to reorder in enough time to insure continuous supply, to order in economical quantities considering costs of procurement and inventory carrying costs, and finally to act as a screening point for alerting the systems analyst to likely candidates for elimination because of decreasing usage or low activity.

Of course, in doing all this the usual procedures of stock control must be carried out. These include maintaining stock records, processing receipts and withdrawals, originating replenishment requisitions, and following up and expediting deliveries, physical storage of forms, and inventory counts when necessary.

Chapter 10 will go into much greater detail on techniques of inventory control. The inventory control function in a forms control program provides a very key control point for early warning of the systems analyst concerned so that action can be taken on forms analysis and redesign, consolidation, or elimination before the amount in stock gets so low that operations pressure forces replenishment of an obsolete or unnecessary form. A forms inventory control and monitoring procedure is essential to an effective forms control program.

RECORDS RETENTION—HOW LONG TO KEEP?

A recent survey shows that about one-third of the records kept by the average organization could be thrown out without impairing operations to the slightest degree. These unnecessary records cost money and effort, measured in terms of filing space, equipment, and administrative servicing. A prime objective of forms control is to expedite the destruction of unnecessary records.

A good example is correspondence. Much correspondence now filed in cabinets really belongs in the wastepaper basket. The simplest disposal method for letters and similar forms is to file them in separate folders with different colored labels indicating the length of time they are to be kept. Determine at the time of original reading whether the material should be eliminated immediately (wastebasket) or held for thirty days, one year, or longer. Place in a folder with a correspondingly colored marker. The advantages of this simple method are that the weeding of files is reduced and entire folders can be destroyed without glancing at their contents.

There are certain records, of course, that must be retained for varying periods of time. These are covered by the statutes of limitations in each state and the regulations of the government agency concerned. A relatively foolproof method of determining type and time is to consult the organization's lawyer, since requirements vary from state to state.[1] But many records, particularly those used mainly for internal consumption, have no legal strings attached. The organization created them and

---

[1] A very useful reference is the *Guide to Record Retention Requirements*, Superintendent of Documents, Washington, D.C. 20402, which contains about one thousand digests and describes (1) what type records must be kept, (2) by whom, and (3) for how long. Each digest also carries a reference to the full text of the basic law or regulation providing for such retention.

is keeping them for its own convenience. Some organizations attach a slip to all such records over one year old. Each user notes the date of use on the slip. Records that show a pattern of infrequent use are removed to permanent storage; records that are not referred to at all are destroyed at the end of their use period.

Many factors are involved in the decision to destroy or to retain records. Before completing any overall organization records retention plan, it should be carefully checked by a competent lawyer to make certain it satisfies the statutes of limitations that apply.

The basic questions to be asked in determining whether to retain or to destroy are:

1. What is the document and why should it be retained?
2. Is the material summarized in some other record?
3. Do other files hold copies of the record?

The following gives a portion of one organization's retention schedule.

AMI, Inc., Records Retention Schedule
(Excerpted)

Record Title	Years
BANKING	
1. Statements from depositories regarding funds received, disbursed, and transferred	3
2. Records of periodical receipts and disbursements	6
3. Bank deposit books, stubs, ledgers, check records	6
4. Copies of bank deposit slips	1
BILLS COLLECTIBLE	
1. Record of register of accounts receivable bills and indexes, and summaries of distribution of credits through bills for entry in general books	permanent
2. Copies of bills issued for collection and supporting papers which do not accompany the original bills	2
3. Periodical statements of unsettled accounts, except trial balance sheets	1
BOOKS	
All books—cash books, code books, and the like	permanent
EXPENDITURES	
1. All estimates, completion reports, authorities for expenditures and records	permanent
2. Memoranda or detail records used in preparation of No. 1	1

3. Records showing comparisons between estimated and actual expenditures   3
4. Records showing progress of work, order of completion (which do not form a basis of charges or credits to the accounts)   1

CONTRACTS AND AGREEMENTS

1. Book records of contracts, leases and agreements, of expirations and renewals   permanent
2. Contracts, leases, and agreements   8
3. Summaries and abstracts   8

EMPLOYEES' RECORDS

1. Applications, examinations, service records   permanent
2. Applications and replies not resulting in employment   2
3. Schedules of working hours and efficiency and identification records   permanent
4. Pension records and pertinent data   permanent

CONSULTING RECORDS

Most such proposal records, plans, unit cost data, etc., should be filed permanently whether project was completed or abandoned   permanent

AUTHORIZED EXPENSES

All authorized statements of expenses forming basis of charges to accounts   permanent

MATERIALS AND SUPPLIES RECEIVED

1. Vouchers covering payment   1
2. Records of inspection and testing of materials and supplies   3
3. Requisitions, issue records, and receipts   1

MATERIALS AND SUPPLIES AND SERVICES PURCHASED AND SOLD

1. Copies of purchase orders   6
2. Requisitions that formed basis of the order   1
3. Bids and offers   3
4. Contracts for sale or purchase (after expiration)   3
5. Bills of lading, shipping orders   7

PAYROLL RECORDS

1. Payroll and summaries   permanent
2. Application and authorities for changes in payroll   2
3. Deductions, records, and memoranda   6
4. Receipted pay checks   6

PROPERTY RECORDS

permanent

REPORTS

1. Financial statements, supporting papers, reports to stock-holders, statistical operating reports, etc.   permanent
2. Statistical reports used for administrative purposes, not as basis for account entries   3

AUDITORS' REPORTS

All accountants', auditors' reports   6

GOVERNMENT REPORTS   6

TABULATING CARDS

When results are transcribed to other records   1

MISCELLANEOUS

Record of securities   permanent
Tax records   permanent
Titles and franchises   permanent

The destruction date for each record should be clearly marked when that record is stored. It is vitally important to have a retention schedule of this type drawn up and posted prominently, otherwise it may be ignored. Remember, the path of least resistance is for the executive to mark material destined for storage "permanent."

REVIEW QUESTIONS

1. What is the definition of *printed form?* What is its function in the MIS?
2. What are the objectives of forms analysis, design, and control?
3. What are the two basic principles of forms analysis?
4. Describe a summary chart for forms analysis. Why is it used?
5. What is forms design?
6. Select an application that already has an existing form. Apply some of the principles of forms analysis and design outlined in this chapter and present your findings in the form of specific recommendations.
7. Where should what type of instructions appear on the form?

8.   Where is the preferred postion for file or reference data on a form?
9.   List the five requirements of a serious forms control program.
10. What three key questions help determine how long to keep a record?

BIBLIOGRAPHY

ADMINISTRATIVE OFFICE, NAVY DEPARTMENT, *Forms Management*, AOINST 5213.31. Washington, D.C.: Government Printing Office, 1966. Provides a useful guide for the systematic analysis and control of all forms and related procedures.

BENEDON, WILLIAM, *Records Management*. Englewood Cliffs, N. J.: Prentice-Hall, Inc., 1969. Up to date and comprehensive. A worthwhile guide.

CAMERON, C. A., and E. J. LEAHY, *Modern Records Management*. New York: McGraw-Hill Book Company, 1965. A comprehensive survey of the field.

KNOX, FRANK M., *Knox's Standard Guide to the Design and Control of Business Forms*. New York: McGraw-Hill Book Company, 1965. One of the authoritative guides in the field.

LAZZARO, VICTOR, *Systems and Procedures* (2nd ed.). Englewood Cliffs, N. J.: Prentice-Hall, Inc., 1968. The section on forms design and control is written by a recognized authority in the field.

NATIONAL ARCHIVES AND RECORDS SERVICE, *Forms Analysis*, Federal Stock Number 7610–655–8220. Washington, D.C.: Government Printing Office, 1960. A concise yet comprehensive treatment of the subject.

———, *Forms Design*, Federal Stock Number 7610–753–4771. Washington, D.C.: Government Printing Office, 1960. Step-by-step development of the design of a form. Thorough and practical.

———, *Guide to Record Retention Requirements*, Federal Register Vol. 35, No. 37. Washington, D.C.: Government Printing Office, 1970. A detailed, specific digest of the provisions of federal laws and regulations relating to the keeping of records by the public.

PRENTICE-HALL EDITORIAL STAFF, *Handbook of Successful Operating Systems and Procedures, with Forms*. Englewood Cliffs, N. J.: Prentice-Hall, Inc., 1968. Includes many actual samples of forms, reports, charts, and graphs.

SYSTEMS AND PROCEDURES ASSOCIATION, *Business Systems*. Cleveland, Ohio: Systems and Procedures Association, 1966. Prepared by practitioners in the field and contains many practical and useful recommendations.

9

STATISTICAL TECHNIQUES FOR MANAGEMENT INFORMATION SYSTEMS

MEASUREMENT—THE BASIS FOR STATISTICAL ANALYSIS

A common characteristic of all quantitative systems analysis tools is that they depend on some kind of measurement—measurement of time, of distance, of manpower, of costs, of productivity and so forth. Early in this century, managers began making and keeping extensive records of the measurements of these parameters. And these records, reflecting the state of these parameters over a long period of time, developed into a large reservoir of measurements of the past performance of their organizations.

As this body of numerical measurement data, these *statistics*, built up, some managers became intrigued with the idea that an analysis of these statistics would improve their understanding of the underlying patterns of the cause systems intrinsic to their organization's operations. Since the operations generated the statistics, the statistics should reflect the operations. At first, their attempts at analysis were primitive and crude. But, little by little, their many attempts at manipulating the masses of statistics coupled with the gradual emergence of professional statisticians led to the development of effective analysis and control techniques based on statistical theory. Intuition, experience, and judgment had been augmented by measurement. Management's own search for something better helped add statistical measurement and analysis to management's repertory of tools and techniques.

The body of techniques that evolved out of the experimentations with the masses of recorded operational data is generally categorized under the generic name of *statistical analysis*. Statistical tools and techniques represent one of the major success stories of the application of quantitative techniques to the problems of Management Information Systems.

The systems analyst planning to do statistical analysis must weigh the costs of collecting, organizing, and storing the data against the probable benefits to be derived from analyzing the data. Fortunately, much valuable data is normally recorded in many organizations and business operations as a by-product of normal activity. This means that statistical analysis can often be applied to many management systems problems without significant additional cost for collecting and storing the raw data. Analysis of direct labor costs, unit sales, absenteeism, inventory turnover, sales expenses, and demand are all cases in point.

Although much statistical data is readily available, in many situations it is almost impossible or prohibitively expensive to collect all the data pertinent to a particular decision. For instance, if management had to decide on the color preference of consumers for the package of a new product it would be very helpful to ask all potential consumers. But that approaches the impossible as well as being too expensive.

The same thing holds true for maintaining the uniformity and dependability of a production process or a particular quality level of outgoing product. It is usually too expensive and operationally impossible to measure every item (the *population*). Therefore, based on the theoretical work of Walter A. Shewhart, it is possible to measure a much smaller, carefully selected part of all the data. This portion is called a *sample* of the population of the particular measurement (statistic) of interest.

If the sample is selected in accordance with the rules of statistical theory, it is possible to infer certain characteristics about the population from the statistical analysis of the sample. It must be emphasized that the ability to do this rests on the rigorous application of statistical theory. One example of this requirement is that the sample must be selected utilizing a generally accepted random selection procedure. The insuring of this precondition is a significant aspect of sampling design. It is only under such carefully controlled conditions that samples permit dependable generalizations with known precision. In general, it is necessary that the sample be selected at "random." A sample is considered to be random if every element of the population from which it was taken had an equal chance of being selected. The basic procedure for ensuring randomness is the use of an authorized random number table and a standard procedure for using it to select elements for the sample. If the sample is random, the laws of statistical theory hold and valid inferences can be made with calculable precision.

A particularly useful and widely know application of the use of sampling for statistical inference is the management tool known as *quality control*. It is one of the fundamental building blocks of mass production. A related tool known as *work sampling* is particularly useful for measuring nonroutine, nonrepetitive jobs. Both these tools will be discussed later in this chapter.

But a variety of other, less well known, management tools depend on statistical theory and methods, and the following section describes some general areas where their application has been of particular help to management.

GENERAL APPLICATIONS OF THE STATISTICAL METHOD

1. Better Design of Product

The application of statistical sampling techniques to research consumer preferences provides a useful feedback for product redesign in order to meet changing consumer tastes with regard to quality, uniformity, and quantity. Statistical tests and surveys also provide an excellent means of communication with customers and potential customers. Results of statistical analysis, with their accompanying specification of precision, provide management with predictive guidelines to improve the design of product to meet the forecast changes in demand.

Furthermore, the predicted changes in consumer demand that are reflected in product redesign will, in turn, affect production methods and production levels. To meet these changes, statistical methods allow the testing of product manufacture on a pilot basis, if necessary, to insure that product redesign will not be at the expense of manufacturing economy and quality.

The great contribution of statistical methods is their replacing of fallible human judgment by precise measurement and their ability to do it quickly and economically.

2. Better Use of Material

Statistical methods can be and are being applied very effectively in determining whether a needed quality characteristic is possessed by the material that is being considered for use. These methods can also determine whether there is a difference in a specification between one material and another. The statistical test, with its specified range of precision, may very well result in the substitution of one less expensive or more available material for another. Similarly, statistical methods can be used to test the efficacy of material forming methods, or metal treating, or a variety of industrial processes that affect the use of material. The great advantage is that statistical methods provide this needed help reliably and economically.

3. Greater Dependability of Product

Statistical methods include testing a sample drawn by a random selection procedure from an outgoing shipment of product to determine its acceptability. The percentage of defectives in the shipment can be estimated, and it can be stated, for example, that on the average only one sample in hundreds drawn and tested by the same method will vary more than 5 percent from a complete test of all the pieces in the shipment. In essence, the method determines whether the lot being shipped falls within the acceptable quality limits agreed to by the producer and the purchaser.

The desired quality, dependability, and uniformity of a product are definable only in statistical terms, that is, by statistically specified procedures and measurement techniques. Statistical methods not only help to produce uniform and dependable quality but also provide an internationally understood language that both buyers and sellers understand.

4. Lower Price

Price has no meaning unless it is referred to in terms of quality. Quality in turn depends on statistical theory for expression in a way understandable to both buyers and sellers. Therefore, price is inextricably bound to statistical methods to have any real meaning. Price is miles per gallon, dollars per pound of output, BTUs per cubic foot. It therefore requires the statistical methods of quality control to provide the uniformity and dependability of product without which price would be a "rubber yardstick."

Statistical techniques assist management in selecting courses of action that are more efficient and economical, which means that costs of manufacture are lower than they might otherwise be, and in a competitive context this will result in a lower price to the consumer. This lower price is a direct benefit to the consumer because of the uses of statistical techniques.

5. Better Competitive Position

An organization's basic objective is to survive and grow. It approaches this objective by the sequence of management decisions involving the combining of men, materials, machines, and money. Statistical methodology can provide management with quantitative measurements and associated estimates of precision in just about every area in which decisions are necessary, thus improving the organization's competitive capability.

The area of consumer research is a case in point. Effective consumer research will help management in areas such as product design, production levels, materials management, and financial planning. Statistical tests and surveys can also provide management with a feedback channel from customers and potential customers. All this gives the management of a company critical input for decision making and in turn provides the company with a competitive edge over those who may not use statistical techniques to aid in decision making.

Obviously, all the advantages of statistical techniques, that is, reliable and economical methods of producing a uniform and dependable product, efficient utilization of materials and machines, increased safety, aids to auditing and financial management, and the many other advantages that accrue to an organization that utilizes statistical methods also improve its competitive position.

6. Better Use of Machines

The application of statistical techniques in industry has provided an almost unbroken string of successes where they have been applied with competence and vigor. Reports of increases of 50 percent, and 100 percent in production have not been uncommon, without increased investment in machinery. This result occurred because of more efficient use of machines, improved quality, and less scrap and rework. Statistical techniques provide the only accurate and reliable method of defining machine-processing capacity, capability, tolerance-holding ability, and production rate, as well as other key parameters that are required to better utilize machines.

OTHER APPLICATION AREAS

1. Organizing and analyzing raw data so as to extract maximum useful information
2. Establishing cause-and-effect relationships
3. Assessing the reliability of conclusions
4. Monitoring events, trends, and processes
5. Designing effective data collection procedures
6. Forecasting variations of key indicators

The systems analyst owes it to his own professional growth to become familiar with the wide array of tested statistical tools. An introduction to some of these tools will be provided in the balance of this chapter. However, the serious student will utilize the Bibliography to gain a much broader exposure to this rich field.

THE CRITICAL MANAGEMENT QUESTION— WHAT ARE THE CHANCES?

Very few aspects of living are not affected by chance—for instance, the grouping of genes that determines a person's physical makeup, or each man's time of exit from this world, or, in fact, much of what happens in people's private lives. The same is true in the life of organizations. A manager cannot predict when a particular machine will break down, or the quantity on the next order from a customer, or the number of patients a hospital will be faced with next week, or what products a company will be making five years from now. All of these are examples of things that depend on chance occurrence. They represent the unpredictable element in all human activity.

Since man knows that he is often the pawn of circumstance, he has always tried to evaluate the chance, or likelihood, of a particular future event happening. It is a general human trait. It often takes the form of trying to figure out the chances of something occurring out of the total number of things that will occur—the number of "successes" out of the total number of "outcomes." The expression "there's a fifty-fifty chance" is part of the language. Weather reports are another example. They often contain such phrases as "30 percent chance of rain," "40 percent chance of snow," and so forth. This evaluation of likely outcomes, of the probability that something will occur, has attracted the attention of mathematicians for centuries. Their interest and experimentation built up a body of knowledge known as the *mathematics of probability*.

To the mathematician, probability is simply a percentage. It is the frequency with which one event takes place in relation to all the possible alternatives. Examples might include the probability of a head on the flip of a coin or the ace showing on the turn of a card or a machine breaking down or an order arrival or a stock-out occurring. To deal with these situations, certain basic rules and techniques have been formulated and have come to be known as the *laws of probability*. An example of the laws of probability with which everyone is familiar is the tossing of a coin and the guessing of whether it falls heads or tails. Everyone feels he has a fair chance of guessing the outcome because the chance of either a head or a tail is one chance out of two possible outcomes. The probability of guessing correctly is one out of two, that is, one-half. But no one expects a coin to fall heads once in every two tosses. Intuitively, however, people do expect that in a large number of tosses the results will tend to even out, that is, as many heads will turn up as tails. This is an example of a particular law of probability known as the *law of large numbers*. It states that as the number of trials increases, the actual outcome approaches the expected value. It is a particularly useful law in the application of statistics and probability to management problems.

Other examples of this law are all around us. Atoms, molecules, and other tiny units in nature move about in a random fashion that apparently is not predictable. But because they act in such tremendous numbers, it has been proved that their collective behavior is thoroughly predictable. Not only that, but it can be predicted within a known accuracy, that is, a known margin of error. The size of the error can be evaluated by using the laws of probability.

A population of trillions of gas molecules in a jar or a population of millions of Americans behind the wheels of their cars, or a population of thousands of machine parts, or of hundreds of customer orders, or of tens of thousands of library books, or a population of dozens of machine breakdowns are all predictable with known precision using the same analytical approach. It is impossible, of course, to foresee that molecule A will bump into molecule B, or that driver X will crash into driver Y, or that machine #372 will have the next breakdown, or that customer M will order four thousand widgets tomorrow. It is, however, possible to say with a very high degree of accuracy *about* how many molecules will collide in a second or *about* how many drivers in a month. It is possible to give management a forecast, with a stated margin of error, of the number of machine breakdowns per production cycle or the number of orders for four thousand units from all customers during the next selling season.

These educated guesses based on the laws of statistical probabiliy are accurate enough to let the scientist reach a useful conclusion, or to let an insurance company establish its accident policy rates, or to provide management with a basis for setting up the machine maintenance crew, or to forecast the size of finished goods inventory.

This discussion of the laws of probability does not preclude the possibility that an individual will enjoy a stroke of luck, or that a person will play hunches, or that an "act of God" may change schedules. These laws of probability begin to act as laws only when many instances are involved—many throws of the dice, many deals of the cards, many car collisions, many lifetimes, many machines, many customer orders. This aspect of probability, the law of large numbers, interestingly enough, does not decrease the chance that an individual will again be lucky on any one occasion even though he has enjoyed a long run of good luck. Happily, an executive who flies thousands of miles a year without an accident does not incur a greater risk of crashing every additional time he boards a plane. Airplane engines and navigational radar have no "probability" memory, and his chances of surviving a specific flight remain as good after 2,001 times as they were the first time he flew.

The laws of probability, in their practical applications, are major ingredients of the science of statistics. Statistical probability is used to estimate the inventory that a manufacturer should hold in reserve in his warehouse to meet unusual fluctuations in the demand for his products. In communications, it reveals the number of connections and therefore the size of the telephone exchange or telegraph network. In marketing, it indicates whether the reported results of a market research study are statistically meaningful and can therefore justify extensive investments in equipment and advertising or whether the research indications are merely the results of chance.

These more complex, real life applications of probability are fundamentally different from the games of chance from which the laws of probability evolved. The basic reason they are different is that in games of chance all the cards in the deck are known, as are all the faces on the dice, whereas in predicting the twists and turns of real life it is seldom possible to know in advance all the possible outcomes.

This also holds true in most management applications of mathematical probability. All the possible outcomes are rarely known at the start. Yet, *probability* is defined as the ratio of the desired outcome to all the possible outcomes. If all the possible outcomes are not known, how can the probability be calculated? The technique that is used when all the outcomes are unknown is to take a carefully planned experimental sampling from the available outcomes and then evaluate the probability of estimating the parameters of the entire population of probable outcomes with a specified precision. If the probability is high enough, the sample can be used to draw very useful conclusions about the population from which it was taken.

In order that this scheme make sense it would be useful to remind ourselves that there is a great deal of uniformity in nature—in the awe-inspiring regularity of the solar system, in the fantastic structuring (Fibonacci ratios) of the spirals of a seashell and the petals of a flower and in the pattern of the snowflake and of the honeycomb. They all reflect a sense of the underlying order of nature. There is a similar order in the affairs of men and of organizations.

This is one of the most fascinating aspects of the application of statistical techniques to management problems. In many situations that seem hopelessly erratic and completely unstructured—when managers cannot seem to find a "handle" to resolve them—statistical analysis can often provide insights that bring out the hidden patterns that exist in many management problem areas. A good example is the "normal distribution," a pattern that occurs with surprising frequency in many situations.

THE NORMAL CURVE—A DESIGN FOR DECISION

A basic tool that helps statisticians to investigate unknown groups of statistical data (populations) is the so-called normal distribution graphically represented by the "bell-shaped" curve (Fig. 9-1). This bell-shaped

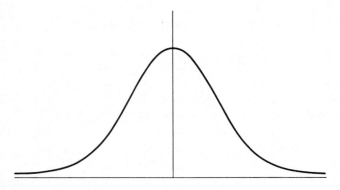

FIGURE 9-1

The Normal Distribution

curve is the most common graph in probability theory. It graphically represents the distribution of the frequency of occurrence of all the variations of certain measurements of a group of events or quantities. Examples include the variations in the life-span of light bulbs, the different sizes of leaves on a tree, the various heights in a regiment of troops, or the variations in product dimension such as the outer diameter of a shaft or the length of a fitting.

The natural occurrence of relatively close approximations of this bell-shaped arrangement of data is dramatically illustrated by such common phenomena as the distribution of spectators at a football game or patrons in a theater (see Fig. 9-2). If the center line in the illustration were the 50-yard line in a football stadium and the crowd of spectators did not fill the stands, they would probably distribute themselves as indicated by the curve. The same thing would occur in a theater. If it were not filled to capacity, once again the crowd would probably distribute itself in much the same way. This same pattern is the basis for a number of very useful management techniques. Statistical quality control, con-

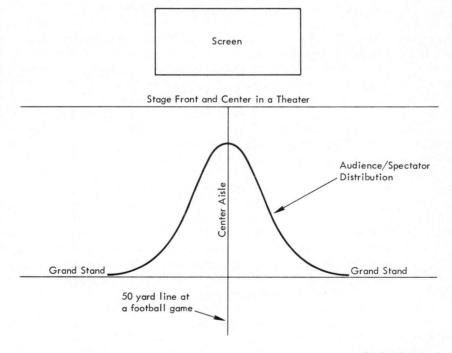

FIGURE 9-2

The Normal Distribution

sumer sampling, acceptance sampling, opinion polls, work sampling, and a host of other tools depend on it.

One particularly important characteristic of the normal distribution is that certain statements can be made about the percentages of the total group being studied (the population) that fall within certain variations from the center of the distribution. These limits, or intervals, are calculated in terms of two important specifications of the distribution, the *mean* and the *standard deviation*. If these two specifications about any normally distributed population of data are known, the distribution can be described completely.

The Mean

The *mean* of the data is the sum of all the values (measurements) divided by the number of values. It is simply the arithmetic average of the values.

$$Mean = \text{Sum of all measurements/Total number of measurements}$$
$$Mean = \Sigma X/N$$

The mean of a population is usually indicated as $\overline{\overline{X}}$ and the mean of a sample as $\overline{X}$.

For example, suppose a count was taken of the number of machine breakdowns per day for a week.

Day of week	Number of Machine Breakdowns
Monday	3
Tuesday	5
Wednesday	2
Thursday	4
Friday	1

The average number of breakdowns per day for that week can be calculated by taking the sum of all the breakdowns in the week and dividing by the number of days. If we consider the week's breakdowns as a sample of all the breakdowns that may occur in a year, the average is the sample mean and will be used in this example as an estimate of the population mean.

$$\overline{X} = \Sigma X/N$$
$$\overline{X} = \frac{3 + 5 + 2 + 4 + 1}{5}$$
$$\overline{X} = 15/5 = 3$$

The mean that has just been calculated is then used to develop the standard deviation.

The Standard Deviation

The *standard deviation* is a measurement of the spread of the values in a distribution. It is a measure of how the various values differ from the mean. In fact, it is really a kind of average of the distances of all the observations from the mean. These distances can be represented as $X - \overline{X}$ and are called the *deviation from the mean.*

For many applications in statistical analysis it is important to know the deviation, on the average, of all the observations from their mean. This measurement is called the *standard deviation.* It is important because it is very useful in determining how much of the total population falls within the certain intervals as dimensioned by the standard deviation. This is a key factor in utilizing the normal curve in solving management problems.

The average of all the deviations from the mean is calculated by dividing their sum by the number of observations, N. It is interesting to note that the sum of the deviations of a symmetrical distribution (like the normal) is zero and therefore to avoid this result the deviations are squared. In mathematical notation this can be shown as:

$$\Sigma(X - \overline{X})^2/N$$

This average of the sum of the deviations squared is called the *variance* (S^2).

$$S^2 = \frac{\Sigma(X - \overline{X})^2}{N}$$

The square root of S^2 is the standard deviation (S):

$$S = \sqrt{\frac{\Sigma(X - \overline{X})^2}{N}}$$

A simple example of calculating the standard deviation follows: Observations (X), are 6, 3, 4, 7, 3, 6, 2, 4, 2, and 3, and the number of observations is 10.

the mean, $\overline{X} = \Sigma X/N = \dfrac{6 + 3 + 4 + 7 + 3 + 6 + 2 + 4 + 2 + 3}{10}$

$\overline{X} = \dfrac{40}{10} = 4$

Now calculate the deviations and square them (Table 9-1).

TABLE 9-1

Calculation of Deviations

X	$X - \overline{X}$	$(X - \overline{X})^2$
6	+ 2	4
3	− 1	1
4	0	0
7	+ 3	9
3	− 1	1
6	+ 2	4
2	− 2	4
4	0	0
2	− 2	4
3	− 1	1
		28

$$\Sigma(X - \overline{X})^2 = 28$$

Knowing $\Sigma(X - \overline{X})^2$ and N, calculate the standard deviation:

$$S = \sqrt{\frac{\Sigma(X - \overline{X})^2}{N}}$$

$$S = \sqrt{\frac{28}{10}} = \sqrt{2.8}$$

$$S = 1.67$$

THE USEFULNESS OF THE STANDARD DEVIATION   First of all, one standard deviation on each side of the mean $(\overline{\overline{X}})$ always marks off 68.27 percent of all the observations under every normal curve. Furthermore, 95.45 percent of all observations fall under the curve within two standard deviations of each side of the mean. Three standard deviations each side of the mean will encompass 99.73 percent of all values. Figure 9-3 shows these dimensions laid off on a normal curve.

The amazing uniformity exhibited by this distribution coupled with the frequency of its occurrence in every organization provides management with a powerful tool for analyzing those operational patterns that can be closely approximated by the normal curve. Furthermore, there are a number of other "standard" distributions that have also been thoroughly researched and documented by statisticians. These include the binomial, the Poisson, and the chi-square. Even when data patterns do not fit these standard distributions exactly, they are usually close enough to be adequately approximated by one of them. This means that the systems analyst has access to a wealth of previously worked out data to help him solve his problems.

Although the normal curve is the only distribution that is discussed here in some detail, the other distributions that occur in management problems are also uniquely useful in those applications where they apply. The great work of statisticians such as Ronald Fisher, Walter A. Shewhart, and W. Edwards Deming has blazed a broad trail for the knowledgeable utilization of a wide spectrum of powerful statistical tools. A number of these tools will be discussed in the paragraphs that follow.

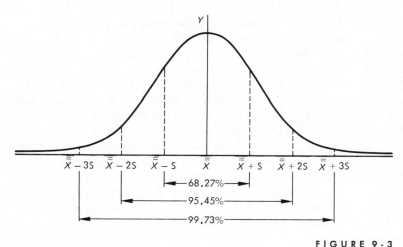

FIGURE 9-3

The Normal Distribution

SPECIFIC STATISTICAL TOOLS AND TECHNIQUES

Statistical Quality Control

Control of the quality level of the product of a company or the services of an organization is an example of the application of the normal curve, the mean, and the standard deviation to a management systems problem. It utilizes one of the most widely accepted of all the statistical management tools, the *quality control chart*, which was developed and applied by one of the greatest of statisticians, Walter A. Shewhart. The reason it is one of the most successful of the statistical analysis tools and has won such widespread management acceptance is simple—it works!

Statistical quality control is generally defined as a systematic method of applying statistical principles and techniques in all stages of input, processing, and output of an operating system with the objective of minimizing the cost and maximizing the utility of the product or service. An operating system brought to a state of statistical control by the analytical methods pioneered by Walter A. Shewhart will continuously produce products or services with variations in quality characteristics that can be predicted with precision. This is possible, since the cause system producing the products or services is rendered stable and constant by the application of statistical quality control techniques.

The basis of the statistical quality control techinque is the testing of random samples of the process against a predetermined quality standard. Variations greater than those specified by the quality control chart limits indicate trouble. The samples must be selected in such a way that every item in a particular lot has an equal chance of being selected. As was mentioned previously, this is the definition of random sampling and provides the basis for the operation of the laws of probability. Although practical considerations often require approximating randomness rather than insisting on it, statisticians have provided useful guidelines to insure the integrity of the technique.

It is important to recognize that the term *quality* has nothing to do with "good" or "better." Quality is simply the adherence to a standard. The standards are set by engineering or manufacturing or the user or a combination of the interested parties. Since these standards can only be verified statistically they are defined statistically. Once set, random samples of the product are selected and tested against this standard. The results of these tests are then analyzed using carefully worked out techniques of mathematical statistics. One of the most useful of these techniques is the statistical quality control chart.

QUALITY CONTROL (OR SHEWHART) CHARTS   The sources, or causes, of quality differences in products or services are of two distinct types—random causes and assignable causes. The random causes include such things as the slight variations that occur from one machine cycle to the next because the gears mesh differently, the infinitesimal variations of crystalline structure or thickness or metallurgical composition in the material being used, the variations of temperature and humidity in the working environment, and the host of other uncontrollable variations involving the interaction of men, materials, or machines in any process.

These random causes are considered unassignable to an identifiable source and they are, for all practical purposes, uncontrollable.

The identifiable, assignable, controllable causes are those involving variations in significant aspects of the production process. For example: machine settings, feeds, and speeds; material specifications; tool wear; wrong tools; wrong materials; wrong specifications; in general, all the factors that can be affected by human decisions.

When all the variations in production are due to chance, that is, due to unassignable, uncontrollable causes, there is no point in spending money and time to attempt to control them. Such a production process is considered to be operating in a state of *statistical control.*

When the variations in the process are due to assignable, controllable causes, the production operation is considered to be *out of control* and action can be taken to identify and eliminate the causes of the variations.

Statistical quality control's objective is to provide an analytical tool to detect the existence of a cause of variation and to indicate whether it is a random or an assignable cause. This distinction is very important inasmuch as searching for an assignable cause when none exists or failing to search for one when it does exist can be expensive mistakes indeed. Both types of mistakes can be avoided by the effective analysis of quality control charts.

A statistical quality control chart (Fig. 9-4) is a graphical representation of the expected variation in the specifications of the items being produced due to random (not assignable) causes.

In practice, the use of a quality control chart works something like this: Random samples of the items being produced are selected and the specification that is to be controlled is measured. The measurements of the items in the sample are then averaged, and this average of the sample is plotted on the quality control chart.

The theoretical relationship to the previous discussion of the normal distribution now becomes obvious. All variation within the limits of three standard deviations from the mean is considered the result of random, unassignable causes. When a point falls outside these limits, the laws of probability guarantee that 997 times out of 1,000 it is due to an assignable cause.

Once this analytical tool indicates the probable existence of an assignable cause, the persons directly responsible must take action to investigate, discover, and correct the cause of the variation and restore statistical stability.

Setting Up the Control Chart.   The usual procedure for setting up a quality control chart (Fig. 9-4) is as follows:

1. As a general rule, to be statistically reliable, the initial computation of control limits must be based on at least twenty-five sets of sample observations.
2. The frequency of drawing the samples may be either in terms of time, such as once every hour, or in terms of the proportion of outputs produced, such as five out of one hundred.
3. A decision must be made as to the selection, number, size, and frequency of the samples. Helpful guidelines can be found in any standard statistical quality control book.
4. All types of control charts have a general form that consists of a set of three horizontal lines drawn on graph paper. The central line is the calculated process average (the mean). The other two lines, which are customarily three "standard deviations" from the central line, are the upper and lower control limits.
5. Sample observations are made, their mean is calculated, and a point is plotted on the chart equal to the mean of the sample. These points are called *sample points*.
6. When a point falls outside the control limits it is the signal for investigation, analysis, and corrective action.

Application of Quality Control Charts.   Quality control charts can be applied to all areas of an organization to maintain a certain quality level of performance. They have generally been applied in manufacturing areas, but they should be used just as extensively in administrative areas. In particular, their intelligent use at various control points in a Management Information System could provide early and reliable warning of a buildup of errors, or missed deadlines, of the development of processing bottlenecks within the information system.

The many similarities between production (machine) and administrative (human) operations (input-processing-output) make possible the application of control charts to both types of processes without any special modifications. In either type of operation, control charts give reliable, precise, and timely evidence regarding the quality level, its variability, and the presence or absence of assignable causes as the source of variations in the process. Once spotlighted, assignable causes can be tracked down and corrected by management action.

Quality Control Chart Example (A Simplified Calculation)   To demonstrate statistical quality control, the quality control chart shown in Figure 9-4 will be discussed. This particular chart was constructed to monitor the output of a machine that produces a particular engine part. The mean or average diameter of these parts has been calculated to be 0.574 inches with a standard deviation (that is, the expected variation from the average) of .0033 inches. These figures were calculated from sample data using the formulas that were discussed previously.

Process Mean = $\overline{\overline{X}}$ = .574 inches $\overline{\overline{X}}-3\sigma \leq \overline{X} \leq \overline{\overline{X}} +3\sigma$ Sample Mean = $\overline{X}$

Standard Deviation = σ = .0033   With 99.73% Confidence   Sample Std Dev = S

Number of Samples = N $\overline{X}$ Lies between .564 and .584 in. $\sigma \cong \Sigma S/N$

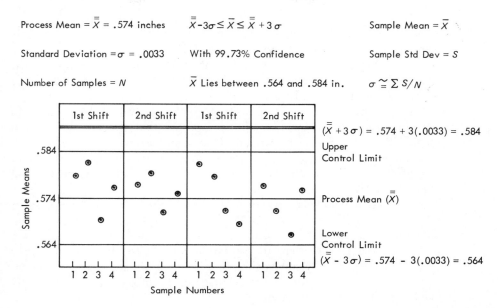

$(\overline{\overline{X}} +3\sigma) = .574 + 3(.0033) = .584$
Upper
Control Limit

Process Mean $(\overline{\overline{X}})$

Lower
Control Limit
$(\overline{\overline{X}} - 3\sigma) = .574 - 3(.0033) = .564$

FIGURE 9-4

Quality Control Chart Application

The mean of the sample means $\overline{\overline{X}}$ is the center line of the chart. It is the estimate of the actual population mean.

$$\text{Population mean} = \overline{\overline{X}} = \Sigma \overline{X}/\text{No. of samples} = .574$$

$$\text{Sample standard deviation} = S = \sqrt{\Sigma(X - \overline{X})^2/N}$$

The standard deviation of the population of engine parts (σ) is estimated from the sample standard deviations.

$$\sigma \cong \Sigma S/\text{No. of samples} = .0033$$

Using the calculated value of the mean, the center line of the chart is drawn. The standard deviation (σ) is multiplied by 3 and the result is added to and subtracted from the mean to determine the upper and lower control chart limits respectively. Then a random sample of six of the parts is taken every two hours, their diameters are measured, and the mean diameter of the sample is computed. These sample points are then plotted on the chart.

Based on previous experience and statistical theory, it can be assumed that the output variations are normally distributed. Therefore, it can be said with 99.73 percent confidence that the average of the sample, that is, the sample mean $(\overline{X})$ must lie within three sample standard deviations of the process mean $(\overline{\overline{X}})$.

Substituting the values given, it is seen that the sample mean should lie in the range of .564 to .584, and any variation outside these limits can be interpreted as an assignable failure that requires corrective action. In only .27 percent (100.00 − 99.73), about three chances in one thousand, of the cases can it be expected that the sample will fall outside these limits due to random (unassignable) variations. The overwhelming probability of the existence of an assignable cause is a very powerful incentive to stop the process (if necessary), investigate, and apply corrective action.

It is a relatively simple matter, once the chart is set up, for a relatively unsophisticated person to plot the sample means on the chart. This indicates that quality control charts can be installed at the operating level with the proviso that any deviation outside the limits will trigger further investigation by supervision. Systems control can be applied at the source for early warning to the Management Information System specialist or the responsible manager.

Work Sampling

Statistical quality control is based on the laws of probability and the theory of sampling, and without them the control chart technique could not have been developed and applied. The application of the theory of sampling independent of control charts is also a powerful systems tool. Using sampling theory, a small number of items can be inspected as generally representing the variation that would be found if 100 percent inspection was used. A particularly useful adaptation of sampling theory is known as *work sampling*.

This technique is especially useful in situations that do not appear to have a cycle or a repetitive pattern. The work of engineers, programmers, and most professional activity falls into this general category. In studying these elements of the Management Information System it is often very difficult and cumbersome to use the flow process chart, the flow diagram, the work count, or many of the other tools already discussed or that will be discussed. The absence of a repetitive cycle clutters up any attempt at fact gathering with a great deal of confusing detail.

Work sampling utilizes the power of sampling theory to make inferences about an activity based on observations taken at random intervals of the nonrepetitive operation under study. The observations taken at random intervals are categorized into specific activities that are significant to the operation. For instance, in analyzing the programming function in a particular organization, the categories were defined as:

1. Coding
2. Testing on the computer
3. Desk checking
4. Make ready/Clean up
5. Personal
6. Computer delays
7. Other delays
8. Documentation

Each category, in turn, was defined objectively and clearly so that observations could be categorized with a minimum of speculation.

It may be interesting to note that the method was developed in 1934 by L. H. C. Tippett to measure operator and machine delays in the textile industry in England. He called it his *snap-reading method*. R. L. Morrow was one of the first statisticians in the United States to use Tippett's method, which he called *ratio delay*. In 1952, H. L. Wadell decided that the name *work sampling* would be more descriptive, and this name is generally used today.

Before the use of work sampling, the most common method for obtaining information about the productive or nonproductive activity of a man or of a piece of equipment was by continuous stopwatch time study. This required direct observation of the activity by an analyst for an extended number of hours, timing and recording the activities and the delays as they occurred. This was expensive, irritating to those observed, and very time-consuming. Work sampling enables the analyst to obtain information on activities and on delays simply by making random observations (taking "snapshot" samples) without the use of any timing device.

THE METHOD OF USING WORK SAMPLING

1. Define a set of activity categories for the operation, including idle, delay, or nonproductive categories.
2. Determine the number of sample observations to be made.

$$\text{No. of observations} = \frac{4(1-P)}{(\text{Accuracy})^2(P)} @ 95\% \text{ Confidence level}$$

The number of observations depends on the proportion of occurrence of the category being measured (P), the degree of confidence desired (usually 95 percent), and the required accuracy in the results (usually ± 5 percent). A sample of about one hundred observations is usually taken to approximate the proportion that is to be measured. Taking one hundred observations insures that the distribution approaches the normal and allows the use of the statistical relationships discussed earlier in this chapter.

Rather than use the formula indicated, the *nomograph* shown in Fig. 9–5 can provide the answer as to how many observations much more quickly.

3. Use a table of random numbers to determine when to take each observation. One approach is to assign the number 001 to the first minute of the day and 480 to the last minute (if an eight-hour shift). Then, the last three digits of each entry in the random number table will indicate the exact time to take the observation.

4. Make the observations and record on a previously prepared category-scoresheet.

5. Summarize the data.

6. Analyze the data based on objectives, timing, and results expected.

7. Generate an improved general pattern of the activity studied.

Using the Work Sampling Nomograph.   The number of observations is very important to the reliability of the results. However, beyond a certain point, additional observations cost more than they are worth in terms of improving the accuracy of the results. The nomograph will quickly indicate the number of observations needed to attain a given level of accuracy.

1. Estimate from previous experience or from a sample of one hundred observations the proportion of occurrence (percent) of the element in the activity that is to be measured. This is the left-hand column of the nomograph.

(In the example of the nomograph, this is 80 percent.)

2. Decide on the degree of accuracy desired. Multiply the percent of occurrence and the percent of accuracy to get the *precision interval.*

In the example:

Degree of accuracy   = 5%, or .05
Proportion of occurrence = 80%, or .80
(.05) × (.80) = .04, or 4%

This is the value on the middle column of the nomograph.

3. Lay a straightedge at 80 percent in the left-hand column and at 4 percent in the middle column and read the number of observations where the straightedge crosses the righthand column.

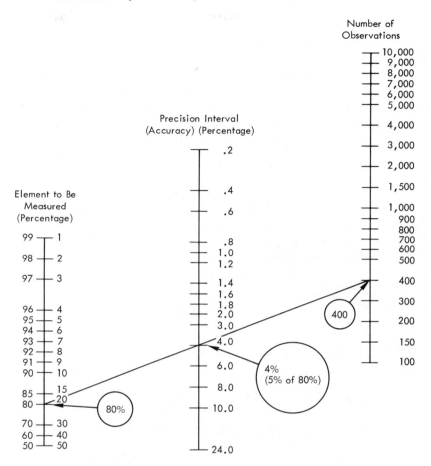

FIGURE 9-5

Work Sampling—How Many Observations?

In the example, for a work activity that takes 80 percent of the time, and with an accuracy of 5 percent, a sample of four hundred observations is necessary.

Other Statistical Techniques

1. Testing of Management Predictions

Using techniques related to what has already been discussed, probability statements can be made about the truth or falsity of certain predictions, which in the language of statistics are called *hypotheses*. For example, if data on inventory stock-outs was from one plant and similar data was available for the same type of inventory item at another company plant, statistical tests could be performed to determine if any differences between the data were "significant" or merely "random" variations. This is known as *hypothesis testing*. Probabilities can be calculated for the testing of hypotheses based on well-detailed techniques that allow management to take carefully calculated risks.

2. Establishing Cause-and-Effect Relationships

It is often desirable to determine the relationships, if any, between a number of factors or variables. For example, is there a relationship between the failure time of electronic circuits and the ambient temperature? Or, does the position of gunpowder within a cartridge have an effect on bullet velocity? Or, does the frequency of a salesman's calls affect the number of sales orders placed? Statistical techniques such as the calculation of *correlation coefficients, regression analysis,* and *analysis of variance* can be used to provide management with the answers.

REVIEW QUESTIONS

1. What statistics would you be interested in seeing if you were appointed manager of:
    a. A company manufacturing Christmas toys?
    b. A hospital treating the aged?
    c. A company manufacturing computers?
2. What can statistical analysis provide to assist management?
3. Define *sample, population, statistics, probability.*
4. Assume that you are managing a plumbing supply store. There are one thousand different items in your catalog. Unfortunately, there is space for only eight hundred different types of items in your store. How can probability help you to decide what items to stock?
5. Give three examples of the normal distribution that one can observe in a department store.
6. A particular IQ test has a mean of 100 and a standard deviation of 14. What observation can you make from this data?
7. What is statistical quality control? How is it used?
8. Give two causes of quality variation. Which is the easier to improve?

9.   Define *work sampling*. How is this technique related to statistics?
10.   What benefits can work sampling provide to industry?

BIBLIOGRAPHY

BARNES, R. M., *Work Sampling*. New York: John Wiley and Sons, Inc., 1957. A comprehensive and detailed treatment of this useful tool.

DEMING, W. EDWARDS, *Sample Design in Business Research*. New York: John Wiley and Sons, Inc., 1960. A truly great book written by a master in the field. Actual examples from the author's wide-ranging consulting practice are scattered profusely throughout the book.

FREUND, JOHN E., *Mathematical Statistics*. Englewood Cliffs, N. J.: Prentice-Hall, Inc., 1962. A standard treatment of the subject matter by a recognized authority in the field.

GRANT, EUGENE L., *Statistical Quality Control* (3rd ed.). New York: McGraw-Hill Book Company, 1964. The author sets the tone for the book when he refers to it as a practical working manual. That it is and by an acknowledged authority in the field.

MCCOLLOUGH, CELESTE, and LOCKE VAN ATTA, *Statistical Concepts*. New York: McGraw-Hill Book Company, 1963. The programmed, self-instructional approach makes for painless review and learning. Most useful for someone learning the concepts for the first time or coming back to them after a long time away.

PETERS, WILLIAM S., and GEORGE W. SUMMERS, *Statistical Analysis for Business Decisions*. Englewood Cliffs, N. J.: Prentice-Hall, Inc., 1968. A thorough treatment of probability and statistics. Answers to many of the exercises are included and provide a useful stimulus to self-study.

SPIEGEL, MURRAY R., *Statistics*. New York: McGraw-Hill Book Company, 1961. This is one of the famous Schaum's Outline Series that have helped many a student through many a statistics course. Excellent for basic review purposes.

YAMANE, TARO, *Statistics, An Introductory Analysis*. New York: Harper & Row, Publishers, 1964. A clearly written text on modern statistics. A good book on an elementary level.

10

SYSTEMS CONTROL
TECHNIQUES

Once the objectives of an organization are set, management develops and implements plans to reach these objectives. These plans are designed to utilize the resources of the organization in terms of the realities of its internal and external environment. But these realities are constantly changing. The function of the Management Information System is to provide data on all aspects of the organization's operations and its environment so that management can compare reality with plans and make the necessary action decisions. These action decisions when transmitted through the information network to the critical points in the organization are the essence of control.

The action decisions derive from management's judgment as to what should be done when actual results vary from the expected. These action decisions may change the specific plans involved or the operating conditions that produced the variance in the results. Once again, it is important to emphasize that only when management's decisions are implemented is there the reality of management control.

A number of the tools and techniques already discussed in previous chapters are readily identifiable as useful in the management control process. Yet, a number of particular systems control concepts could be very helpful to the systems analyst in designing and implementing a Management Information System. A case in point is the ABC concept of control.

THE ABC CONCEPT OF CONTROL

Some years ago a bank robber by the name of Willie Sutton was asked the tongue-in-cheek question, "Why do you rob banks?" His answer embodied a philosophical truism that (with slight modification) every manager could usefully include as his personal motto. He said, "That's where the money is!" The interpretation that makes his answer a management maxim is, "Put your efforts where the results are maximized." Figure 10-1 gives a graphical representation of what could be called "the Willie Sutton principle." A amount of effort produces X amount of results. B amount of effort produces only Y amount of results. A careful selection of where to put the effort can produce a significant difference in the amount of results. An extension of the principle of putting the effort where the results are maximized is often referred to as "the ABC concept of control." The premise of the ABC approach is that management should concentrate its energy on controlling those items that most effect the organizational objectives. Conversely, management should pay proportionately less attention to those matters that have proportionately

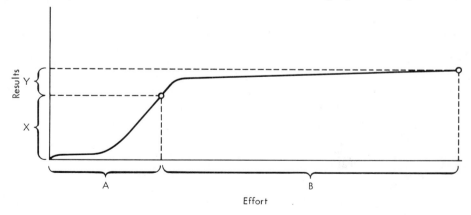

FIGURE 10-1

The "Willie Sutton" Principle

less effect on the organization's objectives. A dramatic application of this ABC concept is in inventory control.

The ABC Concept of Inventory Control

There is a pattern in just about every inventory system that lends itself to the application of putting the effort where the results are. The items in every inventory can usually be broken down into three relatively arbitrary categories. The A category is for those inventory items that are the most active or the most costly, or in some way have the greatest impact on results. The C items are the most inactive or the least costly, or they have the least effect on results. The B category is for those items that are neither A items nor C items.

An inventory control system that applies the *efforts-results* management principle discussed earlier would have A items controlled by sophisticated tools, with close and frequent management analysis. B items would be controlled by means of rigorous, more traditional control tools, with routine monitoring by management. C items would be handled on a routine, repetitive, exception basis, with management attention only when and if necessary.

The actual prevalence of this phenomenon has been attested to by many surveys and reports. In manufacturing companies, for instance, 20 percent of the items account for 90 percent of the dollar usage per year. Wholesale companies find that 20 percent of the items account for 80 percent of the dollar usage per year. In high technology industries, with high unit costs and high obsolescence rates, 20 percent of the items account for 98 percent of the total dollar usage per year.

Implementing ABC Inventory Control:

1. Calculate the dollar usage per year for each item in inventory.
   (Year's Activity in Units) $\times$ ($ value per unit) = ($ usage per year)
2. List all the items in inventory in the order of their annual dollar usage—from highest to lowest dollar usage.
3. Total the dollar usage of all items in the inventory.
4. Calculate the percentage of each item's annual dollar usage to the total dollar usage of all the items in inventory.
5. Calculate cumulative percentages.
6. Management decides on the cutoff points for A, B, and C categories.
7. Apply the applicable inventory control tools:
   A Items—Perpetual inventory monitoring, simulation, Monte Carlo, close-in management control reports

B Items—Periodic inventory monitoring, economic ordering quantity formulas, min-max controls, exception reporting to
management

C Items—2-bin system, minimum stock reordering, quarterly
summary reports to management

Of course, the real significance of the ABC concept is not in its
application to inventory control but in its application to all areas of
management planning, analysis, and control. The key concept it embodies is that there exists a law of diminishing returns affecting management's efforts. The Management Information System must integrate
this concept in order to enhance management's ability to put the effort
where the most results can be expected.

THE LEARNING CURVE

Closely related to the "Willie Sutton principle" and the ABC concept
of control is another very useful management systems tool popularly
known as the *learning curve*. It was developed by the aircraft industry
during World War II as a means of forecasting labor requirements to
meet stringent production schedules.

It is a reflection of the principle that an organization learns from
experience. Specifically, it was found that as production doubles the
average effort required per unit produced decreases at a constant rate.
For example, the first ten units produced required an average of 100
man-hours per unit, the first twenty units required an average of 80
man-hours per unit, the first forty units required an average of 64 man-
hours per unit, the first eighty required 51.2 man-hours per unit, and
so forth. This would be an example of an "80 percent learning curve."
That is, for every doubling of the quantity of units produced, the cumulative average man-hours of effort expended per unit tends to be 80
percent of its preceding value. In tabular form the factor relationship is
even more obvious.

Units Produced		Average Man-Hours per Unit
10		100
20	$(100 \times .80) =$	80
40	$(\ 80 \times .80) =$	64
80	$(\ 64 \times .80) =$	51.2

This relationship can be expressed graphically on regular arithmetic
(rectangular coordinate) graph paper (Fig. 10-2).

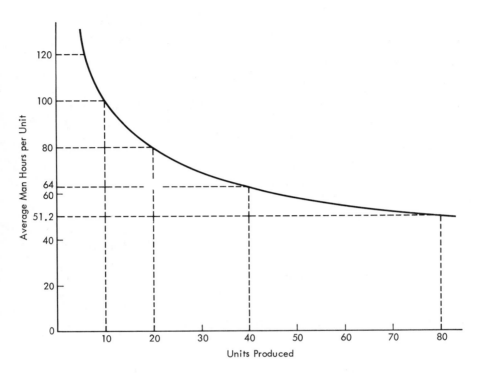

FIGURE 10-2

Eighty Percent Learning Curve on Arithmetic Graph Paper

The usefulness of the learning curve concept is in the assistance it gives management in forecasting labor requirements and production schedules. Plotting the results of production experience on arithmetic graph paper limits the quantities that can be shown, and because the relationship follows a curved path, it is difficult to extend the curve accurately. For these reasons. learning curves are usually plotted on geometric (log-log) graph paper. The result, for the same relationships used previously, is a straight line (Fig. 10-3). It can accommodate much larger quantities and can be read much more accurately.

The learning curve is essentially a statistical expression of a basic law of economics known as *the economies of scale*. As production quantities increase, average unit cost tends to decrease. Based on an analysis of cost experience over a particular quantity of production, it is possible to compute the pattern of cost performance and to project the expected performance over future production quantities.

The term *learning curve* places an inordinate amount of emphasis

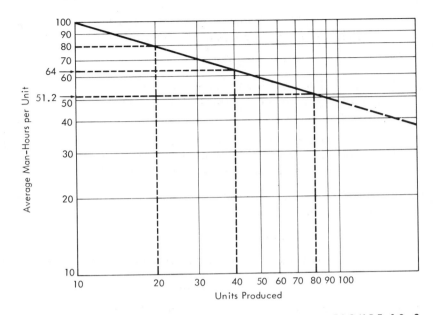

FIGURE 10-3

Eighty Percent Learning Curve on Geometric Graph Paper

on the effect of human learning on costs. Depending on the circumstances, a great many factors besides labor costs may generate the downward trend of unit production costs. Some of these other factors are:

1. Improved flow of materials
2. Reduction in scrap, rework, and rejects
3. Improved tools and work methods
4. Elimination of initial "bugs" and mistakes
5. Work simplification results
6. Identification and elimination of "idle time" and delays
7. Improved management controls
8. Scheduling economical production quantities

All the above factors have greater impact on costs as production quantities increase. Therefore, the sum total of the effects of all these factors is reflected in the learning curve, not just improved worker know-how.

Learning curves vary by industry and by type of work in specific companies. The learning rate can, theoretically, reach a "maximum" of 100 percent (no learning at all) and a "minimum" of 50 percent (production doubles without requiring additional labor). The following examples will clarify the reason for these theoretical limits.

100% Learning Rate

The first 10 units required an average of 100 man-hours per unit. With a 100 percent learning rate, the first 20 units would require an average man-hours per unit as calculated below:

(Average man-hours per unit for first 20 units) = (Average man-hours per unit for first 10 units) $\times$ (Learning rate) $(100) \times (1.00)$ = 100 average man-hours per unit for first 20 units

In other words, there was no decrease in effort per unit since there was no "learning" at all.

50% Learning Rate

Average man-hours per unit of first 10 units = 100

Learning rate = 50%

Average man-hours per unit of first 20 units = (Average man-hours per unit of first 10 units) $\times$ (learning rate) = $(100) \times (.50)$ = average of 50 man-hours per unit for first 20 units

Total production man-hours for first 10 units = (Number of units) $\times$ (average man-hours per unit) = $(10) \times (100)$ = 1,000 man-hours

Total production man-hours for first 20 units = $(20) \times (50)$ = 1,000 man-hours

Since it took one thousand man-hours to make the first ten units, it is clearly unreasonable to have ten more units made without the expenditure of any effort whatsoever. A learning rate below 50 percent would actually have "negative work" occurring. The theoretical limit of the learning rate is therefore 50 percent, but of course it is never approached.

In industries with a great deal of hand assembly, the learning rate has approached 70 percent. The aircraft industry has often experienced 80 percent learning curves, and in situations involving highly complex operations, the learning rate is often in the area of 95 percent.

Determining the Learning Rate

The learning rate can be determined from accumulated production data.

Let
$$X = \text{Number of units}$$
$$R = \text{Learning rate}$$
$$R = \frac{\text{Average unit time for 2 X units}}{\text{Average unit time for X units}}$$

Using the previous data: First 10 units—100 man-hours/unit
                         First 20 units— 80 man-hours/unit

$$R = \frac{80 \text{ man-hours/unit}}{100 \text{ man-hours/unit}} = .80 = 80\%$$

The potential areas of application of learning curve techniques in management systems are substantial. The probable reason for their lack of use is that the subject is not widely known. Its very simplicity mitigates against its acceptance by some of the "experienced" production men. However, its power should be self-evident once it is effectively applied.

The following characteristics should alert the systems analyst to the possibility of using the learning curve technique.

1. A rigorous and reliable production cost accounting system is in effect.
2. Production quantity and schedule provides a reasonable expectation that the "learning" effect will be experienced.
3. The product is relatively complex and requires special design and specification.
4. Direct labor cost is a significant element of total manufacturing cost.

INVENTORY CONTROL SYSTEMS

Inventory plays a key role in all organizations, even those that are service oriented rather than product oriented. Hospitals, orphanages, schools, social agencies all must pay careful attention to maintaining an adequate supply of necessary operating items as well as providing this supply at minimum cost. Product-oriented organizations are more obviously concerned with inventory, but the techniques of control are quite similar.

Interestingly enough there are but two basic questions that must be answered if an organization is seriously interested in setting up an inventory control system: When to order? How much to order?

The answer to the question When to order? is based on the current demand plus the length of time it takes to obtain supplies from their sources (lead time) plus an allowance for protection against inordinate demand for stock during the lead time interval.

A number of statistical techniques have been developed to assist management in arriving at a feasible answer to the question of *when* to order. A useful approach to developing a reordering strategy will be presented after explaining the tool that answers the question, How much to order?

Inventory Control—How Much to Order

The question of how much to order is answered by the economic ordering quantity formula. This formula is a simple mathematical expression of the relationship of all the factors involved in determining a reorder quantity.

There are really only two major considerations in deciding how much to order: (1) the cost of administering the procurement of the quantity to be ordered (procurement costs) and (2) the costs of carrying that quantity in storage (carrying charges).

1. Procurement Costs—all office and shop costs that occur when an order is placed. The total of these costs varies with the number of orders that are placed each year. They include:
   a. Requesting and evaluating quotations
   b. Setup costs
   c. Expediting
   d. Tooling or design charges
   e. Acceptance and inspection charges
   f. Purchase order initiation and administration costs
   g. Costs of processing the invoice
2. Carrying Charges—the costs involved in storing an item.
   a. Interest on investment in inventory
   b. Taxes on inventory
   c. Insurance
   d. Storage and handling (rent, light, heat, protection costs, etc.)
   e. Maintenance of records
   f. Obsolescence, deterioration, shrinkage
   g. Repackaging and rehandling

As might be expected, procurement costs per item vary inversely with the quantity (Q) ordered at any one time. The greater the quantity on the order, the less the per item cost. Suppose the procurement costs per order detailed above are represented by the symbol P.

If the total requirement for inventory in one year is (R), the total annual cost due to these procurement costs is $R/Q(P)$.

Notice that the total inventory requirement for the year (R) divided by the quantity per order (Q) gives the number of orders per year. When multiplied by the procurement costs per order (P), the result is the total annual procurement costs.

These total annual procurement costs depend directly on the number of times an order is generated. Inventory costs could be minimized by ordering once a year if they were the only costs to be concerned about. But procurement costs are not the only costs that are involved—carrying charges must also be considered. The dilemma faced by management is that decisions that minimize procurement costs tend to increase carrying charges, and vice versa. For example, a company uses 120 units of a particular part each year at a constant rate. That would be 10 a month. If these parts were ordered once a year, say on January 1, and were completely used up by December 31, the average inventory would be one-half the number ordered. That is, $Q/2$, which in this case would be 60. The usage rate and the average inventory of this item for the year is represented on the graph in Figure 10-4.

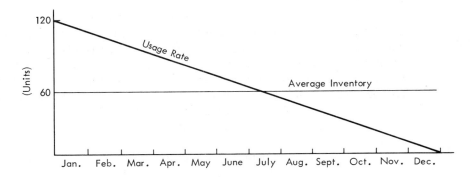

FIGURE 10-4

Continuing the example, if it costs $3 a year per item to carry these parts in inventory, and it costs $50 to administer the ordering cycle, that is, procurement cost, even a casual analysis would indicate that with carrying charges of $(60 \times \$3 = \$180)$ and procurement costs of $50, it would be sensible to order more often and cut down on average inventory and the attendant carrying charges. Suppose orders were put in twice a year, 60 each time. Average inventory would be ½ $(Q) = 60/2 = 30$. See Figure 10-5.

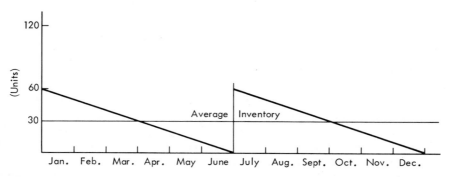

FIGURE 10-5

If an order of 120 is placed once a year, the procurement cost of $50 for the order plus the total carrying charges of $180 add up to $230 for total inventory costs. If an order is placed twice a year, procurement costs come to $100, while carrying costs (average inventory of 30 times $3 per item) drop to $90 for a total of inventory costs equal to $190.

The more times a year an order is placed, the lower the order quantity, the lower the average inventory, and the lower the total carrying charges. But on the other hand, the more orders placed each year, the more the administrative work, order processing, and receiving activity, resulting in higher total procurement costs. The quandary is this: Should less be ordered each time—but ordered more often, or should more be ordered each time—but less often? The formulas for total annual procurement costs and total annual carrying charges can help develop an answer.

$$Q = \text{Quantity per order}$$
$$P = \text{Procurement cost per order}$$
$$R = \text{Annual inventory demand}$$
$$C = \text{Carrying charge per item per year}$$
$$\text{Average inventory} = Q/2$$
$$\text{Annual procurement costs} = \frac{R}{Q}(P)$$
$$\text{Annual carrying charges} = \frac{Q}{2}(C)$$

If various ordering quantities are substituted in the annual procurement cost and annual carrying charge formulas, and if the results are plotted, the curves are developed as shown in Figures 10-6 and 10-7.

The graphs dramatize our quandary. The smaller the order

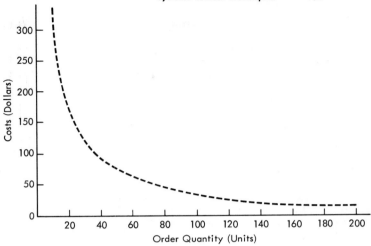

FIGURE 10-6

Procurement Costs

quantity, the more times a year we order, the lower the average inventory, and therefore the lower the total carrying charges. But on the other hand, the more times a year we order, the higher will be the total procurement costs. As the question was posed previously, should we order less each time—more often, or order more each time—less often? Putting both the procurement cost curve and the carrying charges curve together gives us the answer!

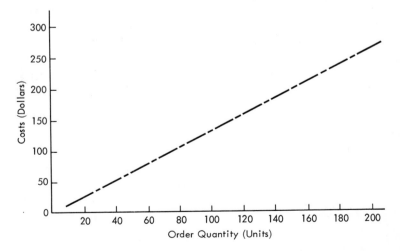

FIGURE 10-7

Carrying Charges

As shown in Figure 10-8, the intersection of the procurement costs curve and the carrying charges curve is the point of minimum total costs for inventory. It identifies the Economical Order Quantity (EOQ).

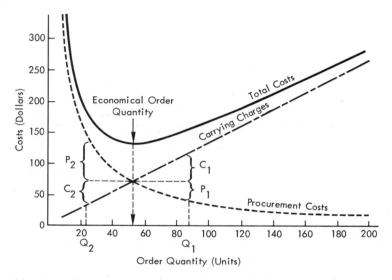

FIGURE 10-8

Economical Order Quantity

The best operating point is where procurement costs equal carrying charges. If any more than this quantity is ordered each time (Q_1), the amount saved because of lower procurement costs (P_1) is more than offset by higher carrying charges (C_1). If less than this amount is ordered each time (Q_2), the amount saved because of lower carrying charges (C_2) is more than offset by higher procurement costs (P_2).

The point of minimum total costs is known as the Economical Ordering Quantity (EOQ). This is the point at which carrying costs $\left(\dfrac{Q}{2}\right)(C)$ are equal to procurement cost $\left(\dfrac{R}{Q}\right)(P)$.

Equating these to each other and solving for Q:

$$\left(\frac{Q}{2}\right)(C) = \left(\frac{R}{Q}\right)(P)$$

$$Q_2 = \frac{2\ RP}{C}$$

$$Q = \sqrt{\frac{2\ RP}{C}}$$

This, then, is the Economical Order Quantity formula. If annual demand (R), procurement cost (P), and carrying charges (C) are accurate, the EOQ will be accurate and the total costs will be minimum. Many different variations of the basic formula have been developed to cover specific situations.

For instance, it is quite common for a company to generate carrying charges per year as a percentage of the unit price of the item. In that case the carrying charge would be calculated by multiplying the percentage times the unit price. Let K represent the carrying charge percentage and I the unit price of the item. The carrying charge $= KI$, and the EOQ formula would be:

$$Q = \sqrt{\frac{2\ RP}{KI}}$$

In actual practice, the EOQ formula itself is not often directly used. Rather, charts, graphs, and tables based on the formula are used because they eliminate repetitive calculations by inventory personnel.

The EOQ Nomograph

The nomograph is a particularly useful device to eliminate calculating EOQ. For this example, assume that the company uses monthly rather than annual requirements. Three scales are set up—monthly requirements, EOQ, and unit price (see Fig. 10-9). Select a logarithmic scale that covers the range of unit price values needed and another that covers the range of monthly requirements.

Put the monthly requirements scale on one side of the page and the unit price scale on the other. The values must run in opposite directions. Exactly halfway between the two scales draw a vertical line. Select a unit price and a monthly requirement; calculate the EOQ with the formula. Using a straightedge, connect the unit price and the annual requirements. Where it crosses the center line, mark and identify with the EOQ you have calculated. From this point on the center line, simply plot another logarithmic scale and have it run in the same direction as the monthly requirements scale. You now have an EOQ nomograph.

A Last Word About EOQ

The subject of economical order quantities has been explored for many years and is universally respected as a very useful tool. But like all tools, it must be used with judgment. For instance, the formula makes no provision for stockouts—it assumes immediate delivery. The person using the formula has to use common sense to adjust the results of the formula to conditions as they actually are. Formulas and mathematical techniques are objective quantitative guides to assist manage-

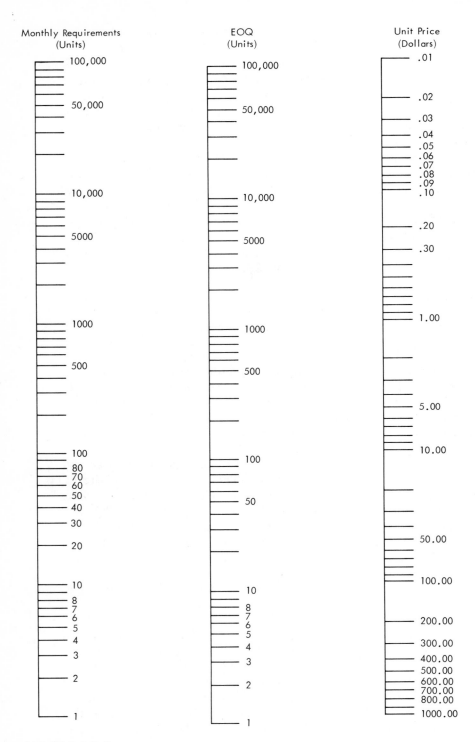

FIGURE 10-9

EOQ Nomograph in Unit Quantities

ment in making decisions. They reduce the area of uncertainty in management decision making, but they certainly are not substitutes for judgment.

For example, in many situations inventory replenishment occurs over a period of time dependent on the production rate (A). In such a case the EOQ formula is modified as follows:

$$EOQ = \sqrt{\frac{2P}{C}\left(\frac{A-R}{A}\right)}$$

There are many different EOQ formulas to fit different conditions. But for the systems analyst, the important thing is to understand the concepts and to be aware that a growing body of literature is available to help in setting up inventory control systems. The Bibliography will provide a number of sources that give useful details on a variety of inventory applications.

Inventory Control—When to Order

As was mentioned earlier in this chapter, inventory control depends on the answers to two questions—How much to order? and When to order? The Economical Order Quantity technique helps answer the first question. In this section, tools related to statistical analysis will be shown to be very helpful to management in developing an effective answer to the question, When to order?

If inventory replenishment quantities could be obtained instantly, there would be no problem as far as determining when to order. The Economical Order Quantity formula would tell the manager concerned how much to order, and when the quantity on hand reached zero this would trigger the reorder cycle. Since the quantities desired could be obtained immediately there would be no danger of interrupted customer service or a shortage of materials and supplies anywhere in the organization.

But real life is not that easy. The usual situation is that a reorder must be initiated when there is still enough stock on hand to cover anticipated demand until the quantity ordered is received. Usually, this reorder cycle includes:

1. Time for the paperwork involved in requisitioning.
2. In some cases, the processing of quotations from vendors is necessary.

3. If the item is made in the shop, time is needed to make the quantity ordered.
4. If it is a purchased item, the time may include the making of the part by the vendor.
5. Purchased parts require time for shipment, receiving, inspection, and restocking.

When all the times in the reorder cycle are added up, they represent the reorder *lead time*, which can run into weeks or even months.

If demand in a company were two hundred units a week, and if the reorder lead time were three weeks, a prudent inventory manager might reorder when he had some six hundrd units in stock (3 weeks × 200/week = 600).

Of course, in actual inventory situations, actual demand usually varies from expected demand. Therefore, to protect himself from stock-outs, the manager will provide some additional stock as a margin of safety. In other words, he might reorder at seven hundred units rather than at six hundred. This gives him a margin of safety of one hundred units to take care of any unexpected increase in demand.

But this "safety stock" can be expensive. Especially if the safety stock (which in this case is one hundred units) is more than necessary. But inventory managers, being human, are responding to the fact that the amount of criticism received when a stock-out occurs is overwhelming compared with the vague, generalized pressure to "hold down inventories" that exists in many organizations. Most managers would agree that the safety stock is usually higher than it should be.

But what should the safety stock be? The answer to that question is intimately connected to the answer to the quesion, When to order? The more safety stock that is carried, the higher the inventory carrying costs such as taxes, interest, insurance, storage, handling, record keeping, and obsolescence. The less safety stock, the more chance of a costly stock-out. Where should the manager set the level of safety stock?

One important factor in the amount of safety stock needed is the variability in demand. Therefore it will be very helpful for the systems analyst to make an analysis of this variability in demand and develop guidelines as to the range of demand he can probably expect. He does this by examining records of past performance of forecast and actual demand. Table 10-1 gives a hypothetical example of forecast demand and actual demand for a twenty-four month period.

This organization's inventory control program provided for a re-order every month. The statistics in Table 10-1 provide the raw material for an analysis of the effectiveness of this monthly reorder cycle.

TABLE 10-1

Forecast versus Actual Demand
(Twenty-Four Month Period)

Month	Forecast Demand	Actual Demand	(Actual − Forecast) Difference
1	200	162	− 38
2	200	222	+ 22
3	200	148	− 52
4	200	183	− 17
5	200	235	+ 35
6	200	192	− 08
7	200	255	+ 55
8	200	203	+ 03
9	200	159	− 41
10	200	272	+ 72
11	200	201	+ 01
12	200	115	− 85
13	200	217	+ 17
14	200	199	− 01
15	200	214	+ 14
16	200	135	− 65
17	200	175	− 25
18	200	103	− 97
19	200	309	+ 109
20	200	227	+ 27
21	200	176	− 24
22	200	248	+ 48
23	200	209	+ 09
24	200	192	− 08

1. Calculating Variance

Subtracting forecast demand from actual demand will provide a quantitative measure of the degree of variation that occurred. The difference between forecast demand and actual demand identifies the reorder cycles in which shortages (stock-outs) or surpluses occurred. A negative difference indicates a surplus; a positive difference indicates a stock-out. A simple count of the number of times either condition occurred during the twenty-four reorder cycles might be informative, but it would not prove very helpful in setting up a system of management control. Specifically, it would not tell management how much safety stock was necessary—the essential ingredient for answering the queston, When to order?

2. Organizing the Data

The data that has been developed must now be organized. This is done by first grouping the data into equal divisions called *cell intervals*. The size of these intervals is arbitrary, but practice indicates that about eight to twenty cells should be provided for in the range of the data. Since the difference between the largest and the smallest difference (forecast error) is equal to 206 (−97 to +109), cell intervals of twenty seem reasonable.

3. Develop the Frequency Table (Table 10-2)

The *frequency table* summarizes the calculations involved in organizing the data. The first column, labeled *cell interval*, dimensions the cells, and each cell interval is numbered for ease of reference. The second column, labeled *tally*, is where a stroke is made every time the forecast error (actual demand—forecast demand) falls within the interval. The column labeled *relative frequency* is the frequency divided by the total number of observations (twenty-four reorder cycles). The next-to-last column is labeled *cumulative frequency*. *Cumulative relative frequency* is the label of the last column and is the running total of *relative frequency*.

TABLE 10-2

Frequency Table

Cell Interval	Tally	Frequency	Relative Frequency %	Cumulative Frequency	Cumulative Relative Frequency (%)
1. − 109 to − 90	1	1	4.2	1	4.2
2. − 89 to − 70	1	1	4.2	2	8.4
3. − 69 to − 50	11	2	8.3	4	16.7
4. − 49 to − 30	111	3	12.5	7	29.2
5. − 29 to − 10	111	3	12.5	10	41.7
6. − 9 to + 10	1111	4	16.7	14	58.4
7. + 11 to + 30	1111	4	16.7	18	75.1
8. + 31 to + 50	111	3	12.5	21	87.6
9. + 51 to + 70	11	2	8.3	23	95.9
10. + 71 to + 90		0	0.0	23	95.9
11. + 91 to + 109	1	1	4.2	24	100.0

4. The Frequency Histogram (Figure 10-10)

The *frequency table* is the basis for the preparation of a bar chart (called a *frequency histogram*) of the frequency of occurrence of the differences between forecast and actual demand. The cell intervals make up the horizontal scale and the frequency makes up the vertical scale. The height of each bar is therefore determined by the number of forecast errors that fell into each cell interval.

5. The Frequency Distribution (Figure 10-10)

Then the midpoints of the tops of the bars are connected (approximately) by a smooth curve (dashed line) which is the running total of observed frequencies.

It is useful to recall the definition of *probability* at this time. If

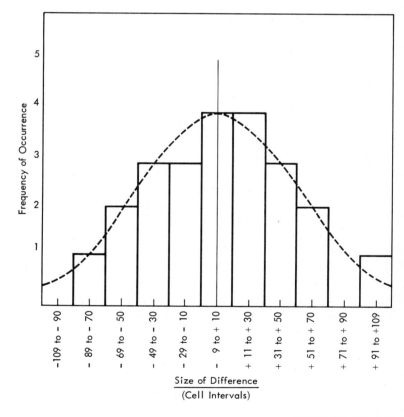

FIGURE 10-10

Frequency Histogram

you remember, it is the number of successes out of the total number of outcomes. This is very much like the definition of *relative frequency* —the frequency of occurrence in each cell interval divided by the total number of all occurrences. It is, in fact, the probability of occurrence of the particular span of forecast error represented by the cell interval. This is an important point to remember in using the tool being developed.

Furthermore, cumulative relative frequency is also important because it quantifies the probability of forecast errors less than or equal to the upper boundary of that cell interval. The reason for the importance of this concept will be self-evident as this explanation develops.

There should be something very familiar about the curve traced by the dashed line. It looks a lot like the normal curve discussed in Chapter 9. But how to be sure? It is the result of a two-year history (twenty-four reorder cycles) of forecast and actual demand of one item of inventory. There is nothing in that to guarantee that it is a normal curve. But even if it were, how can it be concluded that the distribution of forecast errors in the future will be normally distributed as it must have been in the past? The problem is to determine if the distribution developed is normal or very close to it, and if the distribution that was developed reflects what may happen in the future. (A standard statistical test called the chi-square can determine if the distribution is normal.) This is a very crucial point in the development of this tool. Although statistical theory can determine normality, management must decide whether the conditions in the future can be considered to be approximately the same as those in the immediate past. It is a decision that can only be made by management, based on experienced judgment. Yet the application of this tool as well as a very wide spectrum of other quantitative management tools depends on the answer to the question of how well the past presages the future—how much the system is in a condition called *statistical stability*. Statistical tools can help management in this area also, but it ultimately becomes a question of management judgment.

Inventory theory, based on the experience of many inventory analysis situations, states that the distribution of forecast errors can be considered as approximately normal for analysis purposes. Furthermore, in this example, management's evaluation as to whether or not conditions in the future will be the same as in the past, has resulted in the considered judgment that statistical stability exists. Since both conditions hold, the known characteristic of the normal distribution can be used!

Of course, the distribution of forecast errors over the past twenty-four reorder cycles did not give an exact normal curve. But if more and more historical data were gathered, and if more and smaller cell intervals were set up to organize the data, the curve connecting the midpoints of the bar in the frequency histogram would come closer and closer to the standard normal curve. Statistical theory provides rigorous methods (i.e., the chi-square test) to test normality so that there need be no guesswork on that score.

The frequency histogram is specifically a reflection of the results of the twenty-four observations in the particular historical period concerned. But if the relative frequency data were used to develop a histogram. a more general picture of the distribution of forecast errors over any period of time would be available. In point of fact, the relative frequency histogram would be an exact duplicate of the frequency histogram except that the vertical scale would read relative frequency instead of frequency. The basic difference is that the relative frequency histogram is generally applicable to any number of observations and not just to the twenty-four that were actually used.

The cumulative relative frequency histogram will be useful later on and can easily be constructed from the table. It specifies the probability of differences between actual and forecast demand that are equal to or less than each cell interval. This is particularly helpful when it is necessary to decide on an amount of safety stock as protection from stock-outs a certain percentage of the time (say 95 per cent or 96 percent). More about this later. The *cumulative relative frequency histogram* is a direct outgrowth of the *relative frequency histogram* (see Figs. 10-11 and 10-12).

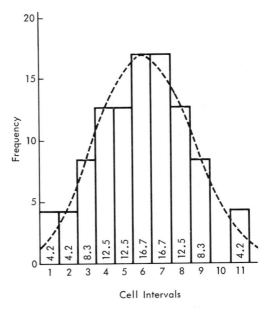

FIGURE 10-11

Relative Frequency Histogram

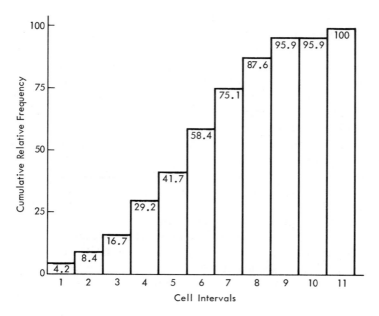

FIGURE 10-12

Cumulative Relative Frequency Histogram

The bars of the relative frequency histogram actually represent the probability of forecast errors in each particular interval. The area of each bar is the proportion of the total area of all the bars in the histogram. Adjacent bars can be combined so that the proportion of errors contained in bigger and bigger areas can be calculated. The area of all the bars totals the area under the smooth curve. That total is unity. This is a further indication of a direct relationship to probability theory. One of the basic laws of probability is that the sum of all the probabilities of all possible outcomes is certainty, that is, one. The total of all the relative frequencies in the tally table is, of course, one. This can readily be checked by referring to the cumulative relative frequency column in Table 10-2.

The area of the histogram is the area under the normal curve. One is the same as the other. But the histogram is very specific. The cell intervals apply specifically to the twenty-four-month sample. The normal curve, on the other hand, is very general. It will apply to all distributions of inventory forecast errors. Therefore, rather than be tied to the specific discrete increments of the histogram's cell intervals, the general and continuous areas under the normal curve will be used.

Since statistical stability has been assumed, that is, the past is representative of what can be expected in the future, the normal distribution can be used to estimate the probability of forecast errors (stock-outs and surpluses) in the future. Since the normal distribution occurs so often, tables of areas (probabilities) under the curve have been developed and are available in just about any text on statistics analysis.

Management can ask questions about the area (probability of forecast error) under the normal curve and use the table to get specific answers. It is also possible to get general information by simply examining the curve itself (Fig. 10-10). For instance, what proportion of the total area under the normal curve is to the left of zero error? Half, or .5 is correct. Forecast errors to the left of zero (−differences) indicate that actual demand was less than forecast demand. This means that a surplus was generated. Supply had more than met demand. No safety stock would have been needed 50 per cent of the time. Forecast errors to the right of zero means that actual demand was greater than forecast demand and a shortage was generated. A stock-out occurred. A safety stock would have prevented the stock-out because it is designed to guard against the possibility that actual demand is greater than forecast or that actual lead time is longer than expected. In usual practice, because management has such a dread of stock-outs, the investment in an overabundant safety stock over long periods of time is far more expensive than the cost of stock-outs. It is the exceptional manager who has ever made a rigorous attempt to determine the actual cost of stock-outs. Rather, the cost of carrying extra stock (which can easily be calculated) seems a small price to pay when compared to the "horror" of a stock-out. So the imbalance is extreme and the cumulative cost is exorbitant.

The attempt to maintain a safety stock that provides for protection against all possible variations in lead time or demand is, therefore, unreasonable and very expensive. A more intelligent systems approach is to set a predetermined number of stock-outs out of so many reorder cycles as an acceptable limit and then design an inventory control system on this quantitative basis.

For instance, in the example, the reorder cycle is four weeks. If management is prepared to accept one stock-out in every twenty-four reorder cycles, this can be a reasonable basis for calculating the amount of safety stock needed. This represents about a 4 percent probability of stock-out, that is, one out of twenty-four reorder cycles, or a 96 percent probability of not having any stock-outs.

From previous discussion of the mean and the standard deviation in Chapter 9, the mean ± two standard deviations encompasses 95.45 percent (quite close to 96 percent) of the area under the normal curve. However, the probability of no shortage is the objective; therefore, the area equivalent to 96 percent must be measured from one extremity (the left, or surplus part) of the curve not on each side of the mean. Looking up the amount of standard deviation from the mean that encompasses 96 percent of the area (in a standard table), it is found that 1.65 standard deviations from the mean (plus the other half of the area) encompasses 96 percent of the total area. Calculating the standard deviation of the distribution of forecast errors (42.5) and multiplying by 1.65 indicates that a safety stock of some seventy units will provide enough protection so that stock-outs should not occur more than once in every twenty-four reorder cycles.

Representing what has been developed in graphical terms and referring to Figure 10-13, it can be seen that it is the graph for a typical inventory situation. There is a certain amount in inventory at the beginning of the cycle (800 units). A certain amount of stock is used each time period. The sloping line indicates the rate of usage. If the reorder quantity comes in just when the amount of stock gets down to zero, the usage during the inventory cycle was just equal to the manager's estimate and there is no forecast error.

It is important to note that the most critical period is during the lead time. If the usage rate changes after the reorder cycle begins, there may be trouble. That is, from the time the replenishment order is

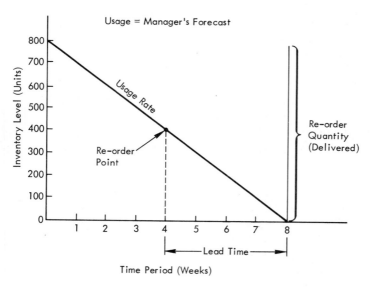

FIGURE 10-13

Inventory Control

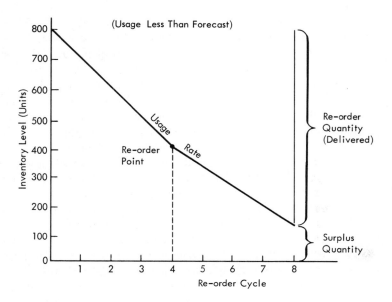

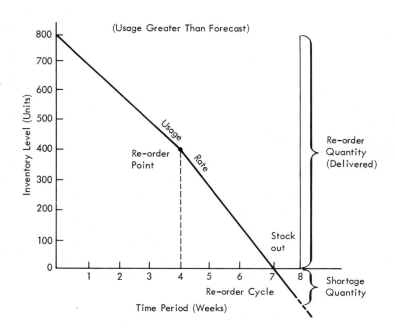

FIGURE 10-14

Inventory Control

initiated (the reorder point) until it is delivered (the reorder cycle) is the period of greatest vulnerability for a stock-out to occur if the usage rate were to increase. A surplus would occur if the usage rate decreased.

If the usage rate was not exactly equal to what was forecast, the usage line would not go to zero at the time the reorder was delivered. It would show some quantity in stock (surplus) or show a stock-out condition (zero stock) when the reorder was received.

The two sawtooth patterns in Fig. 10-14 show two inventory cycles. The first shows a usage rate less than expected (surplus); the second shows a usage rate more than expected (stock-out).

Notice that the usage rate is shown to change during the reorder cycle. This is the most critical time in that it is the time when the inventory control system is most vulnerable. If the usage rate had changed prior to that time, it would have been reflected in the later or earlier reorder point and in a possible adjustment of the reorder quantity. But after the reorder cycle begins, the control system is committed. It is during this period that safety stock can be most useful.

A stock-out is generally considered the most costly, by far, in most inventory situations, and therefore it will be the subject of the example that follows. In the case of a surplus being the more costly, the same approach can be followed, but with the minimizing of the surplus as the objective.

To come to a decision on when to order, that is, the size of safety stock to carry, from a quantitative point of view (as has been discussed before), it is necessary that the normal curve be viewed not only as a graphical representation of the distribution of forecast errors but also as a measure of the chances that particular forecast error will occur. In other words, the normal curve can be used to determine the probability of occurrence of forecast errors of a certain size. This in turn will give the necessary information to provide an adequate safety stock commensurate with a reasonable investment in such safety stock.

Combining the normal curve and the sawtooth wave form of inventory performance (Fig. 10-15) will provide a clearer idea of how the setting of a certain acceptable maximum (4 percent in the example) of stock-outs can be converted into the necessary safety stock.

If a manager wanted to protect himself from stock-outs, say 96 percent of the time (about once in every twenty-four reorder cycles), he could read the required safety stock of seventy units from the graph. Of course, the relative cumulative frequency histogram would give him the same answer. If he wanted to take the time and make the effort required, he could go through the mathematics of calculating standard deviation and get an even more accurate answer. But it would be almost the same (seventy units), give or take a few units.

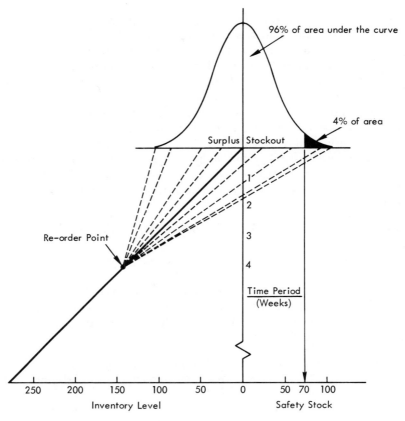

96% of area under the curve

4% of area

Surplus | Stockout

1

2

3

4

Time Period
(Weeks)

Re-order Point

250   200   150   100   50   0   50 70 100

Inventory Level   Safety Stock

FIGURE 10-15

Combined Normal and Sawtooth Curves

The answer to the question, when to order?, therefore, depends on the variation, if any, of demand and lead time. If neither varies, it is child's play to multiply demand per unit time by lead time to arrive at the quantity of inventory on hand (the reorder point) at which to reorder. But if demand or lead time varies, statistical analysis and the laws of probability must be considered. Using the techniques outlined in this discussion, the systems analyst can determine the safety stock needed to provide the level of inventory performance (percentage of stock-outs) commensurate with cost and service standards. This safety stock added to the previously determined quantity of inventory (at static demand and lead time) determines the reorder point and answers the question, When to order?

Varying Demand and Varying Lead Time.   When both demand and lead time vary, a compound analysis with interacting normal distributions is a necessity. Luckily, techniques of inventory analysis using numerical methods developed by experts in the field have been worked out and are available. Many of the methods have been programmed for the computer so that historical data, decision criteria, and quantitative cost and service constraints can be input to the program and run on the computer, and a customized inventory control system can be produced. As easy as it may sound, the implementation of such a program requires accurate data, sound judgment, and nerve. The Management Information System that integrates inventory control into its structure will have provided a major element in a total systems approach.

PROGRAM EVALUATION AND REVIEW TECHNIQUE (PERT)

Management has used a variety of project control techniques over the years. Variations of the Gantt chart discussed in Chapter 7 have been used for scheduling and control. However, this most universal of scheduling and control tools has serious shortcomings, which were listed in Chapter 7 as part of the introduction to the Line of Balance study. Recapping, they are:

1. It does not relate tasks and subtasks to other tasks and subtasks. That is, there is no easy way to relate delay in one task to its effect on any other task.

2. The Gantt chart does not identify the sequence of critical tasks that determine the overall time span of the project. The critical tasks are those that if completed on schedule will insure that the overall project is completed on schedule.

3. There is no provision for identifying reallocatable resources from one task to another—no way to identify idle resources for redirecting to another task that may have need for them.

The PERT technique, developed initially for managing the Polaris weapons system, overcomes all these shortcomings.

What is PERT?

PERT is normally referred to as a planning and controlling device for use on complex projects. In essence, PERT is partially evolutionary and partially new. It draws upon Gantt charting, Line of Balance, and milestone reporting systems. The PERT system is a technique that simulates a complex project by use of a rigorously defined quantitative/symbolic model. It is a dynamic rather than a static model in that it reacts auto-matically to changes.

The PERT model consists of an estimated network of activities and events providing information from which the manager can determine whether schedule requirements will be met. It also permits him to deter-mine which activities (jobs or tasks) are most critical and should have close scrutiny. It also informs management of non-critical jobs so that manpower and other resources can be used more economically.

Also, after the project is in progress and changes to the plan be-come apparent because of the introduction of new requirements, slippages, and so forth, the PERT model can be adjusted and experimented with to determine the necessary action that must be taken to meet the project schedule.

PERT Definitions

Two simple conventions are used in PERT networking. An activity is shown as an arrow and represents the application of a resource over a period of time for some specific purpose. Design of a tool, assembly of a component, machining of a part, and final inspection are all examples of activities.

An event, usually shown as a circle, represents a definable instant in time at which something happens. Completion of final inspection, start of manufacturing, and completion of engineering design are all examples of events.

Event circles are often identified by a C or an S to identify the event as the "completion" or "start" of a particular activity. They also often contain a descriptive legend plus a number for ease of reference.

A final symbol used in a PERT network is the dashed arrow representing a "dummy activity." It connects events that require no expendi-

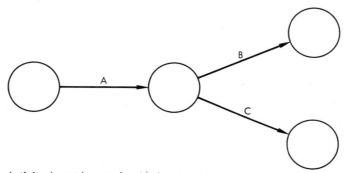

ture of resource between them but have some constraint connection. That is, one event must occur before the second (connected by the dummy activity) can be considered to have occurred. In a very real sense, a dashed arrow acts as a constraint on the event the arrowhead touches.

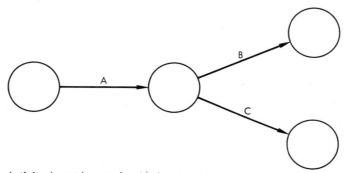

Activity A must be completed before B or C can start.

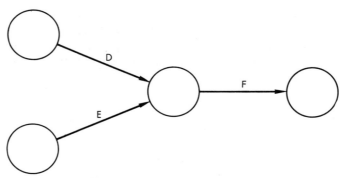

F cannot start until both D and E are completed.

PERT networks consist of combinations of interrelated activities and events indicating the sequence in which resources will be applied. Using the symbolic conventions described, the complete logic, that is, the sequence of planned jobs, tasks, and subtasks (activities) can be represented by a PERT network. Figure 10-16 demonstrates, for a simple project, how a PERT network represents the planned sequence of activities.

This network can be interpreted as follows: At the outset, work

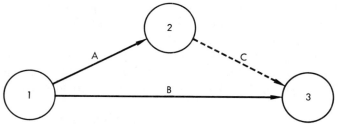

Event 3 cannot be considered to have occurred until Event 2 has occurred. The dummy activity arrow C provides this constraint.

can start on the design of the product. Since the test facility is not dependent upon product design characteristics, its construction can also be started immediately. When the product is fully designed, the manufacture of the product and its shipping container (which must fit its dimensions precisely) can begin. When both the product and the test facility fabrication are complete, the product testing is performed. Finally, when the tests and the container fabrication are both complete, the product is packed.

It is important to notice that the description in each event represents the start or completion of an activity and not the activity itself. For example, event No. 6 described as "Product X Test Complete" indicates that activity 5–6 represents the job of testing Product X.

After the network has been set up and the events and the sequence of activities have been reviewed for accuracy, time estimates

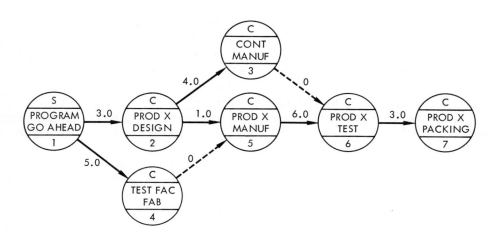

FIGURE 10-16

A PERT Network

are made for each activity. Estimates of the number of weeks required to complete activity are shown in the center of each activity arrow of the sample network. The time estimates represent elapsed time that will be required to perform the effort at normal manpower levels, working straight time only and assuming the availability of required machine time. The estimates are made *without* regard to any imposed schedule require-ments.

This last point is one of the major advantages of the PERT tech-nique. Knowledgeable project members preplan the events and the se-quence of activities and the resources required. This preplanning has proven very valuable in uncovering potential trouble spots even before the project begins.

PERT/Time Scheduling

The scheduling process involves first the determination of the *earliest* time at which each event may be expected to occur and the *latest* time at which each event can be permitted to occur. "Earliest event time" is determined by starting at the first event and working forward answer-ing the question, What is the earliest that this event can occur and still satisfy all the constraints?

"Latest event time" is determined by starting at the last event and working back through the network answering the question, What is the latest that this event can occur and still complete the project on schedule?

Thus, if Event 1 in Figure 10-17 can occur on week zero, Event 2 can occur as early as week three and Event 4 as early as week five. Event 5, which has two activities leading into it, can occur as early as week five. (Note that were it not for activity 4–5, Event 5 could occur by week four.) This process of adding activity times forward through the network is continued to the last event. These earliest event times are indicated by numbers enclosed in rectangles at the left of each event in Figure 10-17. We can see that the project is expected to take fourteen weeks to complete.

If a fourteen-week elapsed time is permissible, the latest event time for Event 7 is fourteen weeks. Now subtracting times backward through the network, starting with Event 7, we can determine the latest time for every other event. The latest event time for Event 6 is week eleven, for Event 5 it is week five, and so forth. (Note that if only activity 2–3 tailed into Event 2, the latest event time for Event 2 would

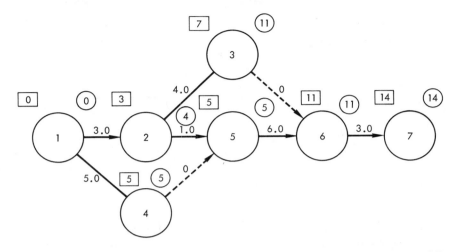

FIGURE 10-17
PERT/Time Scheduling

have been week seven rather than week four.) The latest times are shown to the right of the event enclosed in a small circle in Figure 10-17. If only twelve weeks had been permitted for the completion of the project, the latest event times would have been adjusted simply by assigning week twelve as the latest event time for Event 7 and working backward. Having established the earliest and latest event time for each event, each of the activities can now be scheduled; that is, the date of earliest expected completion and latest permissible completion for each activity can be determined. The reasoning used to determine these earliest and latest completion dates is as follows: If Event 1 occurs on day zero, activities 1–2 and 1–4 can start on day zero. Since Event 2 can occur at the latest at week four, the latest completion date for activity 1–2 is week four. Thus, the *latest completion date* for each activity is equal to the latest event date for the event that it precedes or for the event it leads into. To determine the *earliest completion date* for an activity, we must add the earliest start date of the activity (which is the earliest event date of the preceding event) and the activity duration time. Since activity 2–5 can start as early as week three, week four is the earliest completion date for this activity. The complete schedule is shown in Table 10-3. Now that the total length of the project has been determined to be fourteen weeks, it may be necessary to adjust the plan in order to meet a twelve-week schedule.

TABLE 10-3

PERT/Time Schedule

Activity	Latest Complete	Earliest Complete	Slack	Duration
1–2	4	3	1	3
1–4	5	5	0	5
2–3	11	7	4	4
2–5	5	4	1	1
3–6	11	7	4	0
4–5	5	5	0	0
5–6	11	11	0	6
6–7	14	14	0	3

CRITICAL PATH   Before the plan can be intelligently adjusted, the *critical path* must be determined. The critical path is the longest path from the beginning to the end of the project. It is defined as the path of activities having the least positive or the most negative slack. If every activity on the critical path is kept on schedule, the overall project will meet its schedule. It determines the overall time to complete the project.

Slack is calculated as the difference between the earliest and the latest completion times for each activity. The slack associated with each activity is tabulated in the fourth column of Table 10-3. The tabulations are in activity number sequence. The tabulation in Table 10-4 is identical except that all activities have been arranged in sequence of ascending slack, or critical path. We see from this listing that the path of least slack, the critical path, goes from Events 1 to 4 to 5 to 6 to 7. Additionally, there is a slack path having one week of positive slack going through Events 1, 2, and 5 and a four-week path going through 2, 3, and 6. Since the critical path is the longest path through the network, any cutting of time must be achieved by cutting activity times on the path.

TABLE 10-4

Activity	Latest Complete	Earliest Complete	Slack	Duration
1–4	5	5	0	5
4–5	5	5	0	0
5–6	11	11	0	6
6–7	14	14	0	3
1–2	4	3	1	3
2–5	5	4	1	1
2–3	11	7	4	4
3–6	11	7	4	0

The Meaning of Slack   One important feature of slack should be understood. Though a slack value is shown for each activity, the slack value actually applies to the path of activities rather than to each activity individually. This feature of slack is demonstrated in Figure 10-18. The jobs to be performed in sequence here are activities A, B, and C. Activity A requires two weeks, activity B requires three weeks, and activity C requires two weeks. Activity A can be completed as early as week 2 or as late as week 4 if the other activities are squeezed to the right of the time scale. Consequently, activity A has a slack of two weeks. Similarly, since activity C can be completed as early as week 7 or as late as week 9, it too has two weeks of slack. Moreover, activity B has two weeks of slack, since it can be completed as early as week 5 or as late as week 7. However, it is readily seen that only two weeks of slack exist between week zero and week 9. The slack values of jobs along a particular path are not additive. Each slack value applies to the path as a whole. If two weeks of slack are consumed in performing activity A, activities B and C will have no slack. Slack may be defined in many ways. As has previously been explained, it is calculated as the difference between earliest and latest completion dates for each activity. It can also be defined as the leeway that exists for the activity if all previous activities end at the earliest possible time and all succeeding activities begin at the latest possible time. It can also be defined as the permissive slippage for an activity.

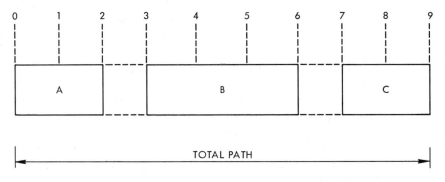

TOTAL PATH

FIGURE 10-18

Slack Value

PERT Monitoring Procedure

Up to this point the PERT process has been used only for initial planning purposes. After the project commences, however, its use can be continued as a dynamic progress monitoring model for decision making. The monitoring procedure requires that periodically each responsible department provide information regarding the status of certain activities within its responsibilities.

First, for all activities that were scheduled for completion during the reporting period, the actual date of completion is reported if completion occurred. If completion of the activities did not occur during the reporting period, a change in time estimates for those activities is reported, projecting a new earliest completion date into the next or subsequent reporting periods.

Second, any activities that have been added to the network during the preceding two weeks because of changes to plans together with their associated time estimates are reported.

Third, any activities that have been deleted from the plan during the previous reporting period are reported.

This is all that is required for the routine monitoring function. With these inputs of information, the network model is revised and recomputed to develop new schedule and slack values and a new expected end date for the program. If the impact of changes on the required dates is undesirable, a suitable change can be made in future plans.

TIME ESTIMATES   It is obvious that a PERT network is an accurate model of the program only if time estimates for each activity are realistic. Times that have arbitrarily been compressed to meet a required delivery are worse than useless in projecting valid future assumptions, since they may have the effect of camouflaging the need for management action. Every effort should be made to make time estimates as objective and as unbiased as possible.

Many projects consist, at least partially, of jobs that have never previously been performed. Accurate estimates for such jobs cannot readily be determined. the PERT method of time estimating overcomes this difficulty by permitting the estimator to provide three time estimates —the optimistic, the pessimistic, and the most likely. This allows the estimator to reflect the degree of uncertainty he feels is inherent in the estimate.

The *optimistic* time (*a*) is defined as the time that would be required if everything went better than usual. If the job were performed one hundred times, without benefit of previous experience, the optimistic time would be met or bettered only once.

The *most likely time* (*m*) is defined as the actual time that would be required most often if the activity were repeated under the same conditions many times.

The *pessimistic* time (*b*) is defined as the time that would be required if significantly worse luck than usual were encountered. If the job were repeated many times, without benefit of past experience, the pessimistic time or longer would be required only about one time out of a hundred.

Where only one time estimate is required, the most likely time is given. It should be noted that many PERT networks use one time estimate because it has been found that all the estimates tend to change as experience is gained and spending too much time developing three time estimates is just not practical. Experience indicates that engineers are usually optimistic and operations people are unduly pessimistic when providing time estimates. A conscientious effort should be made to overcome these tendencies.

The three time estimates are used to calculate the expected time (*te*) of the duration of an activity. This calculation is made by using this formula:

$$te = \frac{a + 4m + b}{6}$$

The expected time is then used to calculate the earliest (*TE*) and the latest (*TL*) completion times discussed previously.

Program Evaluation and Review Technique has proved itself over the years to be a very effective systems control technique. It provides an organized structure for interrelating the resource time schedules of a complex project. It has been applied with significant success to projects as diverse as staging a Broadway musical and producing a prototype airplane. There is much literature available on the subject, and it would be a unique project indeed that could not find a PERT article that described a similar application in some other organization. Intelligent use of this rich body of resource literature will help insure the success of other applications of the PERT technique.

The PERT technique has of course been programmed for the computer. This relieves the user of much of the tedium of the calculations and provides extremely quick response to changes in the network. Prepackaged programs will be discussed in Chapter 13.

REVIEW QUESTIONS

1.   What is meant by the ABC concept of control?
2.   Explain the 100 percent and the 50 percent limits to learning rates.
3.   The first 120 units required a total of 1,440 man-hours. The first 240 units required a total of 2,592 man-hours. What is the learning rate?
4.   What two basic questions are fundamental to every inventory control system?
5.   If the yearly demand is 1,600 units, procurement cost for paper-work preparation and administrative costs is twenty-five dollars per order, and carrying charges are twenty-five cents per unit per year, what is the Economical Ordering Quantity?
6.   Utilizing the EOQ nomograph in Figure 10-9 and the facts in question 5, what is the EOQ if the item's unit price is one dollar?
7.   What are the steps in converting a mass of data on a particular phenomenon into a cumulative frequency distribution?
8.   What is meant by statistical stability?
9.   What is PERT?
10. Identify a possible PERT project. Simulate duration times and the sequence of events and activities. Draw the PERT diagram, identify the critical path, and then calculate latest completion times, earliest completion times, and slack.

BIBLIOGRAPHY

BOCK, ROBERT H., and WILLIAM K. HOLSTEIN, *Production Planning and Control*. Columbus, Ohio: Charles E. Merrill Books, Inc., 1963. Includes a variety of readings integrated with text material to provide an interesting and helpful treatment.

BUFFA, ELWOOD S., *Modern Production Management* (2nd ed.). New York: John Wiley & Sons, Inc., 1965. A very helpful book that provides a great deal of specific explanation in understandable terms. Covers a wide spectrum of tools and techniques.

COCHRAN, E. B., *Planning Production Costs: Using the Improvement Curve*. Scranton, Pa.: International Textbook Company, 1968. A very detailed, how-to approach to the use of the learning curve. Diagrams, actual data, and practical examples illustrate the use of the techniques.

HEIN, LEONARD W., *The Quantitative Approach to Managerial Decisions.* Englewood Cliffs, N. J.: Prentice-Hall, Inc., 1967. Presents a number of systems control techniques in both an understandable and a rigorous way. One of the best treatments available.

McGARRAH, ROBERT E., *Production and Logistics Management.* New York: John Wiley & Sons, Inc., 1963. Examines the quantitative techniques in terms of concrete applications.

MILLER, ROBERT W., *Schedule, Cost and Profit Control with PERT.* New York: McGraw-Hill Book Company, 1963. Emphasizes the problems of program management, especially the planning and control problems associated with special-purpose projects.

ROTHFELD, STUART M., *PERT COST.* Paramus, N.J.; Federal Electric Corp., 1964. The presentation is in the form of programmed instruction and the content is very good.

STARR, M. K., and B. W. MILLER, *Inventory Control: Theory and Practice.* Englewood Cliffs, N. J.: Prentice-Hall, Inc., 1962. Excellent examples and rigorous treatment.

11

OPERATIONS RESEARCH
FOR THE SYSTEMS ANALYST

A COMMONSENSE LOOK AT OPERATIONS RESEARCH

In the preceding chapters a number of Management Information Systems tools and techniques were discussed. A characteristic of almost all of them is that they are generally used in separate applications. That is, they are designed to be applied to solve problems, but with little, if any, attempt to relate the problem and its solution to the organization's overall objectives. In the last thirty years, a body of quantitative decision techniques has been developed that is referred to as *Operations Research*. It uses quantitative techniques and systems concepts to solve problems in terms of the organization's overall systems requirements and objectives.

Operations Research, also referred to as OR and *management science*, originated in England during the early part of World War II. Special teams of scientists, engineers, statisticians, and other technical as well as military experts were brought together to solve difficult problems of logistics, scheduling, and allocation of resources. Their assignments included, for example, establishing the most effective bombing patterns for attacks on enemy targets, finding ways to improve the efficiency of the aerial mining of Japanese-controlled waters during "Operation Starvation," and determining what size merchant convoys would be most effective in terms of reducing losses from submarine actions and requiring a minimum of escort vessels. Military authorities called these groups of specialists "operations research teams."

The many scientists, engineers, statisticians, and other professionals drafted into OR units during the war developed great respect for their new activity. When they returned to civilian life, they promoted Operations Research to industry and other nonmilitary organizations. The first OR programs were established by educational institutions. Case Institute of Technology, Columbia University, Massachusetts Institute of Technology, and others set up courses in nonmilitary applications of Operations Research. Some university professors also began to offer OR consulting services to industry, and as successful applications multiplied, the tools and techniques of OR gradually spread throughout industry.

Definition of Operations Research

There are many definitions of the term *Operations Research* in current literature. One of the best definitions is given by the American Management Association, which calls Operations Research a "scientific methodology—analytical, experimental, quantitative—which, by assessing the over-all implications of various alternative courses of action in a management system, provides an improved basis for management decisions."

A basic concept of Operations Research (and for that matter, the systems concept) is that all the functions of a business or other organization are interrelated. This is a characteristic of the systems concept. So if one key element changes, all are affected. To improve decision making to meet these changing conditions, management would like to know, in advance, what the results of a proposed change would be. But there can be many alternative solutions to a particular management problem, and managers have to decide which of a number of alternative courses of action is the best. This is where the specific techniques of OR apply. They examine the many alternatives to a problem and quantify the probable results.

Operations Research (management science) techniques such as linear programming, Monte Carlo, queuing theory, and simulation, for example, can examine, rapidly and accurately, the many alternatives to a management problem and can quantify the results. Then management can add its own judgment to select the best alternative. It is worth repeating, then—an important function of OR is to test alternative solutions to a problem by using mathematical as well as other techniques and to quantify the results for management evaluation.

GENERAL STEPS IN APPLYING OR

In solving a management problem using Operations Research, two things are usually determined at the start. What is the objective and what are the factors influencing it? Typical objectives might be lowest cost, maximum profit, most efficient use of resources, or shortest production cycle. In the language of Operations Research, the objective is called a *measure of effectiveness* and the influencing factors are called *variables*.

Selecting a measure of effectiveness can often be difficult because of conflicting viewpoints in the organization. Consider inventory level in a company, for example. A manufacturing executive wants to cut costs by having long production runs, resulting in a large inventory of standard items. The marketing manager agrees about large inventories, but he never wants to give up a customer to a competitor, so he also wants many models, types, and sizes. The finance man, on the other hand, concerned with the large amount of money tied up in inventory, wants inventories kept to their smallest possible levels. The executives of this company will have to make a basic policy decision regarding what is an acceptable measure of effectiveness in terms of the company's overall objectives. Without it, all the OR in the world will not help optimize inventory levels.

This need for a carefully defined, measurable objective is a key reason why OR helps management look at problems from an organization-wide viewpoint. OR treats the organization as a total integrated system —which is exactly what it is!

After OR structures problems in terms of overall objectives, the alternatives are tested and measured on a mathematical model. A mathematical model is an approximation of reality—something to stand in place of the real thing. It is necessary because it would be too costly and risky to interrupt operations to try out the possible alternative solutions to a problem. Therefore, to experiment with different approaches, something is needed to stand in the place of the real operations. That is where mathematics comes in. When a basic relationship between separate activities in an organization is expressed in terms of a mathematical equation, we call it a mathematical *model*. One side of the equation is the measure of effectiveness; the other side represents all the variables that can affect it. As specific OR techniques are discussed, a variety of very useful mathematical models will be presented. Each has been developed to fit specific problem situations in management systems.

As was stated previously, the model of a problem in an organization consists of the important variables of the system related mathematically. Its function is to represent the problem situation in a simplified, theoretical form. Once constructed, the model can be manipulated by management to determine the effects on the system of changes in certain variables.

A mathematical model is like a model airplane in a wind tunnel. The model stands for the real thing. They both are used for the same reasons. By changing the variables that affect the model airplane's performance—wind velocity, direction, etc.—the effects of these changes on the real airplane are determined. Many different answers to the same problem can be tried by using different models under different conditions, and much less is at stake if mistakes are made.

TOOLS AND TECHNIQUES OF OR

It may surprise some people, but many techniques that were developed over the years in a variety of disciplines such as mathematics, statistics, and industrial engineering are being used by operations researchers. For instance, charts, graphs, and nomographs are efficient aids in summarizing results of model manipulation, in making visual presentations, and in serving as daily working tools. In addition, many other established tools like statistical inference, work sampling, time-and-motion study, work simplification, flow charting and methods analysis are often very useful inputs to an Operations Research effort. The advent of the new OR tools have supplemented, not supplanted, the old. They have expanded the decision maker's horizon so that he can consider the overall system. OR provides the systems analyst with powerful allies in his campaign for an effective MIS. An overview of the major tools and techniques of OR will give the systems analyst useful insights into their strengths and weaknesses. The Bibliography provides a rich array of reference books for detailed study of any of the following techniques.

Linear Programming (LP)

Linear programming is an Operations Research technique that allocates *resources* (men, materials, machines, money) to *demand* (work orders, customer demand, production orders, budget requests, etc.). It solves problems that involve the allocating of limited resources among many competing demands. Since all the allocation decisions are inter-related, they are made under the same set of constraints. That is, the restrictions of the system apply to all the resources and demands.

Allocating customer work orders to production machines is a case in point. There are only so many machine hours available (resources) and the customer orders require a certain number of hours (demand). Not only must total hours required balance total hours available but each order must compete with every other order for the limited machine time available. Linear programming evaluates the many possible alterna-tives in this situation. An example of the complexity that can develop is to consider a relatively simple production problem involving only nine work orders and nine machines. It can be shown that there are 362,880 possible ways of allocating orders to machines!

LP develops the absolutely "best" solution, such that no other is better, by comparing all the possible solutions and selecting the best solution depending on the measures of effectiveness selected by man-agement.

Mathematical expressions are used to describe the conditions of the problem. The restrictions on the decision variables involved are called *constraints*. The measure of effectiveness that it is desired to maximize is called the *objective function*. The constraints, the decision variables, and the objective function make up the mathematical model that describes the problem to be resolved.

All the mathematical expressions in the model are to the first degree, that is, they each plot as a straight line (they are linear). *Pro-gramming* refers to the step-by-step procedure for developing the optimum solution by selecting the best combination of allocations of resources to demand from all the feasible alternatives. In summary then, linear programming is a technique that utilizes a mathematical model composed of linear functions in order to determine the optimum assignment of resources to demand by selecting the best from among feasible alternatives.

Linear Programming Example: Utilizing Available Capacity to Maximize Profit

A company's production schedule indicates a certain amount of excess capacity in two departments. Management would like to utilize this capacity in order to maximize profit. It is known that the manu-facturing capacity of the departments involved can be utilized for the production of either or both of two different products. Each product requires processing through the two departments. Both of these products are in great demand, and the sales department is sure that all units produced can be sold. The constraints in this situation are the available production capacity in each of the two departments. The decision variables would be the number of units (if any) of each of the two products that would be produced. Profit is the measure of effectiveness to be maximized and therefore the profit per unit of product times the number of units produced and sold would be the objective function. The table below summarizes the specifics of the problem:

	Time Available (Hours per Week)	Time Required (Hours per Unit)	
		Product 1	Product 2
Dept. A	48	3	1
Dept. B	120	3	4
Profit (per unit)		$5	$6

Developing the Mathematical Model

Decision variables.   X and Y will represent the number of units of each product to be produced per week.

Constraints.   The time required to produce one unit of product multiplied by the number of units to be produced per week is limited by the amount of machine time available in each department. The total time required must be less than ($<$) or equal to ($=$) the time available. These constraints can be expressed mathematically as follows:

$$3X + Y \le 48$$
$$3X + 4Y \le 120$$

Furthermore, the mathematical model requires all possible constraints to be expressed; therefore, since "negative product" cannot be made

$$X \ge 0 \quad Y \ge 0$$

Objective function.   The profit function is expressed as the profit per unit multiplied by the number of units to be produced. This is the function to be maximized. Let P represent profit, and so:

$$P = 5X + 6Y$$

SUMMARIZING THE LINEAR PROGRAMMING MATHEMATICAL MODEL:
Maximize

$$P = 5X + 6Y$$

Subject to the constraints

$$3X + Y \leq 48$$
$$3X + 4Y \leq 120$$
$$X \geq 0 \qquad Y \geq 0$$

The method that will be used to solve this problem is the *simplex method*, which solves any linear programming problem. It is an algebraic procedure which arrives at optimality by means of a well-defined iterative process. It is particularly well suited for electronic computers, and real life problems would be solved that way. This problem will be solved manually to illustrate the method.

The Simplex Method.

Maximize

$$P = 5X + 6Y$$

Subject to

$$3X + Y \leq 48$$
$$3X + 4Y \leq 120 \qquad X, Y \geq 0$$

1. Introduce *slack* variables to express the constraints as equations.

$$3X + Y + S_1 = 48$$
$$3X + 4Y + S_2 = 120 \qquad S_1, S_2 \geq 0$$

2. Develop a tableau, from the coefficients and constants.

X	Y	S_1	S_2	$-P$		
3	1	1	0	0		48
3	4	0	1	0		120
5	6	0	0	1		0

3. Select the variable with the largest coefficient in the objective row and identify with a vertical arrow (see above). This is called the *pivot column.*

4. Divide the *constant column* (right-hand column) by the corresponding coefficients in the pivot column (identified by ↑). The ratios are $48/1$ and $120/4$.

5. Select the smaller of the ratios developed above, identify that row (the *pivot row*) by a horizontal arrow ($\leftarrow$). This is the limiting ratio. See below:

X	Y	S_1	S_2	$-P$		
3	1	1	0	0	48	$(48/_1)$
3	④	0	1	0	120	$(120/_4)$ $\leftarrow$
5	6	0	0	1	0	

$\uparrow$

6. The intersection of the pivot column and the pivot row is the *pivot element*. It is converted to 1 and the other elements in the column to 0 by use of matrix algebra manipulation called *row operations*.
7. The next tableau is the result of converting the pivot column to 0s and 1 by means of row operations:

a. Divide second row by 4.
b. Subtract new second row from old first row.
c. Multiply new second row by 6 and subtract from old third row.

X	Y	S_1	S_2	$-P$	
⑨⁄₄	0	1	$-\frac{1}{4}$	0	18 $(18/\frac{9}{4})$ $\leftarrow$
¾	1	0	¼	0	30 $(30/\frac{3}{4})$
¾	0	0	$-\frac{6}{4}$	1	-180

$\uparrow$

Note: *Row* operations rather than *column* because a row is an equation and can be operated on as long as whatever is done is done to both sides. Operating similarly on columns would not be substituting equals for equals and would therefore not be correct.
8. Examine the new tableau for the largest coefficient in the objective function and identify it with $\uparrow$. Then find the smallest (limiting) ratio ($\leftarrow$) by dividing the pivot column coefficients into the corresponding constants. This determines the pivot row and therefore the pivot element (see above).
9. Use row operations to convert the pivot element to 1 and other pivot column elements to 0.

a. Multiply first row by $\tfrac{4}{9}$.
b. Multiply new first row by $-\tfrac{3}{4}$ and add to old second row.
c. Multiply new first row by $-\tfrac{3}{4}$ and add to old third row.

X	Y	S_1	S_2	$-P$	
1	0	$\tfrac{4}{9}$	$-\tfrac{1}{9}$	0	8
0	1	$-\tfrac{1}{3}$	$\tfrac{1}{3}$	0	24
0	0	$-\tfrac{2}{9}$	$-1\tfrac{3}{9}$	1	-184

10. The above tableau is now in *canonical* form. That is, the coefficients of the objective row in the tableau are 0 or —. The solution is optimal. Values can be read directly from the tableau.

Optimal solution: Produce 8 of Product 1 ... (X)
Produce 24 of Product 2 ... (Y)
Maximum Profit = $184

LP DISTRIBUTION METHODS   Interestingly enough, many allocation-type problems are characterized by units of resources having to be allocated to unitary demand.

These are the simplest of the linear programming problems, and the LP techniques used to solve them are generally referred to as *distribution* methods. The key characteristic of such problems is that resources and demand must be handled as whole units (trucks, refrigerators, people, etc.). In LP terms, the coefficients of the variables in the problem are either 0 or 1. When such is the case, the *distribution* methods of linear programming are simple and effective. For example, they can be employed to find an optimum solution to the problem of redistributing empty material-handling skids, unassigned manpower, or critical parts at the lowest cost to various customers or departments according to their needs.

Of course, if the parameters of the problem preclude the use of one of the distribution methods of linear programming, the simplex method of LP can be used. As has been mentioned, it is much more general in scope of application but is also more complex to set up and to solve. All LP methods are extremely time-consuming if done by hand, and this is the reason that electronic computers are, in most instances, a necessity for performing the mechanical calculations. All the popular LP techniques are available in the libraries of most large computer installations. In addition, *approximation* LP techniques have been developed to lighten the load when computation must be done by hand. They do not always give the best result, but they come very close.

The following is a detailed explanation and application of the steps involved in solving an allocation problem using two of the distribution methods (Water-Stone and MODI) and then using one of the simplest of the linear programming approximation techniques. It is called the *Vogel approximation method* (VAM) and is a worthwhile addition to the repertory of any systems analyst.

The *Vogel approximation method* is the only one recommended for pencil and paper solution. All the others should utilize a "canned" LP program on the computer. Remember, the advent of time sharing terminals allows the user to apply computer packages from locations that are remote from any computer installation.

The Transportation (Stepping-Stone, Water-Stone) Method

The Problem: Allocate supplies to customer demand at minimum total transportation cost.

Warehouse Location	Supply		Customer Location	Demand
Baltimore	100 units		Atlanta	70 units
Raleigh	20 units		Columbia	10 units
Savannah	40 units		Jacksonville	30 units
Total Supply	160 units		Richmond	50 units
			Total Demand	160 units

Mileage: From	To: Atlanta	Columbia	Jacksonville	Richmond
Baltimore	640	500	770	140
Raleigh	370	200	480	240
Savannah	250	140	150	480

Shipping Costs: Since it costs 10¢ per unit per mile to distribute this product, the distribution costs per unit are:

From	To: Atlanta	Columbia	Jacksonville	Richmond
Baltimore	$64	$50	$77	$14
Raleigh	37	20	48	24
Savannah	25	14	15	48

Step 1. Express the problem in a distribution matrix. List resources on the left and demand across the top, with quantities opposite. These quantities are called the rim conditions of the problem (Fig. 11-1).

To From	Atlanta	Columbia	Jacksonville	Richmond	Supply
Baltimore					100
Raleigh					20
Savannah					40
Demand	70	10	30	50	160 160

FIGURE 11-1

Rim Conditions

If the total demand is not exactly equal to the total supply (that is, if the rim conditions are not balanced) add a dummy warehouse location to supply the greater demand or a dummy customer location to purchase the excess supply, as the case may be.

Step 2. For a *Cost Matrix* show the unit cost as negative values within each square (Fig. 11-2).

For a *Profit Matrix* profit should be shown as positive values within each square. If a dummy warehouse or customer were needed to balance the

To From	Atlanta	Columbia	Jacksonville	Richmond	Supply
Baltimore	−64	−50	−77	−14	100
Raleigh	−37	−20	−48	−24	20
Savannah	−25	−14	−15	−48	40
Demand	70	10	30	50	160 160

FIGURE 11-2

Distribution Matrix with Rim Conditions and Unit Costs

rim conditions the unit costs associated with the dummy are assumed to be zero.

Step 3.   Establish an initial solution. The 'Northwest Corner' method is a widely used, but arbitrary technique for developing an initial solution. It proceeds as follows: Assign to the upper left hand square as much as possible and then continue along the first row until that resource is exhausted. Then drop down to the second row, etc., until all resources have been assigned and all demand satisfied (Fig. 11-3).

Squares with assignments are called 'stone' squares. Squares without assignments are called 'water' squares.

$$\begin{aligned}
\textit{Total Cost} \\
70 \times 64 &= \$4480 \\
10 \times 50 &= 500 \\
20 \times 77 &= 1540 \\
10 \times 48 &= 480 \\
10 \times 24 &= 240 \\
40 \times 48 &= 1920 \\
\hline
& \$9160
\end{aligned}$$

Note: The number of assignments (stones) should equal one less than the sum of the number of rows (m) and the number of columns (n) in the initial matrix (m + n — 1). If the number of assignments is less than this, degeneracy will occur. It will be discussed later.

To From	Atlanta	Columbia	Jacksonville	Richmond	Supply
Baltimore	—64 (70)	—50 (10)	—77 (20)	—14	100
Raleigh	—37	—20	—48 (10)	—24 (10)	20
Savannah	—25	—14	—15	—48 (40)	40
Demand	70	10	30	50	160 / 160

FIGURE 11-3

Northwest-Corner Initial Solution

Step 4. Evaluate the water squares (the squares with no assignments) one by one, in an orderly fashion (either row by row or column by column) until one is found that shows an improvement possibility, as follows:

    a. Establish a closed path (moving horizontally and vertically only) from the selected water square. A right-angle turn is made only at stones. The path may skip over stone and water squares. If no such path exists (degeneracy), assign a zero (0) stone where necessary to complete the shortest path. This resolves the degeneracy. Where this zero stone is assigned affects the number of iterations but not the final result (Fig. 11-4).

To / From	Atlanta	Columbia	Jacksonville	Richmond	Supply
Baltimore	−64 (70)	−50 (10)	− −77 (20)	+ −14 X	100
Raleigh	−37	−20	+ −48 (10)	− −24 (10)	20
Savannah	−25	−14	−15	−48 (40)	40
Demand	70	10	30	50	160 / 160

FIGURE 11-4

Closed Path to Evaluate Water Square in First Row, Fourth Column

    b. Establish alternate plus and minus signs on the closed path, starting with a plus in the selected water square. The closed path and the alternate plus and minus signs may be established clockwise or counter-clockwise. It makes no difference. The signs are assigned to the initial water square and to squares where turns occur, nowhere else (Fig. 11-4).

    c. Determine the improvement possibility (minimizing costs) by comparing the sum of unit costs in the plus (+) squares in the closed path (increased costs) with the sum of unit costs in the minus (−) squares of the closed path (decreased costs) (Table 11-1).

    d. In this case, we have an improvement possibility, indicated by the fact that the sum of the unit costs of the plus squares (Cost Increase) is less than the sum of the unit costs of the minus squares (Cost Decrease).

TABLE 11-1

Comparison of Sums of Unit Costs of First Closed Path

(Cost Increase) Sum of Unit Cost in Plus (+) Squares	(Cost Decrease) Sum of Unit Costs in Minus (−) Squares
14	77
48	24
$\overline{62}$	$\overline{101}$

Cost Increase − Cost Decrease = Net
$62   − $101   = $39 Net Decrease
                                    per unit

If no improvement were indicated, then repeat Step 4 (a), (b), and (c) with the remaining water squares, one at a time, until an improvement possibility is found. In the unlikely event that none at all were found, then the Northwest Corner guess would be the optimum shipping plan.

Step 5.   When a water square is found that shows an improvement possibility, then add or subtract (as indicated by the + and − signs on the closed path) the amount of the smallest stone in a negative square of the path (Fig. 11-5). This is the candidate for the optimum solution. It must now be tested to see if further improvement is possible. It is a good idea, after each improvement, to add the stones across the rows and down the columns to check with the rim conditions.

Total Costs
First Improved Solution
70 × 64 = $4480
10 × 50 =   500
10 × 77 =   770
10 × 14 =   140
20 × 48 =   960
40 × 48 = 1920
         $\overline{\$8770}$

Net Improvement
$9160 − $8770 = $390

To / From	Atlanta	Columbia	Jacksonville	Richmond	Supply
Baltimore	−64, (70)	−50, (10)	(10) −77, + (20̸)	−14, (10)	100
Raleigh	−37	−20, + (20) (1̸0̸)	−48, −	−24, (1̸0̸)	20
Savannah	−25	−14	−15	−48, (40)	40
Demand	70	10	30	50	160 / 160

FIGURE 11-5

Changes in Initial Solution to Produce First Improved Solution

Step 6.   Begin the evaluation of the water squares of the improved solution. Always start with the first Water Square you come to from left to right, top to bottom of the matrix and proceed in an orderly fashion to avoid missing any. Trace the path, put an alternating + and — signs, evaluate the Water Square (Fig. 11-6).

To / From	Atlanta	Columbia	Jacksonville	Richmond	Supply
Baltimore	— −64 (70)	− −50 (10) +	−77 (10)	−14 (10)	100
Raleigh	−37 x +	−20	−48 (20)	−24	20
Savannah	−25	−14	−15	−48 (40)	40
Demand	70	10	30	50	160 / 160

Increased Costs (+) Sum

77
37
———
114

Decreased Costs (−) Sum

64
48
———
112

No improvement

FIGURE 11-6

Evaluation of First Improved Solution Testing Water Square in Row 2, Column 1

Step 7.   Repeat steps 4, 5, and 6 until no further improvement is possible. (Figs. 11-7 through 11-18). The assignment schedule is then optimum, that is, lowest cost (Fig. 11-18).

To / From	Atlanta	Columbia	Jacksonville	Richmond	Supply
Baltimore	−64 (70)	− −50 (10) +	−77 (10)	−14 (10)	100
Raleigh	−37	−20 x +	− −48 (20)	−24	20
Savannah	−25	−14	−15 (40)	−48	40
Demand	70	10	30	50	160 / 160

Increased Costs (+) Sum

20
77
———
97

Decreased Costs (−) Sum

48
50
———
98

An *improvement!*

$97 − $98 = $1 Decrease per unit

FIGURE 11-7

Closed Path to Evaluate Water Square in Row 2, Column 2

Total Costs
Second Improved Solution

70 × 64 = $4480
20 × 77 = 1540
10 × 14 =   140
10 × 20 =   200
10 × 48 =   480
40 × 48 = 1920
$8760

Net improvement
$8770 − $8760 = $10

To \ From	Atlanta	Columbia	Jacksonville	Richmond	Supply
Baltimore	−64 ⑦⓪(70)	− −50 ⑩(10)✕	+ ⑳(20) −77 ⑩(10)✕	−14 ⑩(10)	100
Raleigh	−37 + ⑩(10)	−20	⑩(10) −48 ⑳(20)✕	−24	20
Savannah	−25	−14	−15	−48 ㊵(40)	40
Demand	70	10	30	50	160 / 160

FIGURE 11-8

Second Improved Solution (Smallest negative stone added and subtracted as indicated by + and — signs.)

Increased Decreased
Costs   Costs
(+) Sum   (−) Sum
50   77
48   20
98   97

No improvement

To \ From	Atlanta	Columbia	Jacksonville	Richmond	Supply
Baltimore	−64 (70)	+ x −50	− −77 (20)	−14 (10)	100
Raleigh	−37 − (10)	−20	+ −48 (10)	−24	20
Savannah	−25	−14	−15	−48 (40)	40
Demand	70	10	30	50	160 / 160

FIGURE 11-9

Second Improved Solution and Closed Path to Evaluate Water Square in Row 1, Column 2

As mentioned previously, after each improvement is made in the solution you must evaluate the water squares in an orderly fashion starting with the first one you come to from left to right, top to bottom of the matrix. Accordingly, after obtaining the second improvement (Figs. 11-8 and 11-9) the water square in the 1st row, 2nd column, is evaluated (Fig. 11-9). In this relatively small scale problem, the need for such attention to detail may not seem important. However, the technique applies to much larger matrices with much more involved paths and then the care taken not to miss a water square is critical to solving the problem.

To From	Atlanta	Columbia	Jacksonville	Richmond	Supply
Baltimore	− −64 (70)	−50	+ −77 (20)	−14 (10)	100
Raleigh	+ −37 x	−20 (10)	− −48 (10)	−24	20
Savannah	−25	−14	−15	−48 (40)	40
Demand	70	10	30	50	160 / 160

Increased Costs (+) Sum
37
77
—
114

Decreased Costs (−) Sum
48
64
—
112

No improvement

FIGURE 11-10

Second Improved Solution and Closed Path to Evaluate Water Square in Row 2, Column 1

To From	Atlanta	Columbia	Jacksonville	Richmond	Supply
Baltimore	−64 (70)	−50	+ −77 (20)	− −14 (10)	100
Raleigh	−37	−20 (10)	− −48 (10)	+ −24 x	20
Savannah	−25	−14	−15	−48 (40)	40
Demand	70	10	30	50	160 / 160

Increased Costs (+) Sum
24
77
—
101

Decreased Costs (−) Sum
14
48
—
62

No improvement

FIGURE 11-11

Second Improved Solution and Closed Path to Evaluate Water Square in Row 2, Column 4

To From	Atlanta	Columbia	Jacksonville	Richmond	Supply
Baltimore	− −64 (70)	− 50	− 77 (20)	+ − 14 (10)	100
Raleigh	− 37 (10)	− 20 (10)	− 48	− 24	20
Savannah	+ − 25 x	− 14	− 15	− − 48 (40)	40
Demand	70	10	30	50	160 160

Increased *Decreased*
Costs *Costs*
(+) Sum (−) Sum
25   48
14   64
—   —
39   112

An improvement!
$39 − $112 = $73 Decrease per unit

FIGURE 11-12

**Second Improved Solution and Closed Path to Evaluate
Water Square in Row 3, Column 1**

To From	Atlanta	Columbia	Jacksonville	Richmond	Supply
Baltimore	(30) −64 (70)	− 50	− 77 (20)	+ − 14 (50) (10)	100
Raleigh	− 37 (10)	− 20 (10)	− 48	− 24	20
Savannah	+ − 25 (40)	− 14	− 15	− − 48 (40)	40
Demand	70	10	30	50	160 160

Total Costs
Third Improved Solution
30 × 64 = $1920
20 × 77 = 1540
50 × 14 =   700
10 × 20 =   200
10 × 48 =   480
40 × 25 = 1000
      ———
      $5840

Net Improvement
$8760 − $5840 = $2920

FIGURE 11-13

Third Improved Solution

After finding the Third Improved Solution we must again evaluate the water squares from the beginning in an orderly fashion. Another improvement is found when the Water Square in Row 3, Column 3 is evaluated (Fig. 11-14).

To / From	Atlanta	Columbia	Jacksonville	Richmond	Supply
Baltimore	+ (30) —64	—50	— (20) —77	(50) —14	100
Raleigh	—37	(10) —20	(10) —48	—24	20
Savannah	— (40) —25	—14	+ X —15	—48	40
Demand	70	10	30	50	160 / 160

Increased Costs (+) Sum	Decreased Costs (—) Sum
15	77
64	25
79	102

An improvement!
$79 — $102 = $23 Decrease per unit

FIGURE 11-14

Third Improved Solution and Closed Path to Evaluate Water Square in Row 3, Column 3

To / From	Atlanta	Columbia	Jacksonville	Richmond	Supply
Baltimore	+ (50) (30)⊗ —64	—50	— (20)⊗ —77	(50) —14	100
Raleigh	—37	(10) —20	(10) —48	—24	20
Savannah	(20) (40)⊗ —25	—14	+ (20) —15	—48	40
Demand	70	10	30	50	160 / 160

Total Costs
Fourth Improved Solution
50 × 64 =	$3200
50 × 14 =	700
10 × 20 =	200
10 × 48 =	480
20 × 25 =	500
20 × 15 =	300
	$5380

Net improvement
$5840 — $5380 = $460

FIGURE 11-15

Fourth Improved Solution

Repeating Steps 4, 5 and 6 . . . the next improvement is shown in Fig. 11-16.

To \ From	Atlanta	Columbia	Jacksonville	Richmond	Supply
Baltimore	−64 (50)	−50	−77	−14 (50)	100
Raleigh	+ −37 x	−20 (10)	− −48 (10)	−24	20
Savannah	− −25 (20)	−14	+ −15 (20)	−48	40
Demand	70	10	30	50	160 / 160

Increased Costs (+) Sum	Decreased Costs (−) Sum
15	48
37	25
52	73

An improvement!
$52 − $73 = $21 Decrease per unit

FIGURE 11-16

Fourth Improved Solution and Closed Path to Evaluate Water Square in Row 2, Column 1

Total Costs
Fifth Improved Solution

$50 \times 64 = \$3200$
$50 \times 14 = 700$
$10 \times 37 = 370$
$10 \times 20 = 200$
$10 \times 25 = 250$
$30 \times 15 = 450$
$\overline{\$5170}$

Net improvement
$\$5380 - \$5170 = \$210$

To \ From	Atlanta	Columbia	Jacksonville	Richmond	Supply
Baltimore	−64 (50)	−50	−77	−14 (50)	100
Raleigh	+ −37 (10)	−20 (10)	− −48 (⌀10)	−24	20
Savannah	(10) −25 (⌀20)	−14	+ (30) −15 (⌀20)	−48	40
Demand	70	10	30	50	160 / 160

FIGURE 11-17

Fifth Improved Solution

Once again, as specified in Steps 4, 5 and 6, each Water Square must be evaluated. When this is done, no improvement is indicated and therefore the Fifth Improved Solution becomes the optimum solution.

To \ From	Atlanta	Columbia	Jacksonville	Richmond	Supply
Baltimore	−64 (50)	−50	−77	−14 (50)	100
Raleigh	−37 (10)	−20 (10)	−48	−24	20
Savannah	−25 (10)	−14	−15 (30)	−48	40
Demand	70	10	30	50	160 / 160

FIGURE 11-18

Final (Optimum) Solution

   The lowest cost shipping schedule to allocate the supply of 160 units in the Warehouses to Customer demand at the minimum cost of $5170 is as follows:

> Baltimore to ship 50 units to Atlanta and 50 to Richmond.
> Raleigh to ship 10 units to Atlanta and 10 to Columbia.
> Savannah to ship 10 units to Atlanta and 30 to Jacksonville.

The overall improvement from the first guesstimate (Northwest Corner Solution) is $9160 − $5170 = $3990. It is important to note that the optimum allocation does not use all the lowest unit cost relationships. Savannah supplies Atlanta at $25 a unit rather than Columbia at only $14 a unit. Raleigh supplies Atlanta at $37 a unit rather than Richmond at $24 a unit . . . and so forth. Attempting to allocate supply to demand on a "common sense" basis, as is done in many companies can easily result in other than optimum allocations. The reason is, of course, that every decision to allocate supplies from one warehouse to a particular customer affects every other possible allocation. The ramifications of each decision are manifold and interrelated. The Transportation Method provides a rigorous (if tedious) method of finding the best solution. In order to reduce the number of iterations (and the tedium) the Modified Distribution (MODI) method was developed. It will be explained next.

THE MODI (MODIFIED DISTRIBUTION) METHOD

This method is similar to the Transportation (Water-Stone) Method but less laborious. You may have noticed in the previous section that a number of relatively small improvements were made before a large improvement was found. In fact, you had the feeling (and you were right) of covering the same ground more than once but were forced to do it in order to be sure of not missing an improvement. The MODI method provides a simple procedure for finding the Water Square with the greatest possibility for improvement at each stage of the solution. The MODI method will be illustrated using the same allocation problem as was used in the Transportation Method.

Step 1.   Establish the problem's distribution matrix and balance the rim conditions just as was done before (Figs. 11-1 and 11-2).

Step 2.   Establish an initial solution using the Northwest Corner technique (Fig. 11-19). It will, of course, be identical to Fig. 11-3. (Vogel's Approximation Method, which will be discussed later, could also be used to establish an initial solution.) The number of assignments must equal m (number of rows) $+ n$ (number of columns) $- 1$. If less,

To From	Atlanta	Columbia	Jacksonville	Richmond	Supply
Baltimore	−64 (70)	−50 (10)	−77 (20)	−14	100
Raleigh	−37	−20	−48 (10)	−24 (10)	20
Savannah	−25	−14	−15	−48 (40)	40
Demand	70	10	30	50	160 / 160

FIGURE 11-19

Initial Northwest Corner Solution

use zero assignments as needed to resolve degeneracy in order to apply the method outlined below.

$$\text{Total cost} = \$9160$$

Step 3.   Compute an R value for each Row and a K value for each Column. Subscripts will be used to indicate the row and column. R_2 means the R value for Row 2. K_4 would mean the K value for Column 4. Double subscripts could be used to specify a square at the intersection of a particular Row and Column. It is the convention when using double subscripts to have the first subscript designate the row and the second designate the column. For instance, if the Water Square in the first Row, fourth Column (Row 1, Column 4) were to be specified by double subscripts it would be shown as Water Square $_{1,4}$ or in abbreviated fashion, $WS_{1,4}$. The following rules are used to develop these R and K values.

Rule 1: $R_1 = O$

Rule 2: $R + K =$ Cost (or Profit) at the intersection of a Row and a Column at a stone square. (As mentioned previously, resolve degeneracy, that is, the inability to solve for R or K, by assigning zero stones.) (See Fig. 11-21)

FIGURE 11-20

Initial solution-R and K Values Established

The steps for determining the respective R's and K's for the initial solution (Fig. 11-20) are:

R_1: $R_1 = 0$ (Rule 1)

K_1: $R_1 + K_1 = -64$ (Rule 2)

     $O + K_1 = -64$ (Substitute O for R_1)

     $K_1 = -64$

K_2: $R_1 = 0$ (Rule 1)

     $R_1 + K_2 = -50$ (Rule 2)

     $0 + K_2 = -50$ (Substitution)

     $K_2 = -50$

K_3: $R_1 = 0$ (Rule 1)

     $R_1 + K_3 = -77$ (Rule 2)

     $0 + K_3 = -77$ (Substitution)

     $K_3 = -77$

R_2: $R_2 + K_3 = -48$ (Rule 2)

     $R_2 + (-77) = -48$ (Substitute the value for K_3 previously calculated)

     $R_2 = -48 + 77$ (Transposing results in change of sign)

     $R_2 = +29$

K_4: $R_2 + K_4 = -24$ (Rule 2)

     $+29 + K_4 = -24$ (Substitution)

     $K_4 = -53$ (Transposing and solving)

R_3: $R_3 + K_4 = -48$ (Rule 2)

     $R_3 + (-53) = -48$

     $R_3 = +5$

Step 4.   Evaluate each Water Square by using the following relationship:

R + K — Cost (or Profit) at the Water Square = Improvement Value of the Water Square

If the result is positive (+) or zero for a Water Square, then no improvement is possible at this time. If the result is negative (—), then improvement is possible. Table 11-2 summarizes the evaluations for each Water Square of Figure 11-20.

TABLE 11-2

Water Square	Equation	Improvement?
Row 1, Column 4	$R_1 + K_4 - (-14) = WS_{1,4}$	
(WS$_{1,4}$)	$0 + (-53) - (-14) = -39$	Yes
Row 2, Column 1	$R_2 + K_1 - (-37) = WS_{2,1}$	
(WS$_{2,1}$)	$+29 + (-64) - (-37) = +2$	No
Row 2, Column 2	$R_2 + K_2 - (-20) = WS_{2,2}$	
(WS$_{2,2}$)	$+29 + (-50) - (-20) = -1$	Yes
Row 3, Column 1	$R_3 + K_1 - (-25) = WS_{3,1}$	
(WS$_{3,1}$)	$+5 + (-64) - (-25) = -34$	Yes
Row 3, Column 2	$R_3 + K_2 - (-14) = WS_{3,2}$	
(WS$_{3,2}$)	$+5 + (-50) - (-14) = -31$	Yes
Row 3, Column 3	$R_3 + K_3 - (-15) = WS_{3,3}$	
(WS$_{3,3}$)	$+5 + (-77) - (-15) = -57$	Yes

Step 5. Select the Water Square with the most negative value (the greatest improvement at this stage of the solution). From Table 11-2, the Water Square with the most negative value is in the third row, third column (WS$_{3,3}$).

Step 6. Apply the Water-Stone method to the Water Square selected in Step 5, that is, draw the shortest complete path, assign alternate + and — signs starting with the Water Square selected, and then add and subtract the smallest negative stone in the path (Figs. 11-22 and 11-23). Having used the MODI method you know this Water Square will result in the maximum improvement at this stage of the solution.

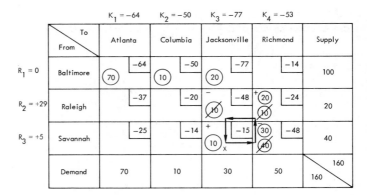

FIGURE 11-21

Changes in Initial Solution

Total Cost

$70 \times 64 = \$4480$
$10 \times 50 = \quad 500$
$20 \times 77 = \quad 1540$
$20 \times 24 = \quad 480$
$10 \times 15 = \quad 150$
$30 \times 48 = \quad 1440$
$\qquad\qquad \overline{\$8590}$

Net improvement
$\$9160 - \$8590 = \$570$

To \ From	Atlanta	Columbia	Jacksonville	Richmond	Supply
Baltimore	-64 (70)	-50 (10)	-77 (20)	-14	100
Raleigh	-37	-20	-48	-24 (20)	20
Savannah	-25	-14 (10)	-15 (30)	-48	40
Demand	70	10	30	50	160 / 160

FIGURE 11-22

First Improved Solution (Recalculating R's and K's and evaluating all Water Squares and making improvements.)

Step 7. Repeat steps 3 through 6 until all Water Square evaluations are positive or zero. That is the optimum solution. Table 11-3 shows the recalculation of the R and K values using the First Improved Solution.

TABLE 11-3

Computation of R's and K's using the First Improved Solution [a]

$$\underline{R_1:} \qquad R_1 = 0$$

$$\underline{K_1:} \qquad R_1 + K_1 = -64$$
$$K_1 = -64$$
$$0 + K_1 = -64$$

$$\underline{K_2:} \qquad R_1 + K_2 = -50$$
$$0 + K_2 = -50$$
$$K_2 = -50$$

$$\underline{K_3:} \qquad R_1 + K_3 = -77$$
$$0 + K_3 = -77$$
$$K_3 = -77$$

$$\underline{R_3:} \qquad R_3 + K_3 = -15$$
$$R_3 + (-77) = -15$$
$$R_3 = +62$$

$$\underline{K_4:} \qquad R_3 + K_4 = -48$$
$$62 + K_4 = -48$$
$$K_4 = -110$$

$$\underline{R_2:} \qquad R_2 + K_4 = -24$$
$$R_2 + (-110) = -24$$
$$R_2 = +86$$

[a] (See Fig. 11-23.)

		$K_1 = -64$ Atlanta	$K_2 = -50$ Columbia	$K_3 = -77$ Jacksonville	$K_4 = -110$ Richmond	Supply
	To From	Atlanta	Columbia	Jacksonville	Richmond	Supply
$R_1 = 0$	Baltimore	−64 70	−50 10	−77 20	−14	100
$R_2 = +86$	Raleigh	−37	−20	−48	−24 20	20
$R_3 = +62$	Savannah	−25	−14	−15 10	−48 30	40
	Demand	70	10	30	50	160 160

FIGURE 11-23

First Improved Solution with new R and K Values

TABLE 11-4

Evaluation of Water Squares of First Improved Solution

Water Square	Equation	Improvement?
Row 1, Column 4	$R_1 + K_4 - (-14) = WS_{1,4}$ $0 + (-110) - (-14) = -96$	Yes
Row 2, Column 1	$R_2 + K_1 - (-37) = WS_{2,1}$ $+86 + (-64) - (-37) = +59$	No
Row 2, Column 2	$R_2 + K_2 - (-20) = WS_{2,2}$ $+86 + (-50) - (-20) = +56$	No
Row 2, Column 3	$R_2 + K_3 - (-48) = WS_{2,3}$ $+86 + (-77) - (-48) = +57$	No
Row 3, Column 1	$R_3 + K_1 - (-25) = WS_{3,1}$ $+62 + (-64) - (-25) = +23$	No
Row 3, Column 2	$R_3 + K_2 - (-14) = WS_{3,2}$ $+62 + (-50) - (-14) = +26$	No

The only Water Square with a negative evaluation is the one in Row 1, Column 4. The result of the application of the Waterstone method to this square is shown in Figure 11-24. This Second Improved Solution is shown in Figure 11-25.

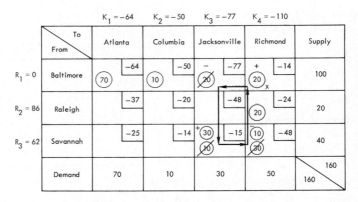

FIGURE 11-24

Changes in First Improved Solution

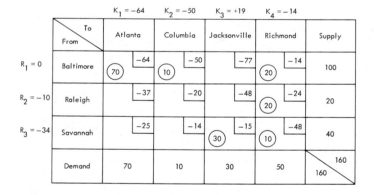

To / From	Atlanta	Columbia	Jacksonville	Richmond	Supply
Baltimore	-64 (70)	-50 (10)	-77	-14 (20)	100
Raleigh	-37	-20	-48	-24 (20)	20
Savannah	-25	-14	-15 (30)	-48 (10)	40
Demand	70	10	30	50	160 / 160

Total Cost
$70 \times 64 = \$4480$
$10 \times 50 = 500$
$20 \times 14 = 280$
$20 \times 24 = 480$
$30 \times 15 = 450$
$10 \times 48 = 480$
$\overline{\$6670}$

Net improvement
$\$8590 - \$6670 = \$1920$

FIGURE 11-25

Second Improved Solution

Using the Second Improved Solution, new R and K values are calculated (Fig. 11-26).

	$K_1 = -64$	$K_2 = -50$	$K_3 = +19$	$K_4 = -14$	
To / From	Atlanta	Columbia	Jacksonville	Richmond	Supply
$R_1 = 0$ Baltimore	-64 (70)	-50 (10)	-77	-14 (20)	100
$R_2 = -10$ Raleigh	-37	-20	-48	-24 (20)	20
$R_3 = -34$ Savannah	-25	-14	-15 (30)	-48 (10)	40
Demand	70	10	30	50	160 / 160

FIGURE 11-26

Second Improved Solution with New R and K Values

The Water Squares are evaluated as usual and the method continues until the improvements result in Water Squares which all have a value of 0 or +. That is the Optimum Solution. Figure 11-27 shows the optimum solution for this problem and the final R and K values that produced this solution as well as the Water Square evaluations that prove this is the optimum solution. Comparing it to Figure 11-18 it can be seen that it is the same as resulted from the use of the Transportation (Water-Stone) Method.

		$K_1 = -64$ Atlanta	$K_2 = -47$ Columbia	$K_3 = -54$ Jacksonville	$K_4 = -14$ Richmond	Supply
$R_1 = 0$	Baltimore	−64 (50)	−50	−77	−14 (50)	100
$R_2 = +27$	Raleigh	−37 (10)	−20 (10)	−48	−24	20
$R_3 = +39$	Savannah	−25 (10)	−14	−15 (30)	−48	40
	Demand	70	10	30	50	160 / 160

FIGURE 11-27

Optimum Solution

VOGEL'S APPROXIMATION METHOD (VAM)

As was mentioned in Step 2 of the MODI Method, there is an excellent alternative to the Northwest Corner procedure for developing an initial solution. It is called Vogel's Approximation Method and was developed by a pioneer in the application of techniques of Linear Programming named Vogel. It is an allocation method in its own right, but because the result of the Vogel Method is sometimes not optimum (it's never worse than 95% of optimum), VAM is often used to develop an initial solution and then MODI is applied to test for improvement possibilities and develop the optimum solution if improvements exist.

By using the Vogel Approximation Method much time and computational effort is saved since the result of the VAM is either opitmum or very close to optimum so that only a very few MODI iterations are necessary.

It should be emphasized that Vogel's Approximation Method usually produces the optimum solution. As you will see, the ease of the method makes it the only practical pencil and paper LP technique to use. All others should use pre-programmed computer packages for practical (large matrix) problems.

This method will be illustrated using the same allocation problem that was solved by the Transportation (Water-Stone) and MODI methods.

Step 1.   Set up the distribution matrix. (See Steps 1 and 2 of the Transportation (Water-Stone) method, pages 233 and 234 (see Fig. 11-2)

Step 2.   Determine the absolute difference between the two most "maximum" elements (lowest cost or highest profit values) for each row and each column of the matrix. This will be referred to as the "Vogel Number". (Fig. 11-29)

Example: The two lowest costs in row 1 (50 and 14) have an absolute difference of 36, which is therefore the Vogel Number of the first row.

		12	6	33	10	
	To / From	Atlanta	Columbia	Jacksonville	Richmond	Supply
36	Baltimore	−64	−50	−77	−14	100
4	Raleigh	−37	−20	−48	−24	20
1	Savannah	−25	−14	−15	−48	40
	Demand	70	10	30	50	160 / 160

FIGURE 11-28

Distribution Matrix—Vogel Numbers Established

Step 3.   Select the row or column with the largest Vogel Number. (If more than one row or column have the largest Vogel Number, see special cases A and B on page 255, but first read step 4 below.) In this example the first row has the largest Vogel Number. (Fig. 11-28)

Step 4.   Assign as much resource as possible to the square with the most "maximum" element (lowest cost or highest profit) in that selected row or column.

Referring to Figure 11-28 we find the square in the first row (selected by step 3) which has the smallest cost, is the one in the fourth column. To this square we assign (by step 4) the maximum number of units possible (50 in this case). (See Fig. 11-29)

		12 Atlanta	6 Columbia	33 Jacksonville	10 Richmond	Supply
	To / From					
36	Baltimore	−64	−50	−77	−14 (50)	100
4	Raleigh	−37	−20	−48	−24	20
1	Savannah	−25	−14	−15	−48	40
	Demand	70	10	30	50	160 / 160

FIGURE 11-29

Distribution Matrix with First Assignment

Special Case—A

If the highest Vogel Number is obtained at the same time in both a row and a column, and the square at the junction of that row and column has the lowest cost or highest profit element, then the assignment is made at that square common to both the row and the column. If the square at the junction does not have the algebraically best cost or profit element, then make an assignment in either the row or column wherever the algebraically best element exists.

Special Case—B

If the largest Vogel Number is obtained at the same time in two or more rows (or columns), then make the assignment wherever the algebraically best element exists in either row (or column).

Step 5.   Cross out the row or column (sometimes both) completely satisfied by the assignment (Fig. 11-30).

	12	6	33	10	
To / From	Atlanta	Columbia	Jacksonville	Richmond	Supply
36 Baltimore	−64	−50	−77	−14 ⊙50	100
4 Raleigh	−37	−20	−48	−24	20
1 Savannah	−25	−14	−15	−48	40
Demand	70	10	30	50	160 / 160

FIGURE 11-30

Distribution Matrix—Column 4, Satisfied by First Assignment, Deleted

Step 6.   Recalculate the Vogel Numbers as may be necessary but omit the crossed out row(s) and column(s) (Fig. 11-31).

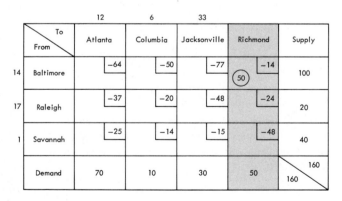

	12	6	33		
To / From	Atlanta	Columbia	Jacksonville	Richmond	Supply
14 Baltimore	−64	−50	−77	−14 ⊙50	100
17 Raleigh	−37	−20	−48	−24	20
1 Savannah	−25	−14	−15	−48	40
Demand	70	10	30	50	160 / 160

FIGURE 11-31

Recalculated Vogel Numbers after First Assignment

Step 7.   Repeat steps 3 through 6 until all assignments have been made (Figs. 11-32 through 34).

	12	6	33		
To / From	Atlanta	Columbia	Jacksonville	Richmond	Supply
14 Baltimore	−64	−50	−77	−14 (50)	100
17 Raleigh	−37	−20	−48	−24	20
1 Savannah	−25	−14	−15 (30)	−48	40
Demand	70	10	30	50	160 / 160

FIGURE 11-32

Distribution Matrix with First Two Assignments

	12	6			
To / From	Atlanta	Columbia	Jacksonville	Richmond	Supply
14 Baltimore	−64	−50	−77 (50)	−14	100
17 Raleigh	−37	−20	−48	−24	20
11 Savannah	−25	−14	−15 (30)	−48	40
Demand	70	10	30	50	160 / 160

FIGURE 11-33

Recalculation of Vogel Numbers after Second Assignment

At this point the second row has the largest Vogel Number. The square in this row with the lowest cost is the one in the second column. We therefore assign to this square the maximum number of units possible, that is, 10 units. (Fig. 11-34)

To From	Atlanta	Columbia	Jacksonville	Richmond	Supply
Baltimore	−64	−50	−77	−14 (50)	100
Raleigh	−37	−20 (10)	−48	−24	20
Savannah	−25	−14	−15 (30)	−48	40
Demand	70	10	30	50	160 160

FIGURE 11-34

Distribution Matrix with First Three Assignments

Inasmuch as columns 2, 3, and 4 are now completely satisfied, the balance of the assignments can be made from the rim conditions. Thus, for example, row 4 requires a total of 40 units and 30 units have already been assigned to that row. The additional 10 units required cannot be assigned to columns 2, 3, or 4 of that row since these columns are completely satisfied. Accordingly, the 10 units must be assigned to the first column of that row. Figure 11-35 indicates this assignment to the square in row 3, column 1 as well as the required assignments to the other squares in column 1.

To From	Atlanta	Columbia	Jacksonville	Richmond	Supply
Baltimore	−64 (50)	−50	−77	−14 (50)	100
Raleigh	−37 (10)	−20 (10)	−48	−24	20
Savannah	−25 (10)	−14	−15 (30)	−48	40
Demand	70	10	30	50	160 160

FIGURE 11-35

Final Solution by Vogel's Approximation Method

Step 8.   When all assignments have been made, then apply the MODI method to test if the solution is optimum and to improve it if it is not. In this example we see that the Vogel solution is identical to the MODI (and Water-Stone) solutions previously found. The solution is therefore the optimum one.

The Monte Carlo Method

During World War II physicists at Los Alamos Scientific Laboratory were faced with a very difficult problem involving the behavior of neutrons. Specifically, the question was, How far would neutrons travel through various materials? Researching the problem by experimental trial and error would have been very expensive, extremely time-consuming, and perhaps hazardous. Furthermore, available mathematical theory seemed inadequate to resolve the problem.

Under pressure of this crisis, mathematicians John von Neumann and Stanislas Ulman proposed what seemed like a wild solution. In effect, it amounted to using a roulette wheel to solve the problem. The probabilities of the separate events were utilized to develop a mathematical model which when manipulated by the "roulette wheel" approach gave an approximate but workable answer to the problem.

The essence of the mathematical technique underlying the method had been known for many years. When it was revived for the secret work at Los Alamos, von Neumann puckishly gave it the code name *Monte Carlo.*

The technique developed at Los Alamos had much in common with the management process in organizations. For instance, one of the key steps in management decision making requires consideration of the probabilities of the different outcomes of each alternative.

Furthermore, managers are continually faced with coming up with "guesstimates" as to the occurrence of future events. This fact of managerial life does point up the role of the laws of probability and forecasting in management decision making and the underlying reason for the success of the Monte Carlo technique in helping to solve management decision problems—specifically, those problems combining elements of probability theory with the simulation of future events. In particular, the Monte Carlo method is used to solve problems where developing exact mathematical models is impossible or where trying out changes in the real world is impractical or too expensive—such as those that occur in forecasting machine breakdowns, inventory control, sales by product line, employee absences, or other occurrences that are often characterized as random. The Monte Carlo technique provides a rigorous approach to help management reduce the area of uncertainty in decision making.

The management problems particularly vulnerable to this technique have the following characteristics:

1. Significant parts of the problems can be expressed in terms of probability.
2. The problems are such that physical experimentation using the real world situation or actual physical samples is not practical, or is expensive, or is impossible.
3. The design and development of a rigorous, specific, mathematical model is too difficult or theoretically impossible.

An Industrial Example:

A practical production example from real life involved the development of assembly specifications for a new product line—even before production began. There was uncertainty about the specifications because the dimensions of the parts that had to be assembled would vary. No part could be machined exactly the same as any other part. Since the dimensions of the parts would vary, their ability to be fitted, one to another, in the assembly operation was unknown. However, past history did provide the probabilities for the variations. Furthermore, physical experimentation was impossible because the parts had not been produced as yet. But, management had to come up with tooling specifications, assembly specifications, inspection procedures, and so forth, in advance. All of which required decisions that were cloaked in uncertainty. The problem combined probabilities with simulation of the future.

Finally, to attempt to develop a rigorous mathematical model of all the controllable and uncontrollable variables involved in the new production line in order to test all the possible alternatives would be close to impossible. It could be done but would take many man-years of effort and more money than it would be worth.

This is typical of the kind of problem that is being solved today by the use of Monte Carlo.

The General Approach to a Monte Carlo Application:

In general, the Monte Carlo method works something like this: The manager or the systems analyst looks at historical records to determine the past pattern of the events he is interested in predicting. He knows that the occurrences of the specific individual events happen at random. Therefore, he must simulate the sequence of random occurrences into the future. This is accomplished by the use of a *random number table*. This table of numbers is similar to the sequence of numbers that would be generated by using repeated turns of a "true" roulette wheel or by using the output of a computer that has executed a program known as a *random number generator*. The basis for the generation of the list of random numbers is that every number has an equal chance of occurring. These random numbers are the basis of the analyst's simulation of the random occurrences that he is interested in predicting.

The random numbers are selected in an orderly manner and are interpreted in terms of the historical record of the events to be forecast, using very simple rules. Through the generation and use of random numbers, which is at the heart of the Monte Carlo technique, the manager has developed specific information regarding the future occurrences of the events he is interested in predicting. Using this quantitative data, plus his own judgment, he can come up with a much better answer to his problem than what might otherwise be a "weighted" guess.

A MONTE CARLO APPLICATION

The Situation: The president of a high-precision machine tool company has been informed by one of his suppliers that the supplier's plant will be shut down for six weeks for major repairs. This will cut off the source of key replacement parts for certain high-precision testing equipment used by the machine tool company. These parts are very expensive, difficult to make, and available only from this one supplier. The shutdown has been carefully planned, and it is certain that it will not extend for more than twenty-nine working days.

The president of the machine tool company is faced with a significant decision. He must order enough replacement parts to last through the shutdown of his supplier. But because of the extremely high cost of the parts, he must be sure not to order too many.

TABLE 11-5

Historical Data on Parts Usage

Part Life (Days)	Relative Frequency (%)
5	5
6	40
7	10
8	35
9	10
	100

Simulation: The parts usage can be simulated by assigning numbers from 00 to 99 in the same proportion as the relative frequency of part life.

TABLE 11-6

Part Life (Days)	Relative Frequency (%)	Assigned Numbers
5	5	00–04
6	40	05–44
7	10	45–54
8	35	55–89
9	10	90–99

The parts usage for each of the five testing machines involved must be simulated over the twenty-nine-day period. This can be done by the standard procedure of using either a table of random numbers or a computer and a random number generating program. As each random number is selected, it is interpreted by means of Table 11-6 into a particular span of part life for that machine. Table 11-7 is the result of one simulation run.

TABLE 11-7

Machine	Random No.	Part Life (Days)		Parts Required
1	04	5		
	60	8		
	67	8		
	89	8	29	4
2	95	9		
	55	8		
	35	6		
	57	8	31	4
3	86	8		
	30	6		
	81	8		
	02	5		
	18	6	33	5
4	87	8		
	68	8		
	28	6		
	44	6		
	86	8	36	5
5	84	8		
	56	8		
	83	8		
	55	8	32	4
Total parts required				22

One simulation will not produce a reliable enough result for a management decision. Statistical theory provides rigorous guidelines for determining the number of simulation runs necessary to provide an answer for management at a certain confidence level.

Assuming a 95 percent confidence level as being a reasonable objective in this case, the following statistical formula may be used to determine the number of simulation runs that will be required for the worst possible situation—that is, when the distribution of historical data cannot be approximated by any of the classical statistical distributions.

$$N = \frac{(k)^2}{(d)^2}$$

$k =$ Constant; 1.36 in this case
$d = (1-\alpha)/2.0$
$\alpha =$ Desired confidence level; 95% in this case
$N = \frac{(1.36\ )^2}{(\ .025)^2} = (54.4)^2 = 2,960$ simulations

The number of simulations required is a dramatic illustration of the key role that can be played by the computer in Monte Carlo applications. What would have been an overwhelming task for hand calculations is a relatively simple effort, using a standard program, for the computer.

The Result: Based on the results of the Monte Carlo technique, the president decided to order twenty-two parts.

Queuing (Waiting Line) Theory

One of man's most common problems is that of waiting. Aside from the purely annoying aspects of waiting, such situations provide management with serious problems of another nature. Waiting means idle time and therefore is unproductive. The manager interested in keeping costs to a minimum must be conscious of idle time, since it represents either higher operating costs or lower output.

Waiting lines (called *queues* by the British) are quite common in industry. Many kinds of management problems—bottlenecks, backlogs, and idle capacity—are the direct result of waiting lines. Parts waiting to be machined, clients waiting for a professional caseworker, machines waiting the service of a repair crew, check-out lines at a supermarket, received parts awaiting inspection, borrowers at a library desk, cars at a tollbooth or at a gas station—all represent common examples of waiting line situations.

If the demand for use of the service facility followed a regular pattern, and if the service times were the same for all units, management could easily arrange for no waiting lines or idle capacity. The trouble is that units to be serviced are very seldom regular in their arrival patterns, and service times also often vary.

This makes it impossible to match the rate of arrivals and the rate of service, and that is how waiting lines are born. The dilemma is compounded by the fact that investment in more service facilities than "necessary" is very expensive, but the alternative of lost customers, unhappy clients, and the costs of idle time, bottlenecks, and backlogs is also unacceptable. Under these conditions of complexity involving probabilities, mathematical relationships, and interactive occurrences, queuing theory was born.

It is interesting to note that very often backlogs and bottlenecks alternate with periods of idleness at the very same work stations. This is one of the most frustrating of the many imponderables faced by managers and systems analysts. Management is constantly trying to discover a method of production or service that will minimize both idle time and backlogs. The general "fix" is to "put out the fire" and wait for the next alarm. But, there must be a better way. The developments in the area of queuing theory hold great promise.

Theoretical research into the properties of queues actually began in connection with the design of automatic telephone exchanges by Dr. A. K. Erlang in the early 1900s. It was important to know the effect of telephone service demands and their fluctuations on the utilization of the automatic switching equipment that was in the process of design for the telephone switching centers. Until relatively recently, most of the work on the theory of queues was done in connection with telephone problems. It has only been since the development of the more general systems approach to management problems that is known as Operations Research that it was realized that the theory developed for telephone system requirements had application to a wide variety of management problems.

COMMON ELEMENTS OF QUEUING PROBLEMS   All waiting line problems include the following elements:

Inputs
Population of possible inputs
Waiting line
Waiting time
Queue discipline
Servicing facility

Service
Service time
Outputs

For example, a basic production operation (machining on a lathe) can be considered as being made up of an *input* (the part to be machined) from a *population of possible inputs* (the parts in the lot), a *waiting line* and *waiting time* (other parts waiting to be machined), *queue discipline* (the role of priority of service—such as first come, first served), a *servicing facility* (the lathe), a *service* and a *service time* (machining), and an *output* (the machined part). There are many such situations in companies and organizations, all of which can be analyzed, and potential improvements can be developed by adapting queuing theory that has worked in similar cases. The following are some examples of areas where queuing theory has proved helpful in minimizing the waiting time of units to be serviced and the idle time of the service facility.

Population of Inputs	Input Units	Service Facility	Service
Trucks arriving at loading dock	Trucks	Dock crew and dock	Unload truck
Machine breakdowns	Mechanics	Attendant and tool crib	Issue tool
Users of toll crossing	Vehicles	Collector and toll booth	Collect toll
Autos needing gasoline	Autos	Attendant and gas pump	Pump gas
Autos needing inspection	Autos	Inspectors and stations	Inspect cars
Supermarket customers	People	Cashier and counter	Collect money and pack
Doctor's patients	People	Doctor and office	Examination or treatment
Customers	Prescriptions	Pharmacist and drugs and Facilities	Fill prescriptions
Airplane arrivals	Airplanes	Runways	Landing clearance

Queuing theory provides mathematical techniques as well as simulation to regulate, interpret, and predict. It provides management with objective yardsticks to combine with judgment for the introduction of improvements to reduce waiting lines or to minimize idle capacity.

Briefly, queuing theory (or waiting line theory) is the theory of efficiently servicing arrivals at a service facility. Too much demand on a service facility results in excessive waiting time for service, or too little demand results in too much idle facility time. The objective of queuing analysis is to minimize the total costs associated with waiting time and idle time. This is accomplished by using mathematical techniques or simulation to forecast the probable length of the waiting line and the probable amount of waiting or of idle time.

The "state of the art" at this point in time analyzes queuing problems that are relatively simple—those involving a few channels for service and a few steps or phases of service. Work is continuing, however, and the learned journals in the field continually report on advances being made.

USEFUL FORMULAS FOR SIMPLE QUEUING APPLICATIONS   For single channel single phase problems with Poisson arrivals $\left[P(x) = \dfrac{e^{-\lambda} \lambda^x}{x!}\right]$ and exponential service times $(P(t) = \mu e^{-\mu t})$.

1. Mean number in the total system $\quad L \;\; = \;\; \dfrac{\lambda}{\mu - \lambda}$

2. Mean number in the waiting line $\quad Lq \;\; = \dfrac{\lambda^2}{\mu(\mu - \lambda)}$

3. Mean time in system $\quad\quad\quad\;\; W \;\; = L/\lambda$
4. Mean waiting time in queue $\quad\quad Wq \;\; = Lq/\lambda$
5. Probability of n units in system $\quad P(n) = (1 - \lambda/\mu)(\lambda/\mu)^n$

STEPS IN SOLVING A QUEUING PROBLEM   The first thing that must be done is to have management collect the basic data that will describe the primary characteristics of a service facility that gives evidence of a waiting line problem. These primary characteristics are *arrival of inputs, service times,* and *queue discipline.*

Arrival of Inputs: These determine the demand for the service. The times at which units arrive at a service facility are therefore recorded. These inputs are from some statistical population which can be described by a frequency distribution specifying the number of arrivals during a particular interval of time. The time between arrivals is also important, and this may be constant, predetermined (as at a doctor's office), or of random length. In the random case, the most commonly used assumption is that the number of arrivals is described by the so-called Poisson distribution. The Poisson distribution occurs when a large number (n) of identical events can occur but the probability (p) of actual occurrence is small $(M = np$ is less than 5).

In mathematical terms, the probability of exactly X arrivals during a time period, *t*, is given by the Poisson distribution as:

$$P(x) = \frac{(\lambda t)^x}{x!} \, e^{-\lambda t}, x = 0, 1, 2, \ldots$$

where λ is the average arrival rate per unit time, and *e* is the natural logarithm base. In this notation, $M = \lambda t$. The distribution of the time *between* arrivals in this case follows a negative exponential distribution:

$$f(t) = \lambda e^{-\lambda t}, t \geq 0$$

Incoming telephone calls, failures of many types of equipment due to random causes, and other similar "arrival" situations have been found to be well described by the Poisson distribution. Other distributions, such as the normal distribution, are used when applicable.

Service Times: Servicing is characterized by such things as the number of service facilities and the distribution of service time for each facility. Service time can be constant (as often occurs at tollgates or for a particular machine operation), or it can be of random length. The negative exponential distribution fits many service time distributions.

Queue Discipline: Queue discipline is characterized by such things as the number of waiting lines, the maximum possible queue length, and the method of selecting a specific waiting item for service. Maximum queue lengths will vary from problem to problem, varying from zero to those having no restriction on length. Times can be selected for service on a first-come-first-served basis, on a random basis, by priority, or by some other management-determined decision rule.

Solution Procedures:

1. The waiting line system is described in terms of arrivals, service, and queue discipline. If possible, and if not already known, samples of arrival times and service times are obtained and analyzed to determine the respective distributions. If not possible, distributions are assumed on the basis of known characteristics of comparable systems.
2. A measure of facility effectiveness is selected, which will vary from problem to problem. For example, in a factory tool crib problem, one may wish to optimize total costs of mechanics waiting for service and the idle time of the tool crib clerks. For tollbooths, one may want the probability that the waiting line of cars does not exceed a certain length.
3. A system of simultaneous equations is set up based on the system characteristics, and these are solved if possible to yield the re-

quired probabilities. The characteristics of interest that are required for the measure of effectiveness are then calculated from these probabilities. Where the direct mathematical solution is not feasible, the relationships of the system characteristics are simulated, usually by computer, and the measure of effectiveness for varying conditions is developed for management review and decision.

4. In the case of "standard" problems, all the necessary formulas have already been worked out. An example of such formulas was given earlier in this chapter.

A Specific Application of Queuing Theory

The client load pressure at a small personnel placement agency has exceeded the capabilities of the facilities and the placement specialist under present operating conditions. Client arrivals are now scheduled at an average rate of one every thirty minutes. Sign-in records indicate that the actual pattern of client arrivals closely approximates a Poisson distribution. The average service rate is one client every twenty minutes, and it also tends to be approximated by a Poisson distribution.

A work simplification study of the facility indicates that an improved layout and simplified forms would decrease client processing time so that the average service rate would be increased to one client every fifteen minutes.

It has been calculated that each client's average contribution to overhead and profit is ten dollars per visit and average waiting time per client is not to be increased by the change. What would the change do to the contribution to overhead and profit?

1. The average arrival rate is now one client every thirty minutes.
$$\lambda_1 = 2/\text{hour}$$
2. The average service rate is now one client every twenty minutes.
$$\mu_1 = 3/\text{hour}$$
3. The average service rate that will result from the change in the layout is one client every fifteen minutes.
$$\mu_2 = 4/\text{hour}$$
4. The mean waiting time per client for the present layout is

$$Wq = \frac{\lambda_1}{\mu_1 \, (\mu_1 - \lambda_1)} = \frac{2}{3(3-2)} = \frac{2}{3} \text{ hour}$$

It has been decided that this will not be increased by the change.

5. The new arrival rate of clients may be determined by relating the projected average service rate and the mean waiting time (which is not to increase).

$$Wq = \cfrac{\lambda_2}{\mu_2\,(\mu_2 - \lambda_2)}$$

$$\tfrac{2}{3} = \cfrac{\lambda_2}{4\,(4 - \lambda_2)}$$

$$\lambda_2 = 2.9 \text{ per hour}$$

6. Calculation of contribution to overhead and profit under the present layout:
   Average arrivals per hour $\times$ Contribution per arrival

$$2 \quad \times \quad \$10 \quad = \$20/\text{hour}$$

7. Contribution to overhead and profit under the new layout:
   Average arrivals per hour $\times$ Contribution per arrival

$$2.9 \quad \times \quad \$10 \quad = \$29/\text{hour}$$

8. Net change in hourly contribution to overhead and profit:

$$\$29 - \$20 = \$9/\text{hour}$$

$$\therefore \text{ an increase of } 45\%$$

Simulation

Perhaps the most useful definition of *simulation* is one of the most concise—"It is an operating representation of a real process." You will note that this is similar to the definition of *model*—"Something that stands in place of the real thing." The difference between simulation and models is that the first (simulation) uses the second (models) to attain its objectives. That is, simulation uses (1) physical, (2) analog, and (3) mathematical models to forecast the results of alternative courses of action.

One of the well-known examples of *physical* simulation already mentioned is the testing of the performance of a model airplane in a wind tunnel. The designers of a new wing are interested in the effect it will have on the airplane's performance. Of course, an airplane could be built at a cost of many millions of dollars and the expenditure of much time and effort and then tested. But, even then, the particular wing configuration tested might be only one of a series before the design was finalized. The idea of building and discarding a whole series of airplanes just to test new wing designs is obviously irrational.

A practical alternative is the physical simulation of the wing configuration on a model in a wind tunnel. It is important to take note of a particular advantage of simulation as illustrated by the above example. The model being tested need embody only those features of the plane and wing design that are important to aerodynamic performance. No attention need be paid to the plane's internal communications systems, passenger seating and service layout, the configuration of its radar, or of a host of other features that are inconsequential to wing design performance. This highlights one of the great advantages of simulation—its ability to simplify a very complex situation by focusing on the elements critical to a decision.

Analog simulation has been used very effectively in engineering studies. Whereas physical simulation seems relatively familiar, analog simulation probably seems quite foreign. It is based on the fact that there are many phenomena in nature that act very much the same although they are in different areas of the physical sciences.

A familiar example might be the comparison of the flow of water through a pipe with the flow of electric current in a wire. Some highly sophisticated analogies have been made of these two phenomena. There are a number of such analogies between electrical and mechanical elements. Torque in mechanics can be shown to act quite like electrical voltage. Velocity is closely related to electrical amperage. The friction encountered by fluids in a pipe is very much like electrical resistance. These are examples of some of the many similar analog relationships in chemical, acoustical, and thermal systems.

The average manager might react by saying, "That's all very interesting, but so what?" The "so what" is that the analogs of one system may differ tremendously in size, weight, and cost from those of another system. Therefore, a representation of a complex, expensive, and massive system might be accomplished by means of simple, inexpensive, and compact analogs of another system. Thus, an inexpensive electrical model on a table-size breadboard can simulate an expensive magneto-hydraulic control system.

The electrical results of experimenting on the model can then be interpreted back into the dimensions of the original system because of the analogies that exist. The savings in time, cost, and effort can be immense.

The third major type of simulation, *mathematical* simulation, may very well be the one of most interest to the systems analyst. In this type of simulation a mathematical model of the situation is developed and then manipulated, and the results are used to sharpen management decisions. Sound familiar? It should, because this is exactly what was discussed when the Monte Carlo method was explained.

The Monte Carlo method provided a way to introduce uncertainty into the testing of alternative solutions. It allows operation in *simulated* time rather than in *real* time.

The mathematical relationships and the quantities that represent the variables in the model stand for the real thing—whether the "real thing" is a production line, an industry, a transportation network, a sales campaign, or a model airplane in a wind tunnel.

Earlier we mentioned a model airplane in a wind tunnel as an example of a physical model. Actually, numbers represented all the significant factors and the results of the test. It would be reasonable to eliminate the physical aspects of the test—the model, the tunnel, and the wind machine—and represent them by numbers, symbols, and mathematical relationships. Complex? Yes. But feasible? Also yes. Especially because of the availability of the services of the electronic computer to do the tedious calculations.

This is often the case today. Physical models are being replaced, in their turn, by a further step of abstraction. They are being represented by mathematical models manipulated by electronic computers as directed by the experimenters.

Simulation, whether physical, analog, or mathematical, provides management with a powerful decision tool. The key to its use is familiarity with the accomplishments in situations similar to those being faced by interested managers. The Bibliography at the end of this chapter will provide a rich vein of tried and proven simulations.

Management Games

Management games are an OR tool and are closely related to simulation. The general characteristic of all management games is that they are played under uncertainty, with competitive pressures, rules and regulations, and penalties, and the outcome depends on skill, judgment, and "a little bit o' luck."

The great amount of interest in management games results from proof of their effectiveness in improving a manager's ability to manage. Decision makers learn to make better decisions by making and then analyzing their decisions.

The old adage Managers Are Made, Not Born is generally accepted as true by most managers. Management decision making can be learned only by experience, but the anomaly is that people have to be managers to gain that experience. This has posed an expensive dilemma for every organization. Will that "hot-shot" systems man or that effective first-line supervisor turn out to be a good manager? Nobody really knows! So top management, since the beginning, has been "promoting and praying." Now, however, management games can provide a much needed tool to evaluate potential managers as well as to improve management performance.

To represent the relationship of the elements in the situation, most management games utilize mathematical relationships and computers to handle the data manipulations and calculations. Individuals or teams are required to make decisions about a particular management problem, usually within a time limit.

The independent decisions are processed by the computer, and since the situation is competitive, each decision affects all the others. Most games have a number of "plays." Therefore, as the results of the latest decision become known, management can "learn" and thereby try to improve its decision and resultant performance the next time around.

Game Theory

Related to management games and to simulation, game theory uses a mathematical approach for dealing with competitive situations, emphasizing the interplay of strategies in the decision-making process of the competitors. It was first developed by John von Neumann in 1928. The objective of game theory is to develop rational criteria for selecting a strategy, that is, a rule for responding to each circumstance at each stage of the game.

Since the operation of business, government, and many other organizations involves competition with others, game theory has its place in Operations Research. All businessmen would swear to the fact that the effectiveness of a course of action in business is inversely proportional to the effectiveness of competition. When a competitor wins, you lose, and under these circumstances the better your strategy, the more effectively can you counter your competitor's actions.

TWO-PERSON ZERO-SUM GAMES   (Most research has been done on this type.) These games involve two adversaries. They are zero-sum because one wins whatever the other loses, so that the sum of their net winnings is zero.

A game is generally categorized by:

1. The strategies of player I
2. The strategies of player II
3. The payoff table

A *strategy* may involve only a simple action or it may involve a series of moves. It is a predetermined rule that specifies completely how one intends to respond to each possible circumstance at each stage of the game.

Before the game begins, each player knows the strategies available to himself, the strategies available to his opponent, and the payoff table. The *payoff table* is usually shown as payoff to player I because the payoff table for payoff to player II is just the negative of player I's payoff table, since the game is zero-sum.

The *actual play* of the game consists of the players simultaneously choosing a strategy without knowing the opponent's choice.

A *primary objective* of game theory is to develop rational criteria for selecting a strategy. This is done under the assumption that both players are rational and that each will uncompromisingly attempt to do as well as possible relative to his opponent. Game theory assumes that both players are actively trying to promote their own welfare in opposition to that of the opponent.

Game Theory—Solution Example   A game has the following payoff to Player I:

		Player II Strategies		
		1	2	3
Player I Strategies	1	3	1	5
	2	3	0	1

Dominant Strategy

What strategy should Player I play? Obviously 1, since it "dominates" strategy 2. It is at least as good as 2, and sometimes better, no matter what the opponent does.

Note: The concept of dominant strategy is very useful for reducing the size of the payoff table and, in some cases, for actually identifying the optimum solution to the game. Simularly, Player II will discard strategy 3, since strategy 2 has uniformly lower payoffs to Player I.

Rationality

Since both players will act rationally, Player II will deduce that Player I will play strategy 1 and, therefore, he should play strategy 2 to minimize his losses.

"Fair" Game

The result is that Player I will always receive a payoff of 1 from Player II. The "value" of this game is therefore 1. If payoff is in dollars, Player I should pay one dollar to Player II to make it a "fair" game. Although decision strategy in a competitive environment is certainly important, there has been little in the way of actual applications because most competitive situations in real life are much more complicated than game theory has been able to analyze. Nevertheless, game theory's contribution to the formulation, logic, and criteria in competitive situations is an important conceptual contribution.

Other Operations Research Techniques

Symbolic logic, search theory, dynamic programming, information theory, factor analysis, and a host of other techniques have been utilized by Operations Research specialists to solve problems. New techniques are under development all the time. It is interesting to note that although mathematics has provided the foundation for most Operations Research techniques, new investigations are probing into the use of such things as expansion of gases, density of fluids, feedback control mechanisms, and other ideas from many of the physical sciences for application to management problems. The possibilities are very exciting.

SYSTEMS APPLICATIONS OF OR

1. Allocating production orders to machines for minimum costs
2. Solving routing (traveling salesmen, warehouse, maintenance) problems
3. Simulating urban transportation networks
4. Balancing assembly lines
5. Designing business decision games for training
6. Determining city planning
7. Determining optimum size of work crews
8. Determining plant layout
9. Allocating scarce material
10. Controlling inventory under certainty and uncertainty
11. Locating plants or warehouses
12. Minimizing waiting time for service
13. Solving equipment replacement problems
14. Scheduling preventive maintenance
15. Designing quality control programs
16. Leveling production and employment in a seasonal industry
17. Forecasting sales
18. Deciding whether to make or buy
19. Selecting advertising media
20. Designing Management Information Systems

ONCE OVER LIGHTLY

Management decisions are what keep operations going. Yet many involve uncertainty, and they all require the selection of the optimum from among alternative courses of action. Many tools have been used in the past to help managers reduce the area of uncertainty in decision making. Operations Research, the name given to a relatively new array of management decision tools, is usefully defined as the scientific study of problems in a management system, often using mathematical models and quantitative analysis to test and select alternative solutions to a problem.

Operations Research provides management with a new approach to decision making. It emphasizes specifics. It evaluates competing courses of action using mathematical techniques. Its relationships, formulas, and models can reflect the impact of individual decisions as well as the integrated activities of an entire organization. Management problems are assessed quantitatively, and the results of alternative courses of action are measured. Since this enables managers to evaluate the results of their decisions in advance, the area of uncertainty in management decision making is greatly diminished.

The better-known and more widely used techniques of Operations Research were briefly described in this chapter—linear programming, Monte Carlo, queuing theory, simulation, and game theory.

Although these have all been used successfully in production, materials management, and sales, the utilization of OR in general management and in nonbusiness applications is still very limited. Many authorities believe that Operations Research will make its greatest contribution when entire organizations with all their interrelationships and complexities are presented by mathematical models. Then will management have the ultimate tool for pretesting its decisions.

Although the application of OR techniques to operations of the entire organization is still a long way in the future, progress toward this goal is being made. Year by year more and more managers are using OR techniques, and the reasons are not hard to find. Organizations are more and more complex, the manager's time is so limited, and so much money is usually at stake that the manager needs all the support he can get to help make the critical decisions.

But regardless of how effectively OR methods help management decision making, it is still the manager who has the final responsibility for evaluating each problem and judging which of the alternative courses of action to select. OR is an aid, but the manager-systems analyst must still make the final and often lonely decision.

REVIEW QUESTIONS

1. Why are models used in many applications of Operations Research?
2. What role does mathematics play in Operations Research?
3. Describe the class of problems vulnerable to linear programming.
4. What are the components of the mathematical model used in linear programming?
5. Solve by the simplex method:

$$\text{Maximize } Z = 6X + 7Y$$

Subject to the constraints:

$$2X + 3Y \le 24$$
$$4X + 3Y \le 36$$
$$X,Y \ge 0$$

6. Solve the following problem of allocating supply to demand at minimum cost. Use the Water Stone method first, then the MODI, then VAM and check for optimality with MODI.

SUPPLY (UNITS)		DEMAND (UNITS)	
A	150	1	90
B	40	2	70
C	80	3	50
	$\overline{270}$	4	60
			$\overline{270}$

$ Cost from/to	1	2	3	4
A	27	23	31	69
B	10	45	40	32
C	30	54	35	57

7. A department manager must distribute computer programming assignments to five senior programmers. The work is divided into four separate areas (FORTRAN, COBOL, PL/1, SYSTEMS DESIGN), and each programmer possesses a different ability in each of the possible work categories. This ability has been evaluated as a cost per hour for each programmer in each category. Each programmer is avail-

able forty hours per week (*resources*) and the total regular weekly work load (*demand*) is as follows:

a. Sixty hours per week of FORTRAN programming
b. Seventy hours per week of COBOL programming
c. Twenty hours per week of PL/1 programming
d. Fifty hours per week of SYSTEMS DESIGN work

Programmer cost per hour is as follows:

Program Languages ($ Cost/Hour) [a]

Programmer	Fortran	Cobol	PL/1	Systems Design
Willa	10	8	14	11
Joshua	11	7	15	9
Serena	14	10	14	15
David	10	14	12	16
Marcus	8	12	9	11

[a] Use VAM and check if solution is optimum with MODI.

8. What are the characteristics of problems that are being solved by Monte Carlo methods?
9. What is the procedure for a Monte Carlo solution?
10. Describe the alternative courses of action that make up all queuing problems.
11. Name at least five elements of all queuing problems.
12. A computer time-sharing terminal usage in a business college is being analyzed (single channel, single phase, first come, first served). Observation indicates that the users arrive according to a Poisson distribution with a mean arrival rate (λ) of ten per hour. Observation also indicates that the usage (service) time has an exponential distribution with a mean service rate (μ) of five minutes. Calculate L, Lq, W, Wq. Also calculate the probabilities of one, two, three, four, or five students waiting to use the terminal.
13. What is a definition of *simulation*? What are the three major types of simulation?
14. Define *game theory*.
15. What is the relationship between electronic computers and Operations Research?

BIBLIOGRAPHY

BRABB, GEORGE J., *Introduction to Quantitative Management*. New York: Holt, Rinehart & Winston, Inc., 1968. Emphasis on the statistical basis for quantitative decision techniques.

CHURCHMAN, C. WEST, RUSSELL L. ACKOFF, and E. LEONARD ARNOFF, *Introduction to Operations Research*. New York: John Wiley & Sons, Inc., 1957. The granddaddy of them all. Although much of it is now outdated, the philosophical discussion and the perceptive comments of the authors maintain the book's position as a classic in the field.

GREENWOOD, WILLIAM T., *Decision Theory and Information Systems*. Chicago: South-Western Publishing Co., 1969. Uses systems analyses and systems models as the common denominator of all decision processes. A useful treatment of the tools of OR and a worthwhile book.

HEIN, LEONARD W., *The Quantitative Approach to Managerial Decisions*. Englewood Cliffs, N. J.: Prentice-Hall, Inc., 1967. One of the best books on quantitative decision techniques. Aimed at being self-explanatory, and except for the simplex method of linear programming, it hits the mark.

HILLIER, FREDERICK S., and GERALD J. LIEBERMAN, *Introduction to Operations Research*. San Francisco, Calif.: Holden-Day, Inc., 1967. A rigorous treatment that will reward careful, thoughtful study. Not for the novice, but an excellent next step.

KIBBEE, JOEL M., CLIFFORD J. CRAFT, and BURT NANUS, *Management Games*. New York: Reinhold Publishing Corp., 1961. Provides a general introduction to the subject of games and probes the questions of why and how to use them, and how to design them.

ROCCAFERRERA, GUISEPPE M. FERRERO, *Introduction to Linear Programming Processes*. Chicago: South-Western Publishing Co., 1967. Reviews basic mathematics for Operations Research and then treats linear programming techniques from a practical and managerial point of view.

SCHELLENBERGER, ROBERT E., *Managerial Analysis*. Homewood, Ill.: Richard D. Irwin, Inc., 1969. This book provides a useful overview of an array of quantitative techniques and decision tools. It includes some provocative philosophical discussion.

12

ADP FOR MANAGEMENT INFORMATION SYSTEMS

Previous chapters of this book have repeatedly emphasized the key/critical importance of automatic data-processing devices in the implementation of many of the tools and techniques already discussed. It is essential that automatic data processing and the electronic computer be better understood by managers and systems analysts so that they can effectively apply these powerful tools.

This chapter and the next will attempt to develop an understanding point of view about automatic data processing in general and the electronic computer in particular. A basic assumption is made. That is, that the reader of this book has little, if any, background or experience in the field. In fact, this chapter and the next will assume that the reader has no prior knowledge of the subject.[1]

[1] Where parts of this presentation tend to brevity and conciseness, and to that extent cause any confusion, the reader may find it to his advantage to refer to William A. Bocchino, *A Simplified Guide to Automatic Data Processing*, 2nd ed. (Englewood Cliffs, N.J.: Prentice-Hall, Inc., 1972), which discusses this same subject area in greatly expanded form.

The basic concepts of data and data processing are discussed first, followed by a brief description of the evolution of punched card data processing, and this chapter concludes with a discussion of the development of the electronic computer. Chapter 13 then explains computer programming and the application of the computer to systems analysis and design.

DATA AND DATA PROCESSING

A good way to begin the discussion of any new subject is to define some key terms. Data is an excellent choice for a beginning. What do we mean by data? A useful definition is that data is any piece of information, any bit of intelligence. Data can be thought of as any number, any letter, or any symbol, or for that matter, any combination of numbers, letters, or symbols. The number 5, the letter R, the symbol $, and the piece of information "$75.00 a dozen" are examples of data. Characters familiar to all of us are used to represent data. Examining the twelve characters used to represent the example of a piece of information

$$\$75.00 \text{ A DOZEN}$$

it is easily seen that they can be separated into three categories—numbers, letters, and symbols. In point of fact, the total of all characters that are commonly used to represent data in a Management Information System will be found to be made up of ten numbers:

$$0, 1, 2, 3, 4, 5, 6, 7, 8, 9,$$

twenty-six letters:

$$\text{A, B, C, D, E, F, G, H, I, J, K, L, M,}$$

$$\text{N, O, P, Q, R, S, T, U, V, W, X, Y, Z}$$

and about fourteen generally used symbols:

$$(\ \$ \ . \ - \ @ \ ^* \ / \ , \ \% \ \# \ + \ \cent \ = \ )$$

These fifty characters (numbers, letters, and symbols) constitute the complete range of "raw material" processed through a Management Information System. They are the *input* that is put through a series of steps to convert the data to some *output* condition. This conversion of input to output is *data processing*.

Often abbreviated DP, data processing is the series of steps that convert input data into output—with or without the use of machines!

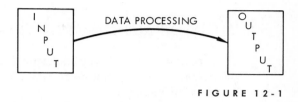

FIGURE 12-1

The conversion of input to output should put the emphasis on "useful" output in order to introduce a basic "law" of data processing. It is known as "GIGO", Garbage In—Garbage Out, a truism of the data processing fraternity. No matter how sophisticated the logic of the processing steps or how advanced the equipment, if the input to a DP system is inaccurate, error laden, and misleading, the output will be inaccurate, error laden, and misleading. Garbage In—Garbage out!

Kinds of Data Processing Systems

When the conversion from input to output is done by human beings without the use of machines, it is known as *manual data processing*. The grocer recording the prices of the items purchased on the back of a paper bag, adding them, and recording the total is a familiar example of manual data processing.

If the grocer in the above example used a hand-operated adding machine in his processing of the data, it would be an example of *mechanical data* processing, that is, human beings utilizing mechanical devices to help them convert input to output.

Electromechanical data processing is the term applied to data-processing systems that utilize electromechanical equipment. The adding cash register at the supermarket check-out counter is a simple example. Desk top calculators, most bookkeeping machines, and much punched card equipment are also in this category.

Electronic data processing (EDP) refers to the processing of data using machines that have electronic circuitry, tubes or transistors, in their design. Computers and most of the other newly developed data-processing devices fit into this category.

Nowadays, the all-embracing term *automatic data processing* (ADP) is apppplied to any DP system that utilizes equipment in converting input to output whether that equipment is mainly mechanical, electromechanical, or electronic.

EVOLUTION OF AUTOMATIC DATA PROCESSING

Now that we have a basic understanding of data and data processing, a discussion of the development of modern data-processing devices should be more meaningful.

It is generally recognized that the initial impetus for the development of modern DP equipment was the stipulation in the U.S. Constitution that congressional seats must be reapportioned, based on the census, every ten years. Since the 1880 census took seven years to compile, the director of the Bureau of the Census was concerned that the 1890 census, with a much larger population, might not be finished by 1900. Therefore, he put a statistician-inventor, Dr. Herman Hollerith, to work on the problem.

Dr. Hollerith had been intrigued by earlier calculating devices such as the abacus, Pascal's calculating device, and especially by the unsuccessful "difference engine" (a wood and metal computing machine) of Charles Babbage of England. In addition, Dr. Hollerith had made a painstaking study of the Jacquard looms of France—textile weaving machines that utilized holes in heavy paper to control the patterns woven. He understood that the position of the holes in the heavy paper represented control information to the looms. Dr. Hollerith's great contribution was his conceptualizing a system of utilizing patterns of holes in cards to represent numbers, letters, and symbols, that is, data, as well as the design of machines whose functions would be dependent on the patterns of holes in cards.

Initially, Dr. Hollerith devised a hole code designed specifically to represent census data in cards. He also developed a simple machine that could "read" the holes in the cards. Lo and behold, counting the census was mechanized and modern data processing was born! His developments and those of his associates and followers provided the basis for the punched card data processing systems that are still very widely used today and that led to the development of the electronic computer.

PUNCHED CARD DATA PROCESSING

Two major classifications of punched card systems developed commercially. One used a round hole and the other a rectangular hole, but otherwise there was really no basic difference in principles. The card code concept, the reading of the cards, the equipment, the effectiveness of the systems, all were essentially the same.

For many years one manufacturer's cards could not be used with the equipment of another manufacturer. This exclusivity was finally breached when a line of Remington Rand equipment (round holes) was produced that could easily be adapted to handle IBM cards (rectangular holes). The general and almost universal trend is to standardize on the rectangular hole system and, therefore, it is the one that will be described in detail.

Today's standard IBM card (see Fig. 12-2), has numbers pre-printed on it in a particular pattern. Each vertical listing of numbers 0 1 2 3 4 5 6 7 8 9 is called a *column*. Each horizontal listing of numbers 3 3 3 3 . . . is called a *row*. There are eighty columns on the card and twelve rows. Ten of the rows are printed; two of the rows, the 11 and 12, are not printed. The tiny numbers below the 9 row and between the 0 and 1 row identify the columns 1 through 80.

The reason the 11 and 12 rows are not printed on the card is that cards are used as basic operating documents in many applications, and the data must be easily readable by human beings. Information punched into the card is often printed on the card, and preprinted identification is also put on the card. It is usually printed at the top of the card in the approximate location of the "11" and the "12" rows.

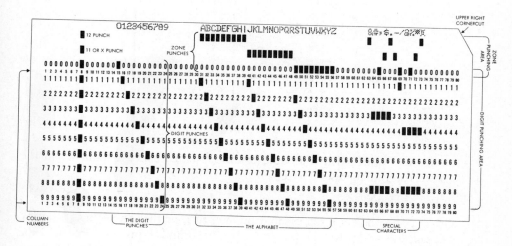

FIGURE 12-2

The Standard IBM Card and Card Code

If a row of 11s and a row of 12s were preprinted on the card, there would be quite a bit of confusion in attempting to read the other printed data on the card.

Card Codes

The alphabet, numbers, and symbols are represented by a hole or combination of holes in the card (refer to Fig. 12-2). The patterns of holes will always represent the same specific characters.

Numbers

Numerical information, that is, any one of the ten basic digits in the decimal system (0–9) is encoded on the card by punching a single hole in any column in the position representing that digit. *Example*: A hole in the 3 position in any column will always mean the number 3 to any IBM punched card machine. Numbers of more than one digit require as many columns as there are digits to be represented. If the number to be punched was 6437, for instance, four columns would be needed.

Letters

Alphabetic information is encoded by using two punched holes in any column—one hole in the 1 . . . 9 positions (numerical punches) and another hole in either the 0, 11, or 12 positions (zone punches) in the same column. *Examples*: A to all IBM punched card equipment is the 12 punch and the 1 punched in the same column. The letter L is the 11

A	12–1	J	11–1	S	0–2
B	12–2	K	11–2	T	0–3
C	12–3	L	11–3	U	0–4
D	12–4	M	11–4	V	0–5
E	12–5	N	11–5	W	0–6
F	12–6	O	11–6	X	0–7
G	12–7	P	11–7	Y	0–8
H	12–8	Q	11–8	Z	0–9
I	12–9	R	11–9		

and the 3 punched in the same column. Remember, two punches in the same column represent letters.

Symbols

Symbols are represented by one, two, or three holes in a column. *Examples*: — by the 11 punch, / by the 0 and 1 punches in the same column, $ by the 11–8–3 punches. See if you can corroborate the above in Figure 12-2.

Reading the Card

The basic principle of card reading is the converting of the distance of the hole from the edge of the card into the timing of an electrical impulse. This is accomplished simply and ingeniously. Each card fed into a punched card (PC) machine passes between a brush and a roller connected to an electrical circuit. The brush is kept from touching the copper contact roller by the card which acts as an insulator. When the brush reaches a hole, it drops through and touches the roller, completing the circuit. The timing of the impulse is proportional to the distance of the hole from the leading edge of the card. (See Fig. 12-3.)

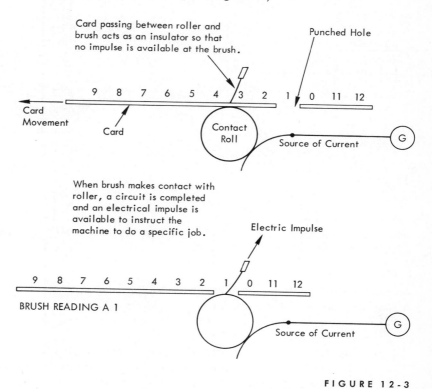

FIGURE 12-3

Control Wiring

Having sensed the holes in the card, there remains the step of directing the electrical or mechanical energy generated in the sensing mechanism in such a way as to produce the required operations by the equipment. Control panels perform this function.

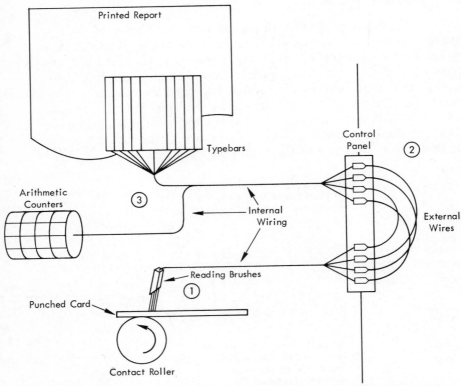

Electrical Impulses from the Brushes ① are routed through the control panel ② to the particular internal components ③ for the desired processing.

FIGURE 12-4

Accounting Machine Wiring. Reprinted from Bocchino,
A Simplified Guide to Automatic Data Processing, p. 33.

The control panel operates in a manner similar to that of a switchboard. The brushes in the sensing mechanism are connected internally to the control panel. Wires leading to other parts of the equipment are also connected internally to the control panel. Plugs are inserted externally, in appropriate holes (hubs) in the face of the control panel, causing contact to be made with the internal connections to the equipment. (See Fig. 12-4.)

The control panel or board is usually removable so that once set up for a particular DP operation it can be stored until needed again.

Punched Card Equipment

Information from source documents, such as bills, job tickets, and sales receipts, is put into the cards by using the card punch machine (see Fig. 12-5). This machine has a keyboard similar to that of an ordinary typewriter, and anyone who types can operate it. The operator reads from the source document, the appropriate keys are depressed, and the correct combination of holes is punched into the cards to represent the numbers, letters, and symbols comprising the desired information.

The recording of data by converting each character on the source document to a combination of holes in a card makes it possible for the information to be processed by other punched card machines—adding, subtracting, multiplying, dividing, sorting, arranging in alphabetical or numerical order, and many other data-processing operations. (See Fig. 12-5.)

This brief discussion of punch card data processing provides a basic idea of its principles and the operation of PCDP equipment. The most important point to remember at this time is that holes in a card represent numbers, letters, and symbols, and a variety of machines were developed that utilize the holes in the cards to process data from input to output.

TRANSITION TO THE ELECTRONIC COMPUTER

The foregoing, although a very condensed introduction to punch card data processing, does provide enough of an exposure to its operation to develop some reservations about the equipment. For instance, the equipment leaves something to be desired in terms of speed. Cards are processed through these electromechanical devices one at a time. Processing great quantities of data, a card at a time, through an essentially mechanical device can take an inordinate amount of time.

Another less obvious point is that whenever the data is to be processed through the next step in the procedure, the deck of punched cards must be physically carried to the next machine. This is necessary because each machine is a special function device usually able to perform but one step in the process. This movement of masses of cards from one machine to the next machine to the next machine, and so forth, is time consuming and also creates material-handling and human-error problems. Cards drop, get out of sequence, get soiled, and they tend to be mutilated the more they are handled.

Another serious limitation of PCDP involves storage ability. In

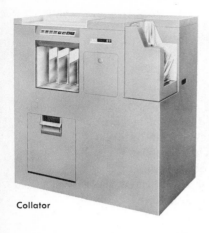

Collator

Accounting Machine

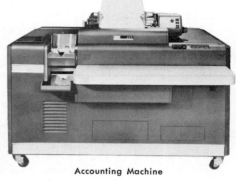

Accounting Machine

Calculating Punch

Key Punch

Statistical Sorter

FIGURE 12-5

IBM Punched Card Machines

Verifier

Tape-to-Card Punch

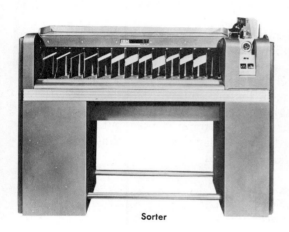

Sorter

Reproducer

Card-to-Tape Punch

Collator

PCDP, the punched cards themselves are the storage devices. The data from source documents is available for processing only if punched into the cards. The PCDP equipment itself has no storage capacity. This is critical because the bulk of the data processed in routine applications such as payrolls, financial reports, inventory and production reports, and cost studies consists of standard reference data such as tax tables, price lists, wage rates, standard costs, employee names and addresses, customer credit ratings, and vendor terms and conditions—data that will not change very much or very often. Therefore, a great deal of the data punched into cards is really standard reference data. But there is no way to store this standard data inside PCDP equipment where it would be readily available during processing. Instead, this data must be punched into cards and the cards laboriously read one by one for the standard reference data to be included in the process. This is a serious and an expensive limitation of PCDP.

Less obvious than some of the other limitations, but of paramount importance to MIS applications, is the inability of PCDP equipment to make decisions—that is, the inability of the equipment to select an alternative sequence of subsequent processing steps based on a testing of the conditions at a certain stage in the procedure.

The argument in support of this position pivots on a fascinating aspect of most data-processing applications. Simply put, the decisions that are an integral part of the day-to-day procedures of all organizations consist of the same three universal steps:

1. Two numbers are compared.
2. A hierarchy of value is generated.
3. The alternative is selected.

A decision is the selection of one from among alternative courses of action. When that selection is based on a hierarchy of values (relative worth of each alternative) it is known as a *logical decision*. Since the operations of all organizations require a multitude of logical decisions in the course of each day's activities, it is only to be expected that data-processing applications contain many of these logical decision steps. For instance, in an inventory control procedure, identification of the quantity level of a particular item at which to reorder (reorder point) starts a chain reaction that results in replenishment of that item in inventory.

Specifically, if the quantity in inventory were, say, 3,600 units, and if the reorder point had been calculated (based on usage and delivery times) at 3,000 units, the subtraction of the reorder point (3,000) from the quantity on hand (3,600) would result in an answer of + 600 and no requisition for more material need be prepared. If the quantity on hand were 2,800, the comparison (i.e., subtraction) of the reorder point (3,000) from the quantity on hand (2,800) would have resulted in a —200 and material would have been ordered. If the quantity on hand were 3,000, the subtraction would have resulted in a zero answer and the reorder would also be initiated.

Recapping:	Quantity on hand	3,600	2,800	3,000
	Reorder point	−3,000	−3,000	−3,000
	Result	+ 600	− 200	0

The foregoing is one example of the kind of ordinary, routine, repetitive decisions that depend on the comparison (subtraction) of one number from another, and the subsequent selection of the alternative course of action is dependent on recognizing whether the result of the subtraction generated a minus or a zero or a plus. The importance of this point makes repeating it worthwhile. The selection of the course of action really depends on whether the answer to the subtraction of reorder point from quantity on hand is — or 0 or +.

Other examples of the number and variety of day-to-day decisions that are based on the comparison of numbers are literally endless: sales performance against target, budgeted expenses against actual costs, patient admissions against hospital forecasts, schedules against actual production, and so forth. Punched card equipment does not have the ability to perform this simple but profoundly important three-step sequence unless a human being assists by recycling the cards, changing the control panel, and pushing some buttons.

Finally, in PCDP the conversion of input data to output involves not only human beings in the movement of cards from one step to the next in the data-processing cycle but also a great deal of "hands on" operation of the equipment. This includes the insertion of control panels, handling of cards, and manipulation of switches.

This means that PCDP is not "a continuous self-controlled operation." That is, even though each step in the process has been carefully predetermined and detailed, human beings must still activate, monitor, and control the processing just about every step of the way. PCDP does not have the ability to direct itself internally through the sequence of steps that are necessary for processing the data. This sequence of steps is just another way of saying program, and therefore this limitation of PCDP can be specified as a lack of "internal programming."

Summary of Limitations of PCDP

1. *Slow*: PCDP was a major step forward, but because PCDP is electromechanical, it is relatively slow in terms of management's needs.
2. *Much material handling*: Each step in PCDP requires handling the cards and moving them from machine to machine.
3. No *internal storage*: Storage of data is extremely limited: the card itself or some few counters in certain parts of some machines— and that is all. Yet a great deal of the data punched into cards and used in routine data-processing applications is standard reference data which, if available within the equipment, will greatly enhance the efficiency of the data-processing application.
4. No *decision ability*: PCDP equipment cannot handle the selection of alternatives that depend on "logicability"—that is, the ability to select a predetermined course of action (decision) as indicated by the hierarchy of values (− or 0 or +) generated by a comparison of numbers (subtraction) at a particular point in a DP procedure.
5. *Internal programming*: Human beings are needed to monitor, interconnect, and control the steps between input and output. PCDP equipment cannot go through a significant number of steps under its own control.

This list of limitations of PCDP equipment provides a natural gateway to the development of operating specifications for a data-processing device that can overcome these limitations. The operating specifications, in turn, will provide an excellent set of guides for designing the new device.

Operating Specifications for a New DP Device

1. *High speed*: It must be as fast as possible in all phases of operation.
2. *Interconnection*: All components of the device must be interconnected in some way to allow for a continuous flow of processing from input to output without human intervention.
3. *Mass storage capacity*: It must be very large, in the order of hundreds of thousands, even millions—perhaps billions—of character capacity to hold large masses of reference data, transaction data, and results.
4. *Logicability*: It must be able to go through the three decision steps under its own control, that is, compare two numbers and decide on a predetermined course of action based on whether the result of that comparison is − or 0 or +.

5. *Internally programmed*: It must be able to follow a long and complex sequence of processing steps, under its own control.

DEVELOPMENT OF THE NEW DEVICE   Knowing the operating specifications required plus using some well-known engineering principles, it may be possible to discuss the design of this new DP device from the inside out. Although simplified, this approach will provide useful insights into the workings of every electronic computer.

MEETING THE "HIGH SPEED" SPECIFICATIONS   A clue as to how to get very high speed in a better DP device is provided by the answer to the question, What is the fastest thing known? The answer, of course, is light, or electricity—about 186,000 miles a second. In other words, electrons travel at the speed of light. If an electronic DP device could be developed, we would have all the speed we need.

However, there is a real problem in applying this idea because all electronic devices, whether television sets or space guidance systems, must be constructed of combinations of four basic electronic components: resistors, capacitors, inductors, and "tubes" (that is, vacuum tubes, transistors, tunnel diodes, etc.). The problem with using these components may best be explained by pointing out that these electronic parts have much in common with an ordinary electric light bulb-switch circuit. Try this experiment. Flip the switch a few times. What happens? The light is either on or it is off. It is always in one condition or the other in its basic stable state. It is a two-condition device. So are resistors, capacitors, inductors, and tubes (or transistors, etc.) if we stretch a technical point or two for purposes of simplification to aid understanding.

In their basic stable state capacitors are either charged or discharged; resistors have a voltage drop across them or they do not; inductors are magnetized in one direction or the other; tubes (or transistors, etc.) are conducting or nonconducting. All exhibit this two-condition, or *binary*, characteristic.

The data-processing device that is under development must be electronic to get the speed that is needed and, therefore, must use electronic (two-condition) components. But this presents an immediate problem because number manipulation is the great bulk of most data processing and the number system in our culture is a decimal system—a ten-condition system (0, 1, 2, 3, 4, 5, 6, 7, 8, 9). Condition 0, unique, separate, and distinct from condition 1, or condition 2, and so on through condition 9. Attempting to design a ten-condition processing machine using obviously incompatible two-condition electronic components raises the specter of insurmountable problems of stability, reliability, and cost. The design of the new device is faced with a serious dilemma.

It would be easier and much more reliable if the data could be represented in two conditions. Such two-condition data would be compatible with the electronic components (i.e., on-off, charged-discharged, magnetized one way or the other, pulse-nopulse, etc.).

The alternatives facing the designers of this new DP device are either to change the laws of physics (not very likely) to make the electronic parameters multistable or to change our familiar decimal (ten-condition) numbering system to a two-condition or binary (two-bi, number-nary) numbering system within the electronic data-processing device. Such a numbering system, because it is compatible with the characteristics of the electronic components, will allow the processing of data at the speed of light. Luckily, such a number system need not be developed from scratch. In fact, a binary numbering system has been known to mankind for a long time.

The design decision will be to utilize the input device to convert decimal numbers to binary for compatible processing by the electronic data-processing device. After all processing steps are completed, the data is converted by the output device back to human-oriented language.

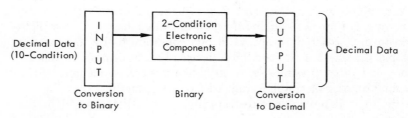

Number Systems

THE DECIMAL SYSTEM   A good place to begin the examination of number systems is with the familiar decimal system. It is a system based on 10. The ten conditions that make up this number system are represented by the familiar numeric characters 0, 1, 2, 3, 4, 5, 6, 7, 8, 9. Interestingly enough, this demonstrates a general rule of number systems. That is, the highest quantity that can be represented by one digit in any number system is always one less than the base of the system. In the decimal system, the highest quantity that can be represented is 9, which is 1 less than 10, the base of the system.

Another general rule of number systems is also demonstrated by use of the decimal system.

DECIMAL

(10)	(0–9)
	0
	1
	2
	3
	4
	5
	6
	7
	8
	9
10	

To represent the next higher quantity after we have exhausted the ten conditions of the system (0–9), a zero is put in the rightmost position and we shift one position to the left and start over again. After listing the number 9, the next quantity is 10. Although, by training, we write it quite naturally, it demonstrates the second general rule of all number systems, namely, that when all conditions representing quantity in one position have been exhausted we represent the next higher quantity by recording a zero, shift one position to the left, and repeat starting with 1.

A third general rule of number systems relates to the value assigned to each position of a number. For instance, 444 in the decimal system is read as four hundred and forty-four. Yet the digit 4 is the same except for its position. What makes it have a value of four hundred in one position, forty in another, and only four in still another position? The answer, of course, is to fall back on our elementary school chant of "units, tens, hundreds, thousands." But these values only apply to the decimal system. What is the general rule? The answer is that each position of a multidigit number has a particular value that is a function of the base of the system raised to a power.

In the decimal system—10^3 10^2 10^1 10^0—10^0 is of course 1, or "units" position, 10^1 is 10, or "tens" position, 10^2 is 100, or "hundreds" position, and so forth. The general rule that can be deduced from this is as follows: In number systems, the value of each position can be determined by raising the base of the system to the zero power for the rightmost (low order) position and then progressively increasing the power of the base as positions are shifted to the left. That is,

$$(\text{Base})^3 \quad (\text{Base})^2 \quad (\text{Base})^1 \quad (\text{Base})^0$$

The final rule that is needed to have a reasonably comfortable grasp of number systems for this discussion is the rule for converting numbers in any base to the value in the decimal system. In fact, the decimal system itself can give us a clue as to the general rule that applies. Suppose we wished to determine the quantity represented by the three-digit decimal number 437. We know about the value of position, so

$$
\begin{array}{rcl}
437 & & \\
\quad 7 \times 10^0 = 7 \times 1 & = & 7 \\
\quad 3 \times 10^1 = 3 \times 10 & = & 30 \\
\quad 4 \times 10^2 = 4 \times 100 & = & 400 \\
\hline
& & 437
\end{array}
$$

Of course, the result is exactly the same as what we started with because it was already a decimal number, but it provides the basis for stating the general rule for conversion to the decimal system. Multiply each digit by the value of its position utilizing the base of the particular number system involved and then add up the individual values to get the decimal equivalent.

Summarizing the general rules for number systems:

Rule 1: The base of a number system is always 1 more than the highest condition that can be represented by one digit in that system.

Rule 2: When all the conditions representing quantity by one digit have been exhausted, you represent the next higher quantity by using a 0, shifting one position to the left, and recycling.

Rule 3: The value of a digit depends on its position. The rightmost position has a value equal to the base of the number system to the zero power (always 1), the next position to the left has a value equal to Base^1, the next has a value equal to Base^2, and so forth.

Rule 4: To convert to the decimal equivalent from any number system, multiply each digit by the value of its position and add.

THE BINARY SYSTEM   Utilizing the general rules for number systems developed by examining the familiar decimal system, we can develop an understanding of the binary system. First of all, it is a two-condition system. The base of the system is 2. The two conditions are 0 and 1. As Rule 1 indicates, the highest condition that can be represented is 1.

BINARY

Base	Conditions
(2)	(0–1)
0	
1	

After listing the digits 0, 1, we find we quickly run out. Utilizing Rule 2, we can write the next higher quantity (two) by shifting one position to the left and placing a zero in the right-hand position and repeating. Applying it to this case, the next higher quantity (two) can be represented in binary as 1 0. Three is one added to two, or 1 1, but we must once again apply Rule 2 to represent the quantity four as 100, and then five as 101, six as 110, seven as 111, eight as 1000, and finally nine as 1001.

Summarizing as follows, we have developed the binary number system's representation of the ten decimal conditions:

Binary		Decimal
0	is	0
1	is	1
10	is	2
11	is	3
100	is	4
101	is	5
110	is	6
111	is	7
1000	is	8
1001	is	9

For uniformity, and to assist in subsequent developments, we rewrite the above adding leading zeros to the binary numbers:

Binary	Decimal
0000	0
0001	1
0010	2
0011	3
0100	4
0101	5
0110	6
0111	7
1000	8
1001	9

Four binary digits, abbreviated *bits,* represent each decimal digit. This system of "coding" decimal digits in binary is referred to as *binary coded decimal* notation, abbreviated as BCD.

Representation of a number greater than 9 requires more sets of four binary digits (bits). For example:

$$
\begin{array}{ccc}
4 & 3 & 7 \\
0100 & 0011 & 0111
\end{array}
$$

It should be pointed out that Rule 3 and Rule 4 are very definitely involved in this presentation. For instance, Rule 3 can be used to convert from binary to decimal. Remember that the values of each of the four binary positions are 2^3 2^2 2^1 2^0. Therefore

$$
\begin{array}{l}
10 \\
\quad \rightarrow 0 \times 2^0 = 0 \times 1 = 0 \\
\quad \rightarrow 1 \times 2^1 = 1 \times 2 = \underline{2} \\
\hphantom{\quad \rightarrow 1 \times 2^1 = 1 \times 2 =} 2
\end{array}
$$

and

$$
\begin{array}{l}
100 \\
\quad \rightarrow 0 \times 2^0 = 0 \times 1 = 0 \\
\quad \rightarrow 0 \times 2^1 = 0 \times 2 = 0 \\
\quad \rightarrow 1 \times 2^2 = 1 \times 4 = \underline{4} \\
\hphantom{\quad \rightarrow 1 \times 2^2 = 1 \times 4 =} 4
\end{array}
$$

finally

$$
\begin{array}{l}
1000 \\
\quad \rightarrow 0 \times 2^0 = 0 \times 1 = 0 \\
\quad \rightarrow 0 \times 2^1 = 0 \times 2 = 0 \\
\quad \rightarrow 0 \times 2^2 = 0 \times 4 = 0 \\
\quad \rightarrow 1 \times 2^3 = 1 \times 8 = \underline{8} \\
\hphantom{\quad \rightarrow 1 \times 2^3 = 1 \times 8 =} 8
\end{array}
$$

and just for practice

$$
\begin{array}{l}
0111 \\
\quad \rightarrow 1 \times 2^0 = 1 \times 1 = 1 \\
\quad \rightarrow 1 \times 2^1 = 1 \times 2 = 2 \\
\quad \rightarrow 1 \times 2^2 = 1 \times 4 = 4 \\
\quad \rightarrow 0 \times 2^3 = 0 \times 8 = \underline{0} \\
\hphantom{\quad \rightarrow 0 \times 2^3 = 0 \times 8 =} 7
\end{array}
$$

The value of each binary position is easily remembered. Whenever there is a 1 in any of the four positions, its decimal value is as indicated.

Binary Position	0	0	0	0
Power	Base^3	Base^2	Base^1	Base^0
Base to the power	2^3	2^2	2^1	2^0
Decimal value	8	4	2	1

Remember that the reason that binary notation is utilized is to overcome the inherent incompatibility of the ten-condition numbering system in use in the human-oriented Management Information System and the two-condition requirement of the components of the electronic data-processing system.

Each binary digit, or bit, that has been represented as a zero or a one could also be represented by any two-condition device. An electric light bulb (on-off), an inductor (magnetized one way or the other), a capacitor (charged-discharged), or a transistor (conducting-nonconducting). For example: think of four light bulbs coding a decimal number in binary (the X in the circle represents "on," that is, the binary 1):

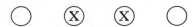

Utilizing your growing familiarity with binary notation, this is obviously the decimal 6.

Binary	*Decimal*
0110	6

The binary device could just as easily have been an inductor, called a *magnetic core*, about the size of the head of a pin, since magnetic cores play a very important role in electronic computers in just this way. More about them later; first let us finish up number systems.

THE HEXADECIMAL SYSTEM   Although not specifically involved in this discussion, the prevalence of the hexadecimal numbering system in many computers makes some familiarity with it quite useful. It is also a natural outgrowth of the use of binary coded decimal (BCD) notation. BCD utilizes four binary digits to represent the decimal digits 0 to 9. But if all the possible combinations of the four binary digits were utilized, it would also be possible to represent the conditions 0 to 15.

(Recalling the value of each binary position will help you to convert to the decimal value quickly.)

8421

Binary	Decimal
1010	10
1011	11
1100	12
1101	13
1110	14
1111	15

Applying Rule 1 we know that a number system involving conditions 0 through 15 will be a base 16, or hexadecimal, number system. However, since the numeric characters in our culture are limited to 0 to 9, it is necessary to use other characters to represent the hexadecimal quantities ten through fifteen. The decision was to use six alphabetic characters and the result is as follows:

Decimal Quantity	Hexadecimal Notation		Binary Coded Hexadecimal
	(16)	(0–15)	(8421)
0	0		0000
1	1		0001
2	2		0010
3	3		0011
4	4		0100
5	5		0101
6	6		0110
7	7		0111
8	8		1000
9	9		1001
10	A		1010
11	B		1011
12	C		1100
13	D		1101
14	E		1110
15	F		1111

The general number system rules still apply, of course. For instance, Rule 2 would result in the quantity sixteen being expressed in hexadecimal notation as 10, and Rule 3 would prove it, as follows:

Hexadecimal 1 0

$$0 \times 16^0 = 0 \times 1 = 0$$
$$1 \times 16^1 = 1 \times 16 = 16$$

Decimal . . . . $\overline{16}$

Now try converting the hexademical number A4F to decimal:

Hexadecimal A4F

$$F \times 16^0 = 15 \times 1 \quad = \quad 15$$
$$4 \times 16^1 = \ \ 4 \times 16 \ \ = \quad 64$$
$$A \times 16^2 = 10 \times 256 = 2560$$

Decimal . . . . $\overline{2639}$

Binary Coded Decimal for Letters and Symbols

Coding the decimal digits into binary numbers solved the problem of incompatibility as far as numbers were concerned, but it also provided, with just a simple extension, for the representation of letters and symbols in binary.

Two more bits were added to the previous binary array, or *byte,* the B bit and the A bit:

B   A   8   4   2   1
○   ○   ○   ○   ○   ○

When the B bit is "on" it is the code equivalent of the 11 punch in the Hollerith code. When the A bit is "on," it is the equivalent of the 0 (zero) punch in the Hollerith code. When they are both on, it is the code equivalent of the 12 punch.

Bit Code	*Equivalent Hollerith Code*
B bit "on"	11 punch
A bit "on"	0 punch
B and A both "on"	12 punch

We are now able to represent letters and symbols, for instance:

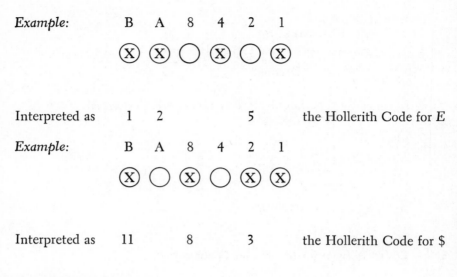

Example: B   A   8   4   2   1

Interpreted as   1   2   5   the Hollerith Code for E

Example: B   A   8   4   2   1

Interpreted as   11   8   3   the Hollerith Code for $

Electronic Processing

What had seemed to be a tremendous obstacle to the design of an electronic data-processing device may have been a blessing in disguise. The binary system has shown itself to be quite adaptable to converting decimal numbers, letters, and symbols into binary coded decimal. The design scheme will introduce an *input* device that will convert numbers, letters, and symbols into binary notation that is compatible with the electronic-processing circuits in the equipment, and when the processing steps are completed, an *output* device will convert BCD back to human-oriented numbers, letters, and symbols.

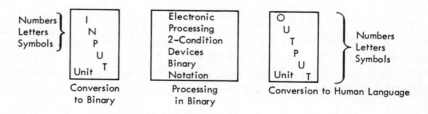

The input conversion may take place in a punched card reading unit, a typewriter input device, or a variety of other devices designed for that purpose. Similarly a printer, typewriter, or similar device could act as the output unit. As will be discussed later, the input and the output units may be a very wide variety of devices depending on whether or not the data is in one form or another.

   Magnetic cores, doughnut-shaped inductors of ferromagnetic material about one-quarter inch in diameter, can be utilized to represent the binary digits. For explanatory purposes it can arbitrarily be decided that when the core is magnetized so that the north pole of the magnetic field is "up" it will represent binary 1 and when magnetized "down" it will represent binary 0. The following configuration, with the Ⓧ representing a magnetic core magnetized "one," that is, a binary 1, and "off" representing binary 0, is the binary coded decimal representation of the dollar sign, $.

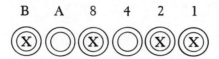

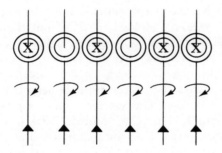

Now let us place a copper wire through each core and indicate current flow in each wire by means of an arrowhead.

The wire is called the *sense* wire and the current is called the *sensing* current. Associated with each current is a magnetic field whose direction is indicated by the curved arrow around the wire. Notice that this magnetic field is in the same direction around each wire because the current flow in each wire is in the same direction.

   Remember that the magnetic cores have the magnetization indicated, and we have designed this circuitry so that when a magnetic core is "on," its magnetic field reinforces the magnetic field associated with the sensing current, causing that current to increase sharply. Conversely, when a magnetic core is magnetized "off," its magnetic field tends to cancel out the magnetic field of the sensing current, causing a sharp drop in current flow in that wire.

Utilizing an oscilloscope (which is much like the picture tube in the home TV set) this effect can be pictorialized:

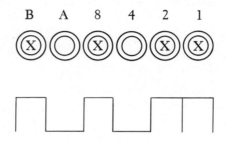

What we see is a train of pulses and no pulses in the exact configuration of the on-off condition of the magnetic cores. What number, letter, or symbol does this pulse train represent? It must be the $ since that is what the magnetic cores represented in BCD notation! At what speed does this pulse train travel? At the speed of light!

Lo and behold, we now have the key to the incredible speed of operation of the computer. The input device converts numbers, letters, and symbols to BCD, and the processing unit utilizes magnetic cores to store them in that notation. The sensing circuits convert the magnetic core (BCD) representation of the numbers, letters, and symbols into pulse train form. These pulse trains are manipulated at the speed of light within the central processing unit. When processing is complete, the output device converts the pulse trains back to the required form for human use or into a form for further processing.

The ability to convert numbers, letters, and symbols into pulse trains is the key to the computer's ability to manipulate data at the speed of light. It also provides the means to overcome another major limitation of PCDP—the lack of interconnection between the different PCDP machines. It was necessary to physically move the punched cards from one machine to the next to complete the steps in the data-processing job. Since pulse trains can travel by wire, all operating components of the electronic system are connected by cable and this second design specification is satisfied.

Now, to recap, input data is converted into binary notation and stored in magnetic core configuration. The cores are "sensed" and the data is converted into pulses and no pulses (pulse trains) of electricity. Manipulating the pulse trains through the sequence of processing steps is equivalent to manipulating the data, since that is what the pulse trains represent. Then, when processing is complete, the pulse trains are converted by the output device into human-compatible printing or into punched cards or into magnetic tape—or into whatever output form is required.

Arithmetic

The device under development must be able to do arithmetic. That, of course, is one of the major data-processing functions. For simplicity in design, we will take advantage of the fact that all arithmetic is really a variation of addition. For instance, subtraction can be carried out by a variation of addition called *complement addition*. It is demonstrated by subtracting 438 from 879.

Usual way:

$$879$$
$$-438$$
$$\overline{441}$$

Now using complement addition, rewrite the lower number, substituting its "nines complement"—the nines complement of 4 (the number that when added to 4 gives 9, which of course is 5), the nines complement of 3 (6), and of 8 (1). So the nines complement of 438 is 561. Replace 438 by its nines complement 561 and add.

Complement addition:

$$879$$
$$+561$$
$$\overline{①440}$$
$$→1$$
$$\overline{441}$$

The final step in complement addition is the "end around carry." Add the 1 on the left to the right (low order position) of the answer. That is, $440 + 1 = 441$.

So you see, it works! What is really important, however, is that in the design of our electronic DP device, we need only provide circuits for addition plus some variations, and we can add and subtract. Furthermore, multiplication is really successive addition and division is really successive subtraction, so we can utilize the high speed of the electronic device to multiply and divide in this simple fashion.

Five times three is fifteen. But, add five to itself three times and you also get fifteen. You get the effect of multiplication by successive addition. Since it is done at electronic speed, doing multiplication of large numbers by successive addition is practical and poses no problem.

Division, in turn, is essentially successive subtraction, which we already know is a variation of addition. Five divided into sixty goes twelve times. Subtract five from sixty and count the number of subtractions and you also get twelve.

Summing up: You subtract by complement addition; you multiply by successive addition; you divide by successive subtraction—which is really successive complement addition. So all that is needed in the new device is an adding capability in order to carry on all the necessary arithmetic of data processing. Although greatly beyond the scope of this book, it can be shown that just about all mathematical processes (integration, differentiation, matrix algebra, etc.), with the aid of the algorithms developed by the great mathematicians, can be accomplished by the combination of high speed and simple arithmetic.

Logicability

Logical decision making was something PCDP equipment could not do. This faculty, as was discussed, pivots on the ability to recognize whether one number is greater than, less than, or equal to another number. The development that has been gone through so far has already covered the subtraction operation and the concept of representing $-$, 0, $+$ in the form of pulse trains. In the discussion of computer programming, in the next chapter, it will be demonstrated that an alternative series of processing steps can be signaled by the $-$ or 0 or $+$ resulting from the comparison of two numbers. The logicability specification can, therefore, be considered to be close to accomplishment.

This may be a good time to recapitulate design accomplishments versus design specifications:

1. *Speed* is provided by making the device electronic. The design complications of using decimal (human-oriented) data with a binary device are avoided by converting to a binary system of data representation at the input, processing the data in binary form, and then converting back to human-oriented characters at the output.

2. *Interconnection* is accomplished by connecting all components by cables, since the data is in pulse train form between input and output.

3. *Logicability* turns out to be a variation of subtraction. Decision making (selecting between alternatives) can be based on the comparison (subtraction) of one number with another and the recog-

nition of a +, 0, or − answer. Some relatively subtle alternatives can be chosen based on successive tests as to whether one number is greater than, less than, or equal to another number.

4. *Arithmetic* ability is provided by having addition with some special features, that is, subtraction by complement addition, multiplication by successive addition, division by successive subtraction.

There are still two design specifications to be met, provision for mass storage and for internal programming of this electronic device. They will be discussed now.

Mass Storage

Magnetic core storage has already been introduced in this chapter. It is characterized by its very high speed (millionths of a second) of accessing information. That is, the speed of getting data from input to core storage or calling for data from core storage and having it ready to be processed. This "access time" is one of the key measures of the relative effectiveness of mass storage devices.

Magnetic core storage also has the very useful ability of having any location of storage accessible in the same amount of time as that of any other location. This is known as *random access*. However, because it is relatively expensive in terms of cost per character, magnetic core storage devices are usually of more limited capacity than other mass storage devices that will be discussed. This is changing as technology provides lower costs, but core storage capacities above one hundred thousand characters are still not as common as lower capacities. Actual core storage is organized in core planes, and these in turn are stacked in core modules (see Fig. 12-6). (Note the C bit in the bit configuration shown in Figure 12-6(C). This check bit is an internal accuracy device to detect bits turned on or off by stray magnetic fields.)

Magnetic core storage, then, is a relatively low capacity, very high speed, relatively expensive, random access storage device.

Magnetic tape storage was a natural outgrowth of the prevalence of home tape recorders. Magnetic tape consists of a strip of plastic tape coated on one side with metallic oxide. Tape width varies. Some are one-inch wide, but tape usually measures one-half inch, and a reel of tape varies from twelve hundred feet to twenty-four hundred feet. Storage reels are about twelve inches in diameter.

Individual characters of data are coded by means of magnetic spots on the tape. The combinations of magnetized spots and non-

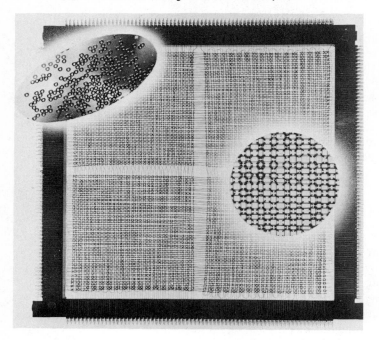

Magnetic Core Plane

FIGURE 12-6
Core Storage

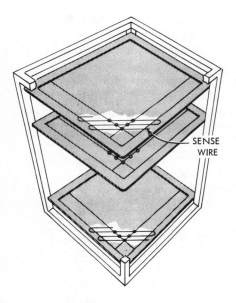

SENSE
WIRE

Sense Wire in Core Plane

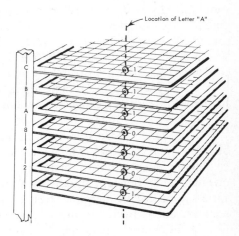

Location of Letter "A"

BCD Character Location

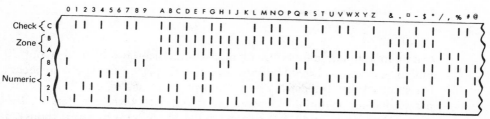

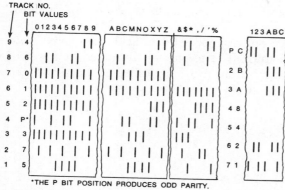

7 Channel (Track) Tape

9 Channel (Track) Tape

*THE P BIT POSITION PRODUCES ODD PARITY.

Hypertape

FIGURE 12-7

Tape Storage

magnetized spots represent a binary code for numbers, letters, and symbols. (See Fig. 12-7.)

The check position in each column on magnetic tape is a self-contained accuracy check inasmuch as it is used to make the number of magnetic spots in each column an even number (even bit parity) or an odd number (odd bit parity), depending on the system.

The recording of data on magnetic tape is similar to that of the home tape recorder. Writing (recording) on tape destroys what was there before; reading does not change the contents. The tape is divided into channels which run parallel to the tape (see Fig. 12-7). A single character is encoded on a vertical frame. A seven-channel tape contains four numeric, two zone, and a parity check position. A nine-channel tape contains four numeric, four zone positions, and a parity check position. Hypertape has ten channels and can record two numbers in a single frame, thereby doubling the characters that can be stored per unit length of tape compared with seven-channel tape.

Tape density is the number of frames per inch of tape. The most common densities are 200, 556, and 800, but can go up to 1,500. A twenty-four hundred-foot reel of tape could theoretically hold about 20 million characters. Effective transmission rate is the tape speed in inches per second times the density per inch. Speeds of 36, 75, and 112.5 inches per second are common. Depending on the particular tape density, this means that information can be transferred at the rate of seven thousand to two hundred thousand (and even higher) characters per second. The average speed of data transfer for most units is about one hundred thousand characters per second.

It should be pointed out that related data fields are grouped into records just as on punched cards. The records are separated by a gap of blank tape about three-quarters of an inch long called an *interblock gap* (IBG). (See Fig. 12-8).

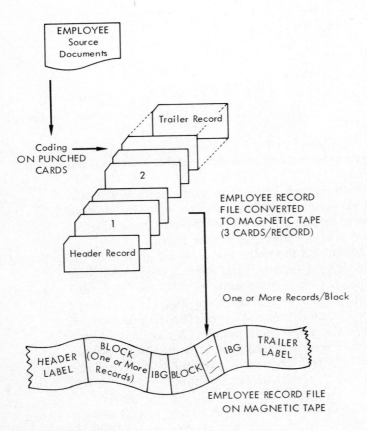

FIGURE 12-8

IBM 2420 Magnetic Tape Drive

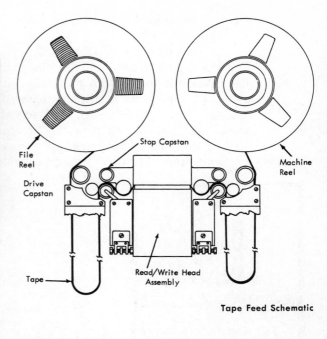

File Reel

Drive Capstan

Stop Capstan

Machine Reel

Tape

Read/Write Head Assembly

Tape Feed Schematic

FIGURE 12-9

IBM 729 Magnetic Tape Drive

The beginning of a magnetic tape file is identified by a control record called a header label which contains date, file number, and other pertinent facts. A trailer label follows the last data record of a file. It contains identifying elements such as file number, file name, and other identification regarding the file that has just been read.

A *tape drive* is the machine that reads and writes on magnetic tape. (Figure 12-9.)

Tapes written on one model of a computer may not be compatible with another because of difference in density, speed, number of channels, recording methods, and so forth.

The most serious drawback of magnetic tape is that all data must be processed sequentially, and it can slow up processing. That is, if the next record to be processed is quite a distance away on the tape, it is necessary to scan the intervening tape till you reach it. This can take expensive time. So the sequential access characteristic of tape can be a serious drawback, but proper structuring of the records on the tape can minimize its effect.

Magnetic tape is a high capacity, low cost, relatively fast storage device. Its major drawback is its sequential characteristic.

Magnetic drum storage was one of the earliest storage devices developed. As the name implies, this cylindrical device (see Fig. 12-10) has its surface coated with magnetic material and rotates at a constant speed. Data is coded on the drum surface by means of the presence or absence of magnetized spots. Data recorded on the drum remains until erased, and just like magnetic tape it can be reused repeatedly.

Read-write heads record or retrieve data from the surface of the revolving drum. The drum surface is divided into individually addressable

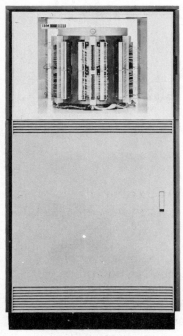

IBM 2301 Magnetic Drum Storage

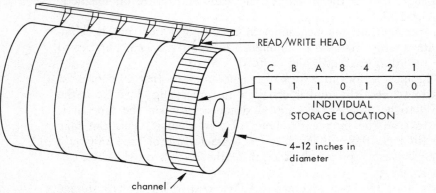

FIGURE 12-10

Magnetic Drum Storage

IBM 2302 Disk Storage

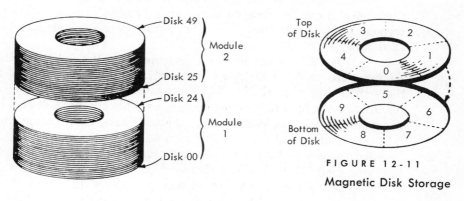

FIGURE 12-11

Magnetic Disk Storage

storage locations. Since the read-write heads are motionless as the drum rotates beneath them, access time depends on the distance the drum must rotate before the data locations are beneath the read-write heads.

Magnetic drum storage (depending on its design) has medium capacity (500,000 to 5,000,000 characters), is moderate in cost, and is comparatively fast (about 10 milliseconds). However, in a number of applications (particularly time sharing) it can be a wise choice.

Magnetic disk storage was developed in answer to the need for a random access storage device with high capacity at moderate cost. The magnetic disk is a thin metal disk, one and one-half to three feet in diameter, coated on both sides with magnetic material. (See Fig. 12-11.) Each side of the disk is divided into concentric tracks. Data can be recorded on both sides of the disk and the read-write head must be positioned over the data location on the disk to read or write data. The disks rotate at about eighteen hundred revolutions per minute.

A disk module is made up of a number of individual disks rotating on a common shaft—from five to one hundred disks. Two or more modules can make up a disk unit (see Fig. 12-11).

Disk access arms with read-write heads move over the disk surface to the specific data location. Data is coded on the disks by means of magnetic spots utilizing the binary system. Each individually addressable disk location (sector) can hold two hundred characters. There are five of these location sectors per track and two hundred tracks on each side of the disk. Therefore, each disk can hold two hundred thousand characters per side, or four hundred thousand per disk. A disk unit of fifty disks could provide storage for 20 million characters. There are disk units that store up to several hundred million characters.

Each segment of two hundred characters is individually addressable and can be retrieved in the same amount of time as any other segment in the disk unit. This is a useful operational definition of a random access device.

Disk pack storage units are very similar to the disk units already discussed except that a disk pack unit can be inserted and removed from the system (see Fig. 12-12). Six disks, smaller than the previous ones discussed, make up a pack. They spin at about fifteen hundred revolutions per minute. Each disk side has one hundred tracks, each track is divided into twenty individually addressable sectors, and each sector contains one hundred characters. Each track, therefore, contains two thousand characters, or a total of two hundred thousand per disk face.

The top and bottom face in each pack of six disks are not usable because they are exposed to physical abuse when the disk pack is removed from the unit. This leaves ten usable sides per disk pack for a total of 2 million characters storage capacity per disk pack. There are disk packs designed and operational that store up to 20 million characters.

Data cell storage (Figure 12-13) was developed to answer the need for a device that would provide storage capacity for the billions of characters represented by large data banks such as technical libraries, the social security system, or a worldwide medical diagnostic network.

In reality, this type of storage device has been known under various other guises over the years, but in essence it consists of an oxide-coated plastic strip on which data is recorded. A number of these strips are put in a box-type container. When a particular unit of data is desired, the strip containing the data is selected and moved under a read-write head, the data is read, and the strip is then replaced in the holder. All

IBM 2316 Disk Pack

FIGURE 12-12

Magnetic Disk Storage

IBM 2311 Disk Storage Drive

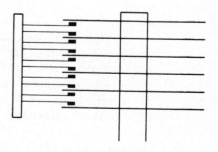

Schematic of Disk Pack and Access

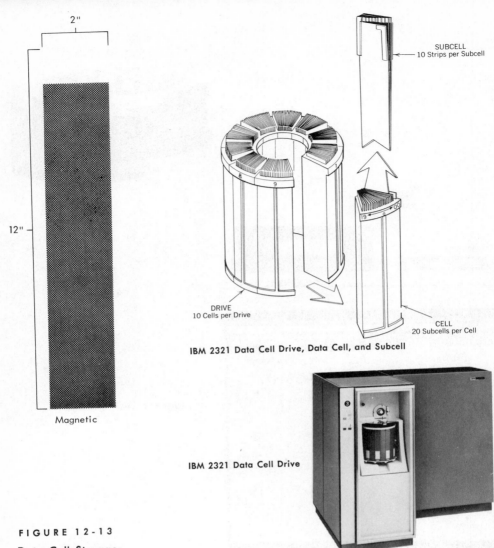

2"

12"

Magnetic

SUBCELL
10 Strips per Subcell

DRIVE
10 Cells per Drive

CELL
20 Subcells per Cell

IBM 2321 Data Cell Drive, Data Cell, and Subcell

IBM 2321 Data Cell Drive

FIGURE 12-13

Data Cell Storage

of this is done electromechanically. The box-type containers are removable, much like disk packs.

The IBM data cell device holds ten data cells, each of which contains two hundred removable and interchangeable strips of mylar tape. Each strip has one hundred recording tracks for data, and each track provides two thousand eight-bit bytes of data. The capacity of the set of ten cells is up to 400 million characters that can be read at a transfer rate of fifty-five thousand characters per second.

The National Cash Register's CRAM system provides storage equivalent to sixty-nine thousand punched cards. Its read-write heads can transfer data at speeds up to one hundred thousand characters per second.

Summary of storage devices:

	Capacity	Access Time (thsds. of char./sec.)	Access Type
Magnetic core	1–2 million	250–2,000	Random
Magnetic tape	1–20 million/tape	15–350	Sequential
Magnetic drum	1–4 million/drum	275–1,200	Random-Sequential
Magnetic disk	2–20 million/pack	100–225	Random
Data cell	100–400 million/unit	25–45	Random-Sequential

Internally Programmed

In our discussion of the limitations of PCDP equipment, a fundamental reason for the ineffectiveness of PCDP was its inability to go through a series of steps under its own control and, therefore, it required human intervention in the data-processing cycle. Since the main reason for developing an electronic device was to gain speed, all would be for naught if human beings would still have to act as links between the steps in the data-processing sequence. Speed could be maintained only if the data, once input, was processed step by step, electronically, under the control or the "stored program" feature of the equipment. It is the key characteristic that separates the computer from all other calculating devices.

The sequence of step-by-step operating instructions is called a *program*. Although programs and programming will be explained in much more detail in the next chapter, the point that should be understood now is that a number (or a letter or a symbol) in pulse train form, put into the control circuitry, will cause the machine to carry out one of its basic operations (add, read a card, etc.). The selection of a particular character (number, letter, or symbol) to cause a certain operation to occur depends on the decision of the designers of the equipment. Once designed into the device, these "operation codes" are set for the life of the particular type of machine.

Internal programming is the final major specification of this new DP device that can be simply described as a high speed adding machine that stores data, can recognize 0 and 1, can tell if one number is greater than, less than, or equal to another number, and can do all these things under its own control. This new DP device is, of course, the *electronic computer*. Simple as it is in concept, it is an awesome data-processing tool and has the potential of being the most powerful management decision tool ever developed.

This self-contained device, this electronic computer, has an input component where punched cards or other data-carrying mediums are converted to binary signals. It has an output device that converts the binary signals back to machine readable printed forms or punched cards or some other medium. It has a STORAGE component of magnetic cores and usually one or more additional storage components (magnetic tape, magnetic disk, magnetic drum, data cell) for masses of data. It has an arithmetic and a logic unit that can do addition, subtraction, multiplication, and division. It can also compare two numbers by subtraction and can determine whether the result is minus, plus, or zero and can thereby signal the internal circuitry of the computer to select an alternative predetermined sequence of processing steps. Its CONTROL unit monitors all the other components and activates them in the necessary sequence to convert input data to useful output. (See Fig. 12-14.)

With the electronic computer, management, for the first time in the history of organizations, has the capability to dominate all the data pertinent to operating the enterprise—a capability that allows a manager to run his operation instead of chasing it.

If the discussion in this chapter has made some sense to you, then you are well on the way to eliminating much of the "language curtain" that has existed between management and the computer. It is not essential to the use of ADP that you understand everything in this chapter, but the more you do, the more your "computer confusion" threshold, or "snow index," will be raised. This means that the application of this powerful decision tool is less in the hands of the so-called computer experts and more in your hands—where it should be.

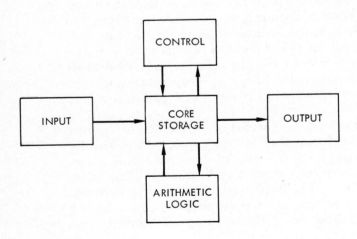

FIGURE 12-14

Computer Components

REVIEW QUESTIONS

1. Define *data* and *data processing*.
2. Differentiate between *manual, electromechanical, electronic,* and *automatic* DP.
3. What is the basic principle on which all card reading is based?
4. What gave the initial impetus to the development of PCDP and who was the man credited with its development?
5. What is the function of the control panel in PC machines?
6. Name five punched card machines.
7. What is the punched card code for the following characters?

D   5   Z $ /

8. What are the five limitations of PCDP equipment and why are they significant weaknesses from the point of view of the MIS?
9. What are the operating specifications of the new device that will overcome the limitations of PCDP equipment?
10. What are the three basic steps in all quantitative decision making? Give an example from real life.
11. What was the dilemma facing the designers of the high-speed DP device?
12. What are the rules underlying all number systems?
13. Give the values of the first four positions of the binary system.
14. Show the binary coded decimal representation of the following decimal numbers:

10   48   146   357   1,000

15. What was the basic design decision that overcame the problem of the incompatibility of the electronic processor and the ten-condition input data?
16. Show the hexadecimal and the binary coded hexadecimal representation of the decimal numbers in Question 14.
17. Represent the following characters utilizing the 6-bit BCD notation:

C $ /   M   5

18. What is the key to converting the static representation of data in magnetic core storage to the dynamic state that allows for data processing at the speed of light?

19. How does the electronic computer subtract, multiply, and divide?

20. List and compare the major storage methods in terms of capacity, access time, and access type.

21. Describe the data cell storage method.

22. Which of the storage methods are random access?

23. What is a computer program?

24. What have pulse trains to do with computer programming?

25. Assess the impact of the computer on the MIS.

26. What are the major components of the electronic computer?

BIBLIOGRAPHY

BOCCHINO, WILLIAM A., *A Simplified Guide to Automatic Data Processing* (2nd ed.). Englewood Cliffs, N.J.: Prentice-Hall, Inc., 1972. Designed for those without any background in the subject matter. Emphasizes the management perspective in developing an understanding and a skill in the use of the computer for decision making.

BRIGHTMAN, RICHARD W., *Practical Data Processing*. New York: The Macmillan Company, 1969. Emphasizes punched card data processing and utilizes case studies for illustrative applications.

DAVIS, GORDON B., *Computer Data Processing*. New York: McGraw-Hill Book Company, 1969. A very well done overview of data processing with many very useful charts and illustrations. One of the best introductory texts in the field.

ELLIOTT, C. ORVILLE, and ROBERT S. WASLEY, *Business Information Processing Systems* (3rd ed.). Homewood, Ill.: Richard D. Irwin, Inc., 1971. Discusses the business information processing systems in use today. Tends to emphasize the accounting aspects, but not at the expense of clarity and scope.

HARTKEMEIER, HARRY P., *Data Processing*. New York: John Wiley & Sons, Inc., 1966. Explains the operation of punched card data-processing machines in detail. Includes very useful full-page illustrations of completely programmed control panels and their input cards and output reports.

HEYEL, CARL, *Computers, Office Machines and the New Information Technology*. New York: The Macmillan Company, 1969. An excellent overview of equipment and applications prepared under the aegis of the Business Equipment Manufacturers Association (BEMA).

LOTT, RICHARD W., *Basic Data Processing*. Englewood Cliffs, N. J.: Prentice-Hall, Inc., 1967. An elementary book for the beginner, with a problem workbook available for testing the student's knowledge of the material covered.

SAXON, JAMES A., and WESLEY W. STEYER, *Basic Principles of Data Processing* (2nd ed.). Englewood Cliffs, N. J.: Prentice-Hall, Inc., 1970. A broad brush treatment of the field by two very knowledgeable practitioners.

13

THE COMPUTER—
MANAGEMENT'S POWERFUL
TOOL

PHYSIOLOGY OF THE COMPUTER

As has been detailed in Chapter 12, the electronic computer can be described as a high-speed adding machine that can recognize 0 and 1, can determine whether one number is greater than, less than, or equal to another number, and can store data—all under its own control. However, its high speed, coupled with its ability to store masses of data and its ability to compare two characters and take an alternate route depending on the result, allows the computer to handle extremely intricate and involved sequences of data-processing steps that can accomplish very sophisticated conversions of input to output. These sequences of individually simple steps are called *programs*, and they are the key to harnessing the power of the electronic computer for management's needs.

A *program* is a series of instructional steps that direct the operating components of a computer to accomplish a particular data-processing or computational task. A useful way to begin to discuss computer programming is by examining the activities of a human being doing a simple clerical task and then relating the same activities to the computer's abilities.

Let us examine the way a clerk might calculate the total price on invoices, that is, multiplying the quantity of items times the unit price per item to get the total price.

$$\text{Quantity} \times \text{Unit price} = \text{Total price}$$

If this were the clerk's regular job and if he were doing it at his assigned desk, he would probably have an "IN" box on one side of his desk and an "OUT" box on the other. The invoices to be processed would be placed in the "IN" box by the preceding operator in the "invoice-processing" procedure. In starting his part of the procedure, the clerk would take an invoice from his "IN" box (input) and multiply "quantity" times "unit price" (arithmetic) to get "total price" (output). This very simple clerical operation used the equivalent of the input, arithmetic, and output functions of the electronic computer.

The clerk would probably check the results of the arithmetic against his previous experience in doing the work to be sure that the results were correct. He would compare his present result against previous results of multiplying similar numbers, and his "logic" comparison would generate a decision to accept the answer or to recalculate.

It should be recognized that the multiplication procedure that he went through involved a series of steps that had been memorized some time before. He recalls the steps of multiplication in their proper order by referring to his memory, or "storage," unit. Furthermore, in doing the process of multiplication he would refer to multiplication tables that he would have memorized previously. Once again, he would have to refer to his "storage" unit as he carried out the multiplication. The clerk's brain acts as the "control" mechanism in determining when he is to take an invoice from the "IN" box, what "arithmetic" or "logic" to perform, when to call on his "storage" (i.e., his memory) as required, and when to put the completed invoice in the "out" box.

The major operations involved in this simple clerical task can be classified as input, arithmetic, logic, storage, output and control. They are shown in block diagram form in Figure 13-1. This same block diagram is identical to the block diagrams of all electronic computers that are used in management applications today. The major components of the electronic computer and their relationship to one another are succinctly represented by the block diagram. The control unit, the storage unit

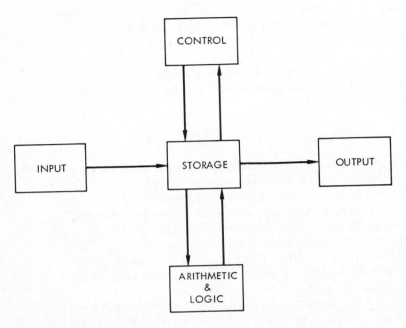

FIGURE 13-1

The Computer Block Diagram

(magnetic cores), and the arithmetic unit are often referred to as the *central processing unit* (CPU).

Numbers, letters, and symbols are converted by the input device into two-condition (binary) representation and put into core storage. These numbers, letters, and symbols in core storage are then manipulated according to a sequence of instructions that the control unit interprets and executes. This sequence of instructions is called a *computer program.* It is also stored in the core storage unit. Therefore, not only are the numbers, letters, and symbols converted to binary by the input device and put into core storage but so is the sequence of steps the computer is to follow.

The computer program, stored in magnetic cores, is therefore available at electronic speed for sequential "reading out" from core storage and transmission as pulse trains over wires for interpretation by the control unit and directing of the other computer components. Step by step the instructions are carried out and the data is processed as directed by the control unit which is interpreting and executing the computer program.

In summary, (1) the input unit converts the data to binary which is stored in magnetic core storage, (2) if arithmetic is required, the numbers are sensed in the form of pulse trains and are transmitted over the cables that interconnect the units to the arithmetic-logic unit where arithmetic is done to them (addition, subtraction, multiplication, division), and (3) they are sent back to core storage for further processing, if any.

If there is a logic step involved, that is, a comparison necessary to choose an alternate sequence of steps at that stage of the processing (depending on the condition of the data at that point), then the three-step decision operation we have previously discussed is necessary. The first step compares two numbers by subtraction. The result of a subtraction is always zero or minus or plus, and depending on whether it is a zero or minus or plus pulse train that results, the control unit is signalled by the result to select the next sequence of processing steps to be executed.

As simple as this may sound, it is actually the way electronic computers work. The input unit converts the instructions and the data into binary form and puts them into magnetic core storage. The instructions are put into a part of core storage first, then the control unit interprets and executes them in the sequence desired and they activate the input unit to bring data into specific locations of core storage or to move portions of the data from one place to another in storage for sorting purposes, or the instructions send parts of the data to the arithmetic logic unit for arithmetic manipulation or the decision process that has been detailed previously. When all the processing instructions have been executed, the final sequence of instructions activates the output unit and the processed data is converted to the output form desired. In essence, this brief description encompasses all the data manipulation possible by the electronic computer—data transfer, simple arithmetic, and elementary logic. But do not be fooled. These individually simple steps when sequenced in a computer program provide the key to this incredibly powerful management tool.

Different input devices are utilized for reading punched cards, punched tape, magnetic tape, magnetic ink characters, light sensitive devices, printed characters, and even handwritten characters. See Figure 13-2.

There are various output devices for producing printed materials, punched cards, punched tape, magnetic tape, graphic displays, microfilm, or whatever output form is required in the particular data-processing system. See Figure 13-2.

Arithmetic and logic units in different computers come in a variety of shapes and sizes, but they all provide the computer with the ability to add, subtract, multiply, divide, and compare one number with another.

Storage devices (also called memory devices) provide facilities to

IBM 2540 Card Read Punch

IBM 2495 Tape Cartridge Reader

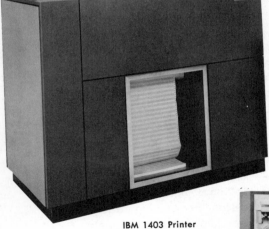

IBM 1403 Printer

FIGURE 13-2
Input/Output Devices

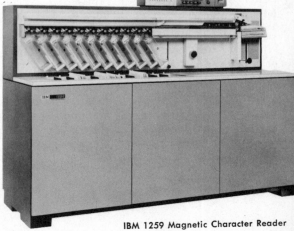

IBM 1259 Magnetic Character Reader

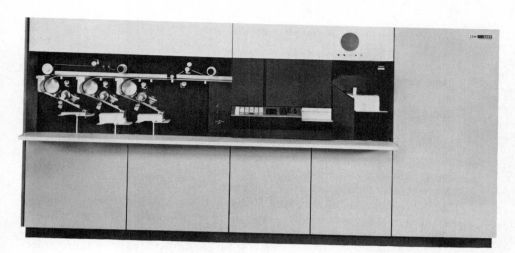

IBM 1287 Optical Reader

IBM 1052 Printer-Keyboard (Model 7)

IBM 1017 Paper Tape Reader

IBM 2260 Display Station

IBM 1018 Paper Tape Punch

store data, reference tables, and instructions. The most widely used types are the drum, disk, tape, data cell, and core storage devices. Examples of these were given in Chapter 12.

The control unit, which directs the operations of all other components, often encompasses the most glamorous-looking part of the electronic computer. It is usually located at the work station of the computer operator and is referred to as the *console*. It quite often resembles an executive-type desk with "space-age" overtones. It usually has banks of lights, colored buttons, and switches relating to the operation of the computer, and sometimes a typewriter to manually introduce data or interrogate the machine. See Figure 13-3.

Sometimes the control unit is physically a part of the memory and/or arithmetic–logic units. That is, the control switches and lights and their associated circuits are mounted on the same frame that contains the other units. In some computers all five components are housed in one frame. There are many combinations and wide variations in outward appearance, but whatever the "disguise," every electronic computer is made

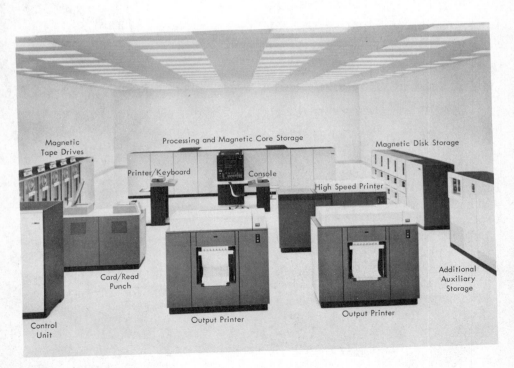

FIGURE 13-3

The IBM 370 Data Processing System

up of the same five basic components—input, output, storage, arithmetic-logic and control. Examples of a complete computer system with its major components identified are shown in Figure 13-3.

PROGRAMMING THE ELECTRONIC COMPUTER

Computer programming, that is, the detailed, step-by-step, sequencing of operations that the computer is to carry out, has become the great mystery of automatic data processing. People refer to it in a way that reveals a certain awe, if not an actual dread of it, and the general numbness that the ordinary layman exhibits about computers is evidently focused on computer programming. Yet the trend in computer programming is toward more simplified and more automatic programming systems. The time is fast approaching when a problem stated in ordinary language will automatically be translated into a computer program. Of course, until that time actually comes, human beings will still have to convert the step-by-step solution of a problem, or the step-by-step DP procedure, into the specific instructions the computer is to follow.

As for the difficulty of a computer programming, it is a mattter of fact that elementary school children are programming large-scale computers. It is also becoming quite common for engineers, accountants, and managers to be given an intensive one- or two-day BASIC language course or a one-week course in the FORTRAN language and, lo and behold, they find they can program a computer. This powerful device becomes a very available and useful tool.

First of all, it must be understood that the computer, like any machine, must be directed by human beings. A telephone system will connect the correct telephones only if the correct number is dialed. Your automatic washing machine at home will start, stop, rinse, agitate, and spin dry your clothes only if you "set it up" to do so. Similarly, a program, prepared by a human being, translates the step-by-step solution to a problem or the step-by-step procedure for processing data into the specific computer instructions that activate the proper circuits within the computer to develop the solution or to carry out the procedure.

Just like a dial telephone or an automatic washing machine, the computer does exactly as it is "told." You "tell" the telephone switching system what to do by dialing a number. Dialing the number generates a series of electrical pulses that open and close various relays and activate exactly the right switching circuits in the proper sequence so that the telephone bell of the party you want begins to ring—you have made your connection. Each telephone number is unique. When dialed it generates a unique sequence of pulses to cause that particular combination of circuits to activate that will cause only that one phone to ring.

Computer designers could have put a large control dial on the face of their machine, and dialing a number (like the telephone) would then generate a train of electrical impulses that would activate the internal circuitry of the computer and would result in an add operation, or subtract, or read a card, or any of the other operations the computer was designed to carry out. But then, the speed of operation would be reduced to that of the person doing the dialing and we would be right back where we started from. Instead of electronic speed, we are back to human-mechanical speed. But, all is not lost. The computer designers borrowed a page from the telephone switching circuit designers and appropriated the concept of utilizing a train of pulses to trigger the internal circuitry to cause a specific operation to occur. Since each number, letter, or symbol has its own unique pulse train, the designers of computers assigned specific numbers, letters, or symbols (actually, the pulse trains representing the specific numbers, letters, or symbols) to cause the computer to add, subtract, multiply, divide, store data, move data, compare or to perform any of the other operations for which the computer was designed.

What the computer designers added to the concept, however, was the idea of storing these "operation codes" in core storage so that they could be accessed at electronic speed, in sequence, to carry out the steps in the conversion of input to output.

Specific numbers, letters, and symbols were assigned to specific computer operations. The computer programmer would translate the data-processing steps desired into these "operation codes" which were then read by the input device, converted to binary, and transmitted to core storage. Then, when the program is to be executed, the data to be processed is made available at the input unit and the "START" button of the computer is pressed. This causes the first instruction to be placed into the control unit where it is interpreted and executed. Then the second instruction is obtained from core storage, sent to the control unit, interpreted and executed, and so on. The computer transmits these operating instructions in careful sequence from core storage to the control unit in the form of pulse trains where they are then interpreted and then executed. This interpretation and execution is accomplished by the pulse trains that represent the instructions triggering the control unit to activate the proper circuits in the required sequence within the computer. The specific operation codes whose pulse trains cause the desired operations are designed into the computer at the factory and are known as *machine language*. If the series of computer instructions (in machine language) is placed into core storage in the proper sequence and if the data to be processed is made available at the input, the desired DP procedure or the problem solution is carried out by the computer.

Each type of computer has designed into it its own repertory of basic operations that it can perform. It also has designed into it the electronic circuitry that will respond to the operation codes in the form of pulse trains that will activate the computer circuitry to cause a specific operation to be performed. For example, in a very popular medium-sized computer, the operation code for "add" is A. In another widely used computer the operation code for "add" is 21. In other words, if a set of instructions were being prepared to process data by one of these computers and if one of the DP steps required data to be added, that particular instruction's operation code would be the letter A on one machine and the number 21 on the other. This illustrates an additional facet of computer programming. Machine languages are different for each machine. This posed a real problem for early programmers. A new computer meant learning a new "language." As we shall see, their solution to this vexing problem provided those of us who came after with a much easier method of computer programming. More about this later.

Most computers have a repertory of some thirty to fifty basic operation codes. Some may have more, some less. (Special operations can often be added at additional cost.) The list of general operations may seem limited, but it is very difficult to come up with a generally accepted step in the processing of data that is not on the list of operations of general-purpose computers. Some of the listed commands may seem strange, and they may not be familiar to the average manager. But, they have been found, by experience, to be needed to adapt DP procedures and management applications to the idiosyncrasies of an electronic machine. Some of the commands are also provided for the maintenance and testing of the computer.

Following is a sampling of the characters that cause specific operations in the computers indicated. (Remember, these command characters are called *operation codes*, more specifically, *"machine language" operation codes*.) Here are some of the approximately forty machine language operation codes for a specific medium scale computer:

Operation Code	Operation
21	Add
22	Subtract
23	Multiply
24	Compare
25	Transfer digit
26	Transfer field
32	Set word mark
33	Clear word mark
36	Read numerically
38	Write numerically
49	Branch unconditional

Following is a sampling of the approximately sixty machine language operation codes for a larger and more popular computer, and it clearly demonstrates the variety of characters used for operation codes.

Operation Code	Operation
1	Read a card
2	Write a line
3	Punch a card
A	Add
S	Subtract
@	Multiply
%	Divide
C	Compare
F	Control carriage
.	Halt

Machine Language Programming

To demonstrate the preparation of a program in machine language, suppose it was desired to calculate the sum of two two-digit fields that are punched into ten thousand cards. As shown in Figure 13-4, each input card has two fields which can be designated J and K. The output is to be one card punched for each input card, with the J and K fields punched into the output card in addition to their sum.

The J field is punched into columns 1 and 2 of the input card. The K field is in columns 3 and 4. The output card will have the same layout with the addition of the sum field, which will be designated as the L field and which will have three columns (5, 6, 7) set aside for it, since the sum of two two-digit numbers can be a three-digit number.

The problem:

1. The input consists of about ten thousand punched cards having two fields—field J in columns 1–2, field K in columns 3–4.
2. Calculations will be carried out to add fields J and K, the answer to be field L.

$$L = J + K$$

3. The output will be punched cards (one output card for each input card) J, K, and L in columns 1–2, 3–4 and 5–7 respectively.

The Systems Flow Chart:

The systems flow chart (explained in Chapter 7) for this application is shown in Figure 13-4. RCD is an abbreviation for "Read a Card."

In data-processing terminology, this is also referred to as a *mnemonic*—something that jogs the memory, helping you to remember. Similarly, PCD stands for "Punch a Card."

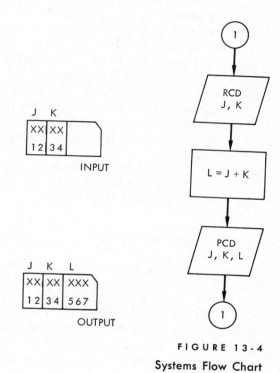

FIGURE 13-4

Systems Flow Chart

The next step in computer programming is the preparation of the program flow chart. This step requires an understanding of the configuration and of the idiosyncrasies of the specific model of computer used. This requires access to the manual that came with the equipment, the "cookbook."

Perusal of the "cookbook" for the particular computer that will be used will reveal the layout of core storage, the format of the computer's instructions, and other pertinent information necessary to prepare the program flow chart, which will in turn lead to the preparation of the computer program.

For instance, when a card is read into core storage of the computer we are using, all eighty columns are read into eighty positions of core storage. But once read into core storage, there is no indication where a field begins and ends. On the card itself we can separate the fields by vertical lines, but in core storage there is no way to draw vertical lines. Instead, the computer designers added an additional bit to each position of core storage, called a *word mark* bit. It is turned on in the high order position of a field to indicate the end of the field. The computer is designed so that when it is sent to a particular position of core storage it will read data from the positions from right to left until it reaches a word mark bit. It will then handle the data from that group of core storage positions as an entity.

Our "cookbook" also alerts us to the fact that each word mark will be converted to an 11 punch in the output punched card unless it is "cleared" by the appropriate operation code before the output instruction is executed. This is an example of an idiosyncrasy of a particular computer.

With the information supplied by the "cookbook," and the general steps represented by the systems flow chart, the program flow chart is prepared (Fig. 13-6).

The Computer Program

The particular computer that will be used to run this program has twenty thousand positions of core storage individually addressable from position 00000 to position 19999. Each position contains eight bits. The core layout (Fig. 13-5) includes the detailed bit configuration in position 00701. Every position has exactly the same bit configuration.

An eighth bit, called the *check* bit (C) has been added to each position of core storage. The check bit is an internal accuracy check that turns itself on or off to maintain an odd number of bits "on" in

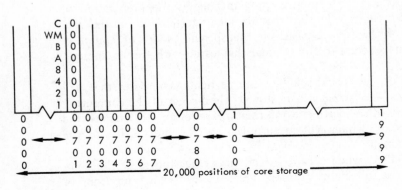

FIGURE 13-5

each position. This is known as *odd bit parity*. It helps to identify any inaccuracies due to magnetic cores being turned on or off by stray magnetic fields.

In preparing the computer program, the correct operation codes in the proper sequence and the correct locations in storage for the data fields must be specified. It is also necessary to designate a location for each instruction in core storage. This is necessary because after writing the program it will be "loaded" into core storage and then executed step by step to get the job done. Unless the instructions are stored in exactly the correct sequence there will be "Garbage Out."

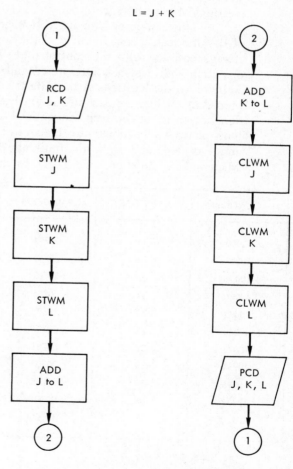

FIGURE 13-6

Program Flow Chart

The programmer must decide on where in storage to read the card (that is, the eighty locations in storage that will contain the data that is on the card) and where to locate the program of instructions. The decision, in this case, is to read the card into locations 00701 through 00780 and put the program into locations 10000 and sequentially higher-numbered locations. The "cookbook" tells us that each instruction for this computer must include the location of the instruction (which is specified by the location of the instruction's high order digit), the operation code, and a P address and a Q address. The operation code tells the computer what to do and the P and Q addresses tell the computer what to do it to. Since each operation code is a two-digit number and the P and Q addresses are five digits each, each instruction will take twelve positions of core storage.

This computer is designed so that when it is sent to the location of the first instruction, it will read the contents of twelve sequential core storage positions into the control unit. The first two will represent the operation code which is interpreted and executed utilizing the P and Q addresses as the locations of the data that are involved in that step of the processing. When the first instruction has been executed, the computer is designed to go to the next sequential instruction location, read the contents of twelve locations into the control unit where they are interpreted and executed, and so forth, until all the steps have been completed, whereupon it stops or is sent back to the first instruction to repeat the

LOCATION	OP CODE	P ADDRESS	Q ADDRESS
10000	36	00701	00500
10012	32	00701	00000
10024	32	00703	00000
10036	32	00705	00000
10048	21	00707	00702
10060	21	00707	00704
10072	33	00701	00000
10084	33	00703	00000
10096	33	00705	00000
10108	38	00701	00400
10120	49	10000	00000

FIGURE 13-7

The Computer Program

process until all the data has been processed or the problem has been solved.

Utilizing the information contained in the "cookbook" and the program flow chart, the computer program is prepared (Fig. 13-7).

Detailed Program Preparation

Step 1   The program flow chart indicates an input operation involving the reading of the data on a card into core storage. Referring to the manual and turning to the table of operation codes, 36 is the operation code for reading numeric data. The "cookbook" also points out that the P address of this instruction must designate the location in storage (we have already decided on 00701) where the data in column 1 of the card is to be placed. The other seventy-nine columns will automatically be placed in the next seventy-nine locations. In addition, the Q address is to designate the input device used. The list of input/output devices and their five-digit designations is also in the manual. The card reader is 00500. With this information plus the decision to start the instructions in location 10000 the complete first instruction is written:

10000   36   00701   00500

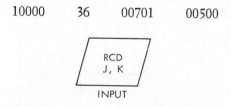

INPUT

Step 2   A word mark bit is to be turned on in the high order position of the *J* field. This field is in columns 1 and 2 of the card, so it will be put into positions 00701 and 00702 of core storage. The Op Code is 32 and the manual also indicates that the location for setting the word mark is to be specified in the P address. The Q address is not involved but must be filled in with five digits, since each instruction in this machine is twelve digits in length. The first instruction was placed in location 10000 to 10011, so this instruction starts in 10012 and goes to 10023:

10012   32   00701   00000

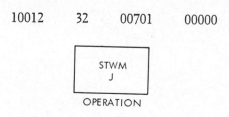

OPERATION

Step 3   Similarly as in Step 2, the Op Code is 32, but the K field which was in columns 3 and 4 on the card is read into locations 00703 and 00704 in core storage by the input command. Its high order position is 00703, so the instruction that will begin in location 10024 is:

10024   32   00703   00000

```
+-------------+
|    STWM     |
|      K      |
+-------------+
```

Step 4   Since the output is to contain the *J* and *K* fields as well as their sum, it is necessary to set up a separate field for the sum. If the *J* field were added to the *K* field and their sum stored in the *K* field, it would destroy the previous contents of the *K* field and make that data unavailable for output. This is the reason a separate *L* field is set up by setting a word mark in its high order position. Since the output desired is the *J* field, then the *K* field, and then their sum, the *L* field is set up to the right of the *J* and *K* fields. Note that the address of each sequential instruction is easily determined. It is simply twelve locations higher than the previous instruction:

10036   32   00705   00000

```
+-------------+
|    STWM     |
|      L      |
+-------------+
```

Step 5   All is now ready for computation. It must be recalled that the writing of the program requires the mental simulation of the operation of the computer to be sure that every possibility has been considered. In this case, when the program is completed, put into core storage, and executed, and when the computer reaches this step, a card will have been read into core and word marks will have been set to dimension the fields. This step will add the *J* field to the *L* field. The *J*

```
+-------------+
|     ADD     |
|    J to L   |
+-------------+
```

field has data read in from the card, the L field has zeros, since blank columns in the card are read in as zeros. The "cookbook" tells us that 21 is the Op Code for "ADD," and the instruction is written with the "receiving" field designated by the P address and the sending field designated by the Q address. The "cookbook" tells us that data fields are addressed by their low order position, and since we want J to add into the L field, the low order position of the J field will be the Q address and the low order position of the L field will be the P address. Assuming the first card has 25 as the J field and 47 as the K field, and using the minus sign (—) as a word mark, core storage would contain the data as shown before this program step is executed.

$\overline{2}$	5	$\overline{4}$	7	$\overline{0}$	0	0
0	0	0	0	0	0	0
0	0	0	0	0	0	0
7	7	7	7	7	7	7
0	0	0	0	0	0	0
1	2	3	4	5	6	7

The instruction would be:

10048   21   00707   00702

Note that the address of the field is its low order position because the computer reads from right to left till it reaches the word mark and that signals the number of digits it is to handle as a unit.

Step 6   Just as in Step 5, only now the K field will be added to the L field:

10060   21   00707   00704

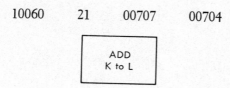

ADD
K to L

Before this instruction is carried out, core storage will be:

2	5	4	7	0	2	5
0	0	0	0	0	0	0
0	0	0	0	0	0	0
7	7	7	7	7	7	7
0	0	0	0	0	0	0
1	2	3	4	5	6	7

After this instruction is carried out, core storage will be:

2	5	4	7	0	7	2
0	0	0	0	0	0	0
0	0	0	0	0	0	0
7	7	7	7	7	7	7
0	0	0	0	0	0	0
1	2	3	4	5	6	7

Step 7   Now that the computation is complete, all that is needed is to clear the word marks and punch out the output. The "cookbook" tells us that CLEAR WORD MARK has the Op Code 33, and just like the set word mark command, the *P* address specifies the location of the word mark to be cleared. *Q* address is to be filled in but is not used:

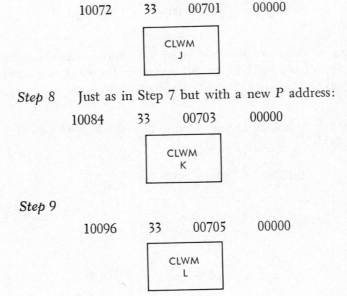

10072   33   00701   00000

CLWM
J

Step 8   Just as in Step 7 but with a new *P* address:

10084   33   00703   00000

CLWM
K

Step 9

10096   33   00705   00000

CLWM
L

Step 10   We are now ready for output and our manual tells us that, just like the input instructions, we must use the P address to designate the location of the high order position of the record in core storage, and the Q address designates the output device used. The Op Code for OUTPUT is 38, the P address is 00701 and the card punch is 00400:

10108   38   00701   00400

/PCD
J, K, L/

The result of this instruction is a punched card as shown below.

Data	25	47	072
Columns	12	34	567

Core storage after output is as shown below:

2	5	4	7	0	7	2
0	0	0	0	0	0	0
0	0	0	0	0	0	0
7	7	7	7	7	7	7
0	0	0	0	0	0	0
1	2	3	4	5	6	7

Step 11   The program flow chart indicates a return to Step 1. That seems reasonable, since we have succeeded in processing just one card. Repeating the cycle until the input cards are exhausted will accomplish our purpose. In order to recycle it would be useful if we could

CONNECTOR

send the computer to location 10000 for its next instruction. If we could do that, the design of the machine would cause it to continue through the sequence of instructions one after the other until it reached this point again, whereupon it would be recycled, over and over, until the job was done.

The computer designers provided us with this ability by designing an operation into the computer called an *unconditional branch*. The Op Code is 49, and when executed it sends the computer to the location specified in the P address for its next instruction. The Q address is not used but must be filled in. Therefore, the last instruction in the program will be:

$$10120 \qquad 49 \qquad 10000 \qquad 00000$$

The result of this step will be to send the computer to location 10000 where it will pick up the first instruction, send it to the control unit, and execute it. This will result in the second data card being read into locations 00701 to 00780, erasing the data from the first card which had remained in core storage after the output card had been punched. Then according to the computer's regular operation, the second instruction would be put into the control unit and executed. That would set a word mark in the J field, then the next would set a word mark in the K field, then the L field. Then J would be added to L, K would be added to L, word marks would be cleared, the second output card would be punched, and the 49 instruction would send the computer to location 10000 to repeat the cycle. This would continue until the input cards were exhausted, and the job would be finished.

Disadvantages of Machine Language Programming

This very tedious and meticulous attention to detail is the hallmark of machine language programming. Yet, it is these specific operation codes and field addresses that generate the pulse trains that activate the circuitry that directs the computer to do what we want it to do. But even a program as simple as $L = J + K$ amply demonstrates the tedium, the almost incredible attention to detail, and the opportunity for error that exists in machine language programming. For these and other reasons which will be explained in the next section, programmers and computer designers devised ways to develop machine language programs (which are the only programs computers can respond to) directly without the incredible detail and tedium that has been demonstrated by this example.

Symbolic Programming

With thousands and sometimes hundreds of thousands (even millions) of memory locations to keep track of, plus the many operation codes to remember and the difficulty of interpreting long programs written in machine language when changes were needed, programmers soon developed tricks of their own to help keep their sanity as well as to keep track of the instructions they were writing and the data they were processing. One of the first of these homegrown aids was the use of mnemonic (memory-jogging) "human language" symbolic codes for the characters that were the machine language operation codes. That is, for the computer that has been discussed, they would write ADD instead of 21 on the program coding sheet to represent an addition operation, CLWM for Clear Word Mark instead of the actual operation code 33, and so forth. Since the programs were usually punched into cards before being read into core storage, the card punch operators were the natural choice to translate these symbolic codes into machine language. They were given some training in the use of the operation code reference tables from the "cookbook," and they would then convert the symbolic operation codes to the required machine language operation codes.

If the machine language program of Figure 13-7 were used as a specific example, the machine language operation codes would be replaced by the symbolic codes (see Fig. 13-8). Furthermore, these same key punch operators could also be told to assign location 10000 to the first instruction of every program, unless instructed otherwise, and to add 12 to develop the location of each succeeding instruction. The programmers would use the word START on the program coding sheet as the location of the first instruction to indicate this. (See Fig. 13-8.)

The programmers also instructed the key punch operators to fill in five zeros in those instructions where the Q address is left blank by the programmer. He will also insert CARDRDR and CARDPCH in the Q address of input/output instructions, and the key punch operator will translate them into their proper code addresses by looking them up in the reference table in the "cookbook."

After some practice with the foregoing, the programmers expanded the translation role of the key punch operators and provided the layout of the input card and the layout of the output card—how many columns were assigned to each field and what their designations would be in the symbolic program. In the sample problem, the input fields were J and K (two columns each). The output card had the J and K fields and the L field (three columns). If the programmer instructed his "translator" that he would always use 00701 as his input/output area unless he indicated otherwise in his program, and that he would use the code word DATARCD to refer to it, then he could designate core storage by means of the names of the fields. For instance, as shown in Figure 13-8, he can indicate setting a word mark in the J field by using the symbolic Op Code "STWM" and "J FIELD" as the P address. He would do likewise for

field and the L field. If the "translator" knows the location in core
storage into which the card is read, it is a relatively simple matter to look
at the card layout and know in which locations the word marks should be
set. The field designations J, K, L allow the programmer to do the same
thing when writing the arithmetic instructions (Fig. 13-8). All the programmer has to do now is specify the field and the "translator" will substitute the address of the field when translating the symbolic program into
the machine language program. In the example shown in Figure 13-8,
after the arithmetic is completed he specifies clearing word marks from
the J field, the K field, and the L field. The only thing left then is to
indicate the output step and then specify branching back (BRU for
BRANCH UNCONDITIONAL) to start, which is the location of the
first instruction.

L = J + K

LOCATION	OP CODE	P ADDRESS	Q ADDRESS
START	RCD	DATARCD	CARDRDR
	STWM	J FIELD	
	STWM	K FIELD	
	STWM	L FIELD	
	ADD	L FIELD	J FIELD
	ADD	L FIELD	K FIELD
	CLWM	J FIELD	
	CLWM	K FIELD	
	CLWM	L FIELD	
	PCD	DATARCD	CARDPCH
	BRU	START	

FIGURE 13-8

The Symbolic Program

Comparing Figures 13-7 and 13-8, it can be seen that the programmer has just translated his machine language program of instructions
made up of seventeen digit numbers into a symbolic language program
consisting of much more human-understandable terms. The symbolic
language program is one that he can look at weeks later and still have a
pretty good idea of what is going on. It is exactly the same program

that was written before in machine language, only now it is in symbolic language. A program in a symbolic language is referred to as a *source program*.

A programmer who knows the "rules" of the symbolic language prepares the source program—the sequence of computer instructions written in human-oriented symbolic language. Then it must be translated into machine language. The reason, of course, is that only machine language when converted by the control unit generates the specific pulse trains that produce the desired operations. Unless the machine language codes are in its control circuitry, it cannot operate. The symbolic language was created to assist programmers in writing programs with less tedium and irritating detail, but they are worthless until translated into machine language. Symbolic programs are also much easier to understand because they are almost like human prose, especially when compared with the strings of numbers that make up the machine language of the example. However, they are useless in getting the computer to do what they say. Symbolic (source) programs must be translated into the machine language of the computer that will be used. In the example it was emphasized that this translation is done essentially by a key punch operator doing a series of table look-ups in the reference tables provided. If the programmer follows the "grammatical rules" of the symbolic language as specified in the reference manual, the translation will produce a machine language program that when put into the computer and followed will convert input to output. The machine language program that results from the translation is called the *object* program.

Someone might well ask, Why use key punch operators to do the translating? Most of it involves table look-up and simple addition. Why not use the computer itself? It is the best table looker-upper and adding machine in the world. Why cannot a group of experienced programmers write a machine language translator program that when put into the computer will process the symbolic language program just as though it were data? This machine language translator program would translate the symbolic source program into the machine language object program. Once this interesting idea was recognized, programmers lost no time in writing a translation program, in machine language, to have the computer itself convert symbolic (source) programs into machine language (object) programs. The object programs would then be loaded into the computer to process the data or solve the problem.

The translation process is as follows:

1. The programmer writes the source program (symbolic language).
2. The translator program is put into computer core storage and the source program is made available at the computer's input.

3. The source program is translated by the computer into the object program (machine language).
4. The object program is put into the computer core storage and the data to be processed is made available at the computer's input.
5. The computer processes the data as directed by the object program.

As soon as the translation program for converting a symbolic program into a machine language program is operational, any program written in this symbolic language can be translated into machine language by processing it through the computer under the direction of the "translation" program. In a very real sense, the computer is helping to write its own program.

As experience with the symbolic language built up, many refinements followed. The "grammatical rules" regarding Op Codes, field sizes, names, and so forth, were standardized, and a whole series of "symbolic languages" developed. Examples include SPS, BAL, AUTOCODER and many others.

Examining the program written in symbolic language (Fig. 13-8), it can easily be seen that (1) Every instruction in the machine language program (Fig. 13-7) has a corresponding instruction in the symbolic program. It is a one-for-one translation. (2) The format of each instruction is similar whether machine language or symbolic. There is a location, an Op Code, a P address and a Q address. The symbolic language is closely identified with a specific computer—just as the machine language was. It cannot be used to prepare symbolic programs to be translated into machine language for other computers. It is oriented to a specific computer.

Symbolic languages with the foregoing characteristics are called *assembly level languages*. They are one step removed from machine languages. These characteristics were the source of problems. For instance, programmers would prepare programs in an assembly language, process them using the computer and a translator program (referred to as an *assembler*), and generate an object program. After all that work they ran the risk of finding that the arrival of a new computer required complete reprogramming. The reason, of course, is that one computer's assembly level language is just not compatible with another's.

Furthermore, programs for routine data-processing applications written in an assembly level language could only be translated and run on the same model computers for which they were written. Standard DP applications (payroll, accounts receivable, inventory control, etc.) had to be reprogrammed for every different computer. As programmers changed jobs they often found themselves working with a different computer, which meant learning another assembly language.

It did not take long for programmers to get together with computer designers and come up with a "universal language," a language with a carefully worked out set of rules which was supplied to every computer manufacturer. Each manufacturer would then prepare a translation program (in machine language) which would translate programs written in the "universal" language into the machine language that would fit the idiosyncrasies of his particular computer.

That is exactly the way it works. These universal languages are called *compiler level languages*. They are not machine oriented as were assembly level languages. Rather, they are problem oriented. Their characteristics are:

1. Machine independent. They are not identified with any particular computer. A program written in a compiler language can be translated by most computers into their own machine language.
2. Many for one. That is, a statement in a compiler language is translated by the compiler into many instructions in machine language. This means a great deal of saving of programming time.

Popular compiler languages include Formula Translater (FORTRAN), Common Business Oriented Language (COBOL), Algorithmic Language (ALGOL), Beginners All-Purpose Symbolic Instruction Code (BASIC), and Programming Language 1 (PL/1).

The sample program in machine language and in assembly language as shown in Figures 13-7 and 13-8 is shown written in FORTRAN in Figure 13-9. The same program written in BASIC is shown in Figure 13-10.

The BASIC language is the simplest to learn, yet it is a very powerful problem-solving language and is particularly suited for use with a time-sharing terminal. It is an excellent language for the systems analyst, and a short introduction to it will follow immediately after a brief introduction to time sharing.

Time Sharing

Time-sharing systems (Fig. 13-11) let many individuals use the computer at the same time and without having to wait. Managers, systems analysts, programmers, research personnel, and many others can have direct access to a powerful computer system just by dialing a telephone number at a remote terminal (a teletypewriter or typewriter or video display unit) which is usually quite close to their work area (Fig. 13-12).

Since today's computer can do millions of operations in seconds, it can do a fraction of a second's work on job 1, a fraction of a second's work on job 2, and so on until every terminal in use has been serviced. It repeats the cycle over and over again until all the jobs are completed. The terminal may be in the same building with the computer or a hundred miles away.

Characteristics of Some Time-Sharing Systems

System	CPU Cost/hr	On-Line Chg/hr	Software
GE–235	$150	$10	FORTRAN, ALGOL BASIC
IBM CALL/360	$500	$12	BASIC
CDC–6600	$1,200	$10	FORTRAN, ALGOL COBOL, OPTIMA
SDS–940	None	$25	FORTRAN, BASIC SNOBOL, CAL

```
                    L = J + K

        15   FØRMAT (12,12)
        17   READ (5,15) J,K
             L = J + K
        20   FØRMAT (12,12,13)
             PUNCH (4,20) J,K,L
             GØ TØ 17
             END
```

FIGURE 13-9

FORTRAN Program

```
                    L = J + K
        10   INPUT J,K
        20   LET L = J + K
        30   PRINT J,K,L
        40   GO TO 10
        50   END
```

FIGURE 13-10

BASIC Program

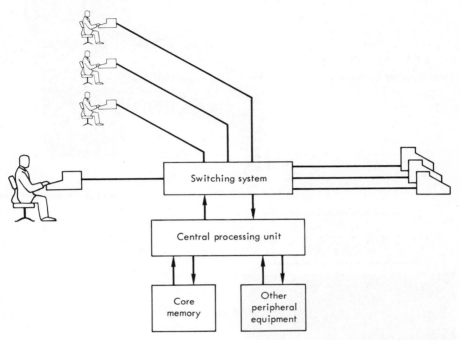

FIGURE 13-11

Computer Time-Sharing System Schematic

PRIMER IN THE BASIC LANGUAGE

1. The BASIC statement: An instruction to the computer telling it what it is to do at a particular point in the program.

2. The three parts of a BASIC statement are:
   a. A Number—Up to five digits. Assigned by the programmer and specifies the sequence of the statements in the program.
   b. A Code Word—An easily understood English word that indicates what the computer is to do with the numbers, letters, or symbols specified in the Operand part of the BASIC statement.
   c. The Operand—The actual numbers, letters, or symbols upon which the computer is to act according to the instruction given in the Code Word.

3. Some additional rules of BASIC:
   a. Variable Names—A letter or a letter and a number that can be assigned various numerical values.

FIGURE 13-12
Time-Sharing Terminals

IBM 2250 Display Unit (Model 4)

IBM 2741 Communications Terminal

Example: A, A5

b. Arithmetic Operations

↑ means raising to a power (Exponentiation)

Example: 10 ↑ 4

* means multiplication

Example: A * B

/ means Division

Example: A/B

+ means addition

Example: A + B

− means subtraction

Example: A − B

( ) are parentheses, and the expressions within parentheses are evaluated before other arithmetic is done.

   c. Hierarchy of Arithmetic Operations—Innermost parentheses first, followed by Exponentiation, then Multiplication and Division, then Addition and Subtraction, in sequence, reading from Left to Right. Multiplication and Division are of the same level. Addition and Subtraction are of the same level. Which is done first depends on its position in the arithmetic expression reading from Left to Right.

Example:

     Algebraic expression: $Y = (A + B) (C/D)/E^3$
     BASIC expression: $Y = (A + B) * (C/D)/E \uparrow 3$

4. Sample BASIC statements:

10 INPUT J,K

When executed, this statement connects the time-sharing terminal being used to the computer's core storage. A ? appears at the terminal, and when two numbers separated by commas are typed, the first is assigned to J and the second to K.

20 LET L = J + K

This statement assigns the value of the expression to the right of the = sign (which can be as complex as the arithmetic operators and creativity can devise) to the variable name on the Left of the = sign.

30 PRINT J,K,L

Results in the numeric values assigned to J, K, L from the preceding steps in the program being printed at the terminal.

40 GO TO 10

Sends the computer to the statement number indicated. In this case, statement 10 will be the next statement executed.

50 END

This statement must be the last statement in every BASIC program.

Note: The BASIC statements discussed above make up the same program as that shown in Figure 13-10.

25 READ A,B,C

This statement is used in conjunction with a DATA statement to assign values to the variables A, B, C.

30 DATA 6,10,15

This statement will assign the values 6, 10, and 15 to A, B, and C respectively.

75 PRINT "THE ANS. IS", L

Whatever is between the quotation marks will be reproduced at the terminal. A useful way of putting labels and headings on the output of your program.

47 IF I = 10 THEN 50

This statement will test the value of I which is developed in previous steps in the program. When I does not equal 10, the next sequential statement is executed. When it does equal 10, statement 50 is the next one executed.

30 FOR I = 1 TO 6 STEP 1
. . . .
. . . .
. . . .

60 NEXT

The FOR and NEXT statements are used together to control the number of times a particular iteration (loop) is executed. The FOR statement starts the loop and provides the variable I (it can be any letter) for counting the cycles. The "1 to 6" tells the computer to go through six cycles from this statement down to the NEXT statement. When $I = 6$ the computer executes the statement after the NEXT statement.

5. This is an example of a relatively complicated arithmetic statement in BASIC: Prepare a program to calculate $X = \dfrac{AB - B^2}{4C \sqrt{D}}$. The values of A, B, C, D are to be put in from the terminal each time this program will be run.

```
10 INPUT A,B,C,D
20 LET X = (A * B − B↑2)/(4 * C * D ↑.5)
30 PRINT "THE ANS. IS", X
40 END
```

THE TIME-SHARING SYSTEM

There are many different time-sharing service companies. The particular one selected will have its own specific rules as to how its system is to be used. However, some general operating procedures apply to all, with little modification.

A teletypewriter or an electric typewriter is the usual means of input and output. Some have a paper tape or a magnetic tape cartridge unit in addition to allow program preparation "off-line," that is, without being connected to the computer.

A telephone and an acoustic coupler are also necessary—the telephone to provide the connection over telephone wires and the acoustic coupler to convert pulses to sound, and vice versa.

A number of operating system commands are needed by the user. These are not part of the BASIC language but are directions to the computer to carry out a particular operation that may be required in connection with preparing and executing the program and signing on and signing off the terminal. These commands are slightly different for each time-sharing system. A sample follows:

HELLO

Used to "sign-on" to the computer. It has three parts:

HELLO—usercode, password

The usercode and password are part of the identification the user must have to show his authorization to use the system. The dash and the comma are part of the command.

BYE

Used to "sign-off" when the user is finished using the terminal.

RUN

Causes the computer to execute the program that has just been typed in or that the user has obtained from the "library" of stored programs.

LIST

Results in the printing at the terminal, by the computer, of all the statements in the program that is now being worked on.

SCRATCH

Causes the computer to erase from storage the program on which it has been working.

In addition to the operating system commands, the user at the terminal should be aware of some of the actions that can be caused by certain keys on the teletypewriter he is using:

RETURN key

This key must be pressed at the end of each statement or command. It causes the computer to act on the statement or command.

BREAK key

Terminates whatever the computer is doing.

← key

Acts like a backspace and erases the last character typed each time it is pressed.

To DELETE a statement

Type its number and press the RETURN key.

To REPLACE a statement

Type its number and the new statement, then press the RETURN key.

A TIME-SHARING APPLICATION

1. The user turns on the teletypewriter and the acoustic coupler and dials the number of the time-sharing service.

2. He should hear the phone ringing and then a high-pitched tone.

3. The telephone handset is put into the acoustic coupler cradle. (In some systems both the telephone and the coupler are integral to the terminal.)

4. The time-sharing system responds by a carriage return or by printing an identifying word or two, the date, and the time.

5. The user types in HELLO—usercode, password and presses the RETURN key.

6. The system responds by typing IDENT. NO.

7. The user types in his identification number (and presses RETURN). It is used by the time-sharing service for billing.

8. The system responds OLD OR NEW.

9. The user can type in OLD and press the RETURN key. This means he wants to use a program he has previously written and stored or he wants to use one of the programs available from the computer's "library."

   The user can type in NEW and press the RETURN key. This means he is going to prepare a new program.

10. In either case the computer responds with NAME: If the user had previously typed OLD, the name he now types in must be that of a program he has stored or that is on the list of "library" programs. After he types in the name of the program and presses the RETURN key, the computer responds READY.

    If he had typed in NEW, he now enters the name he will use to refer to the program he will prepare. Then he presses the RETURN key. The computer responds READY.

11. If it is an OLD program, he will type RUN and press the RETURN key and it will execute.

    If it is a NEW program, he will enter it line by line utilizing the rules of BASIC and the operating system commands and what other keyed operations he may need. When finished writing his program he will type RUN and press RETURN, and it will be executed by the computer.

12. When finished at the terminal, he types BYE and presses the RETURN key. The computer responds with the connect time used and then it disconnects automatically. The user tears off the paper record of his work, turns off the teletypewriter, returns the phone to its cradle—and he is finished.

REVIEWING THE KEY CONCEPTS DEVELOPED IN THIS CHAPTER

1. The computer will only do as it is directed.

2. The data-processing procedure, developed by human beings, is converted into characters called *operation codes* which when combined with the location of the data in storage become a series of detailed instructions called a *computer program.*

3. The detailed specifying of the sequence and the logic of the operations is the principal function left for human beings within the computer system. It is called *computer programming.*

4. Programming is a meticulous job requiring that the electronic system be directed in minute detail, in the proper sequence, and with provision made for handling all possible exceptions in the input data.

5. These directions, like the data, are translated into patterns of electrical pulses (pulse trains) by the computer's control circuitry. These pulse trains move through the system, causing the internal circuitry to be activated in the required manner and in the proper sequence to convert the input into the desired output.

Programming is essentially the analysis of the content and format of source data and the determination of how to convert it by using the available operations of a computer to produce the desired end result. The program defines in complete detail exactly what a computer is to do under every expected combination of circumstance. If it does not, the output may not be usable.

One instruction may tell the computer what operation to perform, another may direct it to the storage location for the factors involved, and still another may tell it what to do with the answer. The number of instructions required for the complete solution of a problem may be a few hundred or many thousands.

These instructions are stored, like the data they will operate on, in the storage areas of the computer, They are referred to in sequence, except in situations where the computer makes a logical decision to skip certain instructions or to introduce others because of intermediate results or changes in the input data.

In developing a data-processing program, the sequence of actions often goes something like this:

1. Analyze the present method of doing the DP job. Utilize process flow charts, work simplification techniques, and other analysis and improvement techniques to better the present data-processing cycle. Uncover all probable exceptions in the sequence of steps and in the data.

2. Prepare a systems flow chart to represent the steps required to convert input data into the required output.

3. Design the necessary forms and records and the procedures for capturing the data and bringing it to the input of the computer's system.

4. Convert the systems flow chart to a program flow chart.

5. a. (Machine language.) Translate the program flow chart into the specific instructions for the computer being used and provide for identifying the locations of the data in storage after input, during processing, and just before output. The assignment of core storage addresses to each instruction step completes the program.

   b. (Symbolic language.) The source program is prepared in a symbolic language and then put through a translation phase using a computer and a compiler (or an assembler) program. The resulting object program is in machine language.

   c. Using a time-sharing terminal, the program is prepared and run using a language such as BASIC. This is generally for short "problem-solving" programs.

6. The program is then run on the computer by using test data and is modified where necessary to correct errors ("bugs") in the instructions or to improve processing efficiency. This is called *testing and debugging* the program.

7. The program is run with regular data, and if the results are acceptable, another program is "on the air."

8. Follow up and improve.

Before a programmer goes on to his next assignment he usually documents his program. That is, he writes a brief description of the program, what the input is, and what the output should be—what the limitations are on input and the possible variations in the output. He also prepares detailed operating instructions so that the actual running of the program, after testing and debugging, can be handled by a less-skilled (and lower-paid) computer operator. This documentation package should at least consist of:

1. The "source" (symbolic language) program punched into cards or on tape.

2. The "object" (machine language) program punched into cards or on tape.

3. A print-out of both.

4. A "write-up" of the program, including detailed operating instructions, plus what the program does and how it does it.

5. The program flow chart and the systems flow chart.

THE COMPUTER AS A MANAGEMENT TOOL

Now that the concept of getting the computer to do a particular job has been explained, it is important to understand its role as an MIS tool. A computer, in its essential nature, is a very high speed arithmetic device that can recognize 0 and 1, can tell if one number is $>$, $<$, or $=$ another number, can store data, and can carry out some few dozen operations under its own control. With these modest-sounding abilities, however, this machine, when coupled with human ingenuity, has the potential of being the most powerful management tool ever developed. However, its potential will begin to be realized only when the managers, who can identify operational problems and can conceive a practical basis for their solutions, learn enough about computers and their use to spearhead computer applications. Managers should learn enough about computers to be able to interpret potential problem solutions into computer programs themselves, if necessary. Even more important, managers should be able to pretest the key/critical subroutines and decision points in their proposed algorithms to crystallize the design of the eventual computer application.

This does not mean that managers need become programmers. Rather, they should build up a workable skill in a language such as BASIC so that they can have direct access to the computer to satisfy themselves about decision points in applications when necessary. In addition, this know-how will help in their ability to work with professional programmers. A host of programs in computer "libraries" make available an array of quantitative decision tools to the manager who has access to a computer time-sharing terminal but just a rudimentary skill in programming.

Managers are in a key position to decide that a useful data-processing application exists, and based on the detailed knowledge of that part of the organization's operations, they can outline the key steps to process the data, to solve the problem, or to get the needed report. A programmer can then convert the general procedure into the computer instructions that will do the job.

Experience has shown that computer programmers can become particularly effective when they develop close associations with operating managers who are by instinct and by experience systems analysts—though, alas, rarely computer-oriented systems analysts. In twenty years, (perhaps ten), the word *manager* may very well mean "computer-oriented systems man."

In order that this view of managers not appear too exotic, it is generally agreed that *managers*, by definition, are people who plan, analyze, and control the interrelationships of men, materials, machines, and money in an organization for optimum results. The same specification defines a systems analyst. The manager, therefore, is in actuality a systems analyst. With the growing importance of the computer in the management of organizations, the manager has little alternative but to become a computer-oriented systems analyst.

The manager often has problems that are not yet crystallized in his own mind, but his instinct tells him that one or more of the advanced quantitative techniques (discussed in Chapter 11) apply. Techniques like Monte Carlo, linear programming, simulation, and so forth, mean little to the average computer programmer, and the manager will therefore find that the computer time-sharing terminal can become his private laboratory, and he the experimenter probing the unknown. The use of an intermediary (a programmer) is not only cumbersome—in a situation like that, it is often impossible.

For instance, if inventory control was the area that the manager desired to improve, he could reap a new understanding of his inventory control policies and practices and the implications of their interplay if he knew enough about programming and the computer to prepare and make the simulation runs personally. Only he knows enough about the subtleties and the interactions of safety stock, reorder points, return on investment, stock-outs, economical order quantities, and so forth, to adjust the controllable and uncontrollable variables to reflect the realities (simulated) of his inventory.

In other words, no one but the manager most intimately concerned can really understand the subtleties of his organization's inventory control environment. Any attempt to transfer this know-how to programmers or to others must result in distortion, "static," or "leakage." The basic reason why it is essential that managers learn computer programming and the use of time-sharing terminals is so that they can personally explore the power of the computer in their areas of particular interest.

If the computer is really the most powerful management tool ever developed, managers must not keep it at arm's length. They must embrace it, physically handle it, and learn how to make it do their bidding, directly—without intermediaries.

REVIEW QUESTIONS

1. Define *computer programming.*
2. Draw the block diagram of the digital computer.
3. Utilize the machine language operation codes and instruction format of the computer used in the sample problem and prepare

a machine language program that will calculate $M = J - K$. Use the same ten thousand cards that were used in the example as the data to be processed.

4. Same situation as above, only this time calculate $L = J + K$ just as was done in the sample problem, but now have the L field precede the J and K fields in the output. That is, punch the L field into columns 1, 2, and 3, the J field into columns 4 and 5, and the K field into columns 6 and 7 of the output card.

5. Differentiate between *machine language* and *symbolic language*.

6. What are the characteristics of an Assembly Level language?

7. What is a compiler?

8. Why were symbolic languages developed?

9. Why were Compiler Level languages developed?

10. What is a source program? An object program?

11. What are the major steps involved in preparing a program in a symbolic language all the way through the producing of output data?

12. What are the three parts of every BASIC instruction?

13. Which is the first arithmetic operation that will be performed in the following expression?

$$A + B * D \uparrow 2/(E + C)$$

14. A has a value of $+50$ in computer storage. What would the value of A be after the following instruction was executed?

$$30 \text{ LET } A = A - 70$$

15. Write a program in the BASIC language that will calculate and print the multiplication tables from 1×1 to 12×12.

16. Write a BASIC language program to evaluate X where $X = B^2 - 4AC$. The values of B, A, and C will be entered on request of the program, from the teletypewriter terminal each time the program is run.

17. Given the equation $Y = 4X^3 - 8X + 23$, write a BASIC language program to calculate and print out the values of Y for the values of X from 1 to 20 inclusive, using increments of 1.

18. Write a BASIC program that will convert a Fahrenheit temperature input at the terminal to centigrade and print the result.

$$C = (5/9)(F - 32)$$

19. Differentiate between *operating system commands* and BASIC *language instructions.*

20. What is the general "sign-on, sign-off" procedure when using a time-sharing teletypewriter terminal?

21. What are the major parts of a computer program's documentation package?

22. What may be a reasonable expectation of an organization president regarding managers' understanding and use of a computer and computer programming?

23. Should managers become professional programmers?

24. How does a manager's access to a computer time-sharing terminal improve the effectiveness of a Management Information System

   a. During the design of the system?
   b. During implementation?
   c. When operational?
   d. For follow up and improvement?

25. Is the manager a systems analyst? Explain.

BIBLIOGRAPHY

ANDERSON, DECIMA M., *Computer Programming FORTRAN IV.* New York: Meredith Publishing Co., 1966. Just about the best presentation of the subject matter around for the beginner in FORTRAN. Development is careful and a step at a time. It reflects dedication and knowledge of the material

BOORE, WILLIAM F., and JERRY R. MURPHY, *The Computer Sampler.* New York: McGraw-Hill Book Company, 1968. Presents a selective sample of the relevant current literature for the layman in the field. Covers selections on problems of introducing the computer into an organization, ways the computer is being used, and future developments in applying computer technology.

BROOKS, FREDERICK P., and KENNETH E. IVERSON, *Automatic Data Processing* (System 360 edition). New York: John Wiley and Sons, Inc., 1969. Illustrates and applies the fundamental aspects of data processing in terms of IBM's System/360 computers.

FARINA, MARIO V., *COBOL Simplified.* Englewood Cliffs, N.J.: Prentice-Hall, Inc., 1968. A carefully structured introduction to the language with plentiful illustrations and understandable development.

———, *FORTRAN IV Self-taught.* Englewood Cliffs, N.J.: Prentice-Hall, Inc., 1966. A self-instructional introduction to FORTRAN IV. Reasonably effective, especially for a first exposure to a problem-oriented language.

———, *Programming in* BASIC. Englewood Cliffs, N.J.: Prentice-Hall, Inc., 1968. A twenty-five-lesson introduction to the BASIC language. Many specific examples and sample programs.

GERMAIN, CLARENCE B., *Programming the IBM 360*. Englewood Cliffs, N. J.: Prentice-Hall, Inc., 1967. As the title implies, the coverage of PL/1, FORTRAN, COBOL, and assembly languages are in terms of the IBM 360. It is a thorough, well-done treatment.

JARCHOW, WILLARD R., *Assembler Language*. New York: ITT Educational Services, Inc., 1970. An easy-to-understand introduction to assembly level languages.

SPROWLS, R. CLAY, *Computers* (rev. ed.). New York: Harper & Row, Publishers, 1968. Provides an understandable overview of FORTRAN IV, COBOL, and PL/1.

———, *Introduction to PL/1 Programming*. New York: Harper & Row, Publishers, 1969. The presentation is geared to the beginner with no prior programming experience.

STARK, PETER A., *Digital Computer Programming*. New York: The Macmillan Company, 1967. A carefully developed exposition of computer programming that does a thorough job of discussing machine, symbolic, and problem-oriented languages.

VAN COURT, HARE, JR., BASIC *Programming*. New York: Harcourt, Brace & World, Inc., 1970. One of the few BASIC texts available other than from manufacturers. It is comprehensive and readable and should enable most users to teach themselves.

14

THE TEN-STEP MANAGEMENT
INFORMATION SYSTEMS
STUDY

Every organization is unique. It has its own unique combination of men, money, machines, materials, and methods. Not only the individual organizational components are different but the degree of evolution of the Management Information System is different. This uniqueness makes it necessary that each organization develop its own specifications for an MIS through a systematic evaluation of its own internal and external environment and from its own point of view and in terms of its own unique requirements. An organized procedure for carrying out this study is the subject of this chapter.

It is a job that each organization must do for itself. Of course, it can obtain the services of technical specialists, systems consultants, and representatives of equipment manufacturers—when, as, and if needed—but the hard core of the study must be carried out by organization personnel.

The reasons for this are twofold. First, from having lived with the evolving MIS, key personnel will come to a better understanding of the subtleties and underlying cause systems in the interrelationships within the organization. Second, the MIS study itself is an intensive, and quite often a profound, educational experience in the realities of the organization's dynamics—an experience that is invaluable for a deeper appreciation of what the organization is and how it works. In fact, the MIS study is an excellent vehicle for management development.

In the conduct of the study, the services of independent systems consultants can be valuable, especially in helping the organization to avoid the mistakes of others. The consultants can provide "the objective outsider" element in the study. Their own enlightened self-interest makes them work for optimum results, since a poor outcome will be detrimental to their long-range relationship with the organization as well as affecting referrals to other consulting assignments.

In this regard, it may be useful for anyone who may be involved in the planning of an MIS study and who may have a voice in the decision regarding the bringing aboard of an outside consultant to consider the following provocative comments of the Institute of Management Consultants, Inc. This organization is concerned with the profession of *management consulting*, which is defined as that work done by management consultants who are associated with a firm controlled by its principals. The institute lists the following characteristics that define the man in the consulting "profession" as opposed to the man in the consulting "business."

1. *Competence.* The professional man has competence to serve his clients, based on specialized training and his grasp of a specialized body of knowledge in his field.

2. *Trust and confidence.* The professional man is trusted by his client—a trust based on good character and adherence to high ethical and moral standards. This trust permits the client to place the confidence in him that is required to make full disclosure of all matters that bear on the affairs in hand. The client also has confidence in the competence and judgment of the professional man. The businessman in the field can also build trust and confidence, but he may be handicapped by his lack of an independent position. Moreover, the tradition of the professions supports the placing of confidence and trust in the professional man.

3. *Primacy of client interests.* The professional man always puts the interests of his client ahead of his own. The businessman in the field can also put the interests of his client first. But again, he may be handicapped by lack of an independent position, and he is not supported by image or tradition.

4. *Independent position.* If the professional is to put the client's

interests ahead of his own and think objectively, he must be in an independent *position*. He may or may not succeed in being objective in his thinking, but at least he should be in a position that does not prejudice his *opportunity* for thinking objectively— or even *appear* to do so.

The individual consultant or the consultant who is associated with a firm controlled by its principals is in such an independent position. The individual is answerable only to himself, and the principals of an independent firm are answerable only to themselves. None of them is expected by an owning corporation or by controlling outside shareholders to increase profits. They are, therefore, in a position to put client interests ahead of their own interests without having to answer to outsiders.

Independence of position is the critical factor in distinguishing the professional man from the businessman.

The client is entitled to have the consultant in a position so independent that there can be no profit pressure from any outside interest and no potential conflict or even *appearance* of potential conflict.

5. *Profit as a by-product.* If the professional man is in an independent position, his profit can come as a by-product of fees for client service. Profit must not be the objective of his service to the client, even though the profession is his vocation.

This is a subtle, subjective, but basic distinction between the businessman and the professional man. Business emphasizes profit for the owners—a profession emphasizes service to the clients. This subjective difference in emphasis and motivation turns on independence of position, which is the watershed between a profession and a business.

These remarks are included because the success of the MIS study may well pivot on the independent and objective judgments of a competent observer. Since the MIS study may result in recommendations for major changes in the organizational structure, and always will result in some changes in the way things are done, it is not a bad investment to provide for a "disinterested observer" to be on the scene to help get the study through some of the tight intraorganizational disputes that are sure to come up.

One of the dangers in any MIS study, especially for the organization without any experience with ADP, is to see the computer as the objective of the MIS study rather than as one possible alternative to evaluate. If any general rule is worth noting at this time, it is to err on the side of conservatism where a first application of ADP is involved. Build on small successes. Prepare the methods, systems and procedures, and the people thoroughly and well. The computer applications will follow that much more easily.

Representatives of a wide array of data-processing equipment manufacturers must also be considered as resource persons for specific information when, as, and if required. This is one of the key points to remember. Each organization must first develop its data-processing equipment needs based on the design of its MIS and in terms of the requirements of its MIS. Not to do as too many others have done, that is, begin with specific hardware in mind, and design the organization's MIS to fit. Rather, the MIS study must develop the detailed set of DP specifications for the company to do the management planning, analysis, and control job required. Then, and only at that point in the study, should equipment manufacturers or service bureaus be contacted. Their equipment or their professional competence can then be evaluated, realistically, in terms of the Management Information System's DP specifications.

Chances are the two will not mesh. The MIS requirements will probably not fit the hardware configurations. This is to be expected, since ADP equipment is designed for general purposes, to fit the needs of as many organizations as possible. At this point, the study group may revise its MIS specifications or may change the time frame of the more sophisticated aspects of the MIS plan to allow the equipment to catch up. But, what a difference! Knowing the MIS specifications in detail, the study group can view all the claims and counterclaims with professional objectivity. It knows what is needed and can make a careful, rational choice.

It is to the organization's best interests to evaluate all equipment specifications with reference to the independently arrived at, predetermined MIS needs. The Ten-Step Management Information Systems Study has as its objective the designing of the organization's MIS, including the operating specifications for DP equipment.

The basic objective of the MIS study is to design a Management Information System that will enhance the survival and growth of the organization. The ten steps that follow are not meant to be exhaustive, but rather are meant to provide general guidelines for an organized approach to this basic objective. The Bibliography will help round out the exposure of the study team to the experiences of others. But the resulting MIS for a particular organization is ultimately a direct function of the intelligence, energy, and integrity of the organization's personnel—those who are on the study team and those who are not. The goal is worth the effort, however, and the recommended procedure that follows will help the study team stay on course in designing its organization's MIS.

THE TEN-STEP MANAGEMENT INFORMATION SYSTEMS STUDY

The general outline of the study is as follows:

Step 1: Organizing the systems study team
Step 2: Establishing the organization's/study team's objectives
Step 3: Surveying the organization's information requirements
Step 4: Setting up the study targets and schedule
Step 5: Analyzing the existing information procedures
Step 6: Developing the improved system's operating specifications
Step 7: Designing the improved information system
Step 8: Evaluating and selecting data-processing equipment in terms of the new Management Information System
Step 9: Detailing the information system's operating procedures
Step 10: Implementing the conversion to the new Management Information System

STEP 1: Organizing the Systems Study Team   The importance of the study team cannot be overemphasized. It need not be large, but it should include representatives of the major functional areas of the organization—personnel with operational experience in performing line functions and personnel with specialist background. Since it is a working group requiring significant time, it should not require the key operating executives themselves. Top management personnel can act as a steering committee. In the smaller organization, however, without staff backup for key executives, the unavailability of a spread of talent poses a real problem. Quite often, the solution may involve the services of an outside consultant. The previous comments on this point may help in the selection of a productive one.

This study team's mode of operation will be a trying-learning experience. The members will feel their way at first, working out the ground rules as they go. For instance, it may meet at least once a week, for half-day sessions at the start. As projects and subprojects are identified, dimensioned, and assigned for investigation, and as the team gets used to working together, the meetings may become two-hour and then one-hour cross-fertilization briefing and decision sessions.

The team leader should report directly to the organization's president. There are few other instances where it is so important that a committee report directly to the chief executive. The very nerve system of the organization will be under scrutiny, and as the study progresses, hard decisions will have to be made that may very well change the organizational relationships that have existed for decades. In the interests of organizational effectiveness, certain private information channels, unique requirements, and special "cases" may have to be discarded or modified. The president is in the position to initiate such changes and give them a reasonable chance of successful implementation.

It has also proved useful to ask the chief executive not to attend committee sessions unless specifically invited. Free-swinging discussion is a great aid in cutting through the fog of practice that often envelops established procedures. Even when invited, he must be cautioned to avoid direct involvement, or the study team's final product may be a distorted version of his own preconceptions.

STEP 2: *Establishing the Organization's/Study Team's Objectives*
Chapter 4 of this book went into a great deal of detail regarding the setting of an organization's objective, and the discussion concluded with the observation that participation in setting the objectives by those who must help reach the objectives is essential for their understanding and enthusiastic cooperation.

Once the long-range objectives of the organization have been agreed to, the shorter-range targets to reach those objectives can be developed and then interpreted by the study team into MIS requirements. The organization's objectives are translated into the MIS study team's objectives. This is done by evaluating the organization's information requirements in terms of the operating structure needed to reach the organization's objectives.

STEP 3: *Surveying the Organization's Information Requirements*
Surveying the organization's information requirements will involve a three-part survey—now, during the near term, and long range. Each part ties into the organization's long-range objectives and their interpretation into MIS needs now and into the future. This survey will cover the following general areas:

1. Review of the overall scope of information recording, processing, transporting, and storing activities of the organization.
2. Compilation of management's needs for problem-solving and decision-making information.
3. Determination of the time frame of information capture, processing, and delivery.

4. Identification of any and all feedback channels within the subsystems and between the subsystems of the organization.

5. Inventory of information-processing personnel and equipment within the organization.

6. Inventory of all reports and forms now being used, planned for use, or that may be required eventually.

7. Compilation of data on the effectiveness and cost of the present system and forecast of probable costs of existing and possible systems.

8. Preparation of general specifications of the information requirements of the organization in terms of identifiable data elements and timing, subsystem by subsystem.

9. Identification of inputs and outputs of definable subsystems within the organization and of all organizational subsystems that interface with the outside environment.

10. Preparation of tentative measures of performance for subsystem elements and the subsystems themselves.

This survey of the organization's information requirements must be based on a thorough understanding of the organization's operations and the key/critical decision points in its operations. The foregoing list is not meant to be all-inclusive, but it will provide a reasonable base for expansion.

STEP 4: *Setting Up the Study Targets and Schedule*   It should be kept in mind that the study targets and schedule will be modular in concept. That is, the initial area of application of the MIS study team's efforts will act as a pilot project for the overall MIS effort. The activities of team members, and through them all elements of the organization, will gradually build up in tempo and outreach until the whole organization will have its attention and its activities attuned to the development of the new MIS.

This modular philosophy will avoid the great bugaboo of all grandiose schemes—trying too much too soon. The study team is both a catalyst and a change agent. There will be times when it must take one role and times when it must take the other. The targets and schedule must reflect this persuasive rather than authoritarian approach.

The sequence of areas for study will be specified and the subsequent steps in the design and implementation of the MIS (outlined in this chapter) will also be specified. Design and implementation will proceed at a varying pace within the organization, and the study team may want to utilize the PERT technique, which is admirably suited to the monitoring of a complex project (Chap. 10).

The targets should be set up in terms of specific information elements, reports, and operational requirements. The schedule should allow sufficient time for the analysis of the existing system, and for the unforeseen and the complications that always come up. The more general targets and dates will gradually be detailed and made more specific as the analysis and the study proceed.

STEP 5: *Analyzing the Existing Information Procedures*   Using the techniques covered in the preceding chapters of this book, the existing information system is flow charted, graphed, and work simplified from the point of view of whether the elements and subsystems are contributing effectively to the organization's objectives. This is a careful detailing and analysis of the information flow from inception, processing, use, and storage or destruction.

The analysis of existing information procedures must be sure to get down to the real "nitty-gritty" of what is actually going on. The following is a useful checklist of the kind of detail that is necessary:

1. List all data elements of all forms and reports with a cross listing by source and user. Evaluate the effort expended to the usefulness of the data element.

2. Evaluate a sample of each format and contents of management control reports. Evaluate in terms of the significance of decisions involved.

3. Specify frequency of occurrence, number of copies, size of the numbers in each category (i.e., field size), type of characters (alphabetic, numeric, symbolic), and any special requirements, such as perforations, carbon, etc.

4. Determine the sources of the data used with particular attention to special types of input such as credit plates, special order forms, and even MICR and optically scanned inputs.

5. Indicate the number of transactions of each type of input per time period. Attention must be paid to variations within a time period or between time periods. Are there peak loads and slack periods?

6. Evaluate samples of each of the input documents with the various data clearly labeled. Chapter 8, "Forms Analysis, Design, and Control," is particularly useful at this point.

7. Determine the sources of the input in terms of department, outside source, or output of another procedure.

8. Specify the operations that are performed on the raw data to convert to information for analysis and control.
   a. What arithmetic operations are necessary? When are they performed? How many times? What are the sizes of the numbers involved? What degree of accuracy is necessary?

   b. What kinds of audit checks of the data should be made as part of the DP procedure? Should input transactions be checked against some total, are crossfooting calculations checked against a total, etc.?

   c. What type of reference data is checked as part of the procedure? Price lists, tax tables, vendor rating schedules, etc.?

   d. What comparisons are made in the procedure and what are the logical alternatives of these comparisons? How many times do they occur? Promised date versus delivery date, actual cost versus budget, actual performance versus forecast, etc.?

9. Determine the time period of the information cycle and of the feedback cycle.

10. Determine what decisions are reducible to a sequence of well-defined alternatives for the conditions at each step of the sequence.

STEP 6: Developing the Improved System's Operating Specifications The new Management Information System is to be developed to meet the requirements and to satisfy the constraints that have previously been specified. The operating specifications will include these requirements and constraints and will also delineate the detailed information system's objectives that must be attained. To accomplish these purposes, the study team must:

1. Develop operating specifications that emphasize the flow of management control information regarding the operations within the organization. This will encompass the determining of the hierarchy of functions, the decision alternatives, and the interrelationships of decision making within the organization. Information-decision activity clusters will begin to take form, and the outline of the interlaced subsystems will begin to emerge.

2. Specify the information-processing system that will insure timely and accurate communication to management and, conversely, quick transmission of their action decisions to the key/critical operations' control points.

3. Set up operating specifications for each of the subsystems that have been identified, utilizing the guides suggested previously.

4. Identify the necessary reporting mechanics and specify content, timing, medium, and recipient of operations analysis reports, operations control reports, and operations planning reports.

5. Make sure that the users of the management information have a key role in developing the operating specifications in their areas of responsibility.

6. Integrate all dollar-oriented procedures and reports with the accounting system.

7. Provide comparisons of forecast with accomplishment and calculation of deviations related to control limits wherever applicable.

8. Combine performance reporting within the structure of possible computer simulation to encourage pretesting of alternatives.

9. Specify a total system reporting structure for interlaced subsystems along with the reporting structure for the subsystems.

10. Emphasize the action-decision portion of the feedback control loop at least as much as the reporting portion.

11. Interpret every aspect of the information system in terms of transactions, records, files, data elements.

12. Calculate data volume per unit time for each processing point in the system.

STEP 7: Designing the Improved Information System

1. Utilize systems flow charts, process flow charts, and layout diagrams to describe the general information-processing steps.

2. Describe the input, output, file requirements, processing steps, test requirements, and documentation for all computer programs and man-machine procedures that are required.

3. Outline the necessary procedures to ensure maintainability, compatibility, and expandability of the methods and procedures that make up the MIS.

4. Utilize the practical guidelines in Chapter 8 to plan for proper forms design and control for the new MIS.

5. Pause and evaluate each of the previous steps and the present stage of MIS development. Make sure that the thrill of innovation has not gained precedence over the basic objective of the study team, which is to provide a "most advanced yet acceptable" Management Information System that will enhance the survival and growth of the organization.

6. Relate all performance standards to quantitative measures.

7. Relate controls to the organizational structure that will exist when the MIS is implemented.

8. Specify origination timing, interaction timing, and process timing of all data elements that are integral to the MIS.

STEP 8: *Evaluating and Selecting DP Equipment in Terms of the New MIS*   It may very well be that no DP equipment is necessary, or that enough is already on hand. Step 8 occurs after the specification steps and before the detailed preparation of methods, procedures, forms, and programs because the equipment characteristics may well affect them.

The study team now knows enough about its requirements, its constraints (including budget), and its objectives to talk to representatives of equipment manufacturers. Remember, the purchase, lease, or rental of DP equipment should be approached with the same down-to-earth practicality as the organization would approach the purchase of a typewriter or a lathe or other equipment. Reputation for service, financial rating, support facilities, location, and attitude are some of the facets to be evaluated along with price and equipment performance.

The MIS study has provided the operating specifications against which the claims of the equipment manufacturers can be measured. It will be the rare study team that reaches this stage of its study without an acute awareness of the many imponderables and unknowns that lurk in even the simplest MIS. Furthermore, the key people involved in designing the MIS have discovered how little they know about the detailed operations of their own organization. This cannot fail to make them move cautiously with regard to ADP equipment, and it will make them want to emphasize flexibility, modularity, and simplicity. Even this is a major advance for their organization.

STEP 9: Detailing the Information System's Operating Procedures

1. All the ingredients of Step 7 (Designing the MIS) should now be detailed, keeping in mind the operating characteristics of any of the DP equipment that may be involved.

2. Prepare program flow charts for each of the computer applications. Divide major program flow charts into detail program flow charts. This modularization of major programs helps to maintain the resultant programs, eases changes and modifications, and allows the programming effort to be more easily handled and supervised.

3. Code the program flow charts into computer instructions in accordance with the rules of the programming language used. The study team will have specified the programming language to be used in order to insure uniformity and standardization to increase the efficiency of initial programming and of program modification and maintenance.

4. Collect sample data; test programs; debug.

5. Prepare documentation including program description, operator instructions, and supporting data.

6. Finalize detailed procedures and forms.

STEP 10: Implementing the Conversion to the New Management Information System

1. Management orientation is the first of a series of explanatory sessions where the MIS will be described to all levels within the organization. These briefings can be set up by management level and then by function including all levels.
2. Management training in the specifics of the new MIS by level and by function and by subsystem within function. The trained managers will in turn be used to train employees in the new MIS.
3. Employee training by their own supervisors and managers so that the MIS is interpreted in terms of their own operating realities.
4. Equipment installation and file conversion.
5. The subsystem that was first chosen for detailed analysis and design may have been superseded by another area during the course of the study. Whichever has been selected for being put on-line first is now launched and its interface with the MIS is carefully monitored. As it gradually develops a smoothly functioning *modus operandi*, a second and then a third system goes on-line until the whole organization is absorbed into the new MIS.
6. This conversion phase will require as much analysis, study, and redesign as all that went before. But now, the analysis, study, and redesign is in terms of the dynamic operating environment. It is for real. The procedures for analysis, study, and redesign should become an integral part of the MIS so that the MIS can grow and change with the organization it serves.

REVIEW QUESTIONS

1. Every organization is unique. Comment.
2. Evaluate an outside consultant's possible contribution to the MIS study.
3. What is the role of the computer with regard to the MIS?
4. How should the study team go about evaluating ADP equipment?
5. Who should be members of the study team? Who should not?
6. Why should the study team leader report to the organization's president?
7. Why is a specific part of the organization selected for detailing the MIS?
8. What is the objective of the MIS study team?
9. What is a useful guideline to follow when evaluating DP equipment suppliers?

10.   Why should analysis, study, and redesign procedures be made a part of the MIS?

BIBLIOGRAPHY

Blake, Robert R., and Jane Srygley Mouton, *Corporate Excellence Diagnosis*. Austin, Tex.: Scientific Methods, Inc., 1968. An in-depth procedure for diagnosing the condition of the total management and organizational system. Ambitious in concept and presentation. Its worth can only be evaluated by implementation in each specific situation.

Glans, Thomas B., Burton Grad, David Holstein, William E. Meyers, and Richard N. Schmidt, *Management Systems*. New York: Holt, Rinehart & Winston, Inc., 1968. A very useful, detailed treatment of the study of design of a Management Information System.

Hartman, W., H. Matthes and A. Proeme, *Management Information Systems Handbook*. New York: McGraw-Hill Book Company, 1968. Not so much a handbook as a detailed step-by-step guide to the design of a computer-oriented MIS. The treatment is technical but understandable, if a bit European in its addiction to detail. Very worthwhile.

Head, Robert V., *Real-Time Business Systems*. New York: Holt, Rinehart & Winston, Inc., 1966. An excellent and detailed guide for a Management Information System study.

McDonough, Adrian M., *Management Systems*. Homewood, Ill.: Richard D. Irwin, Inc., 1965. Additional material on MIS design, using a case study approach and emphasizing man-machine interface.

Murdick, Robert G., and Joel E. Ross, *Information Systems for Modern Management*. Englewood Cliffs, N. J.: Prentice-Hall, Inc., 1971. An up-to-date interrelating of management theory, computers, and the systems approach. Quite good.

Shaw, John C., and William Atkins, *Managing Computer System Projects*. New York: McGraw-Hill Book Company, 1970. This is a guide for the application of the computer to management systems. Emphasis is on a working outline of project management methodology. Both authors have had extensive practical experience.

Withington, Frederic G., *The Use of Computers in Business Organizations*. Reading, Mass.: Addison-Wesley Publishing Co., 1966. Provides a concise treatment of the steps involved in making a decision about the acquisition and use of computers.

Young, Stanley, *Management: A Systems Analysis*. Glenview, Ill.: Scott, Foresman & Company, 1971. Investigates the design and administration of management decision systems. Useful emphasis on the monitoring and maintenance of such a system.

15

THE AUTOMATED MANAGEMENT INFORMATION SYSTEM

THE STATE OF THE ART

The placing of all an organization's operations under the control of a management-designed-and-monitored computer system seems like the natural culmination of combining the MIS and the computer, that is, a computer-based, computer-controlled Management Information System. All the necessary hardware components of such a system are available now. All the software techniques and the computer technology are available now. What is not available in most organizations is the management know-how to go about doing it. Yet, for reasons that have been stated repeatedly in previous chapters, unless managers themselves play a key role in specifying, designing, structuring, and implementing such a system it is foredoomed to failure. The "tools and techniques of MIS" explained in this book can provide the basic building blocks for constructing such a system.

It must be pointed out that the currently popular "total systems concept" is implicit in this discussion. That is, the automated MIS incorporates in its design the fact that the performance of every element in the system affects the performance of the whole. Put another way, the total systems concept is an example of *synergism*—the effect of the whole is greater than the sum of the independent effects of its parts. The computer-controlled MIS discussion that follows is a practical implementation of the total systems philosophy.

Of course, computer-controlled MIS does not mean that management judgment and key/critical decision making are taken over by the computer. These remain, and always will remain, in the province of the human beings who have the responsibility for the survival and growth of the organization. What it does mean, however, is that the day-to-day operations data will be computer sensed, processed, and evaluated and that routine decisions and controls will be implemented within the guidelines and objectives set by management.

Some organizations are well on their way to putting their total information system under some form of centralized computer control, but they are in the microscopic minority. The mainstream of management thinking is still adapting to concepts of scientific management and human relations, though some of these concepts are almost a half-century old. Even the more knowledgeable managers are just beginning to realize that computers are not necessarily synonymous with accounting. In addition, it is unfortunate that most managers are so involved with responding to the crisis-to-crisis atmosphere of most organizations that they do not have the time to keep up with the advanced techniques that are being developed almost daily by computer and Management Information Systems specialists.

It must also be remembered that the major share of the business that is done in the United States (according to the U.S. Small Business Administration) is done by small business (i.e., a company with less than five hundred employees and nondominant in its field). As surprising as it may seem, this means that the bulk of management activity in America takes place in the context of tight budgets, thin profit margins, and the sparse managerial talent of small companies and organizations. The environment of the small company is such as to make technological innovation, especially in the management area, very difficult. The available talent is already stretched thin covering day-to-day problems, and the challenge of undertaking the implementation of an automated MIS is certainly expecting too much.

Typically, these hard-working, "started-from-scratch" managers know their businesses like the palms of their hands, but they have little time or inclination to dabble in the heady atmosphere of computers and advanced management techniques. It is for these and other equally cogent reasons that although the tools and technology are available, the advent of computer-based, automated Management Information Systems is still a long way off.

It is also not a question of large capital investments. There is little need for large-scale, in-house hardware, since much of the ADP activity in a computer-based, automated MIS can utilize the services of a time-sharing company. In fact, time sharing (i.e., more than one user sharing a computer by telephone lines or other such communications facility) is a real breakthrough for the smaller organization interested in harnessing computer power for its MIS needs.

Examining the concept of the computer-based, automated MIS, even though its advent may seem a long way off, is intriguing, however, and will serve as an excellent vehicle for discussing computer applications, present and future, in the context of a Management Information System.

A company or an organization approaching such a massive application of ADP would be involved in an effort measured in terms of years, probably in the order of five to ten years. The greatest part of the effort will be invested in restructuring the organization and its operating subsystems for the automated MIS environment.

Contrary to what might be supposed, the minor part of the effort is involved in the "shakedown" stage after the automated MIS is launched and operating. This is a direct result of the modularized stage-by-stage approach that is the recommended approach for development and implementation of the automated MIS.

Interestingly enough, the actual computer programming required would probably be much less of an effort than the converting of all aspects of the organization's present information system to "ADP compatible." "All aspects of the organization's information system" means exactly that—all! Everything from employee identification numbers to supplier numbers, to form numbers, to part numbers, to department numbers, to account codes, and so forth, would have to be made a part of an integrated, comprehensive, meaningful code structure. In addition, procedures that may have been in use for half a century may have to be drastically modified or discarded. Many of the existing information subsystems will be found to be currently operable only because the human beings concerned have gerrymandered, adjusted, used "Kentucky windage," and made other *ad hoc* arrangements to adapt the ineffective procedures to reality. All the inappropriate, inapplicable, inefficient procedures and the data involved have to be standardized and made homogeneous, integral, logical, and routine. That is part of what is meant by "ADP compatible." Quite a job!

THE USE OF PREWRITTEN PROGRAMS

Another reason that the computer programming effort need not be such a major effort is that many of the basic programs that will be required have already been written and are readily available. They may be considered "canned" programs that may readily be customized to an organization's specific needs.

In these canned programs, the mainstream of the logic design, the program flow charting, the operating specifications, and the actual program language coding have already been accomplished. They will need modification and adjustment to fit the unique conditions of a particular organization, but in most situations the programs are readily adaptable and can be pretested using actual data. Best of all, they are available through the auspices of the people who created them and know them best, the time-sharing companies and service bureaus, the programming companies, the equipment manufacturers, or even the particular organizations who are currently using them. Of course, there will be problems and crises, but nothing like the sequence of obstacles and near disasters that would surely occur if such a massive undertaking were being attempted by one organization's limited resources from "ground zero."

These prepackaged programs are available for a wide variety of applications. Forecasting programs, cost analysis and control programs, accounts payable and receivable programs, payroll and personnel programs, production scheduling and control programs, manpower and machine loading programs, market research and sales analysis programs, purchasing and vendor rating programs, preventive maintenance and machine replacement programs, inventory control and materials management programs, and many, many others. All have already been written, tested, and debugged, at many levels of sophistication and for many sizes and types of organizations. Adapting them to the particular requirements of a specific organization will require intelligence and effort, but the savings in time and manpower and dollars will be considerable. IBM has a telephone-book-sized catalog of such programs called the KWIC INDEX (Key Word In Context). It lists each program by name and by functional area of application and includes a brief description of its purpose. Many other equipment and software organizations have similar compendiums. All are available at a reasonable price.

THE ESSENTIAL INGREDIENTS OF AN AUTOMATED MIS

The real "gut operation" will take place in the detailed systems work on the organization's present information system—in mapping the conversion from the present complex, sprawling coding and data-processing procedures of the disparate elements of the company into the systemized, homogeneous, cohesive requirements of a computer-based, automated Management Information System: *Systemized*, so that all of the elements contribute to the growth and survival of the whole. *Homogeneous*, so that coding systems and terminology in one part of the organization do not conflict with, but instead have constructive relation to, the other codes and terms in the rest of the organization. *Cohesive*, so that the overall information system generates a unified and meaningful picture to the management team entrusted with the destiny of the organization.

A big order indeed! But, one that must be fulfilled if the concept of an automated MIS is to become a reality. Where to start? The answer, as usual, is with planning. But in this case, it is not a question of a relatively simple ADP feasibility study, but quite a bit more extensive and, conceptually, starting well before that. The planning will be organization-wide, that is, total systems planning—the determination of courses of action to optimize survival and growth. The specific role the computer will play comes into its own much later in the planning program. But the frame of reference for the management tool called the computer is structured by a thorough stocktaking of the company's objectives and the means it intends to use to reach these objectives. Chapter 14 outlined just such a study.

The thrust of this book has been to provide the manager-systems analyst with techniques for the specifying, designing, structuring, implementing, and improving of a Management Information System. Each organization has a unique combination of men, materials, machines, and money, and it has its own relationship to its external environment. Those entrusted with the guidance of the organization have the prime responsibility for combining these tools and techniques with their own judgment and experience to spearhead the effort to develop a computer-based, automated Management Information System that best fits their organization's needs.

A CASE STUDY OF AN AUTOMATED MIS

An overview of such an MIS installation may provide some useful insights into the extraordinary flexibility and power of such a system. It may

IBM 50 Magnetic Data Inscriber

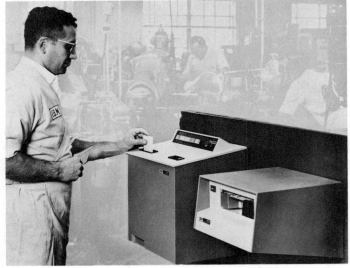

FIGURE 15-1

Source Recording and
Input/Output Terminals

Men Using Source Recording Devices

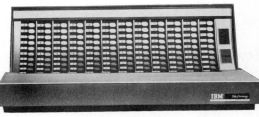

IBM 372 Manual Entry Device

IBM 2740 Communication Terminal

IBM 2265 Display Station

also be a useful vehicle for raising specific questions that will have to be answered, in detail, by anyone seriously contemplating such an effort for his organization.

The presentation is made in general terms with specific details included where their applicability has some general interest. It should be pointed out that feasibility rather than sophistication was aimed at, so that this presentation is by no means to be considered a reflection of "the state of the art" but rather a reflection of a practical, tried and tested, acceptable, and relatively painless approach to the "automated MIS."

Case Study: Overview of a Computer-Based, Automated Management Information System

After a thorough MIS study, much on the lines outlined in Chapter 14, the organization decided to utilize the services of a time-sharing firm's facilities and had a variety of source recording and input/output terminals installed at key points in the company (see Fig. 15-1). It also decided to purchase a small-size in-plant computer for hour-by-hour information on machine loading, production scheduling, and material control on a unit (nondollar) record basis. The rest of the data processing would be done by the time-sharing service which was connected to the plant by leased wires.

Recording of the MIS Data Base

During the conversion phase of introducing the system, all bills of materials, operations sheets, routing sheets, standard costs, payroll data, overhead rates, machine capacities, maintenance schedules, worker and machine allowances, and other pertinent parameters making up the MIS data base were programmed and recorded into the rented storage devices at the time-sharing service bureau.

In addition, the raw material, work-in-process, finished goods inventories, and other in-process data as of a certain date and time (D-day, zero hour, for initiating the system) were also programmed and recorded. At this time, the orders already being worked on in the shop plus any backlog were fed into the storage devices of the in-house computer in a fully planned sequence and were identified in detail. Shop load, department load, and machine load were all keyed into storage.

Capturing the Critical Operating Data

Order Processing

1. An order is received from a customer for one thousand "widgets," one of the many products made by this company.

2. An abstract of this order is typed using a production order format. At the same time, selected data is automatically recorded on magnetic tape.
3. The magnetic tape is used for entering the data into the plant computer and for wire transmission to the time-sharing service bureau.
4. The in-plant computer searches finished goods inventory for the one thousand "widgets." If available, the customer service department is notified, and shipping documents are automatically prepared from preprogrammed routines.

Procurement

1. If one thousand "widgets" are not available, the computer selects the proper bill of materials from the coded identification number for "widgets" and calculates the amount of each item of material required to produce one thousand of the final product. Necessary allowances are included for breakage, scrap, and shrinkage.
2. As each item on the bill of materials is calculated, the computer is programmed to search raw material inventory to check that the quantity required is available.
3. Each item in inventory has a continually updated reorder point which the computer is programmed to compare with the remaining balance after the material for one thousand "widgets" has been deducted.
4. If the reorder point has been reached, the computer is instructed to calculate the economical ordering quantity utilizing the latest data on average demand, procurement costs, and carrying charges, and to prepare requests for quotations or a purchase order, depending on the predecision of management as to how that item should be handled.
5. Each item on the bill of materials is similarly analyzed.

Machine Loading and Job Scheduling

1. The computer uses the operations sheet that is key coded for this particular size and style of "widget." It takes the first operation and computes the amount of time required to produce one thousand "widgets," including setup, tool change, personal time, fatigue, and all other pertinent elements.
2. If machine loading were done by individual machine, it would scan the present status of each machine that manufacturing engineering had indicated could do this operation. As mentioned earlier, the status of every parameter in the company has been "frozen" as of a certain date and time to have a starting point for introducing the automated MIS system. If machine loading were done by department, the department load would be scanned.

3. The amount of machine time required for the order would be preempted from the machine time available. A new balance of machine time "open" would then be indicated. Since machine time versus date and hour would have been preprofiled, the computer would develop the actual date and hour the machine would be available for this unit of work. Maintenance schedules, downtime, and setup time are all included in the computation based on time studies, probability, linear programming, and queuing techniques.

4. The computer continues the machine load analysis for each step on the operations sheet. The result is not only an up-to-the-minute machine load status but an accurate report of just when this particular order will be at each particular phase of its production.

5. The resultant schedule would show the shipping time by date and hour and would also indicate the bottlenecks, if any, in machines or materials. A queuing theory and linear programming package would be included in the program to optimize the routing selected.

6. The computer can also be programmed for alternative courses of action in those cases where a close-in delivery date is required. It includes a priority listing of substitute materials and alternate machines that can do the job, so that, where necessary, management will be given a series of evaluated alternatives to meet the data requested. The manufacturing cost would be higher, but in certain cases it might be very advantageous. Where management wants this prerogative, certain classes of decisions will be referred to management for on-the-spot modification of the systems decisions. Graphic display terminals and light pen input make such interaction feasible.

Production

1. Production orders originate from the time-sharing service computer for inventory orders, from the in-plant computer for scheduled customer orders, or from production order typing for special or emergency orders.

2. Each production order has a code-numbered tag which identifies the order and which also has this code number in magnetic spot code. This tag accompanies the order through its production cycle. Both the plant computer and the time-sharing computer use this number to identify the data pertaining to this order.

3. A worker arrives at the plant at the beginning of his shift and withdraws his badge from a rack. All recording for attendance and payroll takes place automatically when he withdraws his badge. This badge contains his identification in coded magnetic spots.

Within an hour of shift start, all absentee and tardiness reports by section, department, and plant would have been calculated and reported. In addition, statistical analyses would have been made based on historical data to indicate what areas required management attention because of attendance performance outside the statistical control limits.

4. The worker proceeds to his production area and receives his first production assignment from his foreman. He enters his tag and the order tag in a source recording device at his work station. This records the date, time, order, worker, and production step automatically.

5. Upon completion of a production operation he (or the foreman) enters the production count in the source recording device and withdraws the tags. Operation time, production count, order status, and machine load status are recorded automatically.

6. The in-plant computer automatically adjusts the work-in-plant inventory for the operation completed, the machine load schedule is updated, the worker's incentive pay is calculated, and the order status is adjusted. The computer is ready to reschedule on an optimum basis.

7. All data essential to materials management, production control, cost accounting, payroll, and general accounting is automatically transmitted to the time-sharing service bureau.

8. At the end of the shift, the production worker clocks out by returning his badge to the rack.

Generation of Management Information

1. The next morning (it could be hourly if worthwhile) the foreman receives his daily report of completed production and variances from standards and schedules. Production control receives an updated job schedule, materials requirements, manning tables, machine loads, and other pertinent data. At each management level, pertinent reports reflecting the previous day's work are received.

2. At the end of the week the worker receives his pay, and all payroll records are updated. The foreman receives a summary cost report which has applied dollars to his daily report.

3. Management receives reports of production versus schedules, costs versus standard, variances from planned performance, and a forecast of scheduled operations. All management planning, analysis, and control reports designed into the MIS are of course produced to the pre-agreed schedules.

4. All other statistical, accounting, and control reports required by various management functions are completed automatically, in-

cluding weekly profit and loss and balance sheet by product if desired.

Updating of All Standard Reference Data

As new data and parameters enter the system for the first time, such as new product bills of materials and operation sheets, new employees, new customers, new material, new costs, new factors in the formula for EOQ, forecasting, competition, tax regulations, etc., this information is key coded to identify it and is integrated into the MIS data base at the time-sharing service bureau and in the in-plant computer.

Notwithstanding the skeletal outline of the automated MIS described above, it can be seen that such an application, divested of its mumbo jumbo, is well within the competence of most managers and organizations. The great obstacles are the self-imposed. As reflected in a great advertising slogan of yesteryear, Eventually—Why Not Now, management should take a deep breath and begin, right now, on the long but fascinating road to a computer-based, automated Management Information System.

A FINAL WORD

The objective of this book has not been to provide a pretested blueprint that can be applied by any manager-systems analyst in any organization. Rather, it has attempted to present, in understandable terms, an array of tools and techniques that can be applied by such a person or group in conjunction with their own energies and creativity to design and implement a Management Information System, an MIS that will contribute to the survival and growth of the organization. To the extent that this book provides some help along that line it will have achieved its purpose.

REVIEW QUESTIONS

1. How would you characterize the state of the art with regard to hardware and software availability for an automated MIS?

2. Define an automated MIS in terms of management decision making.

3. Relate "small business" and an automated MIS—concept, design, implementation.

4. Where will most of the effort be required in designing and implementing an automated MIS?
5. What role do "canned" programs play in the automated MIS?
6. Describe the KWIC INDEX.
7. Define *systemized, homogeneous,* and *cohesive* with relation to an automated MIS.
8. In the case study, what functions were relegated to the in-house computer and what functions to the time-sharing service?
9. Describe the operation of the automated MIS in a functional area of the company in the case study.
10. Specify some of the methods used for recording, analyzing, and reporting management information in the case study.

BIBLIOGRAPHY

BOORE, WILLIAM F., and JERRY R. MURPHY, *The Computer Sampler.* New York: McGraw-Hill Book Company, 1968. A collection of provocative acticles about the computer as a management tool. Contains a number of interesting treatments that relate to the automated MIS.

DRUCKER, PETER F., *The Age of Discontinuity.* New York: Harper & Row, Publishers, 1969. A very provocative treatment of the impact of key developments in the last third of the twentieth century. Disturbing yet very helpful when considering the philosophy of the MIS in an organization.

ELLIOT, C. ORVILLE, and ROBERT S. WASLEY, *Business Information Processing Systems* (3rd ed.). Homewood, Ill.: Richard D. Irwin, Inc., 1971. In addition to a good presentation regarding the evolution of computers, a significant part of the book discusses aspects of planning, designing, and implementing a business information system.

HEAD, ROBERT V., *Real-Time Business Systems.* New York: Holt, Rinehart & Winston, Inc., 1966. An authority on information systems provides a step-by-step blueprint for the MIS design and implementation.

HEYEL, CARL, *Computers, Office Machines and the New Information Technology.* New York: The Macmillan Company, 1969. The second half of the book is particularly applicable to the concept of the automated MIS. It is handled with know-how and dispatch.

INDEX